Introduction to Cognitive Pragmatics

Cognitive Linguistics in Practice (CLiP)
ISSN 1388-6231

A text book series which aims at introducing students of language and linguistics, and scholars from neighboring disciplines, to established and new fields in language research from a cognitive perspective. The books in the series are written in an attractive, reader-friendly and self-explanatory style. They include assignments and have been tested for undergraduate and graduate student use at university level.

Editors

Carita Paradis
Lund University

Stefanie Wulff
University of Florida

Editorial Board

Rosario Caballero
Universidad de Castilla-La Mancha

Ewa Dąbrowska
Northumbria University

Dagmar Divjak
University of Sheffield

Adele E. Goldberg
Princeton University

Stefan Th. Gries
University of California, Santa Barbara

Martin Hilpert
University of Neuchâtel

Suzanne Kemmer
Rice University

Todd Oakley
Case Western Reserve University

Klaus-Uwe Panther
University of Hamburg

Peter Robinson
Aoyama Gakuin University

Julio Santiago de Torres
Universidad de Granada

Marjolijn Verspoor
University of Groningen, Netherlands &
University of Pannonia, Hungary

Advisory Board

Günter Radden
Universität Hamburg

Volume 4

Introduction to Cognitive Pragmatics
by Klaus-Uwe Panther

Introduction to Cognitive Pragmatics

Klaus-Uwe Panther
University of Hamburg

John Benjamins Publishing Company
Amsterdam / Philadelphia

The paper used in this publication meets the minimum requirements of the American National Standard for Information Sciences – Permanence of Paper for Printed Library Materials, ANSI Z39.48-1984.

DOI 10.1075/clip.4

Cataloging-in-Publication Data available from Library of Congress:
LCCN 2021047258 (PRINT) / 2021047259 (E-BOOK)

ISBN 978 90 272 1062 3 (HB)
ISBN 978 90 272 1061 6 (PB)
ISBN 978 90 272 5821 2 (E-BOOK)

© 2022 – John Benjamins B.V.
No part of this book may be reproduced in any form, by print, photoprint, microfilm, or any other means, without written permission from the publisher.

John Benjamins Publishing Company · https://benjamins.com

To Linda

Table of contents

Abbreviations and symbols — XIII
Corpora and online dictionaries — XV
List of tables and figures — XVII
About the author — XXI
Foreword — XXIII

CHAPTER 1
Cognitive linguistics and pragmatics — 1
1. Introduction 1
2. Pragmatics 1
    2.1 Some basic features of contemporary pragmatics 1
    2.2 The semantics-pragmatics dichotomy: Advantages and drawbacks 4
        2.2.1 Meaning and truth conditions 4
        2.2.2 Truth conditions and (lack of) coherence 8
        2.2.3 Non-declarative sentence types 9
        2.2.4 The role of pragmatic inferences in the assignment of truth values 10
        2.2.5 Deixis 12
        2.2.6 Conventional non-truth conditional meanings 12
        2.2.7 Preliminary conclusion 14
3. A cognitive linguistic view of pragmatics 15
    3.1 Introduction 15
    3.2 Towards a blend of cognitive linguistics and pragmatics 18

CHAPTER 2
Cognitive-pragmatic motivation of language structure and use — 21
1. Introducing the problem 21
2. Some remarks on the history of motivation 21
3. Towards a cognitive linguistic view of motivation 25
    3.1 Preliminaries: Types of signs 25
    3.2 Defining motivation 27
    3.3 Motivated, unmotivated, conventional, and non-conventional signs 29

        3.4   Unmotivated conventional signs   30
        3.5   Motivated conventional signs   30
        3.6   Non-conventionally used motivated signs   32
4.   Semiotic types of motivation   33
        4.1   CONTENT > FORM   34
        4.2   CONTENT$_1$ > CONTENT$_2$ 35
        4.3   FORM > CONTENT   36
        4.4   FORM$_1$ > FORM$_2$ 37
5.   Language-independent factors of motivation   37
        5.1   Sensory-perceptual   38
        5.2   Cultural   39
        5.3   Emotive   40
6.   Demotivation   41
7.   Conclusion   42

CHAPTER 3
The role of inference in the construction of meaning: Entailment and presupposition   43
1.   Introduction   43
2.   Basic modes of inferencing: Deduction, induction, and abduction   43
        2.1   Deduction   43
        2.2   Induction   46
        2.3   Abduction   47
3.   Entailment   48
4.   Presupposition   51
        4.1   Existential and uniqueness presupposition   52
        4.2   Factive presuppositions   54
        4.3   Evaluative presuppositions   55
        4.4   Suspending or canceling a presupposition   57
        4.5   Negation and presupposition   58
        4.6   Discourse-pragmatic presupposition   59
        4.7   The information status of presupposition   60
5.   Conclusion   61

CHAPTER 4
Principles guiding communication: The role of implicature   63
1.   Introduction   63
2.   Two models of communication   64
3.   Gricean principles guiding communication   68
        3.1   The Cooperative Principle and the maxims of conversation   68
        3.2   The Maxims of Quantity   70

        3.3   The Maxims of Quality   73
        3.4   The Maxim of Relation (Relevance)   74
        3.5   The Maxims of Manner   75
4.   Reducing the number of maxims: Neo-Gricean approaches
       and Relevance Theory   77
        4.1   A sketch of Levinson's and Horn's models   77
        4.2   The Principle of Relevance   79
5.   In lieu of a conclusion: The influence of cultural practices
       on maxims of conversation   81

CHAPTER 5
Implicature, entailment, and presupposition:
Differences and commonalities   83
1.   Introduction   83
2.   Conventional implicature   83
3.   Conversational implicature   84
        3.1   Suspendability and cancelability   85
        3.2   Non-detachability   88
        3.3   Calculability   89
        3.4   Non-codability of conversational implicatures   90
        3.5   Reinforceability   90
                3.5.1   Reinforceability of implicature   91
                3.5.2   Reinforceability of entailment   93
                3.5.3   Reinforceability of presuppositions   100
                3.5.4   Conclusion: Reinforced implicature, entailment,
                            and presupposition   103
        3.6   Universality vs. culture-specificity of conversational implicatures   104
                3.6.1   Scalar conversational implicatures: A possible universal   104
                3.6.2   Language- and culture-specific implicatures   105
4.   Conclusion   107

CHAPTER 6
Talking as action: Speech act theory   109
1.   Introduction   109
2.   Folk and expert models of action   110
        2.1   Talk as deficient action   110
        2.2   An expert model of linguistic action: Speech act theory   111
3.   Some examples of infelicitous illocutionary acts (Austin)   113
4.   Searle's speech act theory   115
        4.1   Introduction   115
        4.2   Felicity conditions and illocutionary types according to Searle   116

		4.3	Illocutionary types 118
		4.4	Distinguishing between illocutionary force
			and illocutionary verbs 121
	5.	Coding illocutionary force and propositional content 124
		5.1	Introduction 124
		5.2	Illocutionary force and propositional content coding:
			Mood and constituent order 125
		5.3	Illocutionary force coding 125
			5.3.1	Performative verbs 125
			5.3.2	Performatively used nominal expressions 126
		5.4	Propositional content coding 127
	6.	Illocutionary scenarios and their components 128
		6.1	Introduction 128
		6.2	Assertives 129
		6.3	Commissives 130
		6.4	Directives 131
		6.5	Expressives 133
		6.6	Declarations 136
	7.	Conclusion 138

CHAPTER 7
Metaphor: A figure of iconic and analogical reasoning   139
1.	Introduction 139
2.	Some contemporary approaches to metaphor 140
3.	Metaphor in cognitive linguistics 144
	3.1	Precursors of conceptual metaphor theory 144
	3.2	Lakoff and Johnson's metaphor theory 145
4.	The role of inferencing in Lakoff and Johnson's conception
	of metaphor 151
	4.1	Metaphorical entailments 151
	4.2	The Invariance Principle 153
	4.3	Inferential structure of source and target domain 155
5.	Metaphor and thought 160
6.	Conclusion 162

CHAPTER 8
Metonymy: A figure of indexical and associative reasoning   163
1.	Introduction 163
2.	Metonymy in literary and ordinary language 164
	2.1	Examples of metonymy in literary language 164
	2.2	Examples of metonymy in ordinary language 165

3. Properties of metonymy   167
   3.1 Situation and context   168
   3.2 Metonymy as an indexical and associative relation   170
   3.3 Metonymy as reasoning within a conceptual frame   171
   3.4 Conceptual distance between source and target   172
   3.5 Contingent relation between source and target   173
   3.6 Pragmatic effects   175
   3.7 Experiential and sociocultural motivation of metonymy   176
   3.8 Transparency of metonymy motivation   178
4. Metonymy as abductive reasoning   180
5. Constraining the scope of metonymy   184
6. Types of metonymy   187
   6.1 Referential metonymies   187
   6.2 Predicational metonymies   188
   6.3 Modificational metonymies   189
   6.4 Grounding metonymies   190
   6.5 Illocutionary metonymies   192
7. Conclusion   193

CHAPTER 9
Metonymic inferencing in indirect speech acts I:
Assertives and commissives   195
1. Introduction   195
2. The role of metonymic inferencing in indirect speech acts   196
   2.1 Assertives   197
      2.1.1 Inferences from BEFORE TO CORE   198
      2.1.2 Inference from HEDGED CORE to CORE   202
      2.1.3 Inferences from RESULT to CORE   202
      2.1.4 Inferences from AFTER to CORE   203
   2.2 Commissives   204
      2.2.1 Inferences from BEFORE to CORE   206
      2.2.2 Inferences from HEDGED CORE to CORE   207
      2.2.3 Inferences from RESULT to CORE   208
      2.2.4 Inferences from AFTER to CORE   211
3. Conclusion   213

CHAPTER 10
Metonymic inferencing in indirect speech acts II:
Directives, expressives, declarations   215
1. Introduction   215
2. Directives, expressives, and declarations   215

2.1   Directives   215
    2.1.1   Inferences from BEFORE to CORE   215
    2.1.2   Inferences from HEDGED CORE to CORE   219
    2.1.3   Inferences from RESULT to CORE   220
    2.1.4   Inferences from AFTER to CORE   221
2.2   Expressives   222
    2.2.1   Inferences from BEFORE to CORE   222
    2.2.2   Inferences from HEDGED CORE to CORE   224
    2.2.3   Inferences from RESULT to CORE   225
2.3   Declarations   225
    2.3.1   Declarations of war   226
    2.3.2   Verdicts and sentences   227
    2.3.3   Religious ceremonies   229
    2.3.4   Resigning from a post   230
3.   Conclusion   233

CHAPTER 11
Cognitive pragmatics and grammar   235
1.   Introduction   235
2.   Preposed negative adverbials and auxiliary inversion   237
3.   Felicitous constraint violations: The Coordinate Structure Constraint   239
    3.1   Introduction   239
    3.2   The pattern *go [...] and VP*   241
    3.3   The pattern *sit down and VP*   244
    3.4   The pattern *stand up and VP*   248
    3.5   The pattern *take a step back and VP*   251
4.   Syntactic and conceptual mismatches: More on the pragmatics of *and*   254
    4.1   Introduction   254
    4.2   From coordination to evaluation: The *nice and Adj* construction   254
5.   Conclusion   260

CHAPTER 12
Epilogue   261
1.   To recap   261
2.   Themes and prospects   262
3.   Final thoughts   266

References   267

Name index   279

Subject index   281

Abbreviations and symbols

Lexicogrammatical & semantic-pragmatic labels

A, ACT	Action
ADJ	Adjective
ASS	Assertive illocutionary type
AUX	Auxiliary verb
CL	Clause
COND-CL	Conditional clause (protasis)
COM	Commissive illocutionary type
DAT	Dative
DECL	Declaration (illocutionary type)
DIR	Directive illocutionary type
EXPR	Expressive illocutionary type
F	Illocutionary force
FIN	Finite
GCI	Generalized conversational implicature
H	Hearer
INF	Infinitive
ING	Present participle or gerund morpheme
N	Noun
NEG	Negation
NP	Noun phrase
OBJ	Grammatical object
P	Preposition
p	Proposition *or* propositional content
PCI	Particularized conversational implicature
PTCP	Participle
PRED	Predicate
PRES	Present tense
PRF	Perfect
REFL	Reflexive morpheme
SBJ	Grammatical subject
S	Speaker
SUBJ	Subjunctive
s.v.	Latin *sub voce* 'under the heading'
V	Verb
VP	Verb phrase

Varieties of English

GB	Great Britain (British English)
US	United States (American English)

Symbols and notational conventions

⊩	Entailment
+>	Generalized conversational implicature (GCI)
++>	Particularized conversational implicature (PCI)
⊃	Material implication
→	Metonymic inference
⇒	Metaphorical mapping
>	Relation of motivation
~>	Presupposition
*	Grammatically unacceptable
?	Questionable acceptability
#	Conceptually and/or pragmatically unacceptable
'…'	Informal description of the meaning of a word or expression; e.g. *bachelor* 'unmarried man'
SMALL CAPS	Grammatical, semantic, and functional categories
∀	Universal quantifier 'all'
∃	Existential quantifier 'some'
x, *y*, etc.	Variables (bound or free)

Corpora and online dictionaries

BNC	Davies, M. (2004-) *British National Corpus* (from Oxford University Press). Available online at https://www.english-corpora.org/bnc/.
COCA	Davis, M. (2008–). *The Corpus of Contemporary American English (COCA): One billion words, 1990-2019.* Available online at https://www.english-corpora.org/coca/.
Duden	Wissensnetz deutsche Sprache
GloWbE	Davies, M. (2013). *Corpus of Global Web-Based English: 1.9 billion words from speakers in 20 countries (GloWbE).* Available online at https://www.english-corpora.org/glowbe/.
Google Books	Available online at https://books.google.com.
NOW	Davies, M. (2016-). *Corpus of News on the Web (NOW): 10 billion words from 20 countries, updated every day.* Available online at https://www.english-corpora.org/now/.
iWeb	Davies, M. (2018-). *The 14 Billion Word iWeb Corpus.* Available online at https://www.english-corpora.org/iWeb/.
TV	Davies, M. (2019-). *The TV Corpus: 325 million words, 1950-2018.* Available online at https://www.english-corpora.org/tv/.
DWDS	*Digitales Wörterbuch der deutschen Sprache.* Available online at https://www.dwds.de/
WebCorp	*The Web as Corpus* (Birmingham City University). Available online at http://www.webcorp.org.uk/live/
NOAD	*New Oxford American Dictionary*
ODE	*Oxford Dictionary of English*
OED	*Oxford Dictionary of English*
OGD	*Oxford German Dictionary*

List of tables and figures

CHAPTER 1
Cognitive linguistics and pragmatics

Table 1.	Truth table for logical conjunction	5
Table 2.	Truth table for logical disjunction	6
Table 3.	Truth table for material implication	7
Figure 1.	Continuum between semantics and pragmatics	15

CHAPTER 2
Cognitive-pragmatic motivation of language structure and use

Table 1.	Word order in the world's languages	23
Table 2.	Verbs with the meaning 'laugh' in seven languages	30
Table 3.	Verbs with the meaning 'meow' in five languages	31
Table 4.	The word for 'cuckoo' in five languages	31
Table 5.	The dichotomies 'motivated vs. unmotivated' and 'conventional vs. non-conventional' exemplified	33
Figure 1.	Linguistic signs: Content vs. form	27
Figure 2.	Conventionality and motivation scales	29

CHAPTER 3
The role of inference in the construction of meaning

Table 1.	Deductive reasoning	45
Table 2.	Inductive reasoning	46
Table 3.	Abductive reasoning	48
Table 4.	Entailment	49
Table 5.	Presupposition	51
Table 6.	Logical negation	58

CHAPTER 4
Principles guiding communication

Figure 1.	The code model of communication	64
Figure 2.	The inferential model of communication	65
Figure 3.	Saying and implicating: Misunderstandings	67
Figure 4.	What is said vs. what is implicated	67

CHAPTER 5
Implicature, entailment, and presupposition

Table 1.	Distribution of *entered a/the building/agreement* vs. *entered into a/the building/agreement* in the NOW corpus	98
Table 2.	Defeasibility and reinforceability of three inferential relations	104

CHAPTER 6
Talking as action

Table 1.	Component acts of speech acts	111
Table 2.	Representatives (e.g. *assert*)	119
Table 3.	Commissives (e.g. *promise*)	119
Table 4.	Directives (e.g. *request*)	119
Table 5.	Expressives (e.g. *congratulate, apologize*)	120
Table 6.	Declarations (e.g. *appoint, baptize*)	121
Table 7.	Prototypical directives vs. consultatives	133
Figure 1.	Illocutionary force and propositional content indicators	124
Figure 2.	Illocutionary scenario schema	128
Figure 3.	Scenario for assertives	129
Figure 4.	Commissives (promise)	130
Figure 5.	Directives	131
Figure 6.	Expressives	134
Figure 7.	Apologizing	134
Figure 8.	Congratulating	135
Figure 9.	Thanking	136
Figure 10.	Declarations	137
Figure 11.	Resigning	138

CHAPTER 7
Metaphor

Table 1.	Contrasting literal and metaphorical transfer I	156
Table 2.	Contrasting literal and metaphorical transfer II	157
Table 3.	Ditransitive construction with *give*: THING transfer vs. ACTION transfer	158
Table 4.	Ditransitive construction with *give*: THING transfer vs. FEELING transfer	159
Figure 1.	Conceptual-pragmatic structure of metaphor	147
Figure 2.	The metaphor CHAMELEON ⇒ PERSON	148
Figure 3.	The Shakespearean metaphor STAGE ⇒ WORLD	149
Figure 4.	The metaphor FIDDLER ⇒ LIFE	150

Figure 5.	Some mappings of the metaphor JOURNEY ⇒ LIFE	152
Figure 6.	Metaphorical mapping of PATH topology onto SCALE topology: *way beyond*	154
Figure 7.	Metaphorical mapping of PATH topology onto SCALE topology: *far more*	155

CHAPTER 8
Metonymy

Table 1.	Correspondences between language-independent abductive reasoning (Peirce) and an abductively motivated interpretation strategy for metonymies	182
Figure 1.	Basic metonymic relation	167
Figure 2.	Footprints in the desert as a visual index of the passage of camels	170

CHAPTER 9
Metonymic inferencing in indirect speech acts I

Figure 1.	Metonymic shifts in illocutionary force and propositional content	201
Figure 2.	Asserting *p* by means of asking H to believe *p*	204
Figure 3.	Offers by means of *I can VP / Can I VP?*	206
Figure 4.	Offers by means of Do you want/would you like me to do A?	207
Figure 5.	Promising by means of *I intend to VP*	207
Figure 6.	Hedged performative commissives: *I can promise/offer (you) to do A*	208
Figure 7.	Indirect offers: *Shall I VP$_{ACTION}$?*	209
Figure 8.	Indirect commissives via constructions that denote S's obligation to do A	210
Figure 9.	Indirect commissives: *I will/shall VP$_{ACTION}$*	211
Figure 10.	Inferential structure of *Consider it done*	212

CHAPTER 10
Metonymic inferencing in indirect speech acts II

Table 1.	The metonymy-based metaphor STEPPING DOWN ⇒ LEAVING OFFICE	233
Figure 1.	Directives by means of *You can/could VP$_{ACTION}$* and *Can/could you VP$_{ACTION}$?*	216
Figure 2.	Indirect requests by means of *If you can/could VP$_{ACTION}$*	217
Figure 3.	Directives (suggestions) by means of *Why don't you VP$_{ACTION}$?*	218

Figure 4.	Directives by means of *I want you to* VP$_{\text{ACTION}}$	219
Figure 5.	Hedged directive performatives: *I must ask you to* VP$_{\text{ACTION}}$	220
Figure 6.	Directives by means of *You must/should* VP$_{\text{ACTION}}$	221
Figure 7.	Directives by means of *You will* VP$_{\text{ACTION}}$ or *Will you* VP$_{\text{ACTION}}$?	222

CHAPTER 11
Cognitive pragmatics and grammar

Table 1.	Conceptual and pragmatic properties of *sit down and* VP and *stand up and* VP	250
Table 2.	Additional metaphorical mappings triggered by *take a step back*	253
Figure 1.	Temporal-aspectual structure of *go [...] and* VP	242
Figure 2.	Temporal-aspectual structure of *sit down and* VP	245
Figure 3.	Literal *sit down (and)* as aspectualizer signaling a facilitating/enabling action	247
Figure 4.	Literal *stand up (and)* as aspectualizer signaling a facilitating/enabling action	250
Figure 5.	Metonymic and metaphoric structure of *take a step back and* VP	252
Figure 6.	Metonymic derivation of the target sense of the *nice and Adj* construction	257

About the author

Klaus-Uwe Panther is Professor Emeritus of English Linguistics at the University of Hamburg, Germany. He was a founding member of the German Cognitive Linguistics Association in 2004 and served as its first president from 2004 through 2008. He also served as president of the International Cognitive Linguistics Association from 2005 through 2007. He has been a keynote speaker at various international conferences and a visiting scholar at Indiana University (Bloomington), the University of California (Berkeley), the University Michel de Montaigne (Bordeaux, France), Eötvös Loránd University (Budapest, Hungary), Southern Illinois University (Carbondale), and the University of la Rioja (Logroño, Spain). In 2007, he was granted an Honorary Professorship by the International Studies University in Xi'an (China). From 2012 through 2014 he served as Distinguished Visiting Professor at Nanjing Normal University (China). His research interests include cognitive linguistics and pragmatics, with a special focus on the interaction of grammatical structure and conceptual-pragmatic meaning. His most recent monograph (co-authored with Linda Thornburg) is *Motivation and inference: A cognitive linguistic approach* (2017, Shanghai Foreign Language Education Press).

Foreword

The present work is an attempt to blend a cognitive linguistic approach to language and language use with insights from contemporary pragmatics, in particular, Gricean and Neo-Gricean pragmatics. I believe that the time has come for a synthesis of these paradigms, which, in my view, have more in common than meets the eye, although certain incompatibilities remain, which will be pointed out in due course.

The themes treated in this book range from figurative language and thought, such as metaphor and metonymy, the role of inferencing in meaning construction, and speech acts (especially, indirect illocutionary acts) to the motivation of morphosyntactic structure by conceptual content and pragmatic function. The book may serve as a textbook for advanced students with some basic knowledge of semantics and pragmatics, and my hope is that it might also be of interest to scholars working within a cognitive linguistic and/or Gricean theoretical framework. I am grateful to Carita Paradis and Stefanie Wulff, the editors of the CLiP series, who, for years, have been waiting patiently to receive the final version of the manuscript.

Some earlier versions of the subject matter of this book were presented to doctoral students and interested faculty during my stay as Visiting Professor at Nanjing Normal University and other Chinese universities between 2012 and 2014. I would like to thank all these audiences for their feedback.

In 2018, six draft chapters of the manuscript were tested and assessed by Carita Paradis and her students in a seminar held at Lund University. I am very appreciative of the comments and suggestions for improvement I received from Carita and some of her students, which I have made an effort to take into account. My thanks also go to the external reviewer of the manuscript, Mario Brdar, for his insightful comments. Remaining errors are, of course, my responsibility.

Last but not least, I would like to thank my spouse and frequent co-author Linda Thornburg for her support and encouragement while I was writing this book, and for her thorough review of the manuscript. As the reader will notice, a substantial amount of our joint research has found its way into this monograph. Without Linda's expertise, I could not have written this book. It is with gratitude that I dedicate this work to her.

Kendal, Cumbria, UK
July 2021

CHAPTER 1

Cognitive linguistics and pragmatics

1. Introduction

In a book with the title *Introduction to Cognitive Pragmatics* the reader can expect some elucidation and clarification of the key terms *cognitive* and *pragmatics*. To that end, in this chapter, basic notions of 20th and 21st century pragmatics (Section 2) are introduced; then the most important theoretical commitments of contemporary *cognitive linguistics* are presented (Section 3), and finally a case is made for a blend of pragmatics and cognitive linguistics, which lays the foundation for what this book is mainly about, namely, a *cognitive-linguistic approach to pragmatics*, in particular, to *speech acts*.

2. Pragmatics

2.1 Some basic features of contemporary pragmatics

In order to get a grip on the field of pragmatics, it is helpful to situate it in the broader context of *semiotics*, i.e. the theory of signs, including linguistic and non-linguistic signs. One of the leading semioticians of the 20th century, Charles Morris (1938: 67), distinguished the following three dimensions in the study of signs: (i) *syntactics*, i.e. the formal relations that obtain among signs; (ii) *semantics*, i.e. the relation between signs and the objects they denote; and (iii) *pragmatics*, i.e. the relation between signs and their users (see also Cobley 2010: 318; Nöth 1990: 50).

For the time being, we can ignore syntactics, or, as this discipline is called in linguistics, *syntax*, and focus on semantics and pragmatics. In modern pragmatics, it is commonly assumed that there exists a division of labor between semantics, the discipline that deals with the *meaning* of linguistic expressions, and pragmatics, which is concerned with *meaning-in-use* of a linguistic unit, i.e. the influence that the communicative situation and the discourse context exert on its meaning. I postpone the question whether this distinction can be justified, or whether it should be modified or even abandoned until Section 2.2.7.

The conception of pragmatics described in the preceding paragraph as the study of meaning-in-use is characteristic of the *Anglo-American* tradition of pragmatics.

It contrasts in certain respects with what has been called the *European Continental* tradition, one of whose best-known representatives is a founding member of the International Pragmatics Association, Jef Verschueren. Verschueren (1999: 6) characterizes pragmatics as the study of "people's *use of language.*" Pragmatics is "intended to give insight into *the link between language and human life in general*" (ibid.: 6–7), i.e. assumes "a functional perspective on every aspect of linguistic behaviour" (Huang 2007: 4). In the present book, in accordance with the Anglo-American tradition, the focus is mainly on the study of meaning-in-use, although its relation to other components of the architecture of language, in particular, morphology and syntax is also considered in due course (see in particular Chapter 11).

In the Anglo-American tradition of pragmatics, a clear borderline is usually drawn between semantics (the study of meaning) and pragmatics (the study of meaning-in-use). One leading proponent of this view, the British linguist Geoffrey Leech (1983: 6), formulates the distinction between semantics and pragmatics in terms of the following two questions (slightly adapted):

i. What does *X* mean? [semantics]
ii. What do you mean by *X*? [pragmatics]

Question (i) is about the *conventional* meaning of some expression *X*, i.e., it is a matter of semantics, whereas (ii) is a question about which meaning the speaker of *X intends* to convey to the hearer. Leech points out that question (i) implies a *dyadic* relation between an expression *X* and its meaning, where the latter is independent of the context in which *X* is uttered. In contrast, (ii) exhibits a *triadic* relation, i.e. a relation between a speaker, a linguistic expression *X*, and what the speaker means by *X* in a specific communicative situation and linguistic context. The study of speaker meaning and of "context-dependent aspects of meaning" (Horn & Ward 2006: xi) is generally seen as a central task of pragmatics (see also Allott 2010: 1–2).

It is important to keep in mind that in Anglo-American pragmatics, as e.g. Leech (1983: 6) emphasizes, semantics and pragmatics complement each other in the construction of the overall meaning of expressions and utterances. The following piece of narrative fiction nicely illustrates this complementarity:

(1) [Nadine] was immediately greeted by a zealous aesthetician with jet-black hair and lots of makeup, whom Nadine guessed to be in her late forties. "You'd like a manicure and a pedicure?" Nadine rubbed her arms. "It's cold in here." "We're fixing it right away. You'd like a manicure and a pedicure?" she repeated hopefully. (COCA 1993)[1]

---

1. The piece of narrative discourse in (1) is taken from the mystery novel *Snagged* (1993) by Carol Higgins Clarke.

Let us focus on Nadine's utterance *It's cold in here* in (1). This sentence has a clear conventional meaning, in the sense of Leech's question (i). It is a statement about the low temperature in the room referred to deictically by the locative adverb *here*. However, in uttering this sentence Nadine most likely wishes to convey more meaning than is explicitly *coded* in her utterance. Evidence for non-coded additional meaning is readily derivable from e.g. the aesthetician's response to Nadine's utterance: *We're fixing it right away*. Apparently, the beautician interprets Nadine's utterance not just as a neutral statement but also as a *complaint* and most likely as an *indirect request* to do something about the low temperature in the room. These additional meanings are pragmatic in the sense of question (ii) above. They can be *inferred* on the basis of the literal meaning of *It's cold in here*, the surrounding discourse context, and the communicative situation. And indeed, as we have seen, many scholars regard the study of the role of context in the construction of meaning as the most important task of pragmatics. To cite two more scholars with this view, British linguist D. Alan Cruse (2006: 3) contends that "[t]he central topics of linguistic pragmatics are those aspects of meaning which are dependent on context", and, similarly, in her introductory textbook on pragmatics, American linguist Betty J. Birner (2013: 2) characterizes the contrast between pragmatics and semantics as: "**Pragmatics** may be roughly defined as the study of language use in context – as compared with semantics, which is the study of literal meaning independent of context […]."

Some pragmaticists, in addition to defining pragmatics in the same vein as those already mentioned as "the study of meaning by virtue of, or dependent on, the use of language" (Huang 2007: 2), list various phenomena of language use that they consider to be the main objects of pragmatic inquiry. Among them are the study of *implicatures* or "invited inferences", *presuppositions*, *speech acts*, and *deixis*. This "list" approach to defining the range of linguistic phenomena studied in pragmatics is also adopted by British linguist Peter Grundy (2000: 17) in his introductory textbook where additional "features of talk" (i.e. properties of language-in-use) such as *appropriacy* (of speech acts), *relevance, non-literal, indirect meaning*, and *inference* are cited as fields of pragmatic inquiry.

The characterizations of pragmatics given in the preceding paragraphs presume the existence of use-independent and context-free conventional meanings that are elaborated in various ways in actual communication and discourse to yield meanings-in-use. The function and conceptual structure of such non-literal, i.e. implicit or indirect meanings, is one of the central topics of this book, and it will be shown that an integrative approach that combines contemporary pragmatics with cognitive linguistic analyses may yield new insights into meanings-in-use.

2.2 The semantics-pragmatics dichotomy: Advantages and drawbacks

Let us now discuss in more detail the often-presumed division of labor between semantics and pragmatics. A highly influential paradigm in present-day semantics is based on the idea that knowing the meaning of a sentence amounts to knowing the circumstances under which the sentence in question is *true*. In Section 2.2.1, this *truth-conditional* approach to meaning is illustrated with what logicians call sentence *connectives*, i.e. conjunctions such as e.g. *and, or,* and *if*. In Section 2.2.2, the relation between (discourse) *coherence* and truth conditions is briefly examined. Section 2.2.3 discusses various *sentence types*, such as declaratives, interrogatives, and imperatives with the aim of determining whether their respective meanings can be accounted for in terms of truth conditions. Sections 2.2.4 and 2.2.5 demonstrate the influence of pragmatic inferences and deictic expressions, respectively, on the assignment of truth values to sentences. On the basis of the linguistic data discussed in Sections 2.2.1–2.2.5, Section 2.2.6 seeks to provide an answer to the question to what extent the truth-conditional approach can be applied to conventional meanings. Finally, some conclusions are drawn about the pros and cons of a truth-conditional approach to meaning in Section 2.2.7.

2.2.1 *Meaning and truth conditions*

One important pragmatic school of thought founded by the philosopher of language H. Paul Grice (1975, 1989) and named after him as *Gricean pragmatics*, distinguishes between what is *said*, i.e. conventionally signaled by a sentence (the domain of semantics), and what is *implicated*, i.e. the implicit conveyance of additional meanings in certain contexts of use (the domain of pragmatics; for more details see Chapter 4). The basic idea is that knowing the conventional meaning of a sentence (what is said) amounts to knowing under which circumstances that sentence expresses a true state-of-affairs. As already mentioned above, this conception of semantics is called the *truth-conditional* approach to the description of meaning. It is inspired by modern logic and may appear counterintuitive to a linguist not trained in logical semantics. After all, what does language meaning have to do with truth? Yet, it is not unreasonable to assume that certain aspects of meaning are indeed *truth-conditional*. To see this, consider the meaning of the coordinating conjunction *and*, which is ubiquitous in English, appearing tens of millions of times in the *Corpus of Contemporary American English* (COCA). Here is a fictional example from this corpus (italics added):

(2) He was in charge *and* it frightened him. (COCA 2013)

Sentence (2) consists of two clauses that are connected by the coordinating conjunction *and*. In Gricean pragmatics, the meaning of *and* (and corresponding conjunctions in other languages) is regarded as essentially equivalent to the *logical connective* '∧', which is standardly referred to as a relation of *conjunction* between *propositions* (not to be confused with the sense that the term *conjunction* has in grammar!). The logical meaning of '∧' can be represented by means of a *truth table* such as in Table 1.

Table 1. Truth table for logical conjunction

	p	q	p ∧ q
1.	T	T	T
2.	T	F	F
3.	F	T	F
4.	F	F	F

p, q: propositions; ∧ 'and'; T = true, F = false

The letters *p* and *q* are symbols for propositions and *T* and *F* stand for the truth values 'true' and 'false', respectively. In the second and third column of Table 1, the possible distribution of the truth values *T* and *F* for the propositions *p* and *q* is displayed. The fourth column shows the respective truth values of the complex expression *p* ∧ *q*. According to the truth table, *p* ∧ *q* is true if and only if both *p* and *q* are true. In all other cases, *p* ∧ *q* is false. This configuration squares fairly well with the intuitions of ordinary language users about the meaning of the English conjunction *and*, as well as its equivalents in other languages.

By way of illustration, let us check the applicability of the truth table method to a conjunctive sentence, where *p* corresponds to the proposition expressed in the (complex) clause *I told her regretfully I won't be able to make it*, and *q* to *she was hurt*. If it is true that the speaker (*I*) told the female character that he "won't be able to make it" and the proposition expressed in the conjoined clause that the female's feelings were hurt is also true, then the conjunction of these two propositions constitutes a true statement. If however (at least) one of the two clauses denotes a falsehood, e.g. if the female character referred to in (2) is not hurt, then, as predicted in Table 1, the complex proposition *p* and *q* is false. Thus, for the example given and many others, the truth-conditional approach works, and the hypothesis seems reasonable that the English coordinating conjunction *and*, as well as equivalent conjunctions in other languages, shares logical properties with the connective '∧' in the propositional calculus.

While the logical connective '∧' is semantically relatively close to the conjunction *and* in English, and can thus serve as a template for the semantic description of this natural language conjunction, things become more problematic with the logical connective '∨', which is usually equated with the natural language conjunction *or*. Table 2 provides the truth value distribution of the logical connective '∨'.

Table 2. Truth table for logical disjunction

	p	q	p ∨ q
1.	T	T	T
2.	T	F	T
3.	F	T	T
4.	F	F	F

p, q: propositions; ∨ 'or'; T = true, F = false

Table 2 shows that the complex proposition $p \vee q$ is only false if p and q are both false (see row 4 in Table 2). From a linguistic perspective, the "odd man out" is row 1, i.e. the combination of both p and q having the truth value T, in which case $p \vee q$ is true. At first sight, this result is counterintuitive because the typical sense of *or* in English is 'either … or', i.e., *or* has an *exclusive* sense, as exemplified by (3):

(3) John is in the library *or* (he is) in his office.

John cannot be in two locations at the same time; thus, either the proposition 'John is in the library' is true and 'John is in his office' is false, or the former proposition is false and the latter is true. The first combinatorial possibility, i.e. that both propositions are true, yields a falsehood in the case of (3).

There are however other uses of *or* in which the conjunction has an *inclusive* reading:

(4) Wart viruses can easily be picked up in the shower or in the locker room at pools or gyms. (COCA 2005)

(5) Teachers or students can choose from two main-menu options […]. (COCA 2003)

Example (4) admits the possibility that both 'Wart viruses can easily be picked up in the shower at pools or gyms' *and* 'Wart viruses can easily be picked up in the locker room at pools or gyms' are true. Furthermore, the *or* in *pool or gyms* also allows an inclusive interpretation, i.e., it can be replaced with *and*. In sentence (5), *or* is again inclusive, i.e., (5) has as one of its interpretations 'Teachers can choose from two main-menu options *and* students can choose from two main-menu options'.

The relationship between the natural language semantics of conjunctions and logical connectives gets even more tenuous in the case of what logicians call *material implication*. The truth table for this connective, which is often likened to natural language *if … then*, is given in Table 3.

Table 3. Truth table for material implication

	p	q	p ⊃ q
1.	T	T	T
2.	T	F	F
3.	F	T	T
4.	F	F	T

p, q: propositions; ⊃ 'if …then'; *T* = true, *F* = false

The problem with equating material implication in logic with conditional sentences in human languages becomes especially manifest in the third and the fourth row in Table 3. What is stipulated in these rows is that from a false proposition *p* any proposition *q* follows; in other words, it does not matter which truth value *q* has. This logical property runs counter to how language users would most likely interpret sentences like (6) and (7):

(6) If Paris is the capital of Norway, then Madrid is the capital of Spain.

(7) If Paris is the capital of Norway, then Berlin is the capital of China.

In (6) the protasis – the *if* clause, is false, and the apodosis – the consequent clause – is true, i.e., the truth value distribution is as in row 3 of Table 3. Thus logically (6) is true! Yet, native speakers of English would probably consider (6) holistically as false because the content of the *if* clause does not correspond to the facts. However, from the purely formal point of view of propositional logic, what is relevant is not the conceptual relationship between the two sentences, but, independent of their content, the relation between their individual truth values.

In sentence (7), the distribution of truth values corresponds to row 4 in Table 3. To call the whole sentence true, as Table 3 stipulates, seems even more implausible than in the case of (6). Another problem discussed in more detail in Section 2.2.2 is that both (6) and (7) do not "make sense." It is hard to imagine that such sentences would ever appear in a real-life communication; at face value, they look incoherent (see also Birner 2013: 50–51, regarding the counter-intuitiveness of rows 3 and 4 in Table 3).[2]

To conclude, the relevance of truth conditions in an adequate theory of linguistic meaning is somewhat ambivalent. On the one hand, there is some plausibility to the idea that knowledge or beliefs about the circumstances under which propositions describe existing states-of-affairs is part of the semantic competence of

---

2. This statement has to be taken with a grain of salt. One could imagine a context in which somebody might utter sentence (7) as a reaction to another speaker who has said something patently false, with the aim in mind of mocking this speaker.

language users. On the other hand, as we have seen especially in the case of material implication, there are problems with a truth-conditional account because the truth conditions stipulated in logic do not always square with the intuitions that ordinary language users have about the truth values of complex sentences – even with regard to such mundane conjunctions as *and*, *or*, and *if*.

2.2.2 Truth conditions and (lack of) coherence

The most serious flaw of the truth-conditional approach is that it does not take conceptual relations, i.e. *coherence* relations, among propositions into account. As an illustration of this problem, consider (8) (italics added):

(8) The sun is the star at the center of the solar system *and* François Hollande of France meets Fidel and Raúl Castro in Cuba.[3]

The two propositions conjoined by *and* in (8), which have been selected randomly from two different online sources, are both individually true. The first proposition is backed up by scientific evidence, and the second refers truthfully to an event that took place on May 12, 2015. Thus, in accordance with Table 1 (Section 2.2.1), sentence (8) as a whole is true since both conjuncts are true.

Yet, example (8) hardly makes sense in ordinary communication because it is virtually impossible to establish a coherence link between the first and the second clause. The two clauses are grammatical, they are meaningful individually, and they are true; however, if they are conjoined with *and*, they result in a piece of nonsensical discourse. In natural language communication, it is not enough to conjoin two clauses solely on the grounds that both clauses express presumably true propositions. The language user expects the *contents* of two conjoined clauses to be conceptually and pragmatically *connected*. A purely formal logical analysis in terms of truth conditions neglects this important requirement.

If the first clause of (8) is conjoined with a second clause, as in example (9), the result is a perfectly coherent text (example slightly adapted and italics added):

(9) The sun is the star at the center of the solar system *and* is by far the most important source of energy for life on Earth.
(https://en.wikipedia.org/wiki/Sun; accessed May 13, 2015)

In the case of (9), coherence between the first clause and the second clause is achieved by means of *topic continuity*. The second clause is about the same referent

---

3. The first clause is from the Wikipedia article *Sun* [accessed May 13, 2015 at: https://en.wikipedia.org/wiki/Sun], and the second clause was collected from the *New York Times* [http://www.nytimes.com/2015/05/13/world/europe/cuba-france-fidel-castro-francois-hollande-visit.html; accessed May 13, 2015].

as the first clause (*the sun*), and therefore, according to the rules of English grammar, that referent does not even have to be explicitly coded in the second clause – a phenomenon known as *conjunction reduction*.

There are various means available to language users to accomplish coherence. For example, in utterance (2) (Section 2.2.1), the conceptual connection between first clause *He was in charge* (p) and the proposition expressed in the second clause *It frightened him* (q) is not just a matter of the truth conditional meaning of *and*, but an additional (unstated) cause-effect relationship between the contents of the two clauses is implied: the protagonist referred to as *he* is frightened *because* of some presumably important duty or responsibility he is charged with.

But how can the cause-effect sense in (2) be accounted for? An interesting answer to this question has been given by Grice (1975, 1989), and linguists influenced by him, such as e.g. Levinson (1983, 2000), and Huang (2007). They suggest that this meaning is derived inferentially, via (conversational) *implicature*, sometimes also called *invited inference* (Geis & Zwicky 1971; Traugott & Dasher 2002). The notion of implicature is dealt with in more detail in Chapter 5. For the time being, suffice it to say that in *Gricean* pragmatics, a fundamental distinction is made between what is *said* and what is *implicated*. The basic idea is that what is *said* is the subject matter of *semantics* and what is implicated is part of the domain of *pragmatics*. More generally, semantics is conceived of as dealing with truth-conditional aspects of meaning while pragmatics deals with non-truth-conditional properties of meaning. Thus, the causal sense of *and* in (2) is regarded as the conclusion of a usually spontaneous and subconscious *act of inference* performed by the reader in an effort to establish a coherence relation between the senses of the two clauses.

2.2.3 *Non-declarative sentence types*

As we have seen in Section 2.2.2, Grice and his followers assume that semantics is concerned with truth-conditional meaning and that non-truth conditional meanings can be derived via implicatures or invited inferences. Yet, one important problem with this approach remains: there exist sentence types that cannot be analyzed in terms of truth conditions.

A look at the grammar of natural languages reveals that only instances of one sentence type can be assigned truth values in a straightforward way, i.e. *declarative* sentences such as (8) and (9) in Section 2.2.2. But what about *interrogative* and *imperative* sentences? Consider examples such as in (10):

(10) a. How do you like the pie? (COCA 2011)
 b. Do you like opera? (COCA 2011)
 c. What do you like most about your country? (COCA 2012)

Interrogative sentences do not have a truth value *per se*, but the answers to them, which provide the requested information, do – if they are of the declarative type. Note however that it is not uncommon to find interrogative sentences that are not used as genuine requests for information but as *rhetorical questions*. Among other things, such interrogatives may have the function of implicitly asserting something. For example, consider (11) from an American television broadcast:

(11) Goodnight, and take a look at the White House. Isn't it beautiful? Look how gorgeous it is, all lit up at night, the Washington Monument behind it. It looks absolutely spectacular. (COCA 2009)

In the given context, the interrogative *Isn't it beautiful?* functions as an implicit aesthetic judgment that, in principle, can be discussed in terms or whether it is true or false (although beauty is in the eye of the beholder!) Note however that the implicitly assertive sense of rhetorical questions is based on the literal question meaning, which does not have a truth value.

Another major sentence type, imperative sentences, cannot be assigned truth values either. Consider the series of imperatives in (12):

(12) Slide open the window. Step over the transom. Close the window. Lock it up. Pull the shades. Flip the switch. (COCA 2008)

The standard meaning of imperatives, as e.g. pointed out by Huddleston and Pullum (2005: 8) is *directive*, i.e., an imperative is used to induce its addressee to perform a certain action in the future. As such, it is neither true nor false. One can however argue that the concept of truth is involved *indirectly* in imperatives, in the sense that some *agent* (the hearer) will *make* a proposition *true* (or not true) in the future. This is not a 'truth condition' in the narrow sense, but it can be called a *satisfaction condition* (see e.g. Wunderlich 1976: Chapter 3; Vanderveken 2004). For example, the imperative *Flip the switch* in (12) is satisfied if the addressee of the request or order expressed by the imperative sentence *actually* performs the desired action of flipping the switch. 'Satisfaction condition' is a broader concept than 'truth condition', and it is therefore more capable than the latter of capturing important aspects of sentence type meaning.

2.2.4 *The role of pragmatic inferences in the assignment of truth values*

The conception of semantics and pragmatics sketched in the preceding sections still presumes that there exists a clear dividing line between the two: semantics deals with truth-conditional, or, more broadly, satisfaction-conditional meaning, whereas pragmatic meaning, i.e. meaning-in-use, is constructed via invited inferences/implicatures that operate on the basis of truth/satisfaction-conditional meanings. However, on closer examination, it turns out that these conceptions of the respective functions of semantics and pragmatics are too simplistic. For example, the evaluation of the truth (or falsity) of a declarative sentence may depend on what it implies pragmatically – contrary to Grice's assumption that implicatures have no impact on truth conditions. The following sentence, which contains two instances of the connective *and*, illustrates this phenomenon:

(13) Cheryl waved and Luke smiled and held up the sodas to show he couldn't wave back [...]. (COCA 1998)

In (13), the first *and* is most likely to be interpreted as 'and then', or more precisely, as 'and then, as a reaction', i.e., Cheryl waved and Luke responded to Cheryl's waving with a smile, etc. In contrast, the second *and* suggests the interpretation 'and simultaneously', i.e., Luke smiled and held up the sodas at the same time. Do these contextually induced interpretations contribute something to the overall truth value of sentence (13)? The first point to notice is that for the logical connective '$\wedge$' it does not matter whether the order of the propositions is $p \wedge q$ or $q \wedge p$.[4] In the truth-conditional logic of connectives, conceptual relationships between propositions, e.g. temporal order, cause-effect relationships, etc., are not taken into account. However, in example (13), the order of the conjoined propositions is crucial: if Luke smiled and (then, as a reaction) Cheryl waved, (13) is arguably false because the temporal order of the events depicted is not correctly represented.

The influence of pragmatic factors on truth-conditional meaning becomes even more evident when more complex sentence structures are examined. Posner (1980: 194) discusses the following (made-up) example in terms of its truth conditions:

(14) If Annie has married and has had a baby, grandfather will be happy.

Posner observes that the truth value of sentence (14) depends on the temporal order of the events depicted in the *if*-clause. A conservative grandfather will be happy if Annie gets married and *then* has her baby. If Annie has her baby *before* she gets married, her grandfather might not be happy at all. What this example shows is that, first, the pragmatic interpretation of utterances can influence the truth value assigned to sentences. And second, the truth value assigned to sentences like (14) depends on the *cultural model* of marriage that Annie's grandfather happens to value.

---

4. This property of logical conjunction is known as *commutativity*.

2.2.5 Deixis

The British philosopher of language P. F. Strawson argues that *declarative sentences* should be distinguished from *statements*, i.e. declarative sentences-in-use. According to Strawson (1952: 4), only statements can be assigned truth values. The truth value of a statement crucially depends on *when*, *where*, and by *whom* a sentence is uttered. Most sentences contain words or morphemes whose interpretation depends on the context in which they are used. Such units are known as *deictic* or *indexical* elements.[5] Deictic units are e.g. personal, possessive, and demonstrative pronouns, the definite article, temporal and locative adverbs, and markers of tense. The analysis of deixis is considered by many scholars to be a matter of pragmatics (see Huang 2007: 2). If this presumption is accepted, it follows that the assignment of truth values to declarative sentences is not only a matter of semantics, but also of pragmatics.

To illustrate the importance of deixis in the determination of truth values, consider the following small piece of discourse adopted from Blakemore (1987: 106):

(15) A few days ago, my neighbour asked me if I would like to go to her son's school play. I told her I couldn't.

The truth values of the two sentences in (15) depend on the reference of *my*, *I*, and *me*, i.e. who the speaker or writer is, and who the referent of *her* is. Furthermore, the truth values depend on the temporal reference of the phrase *a few days ago* and that of the past tense morpheme *-ed*, i.e. the time when the described event took place – to name just a few linguistic elements that are relevant.

2.2.6 Conventional non-truth conditional meanings

Natural language conjunctions may have both truth-conditional and *conventional* non-truth conditional meanings. The non-truth-conditional meaning is an inherent part of such conjunctions, i.e., it does not have to be pragmatically inferred as in the case of *and* (see Section 2.2.2). Such sentence connectives, once again, pose a problem for a semantics that is exclusively truth-conditional. As an example, consider the following authentic piece of spoken discourse from a television news broadcast on the U.S. network *ABC* in 2012 (read by Andrea Canning). The first sentence provides some context for the second sentence, which contains two clauses conjoined by *but* (italics added):

(16) On December 15th, 1994, McLaughlin, a 55-year-old inventor, was shot six times inside his home. [...]. No arrests were made at the time, *but* 15 years later, prosecutors re-examined the evidence.   (COCA 2012)

---

5. According to the OED, *deictic* is derived from the Greek adjective of δεικτικός 'able to show', showing directly' whereas *indexical* stems from Latin *index* 'forefinger'. These etymologies already point to the fact that the interpretation of deictic or indexical elements is determined by the linguistic or extra-linguistic context.

The coordinating conjunction *but* shares some of its meaning with *and*; however, in addition, it has its own idiosyncratic sense. To see this, consider (17), which is identical to the second sentence in (16), in contrast to (18) (italics added):

(17) No arrests were made at the time, *but* 15 years later, prosecutors re-examined the evidence.

(18) No arrests were made at the time, *and* 15 years later, prosecutors re-examined the evidence.

The statement in (17) is *true* under exactly the same circumstances as the one in (18), i.e. if and only if both clauses conjoined by *but* and *and*, respectively, express true propositions. Thus, from a truth-conditional perspective, sentences (17) and (18) have the same meaning. Yet, intuitively, (17) and (18) are not felt to be synonymous. In addition to having the same truth conditions as *and*, the coordinating conjunction *but* conveys that the contents of the two conjoined clauses are in some *contrastive* relationship. In the given case (17), the event depicted in the second clause introduced by *but*, i.e. the reexamination of the evidence, is somewhat surprising or unexpected, given the truth of the event denoted by the first clause. This contrastive relationship is essential to an understanding of the meaning of *but*; nevertheless, it does not contribute anything to the truth value of the whole utterance. Grice (1975: 44) (see also Grice 1989: 25) refers to such kinds of inherent non-truth conditional meanings as *conventional implicatures*. He claims that the speaker of (17) does *not say* that there is a contrastive relationship between the first clause and the following *but*-clause, but that the contrastive relationship is part of what is implicitly, but still conventionally conveyed, i.e. conventionally implicated.

The Gricean analysis of (17) relies on the assumption that there is a well-defined borderline between what is *said* and what is *conventionally implicated*. However, again, as in other examples that involve implicature, the boundary between saying and implicating seems rather fuzzy. A diagnostic criterion to determine whether the contrastive sense of *but* is part of what is said or what is (conventionally) implicated is to convert the content of (17) into indirect speech. The question is then whether (19) or (20) is a better and more accurate rendition of (17).

(19) ABC journalist Andrea Canning *said* that it is somewhat surprising that, given the fact that no arrests of were made at the time (i.e. in December 1994), 15 years later prosecutors re-examined the evidence.

(20) ABC journalist Andrea Canning *implied* that it is somewhat surprising that, given the fact that no arrests of were made at the time (i.e. in December 1994), 15 years later prosecutors re-examined the evidence.

It seems virtually impossible to make an unequivocal commitment as to whether (19) or (20) is the adequate report of the content of (17).

As a second example of a conventional meaning that is not truth-conditional, consider (21) in contrast to (22). Example (21) differs from example (22) in that it contains the focus adverb *even*:

(21) Recall the disastrous collapse of freewheeling Long-Term Capital Management a few years ago. Even George Soros has had trouble from time to time.
(COCA 2002)

(22) Recall the disastrous collapse of freewheeling Long-Term Capital Management a few years ago. George Soros has had trouble from time to time.

The second sentence in (21) is true under the same circumstances as the second sentence in (22). Under a strictly truth-conditional analysis, the two sentences would have to be considered synonymous. However, the second sentence in (21) conventionally conveys the meaning that, unexpectedly, one of the richest business magnates and investors in the world, George Soros, has been in financial trouble from time to time. Yet, despite the unlikelihood of the event described in the second clause, the proposition 'George Soros has had trouble from time to time' is actually claimed to be true by the speaker or writer of (21) (for a detailed description of the meaning of *even*, see e.g. König 1991: 63–78). Again, as in the case of (17), the question arises as to how (21) should be rendered in indirect speech. Would the speaker or writer of (21) be reported as having *said* or as having *implied* that, somewhat unexpectedly, George Soros has had financial trouble from time to time? It is hardly possible to answer this question in a yes-or-no fashion. There are, as we have seen, cases for which it is easy to draw a clear distinction between what is said and what is implicated, but there are also cases such as (17) and (21) in which the boundary between saying and implicating is not clearly defined.

2.2.7 *Preliminary conclusion*

From the discussion in Sections 2.2.1–2.2.6 the following picture emerges. It has become clear that the function of semantics cannot be reduced to an account of meanings in terms of truth conditions (see e.g. Predelli 2013 for more detailed discussion). On the one hand, there are inherent, i.e. non-inferred, meanings that are not truth-conditional; on the other hand, one finds pragmatically inferred meanings that have an impact on truth conditions. Does it follow that the distinction between semantics and pragmatics should be abandoned? There are indeed many cognitive linguists who believe that the distinction is irrelevant, or they simply ignore it, preferring to use terms such as *conceptualization* and *conceptual structure* to describe both the inherent, i.e. is context-independent, meanings of linguistic expressions *and* the senses that they acquire in particular contexts and communicative situations.

One notable exception to the common view in cognitive linguistics is Ronald Langacker (2013: 40), who, although he rejects the "strictly dichotomous view", argues *against* the "absence of any differentiation" between semantics and pragmatics. Langacker contends that "semantics and pragmatics form a gradation", a view that is also adopted in this book. The meaning and use phenomena discussed in Sections 2.2.1–2.2.6 point to a continuum between semantics and pragmatics, ranging from more conventional (i.e. entrenched) stable meanings to uses in specific contexts and communicative situations that require a certain amount of inferencing on the part of the language user, as depicted in Figure 1.

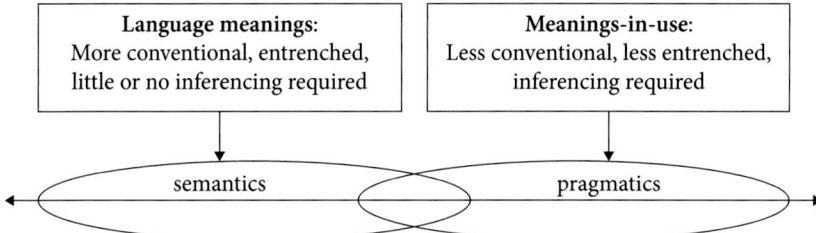

Figure 1. Continuum between semantics and pragmatics
(adapted and elaborated from Langacker 2013: 40)

The nature and different kinds of inferencing involved in the construction of meanings-in-use are discussed in subsequent chapters of this book.

3. A cognitive linguistic view of pragmatics

3.1 Introduction

In her monograph on pragmatics and natural language understanding, Georgia Green (1989: 2) characterizes linguistic pragmatics as an *interdisciplinary* enterprise that incorporates theoretical concepts from various other fields:

> *Linguistic pragmatics* as defined here is at the intersection of a number of fields within and outside cognitive science: not only linguistics, cognitive psychology, cultural anthropology, and philosophy (logic, semantics, action theory), but also sociology (interpersonal dynamics and social convention) and rhetoric contribute to its domain.

Thus, as early as 1989, Green envisaged an approach to pragmatics that integrates insights from e.g. cognitive psychology, cognitive science, and cultural anthropology. But how does contemporary pragmatics relate to the linguistic paradigm that explicitly refers to the notion of cognition in its name, i.e. *cognitive linguistics*? What do contemporary pragmatic and cognitive linguistic approaches have in common? How do they differ? And, how could they be blended into a discipline that could rightfully be called *cognitive pragmatics*? Before examining the relationship between pragmatics and cognitive linguistics in more detail, a few introductory remarks about the cognitive linguistic paradigm is in order.

The first thing to note about cognitive linguistics is that it is far from being a uniform theoretical paradigm.[6] In a *broad* sense, cognitive linguistics goes back to the founding father of generative grammar, Noam Chomsky, whose critical review of the behaviorist approach to language advocated by B. F. Skinner in his book *Verbal Behavior* (1957) is often seen as the beginning of the cognitivist turn in 20th century linguistics. In his review article, Chomsky (1959) regards the language faculty as a *mental organ* that functions according to its own rules and principles, which, in his and his followers' view, are not derivable from more general human cognitive abilities, such as intelligence, perception, experience, or the interaction of humans with their bodies and the environment.

In contrast to Chomsky's *modular* view of the language faculty, cognitive linguistics in the *narrow* sense proposes radically different answers to questions regarding the nature of the linguistic sign, the architecture of grammar, and the language faculty. One of the few common denominators of Chomskyan linguistics and cognitive linguistics in the narrow sense is their anti-behaviorist stance; i.e., both schools of thought consider language to be a *mental* phenomenon that cannot be adequately accounted for in terms of stimulus and response patterns.

As pointed out above, 'cognitive linguistics in the narrow sense' or 'cognitive linguistics', *tout court*, as I call it henceforth, is not a uniform framework; nevertheless, it is possible to identify some properties that various brands of cognitive linguistics share, which distinguish it very clearly from formalist frameworks like generative grammar.

As mentioned above, cognitive linguists reject the hypothesis of a specialized innate language faculty of the sort postulated by generative grammarians. Rather, it is assumed that general cognitive faculties and learning mechanisms suffice to describe and explain language acquisition (Tomasello 2003).

---

6. For a short introduction, on which the following is based, see Panther and Thornburg (2009a). Book-length introductions to cognitive linguistics include Taylor (2002, 2003), Croft and Cruse (2004), Evans and Green (2006), and Ungerer and Schmid (2006).

Cognitive linguists regard human languages as *semiotic* systems in which forms (simple and complex) are conventionally paired with meanings, including the meaning of speech acts and default pragmatic inferences, such as generalized conversational implicatures (see Chapter 4). In Chomskyan theories, the meanings of morphemes, words, and idiomatic expressions are listed in the lexicon, and the concept of construction as a form-meaning pair does not exist.[7] Syntactic structures are regarded as purely *formal* configurations that have to be filled lexically and are ultimately interpreted in a separate semantic component. This assumed property of syntax is known as the *autonomy of syntax* hypothesis.

In contrast to generative grammar, in cognitive linguistics, the form-meaning relation holds not only for individual morphemes or words but also for constructions, which are considered as signs in their own right. Grammatical constructions code more or less abstract (schematic) contents and communicative functions. Constructions are not considered to be epiphenomena of universal grammatical principles (as in generative grammar); rather, they are taken to be the basic units of linguistic description and explanation (Lakoff 1987; Langacker 1987, 1991, 2000, 2008, 2013; Goldberg 1995, 2006). Constructions are organized in networks, not unlike the semantic networks formed by words (lexical fields), as known from structural linguistics.

Another distinctive trait of cognitive linguistics is its emphasis on authentic linguistic data as the basis of linguistic analysis. In theory, although certainly not always in practice, cognitive linguists discard introspective data as unreliable, whereas the use of native speaker intuitions about well-formedness is considered to be legitimate in generative linguistics. In his monograph *Syntactic Structures*, Chomsky (1957) dismisses the study of corpora as irrelevant to the formulation of linguistic generalizations. In contrast, cognitive linguists postulate that the study of language-in-use is a prerequisite to adequate linguistic accounts. Grammars should be "usage-based" (Langacker 1987: 46). As a consequence, and facilitated by the availability of large electronic corpora and search tools, corpus linguistics has seen an enormous upsurge since the 1990s (see the contributions in Janda 2013 on statistical methods, and Paradis 2016 on cross-linguistic corpus-based analyses of antonymy).

Finally, cognitive linguistics also differs from other theories in the significance it attributes to (conceptual) metaphor and (more recently) to conceptual metonymy in the construction of meaning. It is now firmly established that these tropes are not

---

7. There are however, as observed by Goldberg (1996: 4), generativist linguists like e.g. Ray Jackendoff, who "shares many of the foundational assumptions" of cognitive linguistics. See e.g. Culicover and Jackendoff (2005: 34) on "constructional idioms" such as the *Way*-construction exemplified by *Elmer hobbled/laughed/joked his way to the bank*.

merely ornamental figures of speech and writing but that they are crucially involved in human conceptualization. Metaphor and metonymy have been shown to be rooted in human bodily experience and interaction with the environment, a property that is often referred to as *embodiment*. For instance, humans use experientially grounded *image schemata* such as the 'container schema' or the 'path schema' as the basis for the creation of numerous conceptual metaphors and metonymies (see e.g. Lakoff 1987; Panther & Radden 1999; Panther & Thornburg 2003a,b). The cognitive psychologist Ray Gibbs and his collaborators have conducted numerous experiments that strongly support the hypothesis that many metaphorical concepts are embodied (see Gibbs 1994, 2005). It has also been shown that there exists culturally determined variation in the use of metaphor within the limits set by the "human condition" (see Kövecses 2005). The same can probably be said of the uses of high-level metonymies, some of which have been compared cross-linguistically not so much from the perspective of cultural variation as from the vantage point of grammatical differences among languages (see Panther 2015 for a summary of recent research).

3.2 Towards a blend of cognitive linguistics and pragmatics

In the *Handbook of Cognitive Pragmatics*, the editor of the volume, Hans-Jörg Schmid (2012: 3), describes the field of cognitive pragmatics as a "reciprocal relationship between pragmatics and cognition", which "focuses on the cognitive aspects of the construal of meaning-in-context." In this respect, cognitive pragmatics goes beyond "ordinary" pragmatics (my scare quotes), which "is concerned with 'meaning-in-context'." Schmid's characterization entails that an adequate cognitive pragmatic theory should be psychologically plausible. This interpretation is confirmed by the editor's statement that "the aim of this handbook is to identify the general cognitive-pragmatic principles and processes that underlie and determine the construal of meaning-in-context" (Schmid 2012: 3).

But what are the "general-pragmatic principles and processes" at work in the construction of meaning-in-context? Gilles Fauconnier (2006), a leading cognitive linguist, provides us with some guidance regarding the general architecture of the dynamic system of language-in-use.

First, Fauconnier (2006: 2) argues that language "does not represent meaning", but provides "prompts for the construction of meanings with particular cultural models and cognitive resources." Fauconnier's claim is then that language does not code meaning exhaustively but codes linguistic clues that have to be fleshed out by hearers to arrive at the meanings intended by speakers in specific situations and contexts.

Second, Fauconnier emphasizes that the construction of meaning-in-context "draws heavily on 'backstage cognition'", which is "not accessible to our consciousness" (ibid.: 2). The point that linguistic knowledge, often referred to as *linguistic competence*, is usually subconscious was made long before the advent of cognitive linguistics. In particular, Noam Chomsky has to be credited with the insight that the knowledge that native speakers have of their own language, for the most part, resides below the level of awareness.

Finally, as Fauconnier (ibid.: 2) reminds us, "the extreme brevity of linguistic form" contrasts sharply with the conceptual richness of the construction of meaning. As he nicely puts it, "[v]ery sparse grammar guides us along the same rich mental paths, by prompting us to perform complex cognitive operations." The same point is made by the Neo-Gricean scholar Levinson (2000: 6–7, 28), who refers to this contrast as the "bottleneck problem": only a limited amount of information can be phonetically and morphosyntactically coded; most of the content of a message has to be inferred.

In this book, in line with cognitive linguists such as Schmid and Fauconnier, and by relying on analytical tools developed in contemporary pragmatics, my aim is to demonstrate that a blend of cognitive linguistics and pragmatics can lead to new insights into the mechanisms of language-in-use.

CHAPTER 2

Cognitive-pragmatic motivation of language structure and use

1. Introducing the problem

In Chapter 1, a conception of cognitive pragmatics was proposed as a "blend" of contemporary pragmatics and cognitive linguistics. This chapter focuses on one of the key concepts in cognitive pragmatics, i.e. motivation. The notion of motivation is needed for a deeper understanding of many linguistic phenomena, and in particular, those of language-in-use or language-in-context. In this chapter, motivation is discussed from a general perspective; in subsequent chapters, I concentrate more narrowly on inferential motivation, and specifically on one subtype of inferential motivation – motivation based on conceptual metonymy (see Chapter 8). The study of inferences in the construction of meaning is a central subject matter of cognitive pragmatics.

The question whether the structure and/or function of natural language(s) is motivated by linguistic and even language-external (e.g. cognitive) factors has been debated since antiquity, i.e., it is much older than the emergence of linguistics as a scientific discipline in the 19th century. In Section 2, in a kind of *tour de force*, and somewhat selectively, a few landmarks in the study of motivation are presented as evidence that motivation has been a "hot topic" for more than 2000 years in the Western world. Section 3 develops the conception of motivation applied in this book, which is based mainly on previous work by Radden and Panther (2004), Panther and Radden (2011), and Panther (2013), and the literature cited therein. Finally, in Section 4, some data are presented that illustrate the feasibility of motivation as an explanatory concept. Just like inference, motivation plays a key role throughout this book (see also Panther & Thornburg 2017a).

2. Some remarks on the history of motivation

In Western philosophy, the presumably first reference to and discussion of motivation appears in the work of the Greek philosopher Plato (ca. 429–347 B.C.E.). In his dialogue *Cratylus*, Socrates, is asked by his disciples Hermogenes and Cratylus to help them find an answer to the question whether there is "truth" or "correctness" in "names", where the latter term encompasses proper names, common names, and adjectives (Sedley 2003: 4). One of the discussants in this dialogue, Cratylus, can be regarded as a (somewhat naïve) forerunner of the idea that, as Sedley (2013: 1) puts it in the online *Stanford Encyclopedia of Philosophy*, "names belong naturally to their specific objects", a view that is disputed vehemently by Hermogenes, who maintains that linguistic signs are conventional and arbitrary. In the history of ideas, Cratylus' position is usually referred to as 'naturalism', and Hermogenes' view that the form-meaning pairing of names is based on social agreement as 'conventionalism'. In his treatise *De Interpretatione*, Aristotle (384–322 B.C.E.) also holds that the relation between a linguistic expression and its content is conventional, i.e., "no name exists by nature, but only by becoming a symbol" (quoted in Crystal 1997: 408).

Moving beyond "names", i.e. individual words, to the more abstract level of grammatical structure, another puzzle that has preoccupied grammarians for centuries is whether syntactic structure is influenced, i.e. motivated, by thought or, in modern parlance, by cognition. This intriguing problem was already addressed in the 17th century in Antoine Arnaud's and Claude Lancelot's (1660) famous *Grammaire générale et raisonnée*. These authors claimed that the natural order of thinking is reflected in the canonical constituent order *Subject Verb Object* (SBJ V OBJ) of the French clause in transitive sentences such as *La reine aime le roi* 'The queen loves the king' (Arnaud & Lancelot 1660: 49–50). In other words, Arnaud and Lancelot's thesis is that SBJ V OBJ word order is *motivated* by rational thought. But what about languages whose basic word order deviates from this supposedly "natural" order? Are they – from a "logical" point of view – inferior to languages that comply with this pattern (see Lodge 1998 for discussion of the "myth" that French is a "logical language")?

The French writer Antoine de Rivarol (of Italian descent) answered this question with a clear 'yes' in his treatise *De l'universalité de la langue française* (1784), for which he was awarded the first prize by the Berlin Academy. In 1783, the Academy had formulated the following three topics to be discussed in an essay: (i) how French had developed into a universal language, (ii) why it deserved this prerogative, and (iii) whether it could be presumed that it would preserve this status in the future.[8]

Rivarol claimed that French is superior to all other languages (present and past) because:

---

8. In the original French text, the questions were formulated as follows: "Qu'est-ce qui a rendu la langue française universelle? Pourquoi mérite-t-elle cette prérogative? Est-il à présumer qu'elle la conserve?"

> Ce qui distingue notre langue des langues anciennes et modernes, c'est l'ordre et la construction de la phrase. Cet ordre doit toujours être direct et nécessairement clair. Le Français nomme d'abord le sujet du discours, ensuite le verbe, qui est l'action, et enfin l'objet de cette action: voilà la logique naturelle à tous les hommes; voilà ce qui constitue le sens commun. (Rivarol 1857: 109)
>
> 'What distinguishes our language from ancient and modern languages is the order (of its constituents) in the construction of sentences. This order is always direct and necessarily clear. A French speaker names first the subject of discourse, then the verb, which designates the action, and finally the object of this action: this reflects the natural logic common to all mankind; this is what constitutes common sense.'
> (my translation)

According to Rivarol, as for Arnaud and Lancelot, French word order is motivated by the laws of logical thinking. His eulogy of the French language culminates in the famous dictum: "Ce qui n'est pas clair n'est pas français; ce qui n'est pas clair est encore anglais, italien, grec ou latin" ('Everything that is not clear is not French; what is not clear is English, Italian, Greek, or Latin') (Rivarol 1857: 109). Rationality is supposed to be the criterial feature that distinguishes French from other languages like English, Italian, and even Greek and Latin. Rivarol contrasts French with languages that regularly front the object of the sentence, i.e. do not abide by the "logical" order SBJ V OBJ. The speakers of languages with word orders such as OBJ SBJ V or OBJ V SBJ are "plus impérieusement gouverné par les passions que par la raison" (109): they are guided by emotions (passions) rather than rational thinking.

The categorization of languages with the constituent orders OBJ SBJ V or OBJ V SBJ as "irrational" or "gouverné par les passions" sounds unacceptable to the ear of a present-day linguist. Nevertheless, it is noteworthy that, in a typological study, Tomlin (1986: 22) finds that the subject is most frequently found in initial position (see Table 1).

Table 1. Word order in the world's languages (adapted from Tomlin 1986: 2)

Constituent Order	Number of languages	Frequency in %
SBJ OBJ V	180	44.78
SBJ V OBJ	168	41.79
V SBJ OBJ	37	9.20
V OBJ SBJ	12	2.99
OBJ V SBJ	5	1.24
OBJ SBJ V	0	0.00
TOTALS	402	100.00

Notice that 348 (= 87%) out of a sample of 402 languages investigated exhibit either SBJ OBJ V or SBJ V OBJ constituent order. Also notice that the most frequently found word order, according to Tomlin, is SBJ OBJ V. The basic word order of French, i.e. SBJ V OBJ, comes in second. Interesting as these numerical findings are, it should be emphasized that they do not lend themselves to the conclusion that speakers of languages not having SBJ V OBJ (or SBJ OBJ V) order are governed by their emotions while French speakers, because of the SBJ V OBJ constituent order of their language, are paragons of rational thinking!

Since the early 20th century, the debate on the nature of linguistic signs has been dominated by the dichotomy between *motivation* and *arbitrariness*, where the latter term is often equated (erroneously) with convention. The Swiss linguist Ferdinand de Saussure, one of the founders of structuralist linguistics in Europe, postulates in his *Cours de linguistique générale* (first published in 1916) that the linguistic sign is a mental entity (*entité psychique*) that links a content (*signifié* 'signified') with an "acoustic image" (*signifiant* 'signifier') (Saussure 1995: 99). The link between signifier and signified, Saussure contends, is arbitrary (*arbitraire*) (ibid: 100).[9]

It is however important to note that Saussure also maintains that language *must* be motivated at least to a certain extent in order to fulfill its communicative and expressive functions. Saussure refers to this property of natural languages as *relative motivation*:

> Le principe fondamental de l'arbitraire du signe n'empêche pas de distinguer dans chaque langue ce qui est radicalement arbitraire, c'est-à-dire immotivé, de ce qui ne l'est que relativement. Une partie seulement des signes est absolument arbitraire; chez d'autres intervient un phénomène qui permet de reconnaître des degrés dans l'arbitraire sans le supprimer : le signe peut être relativement motivé.
> (Saussure 1995 [1916]: 181–182)
>
> 'The fundamental principle of the arbitrariness of the sign does not prevent our singling out in each language what is radically arbitrary, i.e. unmotivated, and what is only relatively arbitrary. Some signs are absolutely arbitrary: in others we note, not its complete absence, but the presence of degrees of arbitrariness: the sign may be relatively motivated.' (Saussure 1959: 131; translated by W. Baskin)

Saussure recognizes that the notion of relative motivation is especially relevant to the formal and conceptual analysis of linguistic expressions that are more complex than individual bound morphemes or monomorphemic words (on this topic, see e.g. Radden & Panther 2004: 1–2; Panther 2013: 409). As examples of relative

---

9. "Le lien unissant le signifiant au signifié est arbitraire [...]: *le signe linguistique est arbitraire.*" (Saussure 1995: 100)

motivation, Saussure adduces complex cardinal numbers such as German *neunzehn* (lit. 'nine-ten'), and French *dix-neuf* (lit. 'ten-nine'). The constituent morphemes of these numbers – German *neun* and French *neuf* (with the meaning 'nine', respectively) and German *zehn* and French *dix* ('ten') – are arbitrary, i.e., no natural connection between their form and the numeral concepts they convey is detectable. However, the concatenation of German *neun* 'nine' and *zehn* 'ten', which yields the complex expression *neunzehn* 'nineteen', is a motivated process because it makes sense to represent the number *19* as the sum of the single digit *9* plus the double digit *10*. The sequential order, in which the numbers occur is however arbitrary, i.e. language-specific. German (like English) exhibits the order 'single digit + double digit', whereas French has the reverse order 'double digit + single digit'.

3. Towards a cognitive linguistic view of motivation

The question of whether language is motivated by e.g. cognition and communicative function is and should be a central topic of an adequate theory of cognitive pragmatics, and, consequently, in what follows, the notion of linguistic motivation has to be examined and elucidated in more detail. To this end, it is helpful to start with a widely used classification of *signs* before, in subsequent sections, a working definition of motivation is developed. In semiotic terms, two dichotomies are introduced, i.e. the contrast between *arbitrary* (unmotivated) and *motivated* signs, on the one hand, and *conventional* and *non-conventional* signs, on the other. In due course, these distinctions are illustrated with examples from various languages.

3.1 Preliminaries: Types of signs

In present-day linguistics, following American philosopher Charles Sanders Peirce (1839–1914), it is common to distinguish three kinds of signs that are assumed to be linguistically relevant. Peirce's threefold taxonomy will henceforth be used in this book (see also Dirven & Verspoor 2004: 1–4):

i. *Symbols*: A symbolic sign does not exhibit any natural connection between its form and its content. As we have seen, Saussure calls such signs 'arbitrary'. In this book they are referred to as 'unmotivated'. Such signs are found both in language and in the extralinguistic world. A large part of the vocabulary in a language consists of symbols in the Peircean sense. Non-linguistic symbols are e.g. flags, which are supposed to represent a country, or certain traffic signs, such as the inverted triangle, which signifies 'yield' or 'give right of way'.

ii. *Indexes/Indices*: As the Latin origin of the name suggests ('forefinger'), an indexical sign points to some concrete or abstract object. Different from symbols, indexical signs exhibit a natural connection between the form and the content of the sign, i.e., they are motivated. Take a natural phenomenon such as smoke. Smoke can be interpreted as a sign, i.e. an index, of fire. Or consider what doctors refer to as symptoms. A symptom is an index that points to an illness or an ailment. For example, a red face may be an indication of a sunburn, high blood pressure, or a sign of emotional agitation such as excitement or anger. In natural language, there is a special class of words called *deictic*, which, in addition to being symbols, have an indexical function. For example, personal pronouns like *I* and *you*, demonstrative pronouns like *this* and *that*, locative adverbs like *here* and *there*, and time adverbs like *now* and *then* are indexical signs, i.e., their interpretation is dependent on the situation or context in which they are used.

iii. *Icons*: Like indexes, iconic signs exhibit a natural, i.e. motivated, connection between their form and the content they denote. Examples of non-linguistic icons are photographs and (naturalistic) paintings that exhibit a similarity between the picture and what it represents. Examples of iconic signs in natural language are words that imitate what they refer to in the extralinguistic world. Such onomatopoeic words are exemplified in Tables 3 and 4 (Section 3.5).

In what follows, the terms *form* and *content* are used instead of Saussure's 'signifier' and 'signified', respectively. The notion of content covers both 'conceptual (semantic) content' and 'pragmatic (communicative) function'. 'Form' is a convenient cover term for more specific linguistic components: *syntax* (i.e. rules and principles of sentence construction), *morphology* (i.e. the "syntax" of words), and *phonology* (i.e. sound and prosodic structure).[10] The semiotic relation (sign relation) between content and form in natural language can then be diagrammed as in Figure 1. Following Peirce's terminology, this relation can be symbolic, indexical, or iconic, or, which is often the case in language, a combination of different semiotic types.

---

10. Ronald Langacker (e.g. 2008, 2013), the leading figure in the paradigm of Cognitive Grammar, assumes throughout his work that linguistic signs (simple and complex) exhibit a *symbolic* relationship between a *semantic pole* and a *phonological pole*. Different from Peirce, Langacker uses 'symbolic' as a cover term for the sign relation as such.

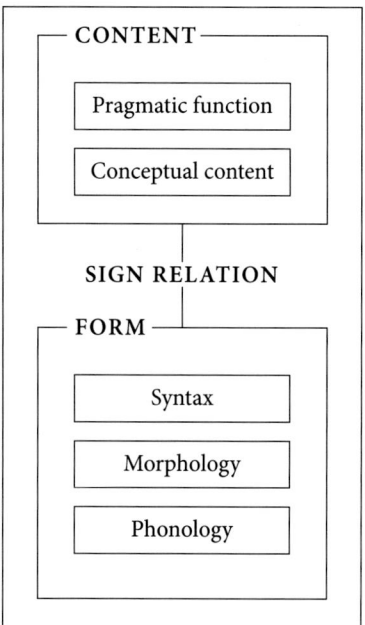

Figure 1. Linguistic signs: Content vs. form

3.2 Defining motivation

The conception of linguistic motivation assumed in this book is based on the one proposed in Radden and Panther (2004: 4), Panther (2008: 6), and Panther (2013: 410):

i. Motivation is a unidirectional relation between a *linguistic source* and a *linguistic target*.
ii. A linguistic target is motivated if and only if at least some of its properties are effectuated by the linguistics source, i.e. its form and/or content, and *language-independent* (translinguistic) factors (see also Heine 1997: 3)

In (ii), it is claimed that not only internal linguistic but also "language-independent factors" may motivate linguistic structure and use. In other words, the motivational forces that shape linguistic phenomena are found not only in language but are operative in other sign systems as well, e.g. in gestures, body language, traffic signs, and the visual arts. Thus, motivating factors "transcend" language and, in this sense, they may be called *translinguistic*.

In formalist linguistic theories, such as generative grammar, motivation has been either ignored or rejected as an unscientific concept (for more detailed discussion see e.g. Panther 2013; Panther & Thornburg 2017a: Chapter 1, and Section 3.2. below). The reason for this critical attitude is that linguistic accounts in terms of motivation are, in general, not *predictive* or, as Goldberg (2006: 217) puts it, *deterministic*. To illustrate this point with words denoting cardinal numerals again (see Section 2 above), in French, two-digit numbers form an "orderly" sequence with distinct lexical items from *dix* 'ten', *vingt* 'twenty', *trente* 'thirty', *quarante* 'forty', *cinquante* 'fifty' up to *soixante* 'sixty'. Then irregularity, i.e. unpredictability, sets in because the lexical item for 'seventy' is coded as a compound *soixante-dix* (literally, 'sixty-ten' in the French spoken in France, where, incidentally, it has to be inferred that the two numbers are added up: there is no explicit coding of the *plus* operation. Another unpredictable form is the French term for 'eighty', i.e. *quatre-vingt(s)* (literally, 'four twenty/twenties'). Regarding this numeral, one might argue that the plural *-s* on *vingt* is an indicator of multiplication, i.e., the numeral is partially motivated, although it is not predictable that this number concept should be coded as 'four times twenty'! Finally, the term for 'ninety' is *quatre-vingt-dix* 'lit. four-twenty-ten', which comes about through a combination of multiplication and addition, i.e. 'four times twenty' plus 'ten'. Note that, in this case, *vingt* is not marked for plural. Furthermore, in *quatre-vingt-dix*, the three numeral terms are simply juxtaposed, i.e., the algebraic operations involved are not explicitly coded.

Obviously, as the preceding (non-exhaustive) discussion has shown, the postulate of predictability does not lead us very far in the analysis of the single and double digit numbers in French: the French number system is idiosyncratic in various respects, but does this mean that the system is completely arbitrary? The answer to this question is "no." The number *quatre-vingts* is historically relatable to a vigesimal system, i.e. to a numeral system that is based on *twenty* (instead of *ten* as in present-day arithmetic). What is more, the number *twenty* is an "embodied" concept (see e.g. Gibbs 2005 for the notion of embodiment), i.e., it is motivated by the fact that humans have ten fingers and ten toes, amounting to twenty digits (for a cultural history of numbers and number systems, see Conant 1931 and Menninger 1969).[11]

In cognitive linguistics, motivation is generally recognized as an indispensable analytical tool in the study of language (see e.g. Radden & Dirven 2007; see also cognitive linguistic handbooks such as Geeraerts & Cuyckens 2007; Littlemore & Taylor 2013; Dąbrowska & Divjak 2015; Dancygier 2017).

---

11. Grevisse and Goosse (2016: 838) note that in certain varieties and dialects of French *septante* is used for 'seventy (e.g. Switzerland, Belgium), *huitante* or *octante* for 'eighty' (Switzerland), and *nonante* for 'ninety' (Belgium, Switzerland), i.e., from a morphological point of view, these numbers are not based on additions or multiplication of single and double digits.

3.3 Motivated, unmotivated, conventional, and non-conventional signs

Let us now turn to some additional distinctions regarding especially the contrasts between 'motivated vs. unmotivated' signs, on the one hand, and 'conventional vs. non-conventional' signs, on the other. There is sometimes a tendency in linguistics to equate 'conventional' with 'unmotivated' (arbitrary).[12] This usage is unfortunate, because conventional linguistic signs can be motivated or unmotivated to varying degrees (see Figure 2 and Sections 3.4 and 3.5 for discussion).

The two relevant dichotomies for our purposes are the oppositions between conventional and non-conventional signs, on the one hand, and between motivated and unmotivated (i.e. arbitrary) signs, on the other.[13] These oppositions are not binary, but scalar; i.e., there are varying degrees of conventionality and motivation. Conventional signs (simple and complex) range from (more or less) unmotivated to (more or less) motivated, but non-conventionally used signs must always be motivated to some extent – otherwise they would be uninterpretable. The claim that non-conventional linguistic signs must be motivated in order to be interpretable needs of course to be bolstered by evidence (see Section 3.6). Figure 2 diagrams the relationship between motivation and conventionality.

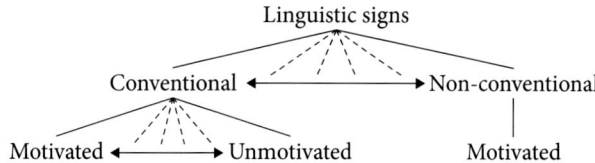

Figure 2. Conventionality and motivation scales
(adapted from Panther 2008: 8; Panther 2013: 409)

The double-headed arrows symbolize the idea that there is a scale, or possibly even a continuum, between the poles 'conventional' and 'non-conventional', on the one hand, and 'motivated' and 'unmotivated', on the other. In what follows, some examples are presented that illustrate the semiotic categories represented in Figure 2.

---

12. This is the case e.g. in Dirven and Verspoor (2004: 1) where it is claimed that a symbol "does not have a natural link between the form and thing represented, but only has a conventional link."

13. I prefer the use of the term *unmotivated* to *arbitrary* because the latter conveys the connotation that any signifier can be coupled with any signified.

3.4 Unmotivated conventional signs

The existence of unmotivated conventional signs can be demonstrated by comparing how the same denotatum is coded in different languages. Consider, for example, how verbs that denote the act of laughing are lexicalized in some European languages (see Table 2):

Table 2. Verbs with the meaning 'laugh' in seven languages

English	German	French	Italian	Hungarian	Danish	Swedish
laugh	lachen	rire	ridere	nevet	grine	skratta
[lɑːf] / [læf]	[ˈlaxn̩]	[rir]	[ˈridere]	[ˈnɛvɛt]	[ˈɡʁiːnə]	[ˈskrata]

As can be seen from Table 2, there is no natural connection between the graphemic and/or phonetic form of the verbs in question and the act of laughing, and this is what Saussure means by his dictum that the relation between signifier and signified is arbitrary.

As another instance of an unmotivated convention, consider the noun *house*, which is a conventional linguistic sign with the meaning 'building for human habitation'. Its phonetic form [haʊs] is obviously not motivated by what it denotes. There exists no natural link between its form and its meaning; and in this sense, *house* is an unmotivated (or arbitrary) sign, a *symbol* in Peirce's terminology. That *house* is unmotivated is also supported by the fact that languages differ in the forms they use for 'house'. Italian codes this concept as *casa*, French as *maison*, Swedish as *hus*, Polish as *dom*, Finnish as *lato*, Hungarian as *(lakó)ház*, and Chinese as *fángzi*. None of these forms for 'house' exhibits a motivated relation with its denotatum.

Cross-linguistically varying forms for the same content are thus evidence against Cratylus' naturalist conception of linguistic signs and they appear to support Hermogenes' view that the relation between form and content is a matter of arbitrary convention. However, there is counterevidence to this claim, i.e., one can also find conventional signs that are motivated.

3.5 Motivated conventional signs

As already noted above, typical examples of motivated conventional signs are *onomatopoeic* words, i.e. cases where the phonetic form of the word imitates the extralinguistic sound(s) it refers to. Such *iconic* forms are listed in Tables 3 and 4.

Table 3 shows that there is some resemblance among the five languages selected with regard to how they code the characteristic sound made by a cat. More importantly, this sound is not coded in an "arbitrary" manner, but each of the five languages codes the act of meowing in a more or less *imitative* way. In this sense,

Table 3. Verbs with the meaning 'meow' in five languages

English	German	French	Italian	Hungarian
meow	miauen	miauler	miagolare	nyávog
[miˈaʊ]	[miˈaʊən]	[mjole]	[mjagoˈlare]	[ˈɲaːvog]

Table 4. The word for 'cuckoo' in five languages

English	German	French	Italian	Hungarian
cuckoo	Kuckuck	coucou	cuculo / cucù	kakukk
[ˈkʊkuː]	[ˈkʊkʊk]	[kuku]	[kuˈkulo] / [kuˈku]	[ˈkɒkukː]

the graphemic and phonetic form of the verbs in Table 3 is clearly *motivated* by a relation of resemblance between the form of the verb in question and its denotatum. Notice however that the five languages do not code the meowing of the cat in exactly the same way. There is thus also an element of language-specific *convention* in the coding.

The same observation holds for the nouns in Table 4, which lists the names for 'cuckoo' in the same five languages. Again, there is clearly a natural, i.e. imitative, connection between the varying language-specific forms for 'cuckoo' and their respective contents; i.e., the forms are not arbitrary but motivated by their denotatum. Nevertheless, language-specific conventions also come into play, as can be seen from the fact that the phonological forms differ in various respects. Finally, it is also important to note that, just as in the case of meowing in Table 3, the forms in Table 4 are "filtered" though the phonological and phonetic system of the language in question. To provide just two examples, the German word *Kuckuck* is pronounced with aspirated *k*-sound [kʰ], i.e., a narrower more accurate phonetic transcription of this lexical item is [ˈkʰʊkʰʊk], while the corresponding French form *coucou* [kuku] is articulated with a non-aspirated plosive consonant [k]. This difference in pronunciation is due to a systematic contrast between the two languages regarding the articulation of plosives. In German, the plosive phonemes /p/, /t/, and /k/ are aspirated in certain positions such as the beginning of a word (before a vowel) whereas, in French, voiceless plosives are never aspirated. Notice also that there is a difference in vowel quality: the vowel in the first syllable of English *cuckoo* is lower, i.e. [ʊ], than the corresponding vowel [u] in French *coucou*.

Interestingly, in the case of the 'cuckoo' words, there is an additional motivating factor at work. The bird is identified via its characteristic call, i.e., an attribute of the cuckoo – its unmistakable sound – *stands for* the bird itself. This relationship between an attribute and the entity that possesses the attribute is an instance of *metonymy*, an important figure of thought that is exploited systematically in natural language. As will be shown in Chapter 8, *metonymic motivation* is ubiquitous in language.

Let us finally review some additional evidence that motivation is a matter of degree (as postulated in Figure 2). Consider the two interjections *ribbit-oops!* and *pippa-eeek!* retrieved from an online *New York Times* article titled "Word of the Day/Onomatopoeia."[14] These two words appear in the children's book *Oh, No!* authored by Candace Fleming and illustrated by Eric Rohmann. To quote the *New York Times* article:

> (1) Fleming's text reverberates with onomatopoeia: a hapless frog tumbles into a deep pit while fleeing a tiger with a "ribbit-oops!," and a tiny mouse attempts to assist with a worried "pippa-eeek!"

Let us focus on *ribbit* and *eeek* in example (1).[15] The interjection *ribbit* ['rɪbət] is defined by the 2010 online edition of the *Oxford English Dictionary* (OED) as 'representing the characteristic sound made by a frog, or an imitation of this'. Since the word appears in the OED, it can be safely assumed that it is conventionally used for conveying this meaning, and for a native speaker of English it is onomatopoeically, i.e. iconically, motivated. However, for a non-native speaker who is not familiar with this interjection it might be quite difficult to infer what the word refers to. This example shows again that there is a language-specific aspect to motivation. Languages differ in how they conventionally code onomatopoeic words (see Tables 3 and 4). As to *eeek* [iːk], according to the OED, it is a conventional expression that imitates a shriek or squeak, and it is derivatively used as an expression of alarm, horror, or surprise. It is a language-specific conventional interjection that is iconically motivated to a certain degree, but it is not an absolutely precise replica of its denotatum (the actual shriek).

3.6 Non-conventionally used motivated signs

But what about the claim that non-conventionally used signs must always be motivated in order to be interpretable? As an example of a non-conventionally used linguistic sign, imagine two friends meeting for a tennis game and one of them says:

> (2) Oh, I forgot my bat.

---

14. Accessed October 25, 2015 at: http://learning.blogs.nytimes.com/2013/10/21/word-of-the-day-onomatopoeia.

15. Whether the interjection *Oops!*, which is usually uttered as the recognition of a mistake, is motivated, cannot be determined here. As to *pippa*, there is no lexical entry of this item in the OED, but it is relatable to *pipsqueak*.

What the speaker of utterance (2) really means is that he forgot his (tennis) racket. According to the NOAE, the (contextually relevant) conventional meaning of *bat* is 'an implement with a handle and a solid surface, used for hitting the ball in games such as baseball, cricket, and table tennis'. The use of *bat* for '(tennis) racket' is incorrect, but it is semantically motivated. The two nouns *bat* and *racket* are conceptually contiguous; both refer to implements with a handle, and they are both used for hitting a ball. In fact, in some languages, rackets and bats are seen as conceptually so closely related that the same form is used for 'racket' and 'bat'. For example, French and German use *raquette* and *Schläger*, respectively, for both 'tennis racket' and 'table tennis bat'. As to the use of *bat* in (2), it is easy for the hearer to reconstruct or infer that the speaker really means 'racket'. The use of *bat* instead of *racket* could be a simple lexical error, but the speaker, in using the wrong term, might also intend to produce a humorous effect in certain contexts.

Now suppose that the speaker, with the intention of referring to his table tennis bat, says:

(3) Oh, I forgot my table.

It would be very hard for the hearer of (3) to infer what the speaker means because 'table' and 'bat' are conceptually not contiguous. The nouns *bat* and *table* share only two high-level semantic components: they both denote concrete objects, but they serve different functions, which have nothing in common.

In conclusion, the examples for the polar contrasts 'unmotivated vs. motivated' and 'conventional vs. non-conventional' can be summarized as in Table 5.

Table 5. The dichotomies 'motivated vs. unmotivated' and 'conventional vs. non-conventional' exemplified (* = unacceptable)

SEMIOTIC DIMENSION	Conventionally used sign	Non-conventionally used sign
Motivated signs	meow cuckoo	*bat* for 'table tennis racket'
Unmotivated signs	laugh house	**table* for 'table tennis bat'

4. Semiotic types of motivation

There are four basic kinds of linguistic motivation, i.e. four ways of defining a motivational relation between the form and the content/function of a linguistic sign (simple or complex) (the symbol '>' stands for 'motivates'):

i. CONTENT > FORM: A linguistic content/function motivates its form.
ii. FORM > CONTENT: A linguistic form motivates its content/function.
iii. CONTENT$_1$ > CONTENT$_2$: A content/function motivates another content/function.
iv. FORM$_1$ > FORM$_2$: A form motivates another form.[16]
v. Combinations of types (i)–(iv).

In what follows, the elementary motivational building blocks (i)–(iv) are illustrated with examples (see Radden & Panther 2004, for more detailed discussion).

4.1 CONTENT > FORM

The motivation of syntactic form by content/communicative function can be illustrated with German conditional sentences such as (4) and (5). These sentences differ in one crucial respect. Sentence (4) shows what Köpcke and Panther (1989) call *integrative* word order; i.e., the preposed subordinate clause (protasis) and the following consequent clause (apodosis) are syntactically closely integrated. In the consequent clause, the positions of the subject and the verb are inverted, i.e., the verb (including auxiliaries) precedes the subject. In contrast, sentence (5) exhibits *non-integrative* word order: the apodosis has the same syntactic structure as a main clause.

Integrative word order: COND-CL VERB SBJ [...]
(4) Wenn Sie es noch nicht wussten, sollten Sie jetzt genau zuhören!
    If   you it yet not   knew   should you now carefully listen
    'In case you didn't know yet, you should now listen carefully'
                        (https://www.wondershare.de/…/einem-pc-oder-speicherkarte-
                                        geloeschte-fotos-wiederherstellt.html)

Non-integrative word order: COND-CL SBJ VERB [...]
(5) Wenn Sie es noch nicht wussten, wir stellen hier die Fragen.
    If   you it yet not   knew   we pose   here the questions
    'In case you didn't know yet, we ask the questions here'
                        (https://books.google.com/books?isbn=3847608673)

The syntactic difference between the two sentences correlates with their distinct meanings and communicative functions. In sentence (4), the speaker establishes a causal link between the protasis (conditional clause) and the apodosis (consequent clause): not knowing something is a sufficient reason for the addressee to

---

16. Radden and Panther (2004) mention a fifth type, i.e. a motivational link between signs, but this type can be derived from a combination of types (iii) and (iv).

listen attentively to the (possibly important) news the speaker intends to convey. Accordingly, the apodosis of (4) is conceptually dependent on the protasis. Examples like (4) are called *content conditionals* by Sweetser (1990): the protasis expresses a sufficient condition for the truth of the propositional content of the apodosis.

In contrast, in example (5), the apodosis is coded as an independent sentence; i.e., it is not causally dependent on the content of the protasis and hence it exhibits main clause syntax. The conditional link between the protasis and the apodosis is one of pragmatic *relevance*. If the addressee of (5) does not know the content of the proposition expressed in the apodosis, then the apodosis constitutes highly relevant (new) information. The main clause syntax of the apodosis is thus motivated by its communicative function as an assertion, which is represented as true, independent of whether the protasis is true or not.[17]

4.2 CONTENT$_1$ > CONTENT$_2$

A standard example of the motivation of one content by another content is known as *polysemy*, i.e. the common phenomenon in natural language that words have more than one meaning and that these meanings are conceptually related. As an example of polysemy, consider the various meanings of the noun *surgery*. According to the online OED, in British English, the word has four senses:

(6) (i) The treatment of injuries or disorders of the body by incision or manipulation, especially with instruments; (ii) a place where a doctor, dentist, or other medical practitioner treats or advises patients; (iii) a period of time during which patients may visit a doctor, dentist, or other medical practitioner for treatment or advice; (iv) an occasion on which an MP, lawyer, or other professional person gives advice.

The four senses listed in (6) are conceptually related. Sense (6)i focuses on the professional *activity* of a surgeon; (6)ii on the location where this professional activity takes *place*; (6)iii on *office hours* held by a surgeon (or other doctor) at the location; and (6)iv refers to any kind of consultation hours provided by a Member of Parliament (MP), lawyer, or other professional.

By way of example, let us examine the relationship between (6)i and (6)ii more closely. The relation between (6)i and (6)ii is *associative* or *contiguous*, i.e. a *metonymic* relation (see Chapter 8). Assuming that meaning (6)i is more basic than that of (6)ii and using an arrow to symbolize the metonymic relation, we can represent

---

17. For additional examples of CONTENT > FORM motivation, see Chapter 10.

the relationship between (6)i and (6)ii as ACTIVITY → LOCATION OF ACTIVITY.[18] In other words, the source meaning ACTIVITY metonymically motivates the target meaning LOCATION OF ACTIVITY.

Moreover, there are metonymic relations between what might be considered the central activity of a surgeon, i.e. the performance of operations on patients, i.e. (6)i, and other activities, such as offering advice during consultations, i.e. (6)iii. Furthermore, between the latter and (6)iv, there exists another conceptual relationship, i.e., the consulting hours of surgeons (or other medical doctors) are related conceptually to the consulting hours of other professionals and members of the British Parliament.[19]

Polysemy is not only found on the level of words but is also productive in morphology. For example, the polysemy of the nominalizing suffix *-er* in English can be accounted for in its entirety in terms of metaphor and metonymic extensions from a prototypical conceptual scenario (see e.g. Panther & Thornburg 2001, 2002).[20] Choi (2012) investigates the polysemy of the Korean nominal suffix *-i* and shows that its meanings are, in many ways, parallel to those of English *-er*: the prototypical agent meaning (like in e.g *teacher*) is metaphorically and metonymically extended to non-human agents, instruments (e.g. *can-opener*), locations (e.g. *sleeper* 'sleeping car' and events (e.g. *groaner* 'event that causes a person to groan').

4.3   FORM > CONTENT

As an example of form motivating content, consider the following sentence pair (from Lakoff & Johnson 1980: 131):

(7)   Sam killed Harry.

(8)   Sam caused Harry to die.

---

18. According to the OED, meaning (6a) is first attested in 1400; the earliest date of attestation for reading (6b) is 1846; and the sense 'office hours' (6c,d) emerges as late as the 20th century (1951).

19. Mario Brdar (p.c.) has suggested to me that the relationship between the two senses 'consulting hours of surgeons' and 'consulting hours of other professionals and members of the British Parliament' is metaphorical; i.e., consulting hours of e.g. members of the British Parliament are, in some respects, *like* consulting hours of surgeons (for a more detailed account of metaphor, see Chapter 7).

20. For the polysemy of the cognate German nominalizing suffix *-er*, see als Köpcke and Panther (2016).

Lakoff and Johnson, as other scholars before them, observe that (7) and (8) differ conceptually in that the former signals direct causation and the latter indirect causation. Sentence (7) codes direct causation as one clause, whereas (8) codes indirect causation by means of a superordinate clause that expresses the cause and a subordinate infinitival clause that codes the effect. Lakoff and Johnson (1980: 131) account for the conceptual difference between (7) and (8) on the basis of the following iconic principle: "The CLOSER the form indicating CAUSATION is to the form indicating EFFECT, the STRONGER the causal link is." In (7), CAUSATION and the EFFECT of dying and death are coded as a single event by the verb formed *killed*, whereas in (8) the act of CAUSATION is coded in the main clause by means of *caused* and the EFFECT is coded in the infinitival clause by *die*. In the terminology used in this chapter, this is a clear case of iconic motivation of content by form; i.e., syntactic distance reflects conceptual distance.

4.4 FORM$_1$ > FORM$_2$

An example of one (phonological) form motivating another (phonological) form is the expressive use of the euphemistic term *heck* [hɛk] for *hell* [hɛl], e.g. in sentences such as (9) and (10):

(9) What the hell are they doing? (COCA 2012)

(10) What the heck are they doing […]? (COCA 2007)

Notice that the two terms *hell* and *heck*, in (9) and (10), respectively, are phonetically similar. They differ only in one sound, i.e. ([k] vs. [l]); i.e., they constitute what phonologists call a 'minimal pair'. The avoidance of the term *hell*, and the use of *heck* as a substitute, was, like the use of *gosh* for *God*, originally religiously motivated.

5. Language-independent factors of motivation

In this section, the focus is on motivational factors that are operative in language as well as in other semiotic and communicative systems; i.e., they are "translinguistic" in the sense that they are not specific to natural language (Panther 2013: 414). In the following sections only a few examples are given that demonstrate the impact of language-independent phenomena on natural language (for more detailed discussion of language-independent parameters of motivation, see Radden & Panther 2004; Panther & Radden 2011).

5.1 Sensory-perceptual

Many expressions in natural language that refer to cognitive processes or states are motivated by sensory-perceptual experiences. To start with visual perception, we find corpus examples like (11), whose interpretation can be paraphrased as (12):

(11) Yeah, okay. I see your point, Prof. The climate's changing and the rate of change is accelerating. (COCA 2006)

(12) Yeah, okay. I understand your point, Prof. The climate's changing and the rate of change is accelerating.

Visual perception is a potent source of knowledge, and hence of the cognitive faculty of comprehending something intellectually. The verb *see* is used figuratively in (11), i.e., its meaning 'understand' is motivated by the metaphor UNDERSTANDING IS SEEING or, equivalently, in the notation used in this book, SEEING ⇒ UNDERSTANDING (see Lakoff & Johnson 1980: 48). Note in passing that, in terms of the types of motivation introduced in Section 4, (11), is an instance of CONTENT$_1$ > CONTENT$_2$ motivation.

Another perceptually motivated use of language is based on the metaphor HEARING ⇒ UNDERSTANDING, which is illustrated in (13) and whose intended target interpretation is given in (14):

(13) […] I hear your message, and I want to give Ms. Stent a chance to respond. (COCA 2013)

(14) I understand your message, and I want to give Ms. Stent a chance to respond.

The following example makes use of the sense of taste to characterize a theory, i.e. a cognitive product:

(15) In his review, Owen tried, unsuccessfully, to undercut Darwin's priority in the discovery of a palatable theory of evolution.
(https://books.google.com/books?isbn=0300165692)

In example (15), the adjective *palatable* literally signifies 'pleasant/agreeable to the palate/taste', as in *a very palatable soup* or *a palatable chicken*, but the interpretation of this gustatory term is metaphorical; its meaning is 'acceptable, satisfactory'.[21] The motivation to use *palatable* for an abstract cognitive construct, such as a theory, is quite transparent. For a scientist, a coherent, descriptively and explanatorily adequate theoretical framework is comparable to an exquisite dish that is pleasant to

---

21. Interestingly, a check of the first 100 hundred entries of *palatable* in the American English corpus COCA yields only 22 examples with the non-metaphorical sense; i.e., the figurative sense appears to be more entrenched than the literal one.

the palate. Note also that theories are often characterized by their proponents as beautiful or elegant; i.e., they are metaphorically likened to aesthetically, in particular, visually pleasing things, such as pieces of art.

As a final example involving the senses as devices of meaning construction, consider the metaphorical interpretation of a lexeme that belongs to the domain of tactile experience:

(16) [P]ostcolonial theory is not easy to grasp. (COCA 2015)

The literal meaning of the verb *grasp* 'seize and hold firmly' is easily relatable to the intended cognitive meaning of (16), i.e. 'get mental hold of' or 'comprehend fully' (NOAD). The metaphorical use of *grasp* as an act of cognitive understanding is a prime example of the role of *embodiment* in the construction of meaning. Gibbs (2005: 1) characterizes the concept of embodiment and its significance in the conceptual analysis of language as follows:

> Embodiment in the field of cognitive science refers to understanding the role of an agent's own body in its everyday, situated cognition. For example, how do our bodies influence the ways we think and speak?

The coding of cognitive processes is often metaphorically motivated by lexemes that denote interactions of the human body with objects in the environment. Here are some additional examples from Gibbs (2005: 98):

OBJECT MANIPULATION ⇒ THINKING

(17) Let's toss around some ideas.

GRASPING ⇒ UNDERSTANDING

(18) She easily grasped the difficult concept.

MANIPULABLE OBJECTS ⇒ IDEAS

(19) Let's reshape that idea.

TAKING APART OBJECTS ⇒ ANALYZING IDEAS

(20) He tore apart the argument.

For more detailed discussion of such conceptual metaphors, see Chapter 7.

5.2 Cultural

Cultural models or folk models (the two terms are use equivalently here) are another important language-independent motivational source that shapes language structure and use. This holds especially for folk beliefs about the character and behavior of animals, such as lions, rats, foxes, sheep, etc. (see Panther & Thornburg 2012a; Panther 2014). Consider the example of *beaver*, which is defined as follows in the OED:

> An amphibious rodent, distinguished by its broad, oval, horizontally-flattened, scaly tail, palmated hind feet, coat of soft fur, and hard incisor teeth with which it cuts down trees; remarkable for its skill in constructing huts of mud and wood for its habitation, and dams for preserving its supply of water.

In Panther and Thornburg (2012a), the conceptual structure of the intransitive verb *(to) beaver away* is analyzed in some detail, and it is shown that certain linguistic properties of this verb-particle construction are shaped by a cultural model of beavers as highly *industrious* animals. This folk model motivates the meaning of *beaver away* as 'work hard' in examples such as the following:

(21) From 2008 to 2010, Allum beavered away in a 2,000-square-foot workshop in Sydney […]. (COCA 2014)

Note that *beaver away* is, among other things, the result of the word-formation process of conversion; i.e., the noun *beaver* is converted into a verb of the same form, and the verb inherits certain characteristic conceptual properties from the noun that are then metaphorically applied to human beings – in example (21), to the person named *Allum*.

5.3 Emotive

The conceptualization and coding of emotions and feelings is, like that of animals, characteristically shaped by cultural models. Lakoff and Johnson (1999: 282) maintain that there exists a western folk model that conceptualizes people's emotions as being potentially in conflict with their preferred role as rational agents. In this model, rationality is given a higher ranking than emotivity, which implies that people should control their emotions, although they are allowed to display e.g. affection, anger, joy, and sadness within socio-culturally acceptable boundaries. In English, the folk model motivates expressions such as:

(22) He struggled with his emotions. (COCA 2013)

(23) [F]or years he struggled with his temper. (COCA 2007)

(24) For years afterward, she struggled with depression and suicidal thoughts. (COCA 2013)

In (22)–(24), emotions are conceptualized as adversaries that have to be overcome by calm and rational thinking (see also Panther & Radden 2011: 4 for similar examples), and it is this folk model that motivates the use of a verb denoting physical effort against an attacker.

Two additional examples in which emotions are conceptualized in terms of split personality and spatial displacement of self, are given in (25) and (26):

(25) Sasha was beside herself with excitement, her entire body trembling with a sense of exhilaration. (COCA 2015)

(26) I received a phone call from Eva Kim, and she was beside herself with worry. (COCA 2011)

In (25), the referent of *Sasha* is literally presented as occupying another spatial position than normal, where the "normal position", which is to be equated with her calm and controlled self, is designated by the reflexive pronoun *herself*. This shifted position is indicative of strong emotions, i.e. of Sasha's feelings of excitement and exhilaration. The experiencer's emotions depicted in (25) are exhilarative, although they are at least partially uncontrolled, as becomes clear from the second participial clause, which refers to an observable symptom of Sasha's mental state, i.e. her *entire body trembling [...]*. Example (26) is conceptually and syntactically structured in the same way as (25), except that no observable symptoms of the feeling of *worry* are overtly expressed.

Notice that the phrase *to be beside oneself* with an emotive meaning has equivalents in other languages as well, such as e.g. German. Consider the following equivalences between English (27) and German (28) retrieved from the online dictionary *Linguee* (www.linguee.de):

(27) Beside herself with rage and fear [...].
(28) Außer   sich   vor   Wut und Angst
     Outside REFL with rage and fear

It is noteworthy that French and Italian code (27) and (28) as *hors de soi* and *fuori de sé* ('outside oneself'), respectively.

6. Demotivation

The motivation of the examples given in Sections 5.1–5.3 are most likely transparent to ordinary language users. In this section, some linguistic data are presented whose motivation is likely to be known only to experts with some background in historical linguistics.

Consider the expression *goodbye*, which the NOAD defines as "used to express good wishes when parting or at the end of a conversation." Etymologically, *goodbye* is a contraction of the wish *God be with you/ye* and a substitution of *God* by *good*, in analogy to greetings such as *Good morning, Good night*, etc. (see e.g. OED; Partridge 1966; Durkin 2009: 39). From a synchronic perspective, *goodbye* is not motivated because speakers of present-day English will not relate this farewell greeting to *God be with you/ye*.

As a second example, consider the term *mortgage* (pronounced [ˈmɔrgɪdʒ] in American English), which the online NOAD defines as 'a legal agreement by which a bank or other creditor lends money at interest in exchange for taking title of the debtor's property, with the condition that the conveyance of title becomes void upon the payment of the debt'. People who buy a house or an apartment often secure a mortgage, usually a bank loan, because they do not have enough cash to cover the entire cost of the property. Purchasers know the meaning of the term (at least, roughly), but they are normally not aware of its origin, which, via Middle English, goes back to Old French. Historically, the term is a compound that literally means 'dead pledge', i.e. *mort* 'dead' and *gage* 'pledge'. The contract between mortgage provider (e.g. a bank) and mortgagee "dies" when the mortgage is paid to its full or in case that the mortgagee is unable to pay back the bank loan (including interest). This legal term is historically motivated but its motivation is not transparent to present-day language users.

The two historically motivated examples briefly discussed in this section illustrate that motivation is not a (logically) transitive relation. As Ariel (2008: 123) aptly puts it: "While […] changes from x to y and from y to z may be motivated, the relation between x and z may not be motivated, so cumulative changes often create synchronic arbitrariness." Motivated form and content *chains* are frequently found in the history of natural languages, but since motivation is not a logically transitive relation, the results of such diachronic developments often appear to be arbitrary or unmotivated from a synchronic perspective (see e.g. Panther 2013: 429; Panther & Thornburg 2017a: 52–53).

7. Conclusion

The aim of this chapter has been to show that an adequate cognitive-pragmatic model crucially involves the concept of motivation. Language structure and language use are heavily shaped by both language-internal and language-independent parameters. Many of the language-independent factors of motivation discussed in the preceding sections are instances, albeit not exclusively, of CONTENT$_1$ > CONTENT$_2$ motivation, and they are ultimately cases of what can be called *inferential motivation*: a *source* meaning is conceptually elaborated and inferentially related to a *target* sense. Often, but not exclusively, these inferences involve metaphor and metonymy (see Chapters 7 and 8). And it is the theme of inferential motivation that links this chapter back to Chapter 1 where the role of inferencing in the construction of meaning-in-use or meaning-in-context was emphasized as one of the central objects of inquiry in pragmatics. The role of inferential mechanisms in the construction of meaning is also discussed in more detail in Chapters 3, 4, and 5.

CHAPTER 3

The role of inference in the construction of meaning
Entailment and presupposition

1. Introduction

In Chapter 2, the notion of *inferential motivation*, was introduced and illustrated with a variety of examples. This chapter and Chapters 4 and 5 focus in more detail on the modes of inferencing that are potentially relevant to the analysis of meaning and use in natural language. There are three basic modes of reasoning, viz. *deduction, induction*, and *abduction*, which are introduced and illustrated with examples in Section 2).[22] But more importantly, in Section 3, two inference types are presented that are especially relevant to the analysis of linguistic meaning and use, i.e. *entailment* and *presupposition*.

2. Basic modes of inferencing: Deduction, induction, and abduction

2.1 Deduction

The noun *deduction* and the corresponding verb *deduce* are often used in an informal and non-technical way in ordinary English with the broad meaning 'inference' and 'infer', respectively. Consider the following example from the iWeb corpus:

(1) When you worry, you try to deduce and predict the future.
(iWeb, wakeup.cloud.com)

The verb *deduce* in (1) is used in the general sense 'draw inferences'. Similarly, the famous fictional private detective Sherlock Holmes is represented by Sir Arthur Conan Doyle as a person with exceptional skills of "deducing", i.e. identifying, the perpetrator of a crime. However, arguably, Sherlock Holmes, relies more on abductive rather than deductive reasoning modes (see Section 2.3).

---

[22]. For a brief introduction to these reasoning modes, see also Panther and Thornburg (2018: 145–149).

In a more restricted sense, a deduction is an inference rule whose conclusion, given the truth of certain premises, follows from these premises by necessity. Classical examples of deduction are the inference patterns that are known by the Latin terms *modus ponens* ('the mode that affirms') and *modus tollens* ('the mode that removes, i.e. denies'), respectively.

Schematically, the inference rule of *modus ponens* can be formulated as follows:

(2) *Premise 1*: p ⊃ q
     Premise 2: p
     Conclusion: q

The letters *p* and *q* in (2) stand for propositions with a truth value. The symbol '⊃' represents the logical relation of material implication (see Chapter 1), which, as we have seen, captures certain logical aspects of conditional sentences in natural language. The inference schema (2) postulates that, given the truth of two premises p ⊃ q and p, the conclusion q follows logically. Its functioning is illustrated with the following example:

(3) *Premise 1*: If the weather is nice, we will take a walk in the woods.
     Premise 2: The weather is nice.
     Conclusion: We will take a walk in the woods.

If the two premises in (3) are true, the conclusion cannot be canceled without contradiction, i.e., (3) is an example of *deductive* reasoning.

We now turn to the inference schema traditionally known as *modus tollens*, whose argumentative structure is given in (4). The negation operator is notated as '¬':

(4) *Premise 1*: p ⊃ q
     Premise 2: ¬q
     Conclusion: ¬p

A linguistic example of this inference rule is (5):

(5) *Premise 1*: If today is Sunday, the shops are closed.
     Premise 2: The shops are not closed.
     Conclusion: Today is not Sunday.

Another classical type of inference schema is known as *syllogism*, which was already systematically investigated by the Greek philosopher Aristotle (384–322 B.C.E.). An example of syllogistic reasoning is given in (6):

(6) *Major premise (generalization)*: Every adult American has a credit card.
     Minor premise (specific fact): John is an adult American.
     Deductive conclusion: John has a credit card.

If the premises *Every adult American has a credit card* and *John is an adult American* are accepted as true, then the conclusion *John has a credit card* necessarily follows.

Deductive arguments have the property of being *non-cancelable* (also referred to as *indefeasible*). Given the premises, the conclusion cannot be denied. Of course, if one of the premises turns out to be false, the argument collapses. For example, if we find out that not every adult American has a credit card and that John is an adult American, the conclusion that John has a credit card cannot be drawn.

A slightly more formal way of representing the logical structure of (6) runs as follows:

(7) *Major premise*: For every x: If x is an adult American, then x has a credit card.
    Minor premise: John is an adult American.
    Deductive conclusion: John has a credit card.

Note that the reformulation of the syllogism (6) as (7) contains a conditional sentence in the major premise. As already pointed out above, the conditional relation in natural language is often represented by the logical relation of material implication. Using the horseshoe symbol '⊃' for material implication and two additional conventions, the structure of (6) and (7) can be more formally represented as follows:

(8) *Major premise*: $\forall x$ (adult American (x) $\supset$ Has a credit card (x))
    Minor premise: Adult American (John)
    Deductive conclusion: Has a credit card (John)

As can be seen from (8), syllogisms like (7) are deductive arguments; they are instances of the inference schema *modus ponens*. The symbol '$\forall$' in (8), is called the *universal quantifier*; *x* is a *variable* that is *bound* by the quantifier; *adult American* and *has a credit card* are *predicates* in the parlance of logic; and *John*, in contrast to the variable *x*, has the status of an *individual constant*.

Following e.g. Pople (1973: 147) and Levinson (2000: 43), the syllogism elaborated in (5), (6), and (7) has the schematic structure represented in Table 1:

Table 1. Deductive reasoning

INFERENCE	Structure of argument		Defeasibility
Deductive	Major premise *or* general law	$\forall x\ (P(x) \supset Q(x))$	No
	Minor premise	$P(a)$	
	Conclusion	$Q(a)$	

$\forall$ = universal quantifier; *a* = individual constant; *P, Q* = predicates; $\supset$ = (material) implication; *x* = individual variable (bound by $\forall$)

2.2 Induction

Inductive reasoning is ubiquitous both in the domain of science and in ordinary life. What scientific inductive reasoning and the inductive reasoning of ordinary people have in common is that inductive conclusions do not follow logically from their premises. Suppose that a European traveler in the United States finds that every adult American he or she meets possesses at least one credit card. From this observation the European visitor might conclude that *every* (adult) American has a credit card. This reasoning process can be informally formulated as follows:

(9) *Premise 1* (specific facts): (i) John is an adult American. (ii) Liz is an adult American. (iii) Mary is an adult American. (iv) Bill is an adult American. […]

(10) *Premise 2* (specific facts): (i) John has a credit card. (ii) Liz has a credit card. (iii) Mary has a credit card. (iv) Bill has a credit card. […]

(11) *Inductive conclusion* (generalization): Every adult American has a credit card.

The inductive generalization (9) is however *falsified* if one adult American is found who does not have a credit card. Inductive conclusions are thus defeasible.

Although inductive inferences are certainly valuable and even indispensable tools for making sense of the natural and socio-cultural world, in practice, people often draw rash inductive inferences. Unfortunately, cultural, religious, and ethnic prejudices are frequently based on faulty inductive reasoning that uses a few (often merely allegedly true) propositions about some members of an ethnic, religious, or otherwise defined group, from which general conclusions are drawn with regard to all members of the group.

Table 2 summarizes the main properties of inductive reasoning (Pople 1973: 147; Levinson 2000: 43).

Table 2. Inductive reasoning

INFERENCE	Structure of argument		Defeasibility
Inductive	Observed fact$_1$	$P(a) \wedge Q(a)$	Yes
	Observed fact$_2$	$P(b) \wedge Q(b)$	
	Observed fact$_n$	$P(n) \wedge Q(n)$	
	⋮	⋮	
	Induced generalization	$\forall x \, (P(x) \supset (Q(x)))$	

$\forall$ = universal quantifier; $a, b, \ldots n$ = individual constants; P, Q = predicates; $\supset$ = (material) implication; x = individual variable (bound by $\forall$); $\wedge$ = logical conjunction ('and')

2.3 Abduction

Abduction – like induction – is logically not stringent, and it is often characterized as inferencing to the best explanation (Lipton 2000). The term *abduction* was coined by the American philosopher Charles S. Peirce (1839–1914) and can be illustrated by means of the logically non-valid syllogism in (12), which again involves our fictitious holders of credit cards:

(12) *Major premise (generalization)*: Every adult American has a credit card.
 Minor premise (specific fact): John has a credit card.
 Abductive conclusion (specific fact): John is an adult American.

The premises of the abductive argument, as illustrated in (12), are a generalization and a specific fact. Let us assume that these premises are true. Obviously, the conclusion does not necessarily follow from the premises because non-Americans may also be credit cards holders; i.e., from the fact that John has a credit card we cannot infer that he is an adult American – he might be e.g. British or Australian. Despite this logical flaw, abduction is a useful heuristic tool for the formulation of scientific hypotheses, which are however in need of further elaboration and testing before they can be (provisionally) accepted.

Peirce revised his conception of abduction several times (Paavola 2005; Deutscher 2002). In his early writings (ca. 1860–1990), Peirce thought of abduction as an inverse and therefore invalid mode of reasoning. He also regarded abductive inferencing as a conscious and controlled cognitive activity. However, later he came to think of abduction as an "instinct" (Paavola 2005: 150) and was reluctant to call instinctual abduction 'reasoning'. At the same time, Peirce was aware of the importance of instinctual abduction in the life of ordinary people. He believed that "abductive suggestion comes to us like a flash. It is an act of insight although of extremely fallible insight" (Peirce, in Buchler 1955: 151).

The "abductive instinct" relies on "small, clue-like signs and the result is a hypothetical idea or interpretation" (Paavola 2005: 147). The premises and the inference are not consciously formulated (either verbally or mentally); in Paavola's words, the link between them is "an associative connection rather than reasoning" (ibid.: 147). The two key notions here are *clues* and (subconscious) *associative reasoning*. It is this conception of abduction that is of high interest to contemporary conceptual metonymy theory discussed in Chapter 8 of this book.

As mentioned at the beginning of this section, abduction can be characterized informally as "thinking from evidence to explanation, a type of reasoning characteristic of many different situations with incomplete information" (Aliseda 2006: 28). A typical example cited by Aliseda is the diagnostic work performed by doctors who routinely draw inferences from patients' symptoms to the ailments or diseases that cause them.

In the same vein as Aliseda, Thagard (2007: 227) emphasizes that abductive inferencing is rampant in both scientific and common sense reasoning. Experimental results in the sciences can be regarded as facts that require some interpretation as to what best "explains" them. For example, crime detection necessitates the abductive interpretation of evidence that leads to reasonable conclusions about "whodunnit" and the perpetrator's motives, etc. Masters of such abductive reasoning are famous characters in crime fiction, such as Arthur Conan Doyle's Sherlock Holmes, Agatha Christie's Hercule Poirot, or Georges Simenon's Inspector Maigret.

Schematically, abductive reasoning can be characterized as in Table 3 (following Pople 1973: 147, Levinson 2000: 43):

Table 3. Abductive reasoning

INFERENCE	Structure of argument		Defeasibility
Abductive	Known generalization or law	$\forall x\, (P(x) \supset Q(x))$	Yes
	Observed fact	$Q(a)$	
	Reasoning to the best explanation of observed fact	$P(a)$	

$\forall$ = universal quantifier; $a, b, \ldots n$ = individual constants; P, Q = predicates; $\supset$ = (material) implication; x = individual variable (bound by $\forall$); $\wedge$ = logical conjunction ('and')

3. Entailment

In Section 2, some basic modes of reasoning have been considered, independent of the medium in which the reasoning takes place. This section and Section 4 focus on types of inferences that are relevant to the construction and comprehension of *meaning* in *natural language*. In this section the central concept of semantic implication, known as *entailment*, is reviewed. Section 4 introduces the notion of *presupposition*, which is both conceptually and pragmatically essential for an adequate theory of linguistic meaning and use.

Entailment can be regarded as a type of conceptually driven deduction, i.e., it deals with the *meaning* of linguistic expressions and with what follows from them. Language users are able to distinguish information that is *deducible* from a sentence from information that is merely *insinuated*, *alluded* to, or *suggested* in a certain *context* or *situation*. Using a term known from generative grammar, we may say that the cognitive ability to draw non-defeasible inferences from expressions, in particular, sentences, is part of the *semantic competence* of native speakers of a language.

As a first approximation, entailment can be characterized in the following way: A sentence *p entails* a sentence *q* if the truth of *q* conceptually follows from the truth of *p*. A convenient method of representing the properties of entailment is again a table, in which *p* and *q* are assigned truth values. In Table 5, the entailment relation is represented as a relation of *conceptual dependence* between *p* and *q*, and vice versa.[23] The arrow indicates the directionality of the truth evaluation; i.e., the symbol '–>' indicates how the truth value of *p* determines that of *q*; conversely, the symbol '<–' indicates how the truth value of *q* affects that that of *p* (adapted from Saeed 2009: 100).[24]

Table 4. Entailment

p	Directionality	q
T	–>	T
F	<–	F
F	–>	INDET
INDET	<–	T

T = true, *F* = false, *INDET* = indeterminate truth value

The first row of the Table 4 states that, if the entailing sentence *p* has the truth value *T*, the entailed sentence *q* also has the truth value *T*. In the following examples the entailment relation is represented by the symbol '⊩':

(13) Mary chatted with Bill. ⊩ Mary spoke with Bill.
(14) Lafontant forced Pascal-Trouillot to resign […]. (COCA 1991) ⊩ Pascal-Trouillot resigned.
(15) […] Eve made Adam eat an apple […]. (GloWbE) –> Adam ate an apple.

In (13)–(15), the second sentence is a conceptual consequence of the first sentence. Given the truth of the first sentence, the truth of the second sentence follows.

The second row in Table 4 stipulates that the falsity of the entailed sentence *q* has the consequence that sentence *p* is also false. This property of the entailment relation is often referred to as *contraposition*. The principle of contraposition, applied to (13), (14), and (15), yields (16), (17), and (18), respectively:

---

23. Recall that the truth conditions of material implication (Table 1) do not require sentences p and q to be conceptually related.

24. Notice the difference between the arrows that symbolize 'directionality', i.e. '–>' and '<–', and the symbol '→', which is used in this book to represent a metonymic relation between source and target meaning (see Chapter 8).

(16) Mary didn't speak with Bill ⊩ Mary didn't chat with Bill.

(17) Pascal Trouillot didn't resign ⊩ Lafontant didn't force Pascal-Trouillot to resign.

(18) Adam didn't eat an apple ⊩ Eve didn't make Adam eat an apple.

But what is the truth value of q if p is false? The third row in Table 5 states that in this case the truth value of q is indeterminate; i.e., it can be either T or F. To illustrate, consider sentence (19):

(19) Mary didn't chat with Bill.

From (19) neither 'Mary spoke with Bill' nor 'Mary didn't speak with Bill' follows. Not chatting with someone does not preclude the possibility that some other form of verbal communication takes place, e.g. conversing, gossiping, negotiating, etc., but (19) is also compatible with a situation in which no verbal communication occurs at all. For example, it is possible without contradiction to assert (20) or (21):

(20) Mary didn't chat with Bill; she had a serious conversation with him.

(21) Mary didn't chat with Bill; she didn't speak with him at all.

Analogously, from (22) we can neither infer with certainty that the Haitian politician Pascal-Trouillot resigned nor that he did not resign:

(22) Lafontant didn't force Pascal-Trouillot to resign.

Furthermore, (23) neither enforces the conclusion that Adam ate the apple nor that he did not eat the apple in question:

(23) Eve didn't make Adam eat an apple.

Sentences like (19), (22), and (23) raise interesting questions about the *scope* of negation. We briefly return to this topic in Section 4.

Finally, the fourth row of Table 4 stipulates that, if q is true, neither the truth nor the falsity of p can be inferred with certainty. This situation can be illustrated with the entailed propositions in (13), (14), and (15), here repeated as (24), (25), and (26), respectively:

(24) Mary spoke with Bill.

(25) Pascal-Trouillot resigned.

(26) Adam ate an apple.

From (24) it is not possible to deduce what kind of conversation Mary had with Bill. Did she chat with him, converse with him in a serious manner, negotiate a contract, or what? Analogously, on hearing the news in (25), without further context, it cannot be determined whether Pascal-Trouillot was forced to resign, was kindly requested to resign, resigned voluntarily (e.g. for health reasons), etc. Finally, it would be fallacious to deduce from (26) that Adam ate an apple as a result of Eve making him do so.

4. Presupposition

The concept of presupposition is as central to a proper understanding of meaning and use in language as entailment. Presuppositions share some characteristics with entailments but, in other respects, they differ markedly from them.

A useful working definition of *semantic presupposition* can be formulated as follows: A sentence p presupposes a sentence q if both p and *not-p* imply that q is the case (see e.g. Cann 1993: 6). Analogously to Table 4, in Table 5 the symbols '–>' and '<–' are used to indicate the directionality of the dependency relation between truth values (see Saeed 2009: 103).

Table 5. Presupposition

p	Directionality	q
T	–>	T
F	–>	T
not (T *or* F)	<–	F
INDET	<–	T

T = true, F = false, *not* (T *or* F) = truth value gap, INDET = indeterminate truth value

As can be seen from the first row in Table 5, if the presupposing sentence p is true, then the presupposed sentence q is also true. This configuration corresponds to what has been noted for entailment (see Table 4). However, the second row shows a crucial difference between presupposition and entailment: if the presupposing sentence p is false, the truth of the presupposed sentence q is not affected. Thus, q remains true independent of whether p is true or false. Another way of formulating this property is to say that presuppositions remain *constant under negation*. To see this, compare (27) with (28):

(27) It is surprising that Bill passed the test. ~> Bill passed the test.
(28) It is not surprising that Bill passed the test. ~> Bill passed the test.

From both the affirmative sentence (27) and its negated counterpart (28), the truth of the proposition 'Bill passed the test' follows.

The third row in Table 5 demonstrates another crucial difference between presupposition and entailment. While, in the case of entailment, from the falsity of q follows the falsity of p, the falsity of the presupposed q has the consequence that p has no truth value at all; i.e., p is neither true nor false. In other words, the truth or falsity of *It is surprising that Bill passed the test* cannot be assessed if its presupposition is false. The third row in Table 5 characterizes what is usually referred to as *presupposition failure*.

The fourth row in Table 5 corresponds to the fourth row in Table 4. If the presupposed sentence q is true, the presupposing sentence p is either true or false; i.e., the truth value of p is indeterminate in this case. This situation is analogous to what we find for entailment: From an entailed sentence q neither the truth nor the falsity of p can be deduced.

After these preliminaries, we can now turn to some data that demonstrate the ubiquity of presuppositional phenomena in language and cognition. By way of example, three kinds of presupposition are considered: *existential* and *uniqueness* presupposition, *factive* presupposition, and *evaluative* presupposition.

4.1 Existential and uniqueness presupposition

Consider the following (fictitious) sentence about financial problems besetting a well-known female monarch:

(29) The Queen of England faces budget cuts.

The speaker or writer of (29) obviously takes for granted, i.e. presupposes, that there *exists* a Queen of England and, furthermore, that there is *exactly one* Queen of England at the time of speaking or writing. These two assumptions are usually called *existential presupposition* and *uniqueness presupposition*, respectively. How is it possible to determine that the assumptions of existence and uniqueness are presuppositions? We know from Table 5 that presuppositions remain constant under negation, and negation can therefore serve as a good diagnostic test to determine whether the existence and uniqueness of the Queen of England is a presupposition.

(30) The Queen of England does not face budget cuts.

From (30), the same inference as from (29) follows, namely, the existence and uniqueness of the queen.

Incidentally, there are other useful diagnostic tests for presupposition. Presuppositions not only remain constant under negation but also within the scope of an epistemic adverb, a conditional conjunction like *if*, or a *yes-no* question. To wit, consider sentences (31)–(33):

(31) Possibly/probably, the Queen of England faces budget cuts.

(32) If the Queen of England faces budget cuts, she will not be amused.

(33) Does the Queen of England face budget cuts?

The epistemic modal adverbs *possibly* and *probably* in (31) have no effect on the presuppositions of existence and uniqueness regarding the Queen of England, and the hypothetical *if* clause in (32) does not suspend or cancel these presuppositions either. Furthermore, the interrogative sentence (33) leaves the background assumption intact that the Queen of England exists and that (at the time of speaking) there is exactly one Queen of England.

The diagnostic criteria of negation, epistemic qualification, conditionality, and interrogativity can be abbreviated as *NECI*. The NECI criteria are a fairly sound methodological tool to identify presuppositions and to distinguish them from entailments or cases that are neither entailments nor presuppositions.

Entailments, in contrast to presuppositions, do not survive in sentences that exhibit NECI properties. To see this, consider first (34), a slightly modified example from the American English corpus COCA (1995), which entails but does not presuppose (35):

(34) Mary had John remove the entire panel and replace it with a fullsize dresser drawer.

(35) John removed the entire panel and replaced it with a fullsize dresser drawer.

The verb form *had* in (34) has a causative sense: 'Mary caused John to remove the entire panel and replace it with a fullsize dresser drawer'. The application of the NECI test to (34) yields the following sentences (the diagnostic criterion used is named in parentheses after the sentence in question):

(36) Mary didn't have John remove the entire panel and replace it with a fullsize dresser drawer. (N)

(37) Possibly, Mary had John remove the entire panel and replace it with a fullsize dresser drawer. (E)

(38) If Mary had John remove the entire panel and replace it with a fullsize dresser drawer, the room would look much nicer. (C)

(39) Did Mary have John remove the entire panel and replace it with a fullsize dresser drawer? (I)

As the reader can easily verify, none of the sentences (36)–(39) implies (34). In other words, entailment, in contrast to presupposition, does not remain constant under negation, epistemic modality, conditionality, and interrogativity.

4.2 Factive presuppositions

Conceptually related to existential presuppositions are *factive* presuppositions. An existential presupposition takes for granted the existence of things, e.g. objects, plants, animals, persons, etc. A factive presupposition assumes the existence or actual occurrence of certain *states of affairs*. For example, in English and other languages, one finds predicates that require complement clauses whose truth is presupposed. The following authentic sentences illustrate this phenomenon:

(40) The group realized that it needed better information to preserve the most critical areas. (COCA 2011)

(41) It is odd that the United States is so often the advocate of elections and plebiscitary democracy abroad. (COCA 1997)

(42) Lucy regretted that she had told Wolf the news. (COCA 1991)

The application of the NECI test shows that the content of the complement clauses embedded under the predicates *realized* in (40), *is odd* in (41), and *regretted* in (42) presuppose the truth of their respective complement clauses. By way of example, this can be demonstrated for sentence (42):

(43) Lucy *didn't* regret that she had told Wolf the news. (N)

(44) *Perhaps* Lucy regretted that she had told Wolf the news. (E)

(45) *If* Lucy regretted that she had told Wolf the news, she should have apologized. (C)

(46) *Did* Lucy regret that she had told Wolf the news? (I)

As (43)–(46) show, negation, epistemic qualification, conditionality, and interrogativity do not affect the *background assumption* 'She (= Lucy) had told Wolf the news'.

It is worth mentioning at this point that the NECI list is by no means exhaustive, but can be augmented by other criteria, as illustrated in (47):

(47) She hoped Michelle realized that Buddy was trying to pick her up. (COCA 2012)

In (47), the factive predicate *realized* is within the scope of the verb *hoped*, which expresses a mental attitude toward the proposition 'Michelle realized that Buddy was trying to pick her up'. Note that it is not the narrator who has this mental attitude but a third party referred to anaphorically or deictically by *she*. Nevertheless, we can attribute to the narrator/speaker a commitment to the truth of the proposition 'Buddy was trying to pick her up', embedded under the factive predicate *realized*.

4.3 Evaluative presuppositions

As a third semantic type of presupposition let us consider the phenomenon of *evaluative* background assumptions. Five decades ago, the American linguist Charles Fillmore (1969) published a pioneering semantic analysis of *verbs of judging*. He studied semantically contrasting verbs such as *accuse* vs. *criticize, apologize* vs. *forgive, scold* vs. *blame, justify* vs. *excuse,* and *credit* vs. *praise,* showing that they differ, among other things, in what they *state* or *assert,* in contrast to what they *presuppose.*

To illustrate, let us examine the contrast between *accuse* and *criticize* by way of two authentic examples, i.e. (48) and (49):

(48) At the summit and in preparatory meetings, the Bush Administration was widely accused of putting the interests of corporate polluters ahead of environmental considerations. (WebCorp)

(49) More recently, Gingrich has been criticized for calling Republican U.S. House Budget Chairman Paul Ryan's Medicare overhaul plan "right-wing social engineering." (COCA 2012)

Accusations are instances of *assertive* (or *representative*) speech acts (see Chapter 6 for the notion of speech act). The propositional content of an accusation may be true or false; which means that accusers, in principle, must be willing to provide evidence for their claims.

The assertive character of accusations is however not the whole story: the use of the verb form *accused* in (48) conveys an *evaluative presupposition* that it is inappropriate and morally questionable to prioritize "corporate polluters" at the expense of "environmental considerations." That this negative evaluation is indeed a presupposition triggered by *accuse* is supported by the NECI diagnostic test, e.g. the negation test:

(50) [...] the Bush Administration was not widely accused of putting the interests of corporate polluters ahead of environmental considerations.

As can be seen in (50), the *assertive* property of *accuse* is affected by negation, i.e. the occurrence of the accusation is negated, but as predicted, the *presupposition* that it is bad, inappropriate, or morally reprehensible to rank the interests of polluters higher than a healthy environment remains constant under negation.

To summarize, the meaning of the verb *accuse* can be characterized as follows:

(51) *Assertion*: ACCUSER claims that ACCUSED performs/performed some ACTION A.

(52) *Presupposition*: ACCUSER *evaluates* ACTION A as BAD (i.e. immoral, illegitimate, illegal, etc.).

Now consider the use of the verb *criticized* in (49). In contrast to an accuser, who *asserts* a proposition whose content is evaluated presuppositionally as bad, a criticizer asserts a negatively evaluated proposition and presupposes its factuality. Thus, in (49), the criticizer explicitly claims that Gingrich's characterization of Paul Ryan's "Medicare overhaul plan" as "right-wing social engineering" is *inappropriate*. At the same time, (49) conveys the presupposition that Gingrich actually did use the words "right-wing social engineering", i.e. performed the corresponding speech act. In other words, the truth of the complement clause licensed by *criticize* is presupposed. More generally, the meaning of *criticize* can be informally represented as in (53):

(53) *Assertion*: CRITICIZER evaluates ACTION A performed by CRITICIZED as BAD.
Presupposition: CRITICIZER *believes* that CRITICIZED performed ACTION A.

To conclude, what is asserted by means of *accuse*, i.e. the factuality of some proposition *p*, is presupposed by *criticize*; in contrast, the evaluation of some action as bad is presupposed by *accuse* and asserted by *criticize*.

A further interesting question arising in connection with verbs like *accuse* and *criticize* is: *Who* holds the presupposition(s) given in (51) and (53), respectively? In the case of *accuse*, the ACCUSER presupposes 'It is bad to do A'. But the ACCUSER is not necessarily identical with the speaker or the author. In (48), the ACCUSER, presumably a politician or group of politicians who do not share the Bush Administration's views on environmental issues, is not explicitly mentioned. The use of the passive voice is a well-known pragmatic device for backgrounding or even concealing the identity of the agent of an action, here a linguistic action. The speaker or author of (48) does not necessarily share the accuser's presupposition that the prioritization of corporate interests over environmental concerns is immoral.

As far as *criticize* is concerned, as mentioned above, it conveys a factive presupposition held by the CRITICIZER. But does the author of (49) share this presupposition? The answer depends on whether native speakers would accept utterances such as the following (the *but* clause has been added by the present author):

(54) Gingrich has been criticized for calling Republican U.S. House Budget Chairman Paul Ryan's Medicare overhaul plan "right-wing social engineering"; but I know for sure that he didn't use the expression "right-wing social engineering."

If the piece of discourse in (54) is acceptable to native speakers, then it provides evidence that the presupposition conveyed by the criticizer is not necessarily regarded as true by the speaker/author. Notwithstanding, in the case of (49), there is contextual evidence that the writer believes that the words *right-wing social engineering* were actually used by Gingrich, because he adds the following sentence:

(55) Gingrich later apologized to Ryan. (COCA 2012)

The verb *apologized* in (55) conveys, like *criticized* in (49), that Gingrich did something inappropriate – the only difference being that criticizing someone for something amounts to an *assertive evaluation* of some action as bad, whereas apologizing to someone for something *presupposes* that the apologizer did something bad.

Apart from the problem of attribution of presuppositions, examples like (48) and (49) raise the interesting question under what circumstances presuppositions can be suspended or even canceled. This problem is addressed in the following section.

4.4 Suspending or canceling a presupposition

We have seen that presuppositions are more "robust" than entailments because they survive within the scope of negation, epistemic adverbs, conditional *if*, and questions, among other things. This generalization is however not completely adequate because it is possible to *suspend* or even *cancel* a presupposition in certain contexts. To see this, consider the contrast between sentences (56) and (57):

(56) Sheriff Bob Galtieri, your team has done so much to crack this case.
 (COCA 2012)

(57) You set a vision for yourself, and you achieve it. If you have a team, your team achieves that vision. (COCA 2005)

The noun phrase *your team* in (56) presupposes the proposition 'You have a team', as the reader can easily verify by applying the NECI test criteria. Now consider the linguistic context of the expression *your team* in the second sentence of (57). In this case, it not possible to determine with certainty whether the proposition 'You have a team' is true or not. The existence of a team is only hypothetically assumed in the *if* clause, i.e. the protasis of (57). Therefore, the team mentioned in the consequent clause (apodosis) of the conditional exists merely in a hypothetical world. The speaker implies that she does not know whether the team exists in the *actual* world as well. Thus, in (57), the presupposition usually associated with possessive noun phrases of the type *your team* is suspended – although it is not necessarily canceled.

The suspension of a presupposition is less dramatic than its *cancelation*. In case of a cancelation, the presupposition does not survive at all, but it is removed from the current discourse space (for this notion, see e.g. Langacker 2008: 281; 2013: 50–60). Suppose (57) were changed into (58):

(58) You set a vision for yourself, and you achieve it. If you had a team, your team would achieve that vision.

The protasis in (58) is *counterfactual*, i.e., it automatically triggers the implication that the addressee (*you*) does not have a team. In other words, the usual presupposition 'You have/had a team' associated with the noun phrase *your team* is explicitly canceled.

Another discourse example, in which a presupposition is explicitly denied by the speaker, is (59):

(59) If you have a bank account in dollars, your money doesn't exist – it's just virtual money. (COCA 2012)

The possessive noun phrase *your money* has the default presupposition 'You have money' but the negated predicate of existence following the possessive noun phrase cancels this presupposition.

4.5 Negation and presupposition

In this section, the notion of negation, which, as we have seen, can be used as a diagnostic criterion to distinguish entailment from presupposition, is scrutinized in more detail. In propositional logic, the negation of a proposition has the effect of reversing its truth value, as shown in Table 6.

Table 6. Logical negation

p	¬p
T	F
F	T

T = true, F = false, ¬ = negation

Table 6 conveys that a proposition *p* that is true becomes false when it is negated; and, vice versa, if it is false, negating it will convert it into a true proposition.

There are however some other interesting and intriguing aspects of negation that deserve mention. Let us return to examples such as (20)–(23) above, by means of which the phenomenon of *scope of negation* can be illustrated. For example, a difference in scope can be observed between (20) and (21), repeated here as (60) and (61), respectively:

(60) Mary didn't chat with Bill; she had a serious conversation with him.
(61) Mary didn't chat with Bill; she didn't speak with him at all.

Example (60) seems more natural than (61). What could be the reason for this intuition? In (60), what is negated is that Mary interacted *verbally* with Bill in a *specific* way; the speaker does not explicitly deny that verbal interaction took place, but she denies that this verbal activity could be characterized as 'chatting'. In contrast, in (61) the speaker asserts that no verbal interaction took place at all (including chatting). Negation thus operates on two different levels in (60) and (61). In (60) only a specific aspect of verbal interaction is negated, namely, the chatting component, whereas in (61) the entire frame of verbal interaction is negated.[25]

To conclude, the scope of negation can differ and this property may have an effect on the (non-)survival of presupposition.

4.6 Discourse-pragmatic presupposition

So far our focus has been on presupposition as a kind of semantic implication that remains constant under negation, epistemic qualification, conditionality, and interrogativity. Notwithstanding, one important function that presupposition has in discourse was already hinted at in Section 4.2: presupposed propositions have the status of *background assumptions*, i.e. information that is usually taken for granted by the speaker and believed to be common knowledge of the interactants in the communicative situation.

To illustrate the notion of background assumption or knowledge, consider the following contrasting conversational exchanges (adapted from Givón 1993: 188):

(62) A: What's new? B: The president resigned. A: Oh, when?

(63) A: What's new? B: The president didn't resign. A: Was he supposed to?

As observed by Givón (1993: 188–189), in (63), B's statement that the president didn't resign suggests that the president's resignation was possible or even likely, and A is surprised because he is not familiar with this background information.

The phenomenon that a negative sentence evokes its affirmative counterpart is often called a *pragmatic* presupposition. Pragmatic presupposition contrasts with *semantic* (sometimes also called "logical") presupposition. For example, an intrinsic conceptual component of the verb *regret*, as exemplified in (42) and (43), is that it presupposes that the content of its complement clause is a *fact*, and this interpretation remains constant under negation, epistemic qualification, conditionality, and interrogativity (NECI). In contrast, from the negative statement made by interlocutor B in (63), i.e. *The president didn't resign*, it does not follow that the president resigned, although there might have been some prior rumor or expectation of the president's imminent resignation, which is discarded by speaker B as unfounded.

---

25. For the notion of conceptual frame see Chapter 6.

4.7 The information status of presupposition

In Section 4.6 it has been pointed out that an interesting discourse-pragmatic property of presuppositions is that they often convey *background knowledge* or *old information* as in the following excerpt from a news interview:

> (64) SCHIEFFER: I take your point on that. But were we surprised that this government collapsed? MCDONOUGH: We weren't surprised that this government collapsed. We knew that this was an ongoing challenge over the course of the last several months. (COCA 2015)

In (64), the proposition expressed by the complement clause *that this government collapsed* is a factive presupposition associated with the predicate *be surprised*. Note that it is affected neither by Schieffer's *yes-no* question *But were we surprised [...]?*, nor by McDonough's negative reply *We weren't surprised [...]*. The content of the complement clause is taken-for-granted background information that is not in dispute. What is discussed is whether this fact was surprising or not.

However, the correlation between presupposition and old information is not a necessary one. Presupposed content may sometimes also be used to convey *new information*, as illustrated in the following excerpts from two pieces of narrative fiction:

> (65) "[...] She's even dating." Eric grinned. "My brother can't forgive her for that." "I didn't know you had a brother." (COCA 1998)

> (66) Alex's heart sank. "That's where my stepsister lives." Letta lifted her brows. "I didn't know you had a stepsister [...]." (COCA 2008)

In using the possessive noun phrase *my brother* in (65), Eric presupposes that he has a brother. Furthermore, Eric's utterance presupposes that he has *only* one brother – otherwise he should have used the noun phrase *one of my brothers*, *my elder brother*, or *my younger brother*, as the case may be. Similarly, the referring expression *my stepsister* mentioned in (66) by Alex presupposes that Alex has exactly one stepsister.

The presuppositions conveyed by (65) and (66) are however not necessarily background information that the narrative characters Eric and Alex, respectively, assume to be shared by their conversational partners. In fact, as the responses of the respective interlocutors in (65) (*I didn't know you had a brother*) and (66) (*I didn't know that you had a stepsister*) show, this is new information to them.

New information is also provided by postings occasionally found in public spaces (like a restaurant or pub) as in (67), although, technically speaking, this information is presupposed:

(67) They were sitting under a sign that said THANK YOU FOR NOT SMOKING, but they were cops and used to ignoring signs and Pete the bartender, who knew them well, ignored their ignoring. (COCA 2003)

The verb *thank* has the (factive) presupposition that the person thanked *did* something, usually for the benefit of the thanker, *before* the time of the utterance. To see this, compare the affirmative sentence (68) with sentences (69)–(72), which have been subjected to the NECI test:

(68) She thanked him for coming to the reading […]. (COCA 1995)

(69) She didn't thank him for coming to the reading. (N)

(70) Perhaps she thanked him for coming to the reading. (E)

(71) If she thanked him for coming to the reading, he was very pleased. (C)

(72) Did she thank him for coming to the reading? (I)

In all of the sentences in (68)–(72), it is taken for granted that the male character referred to by *him* came to the reading. It is thus reasonable to assume that the proposition 'He came to the reading' is a presupposition.

Now reconsider the sign referred to in example (67). Under normal circumstances, i.e. in its literal interpretation, if a person says *Thank you for not smoking*, she presupposes that the addressee(s) did not smoke before the time of the speech act of thanking, and she expresses her gratitude for the addressees' considerate behavior. However, in (67) the sign has a different interpretation. It expresses a *request* not to smoke in a room or other location where the sign is posted. The act of refraining from smoking is not presupposed as a past event but rather refers to an imminent or future event. In this sense, *Thank you for not smoking* conveys new information, more specifically, instructions or regulations regarding how customers should behave in the bar ('Do not smoke!'). The "cops" referred to in (67) do not ignore an act of thanking; rather they do not comply with what every competent native speaker would regard as a strong indirect *request* not to smoke in the pub (for indirect speech acts, see Chapters 9 and 10).

5. Conclusion

The purpose of this chapter has been to demonstrate that inferential mechanisms play an important role in the construction of meaning – both in the analysis of language-inherent meanings (e.g. entailment and semantic presupposition), as well as in the study of language-in-context or language-in-use, as evidenced by the discourse-pragmatic functions of presupposition. The discussion of mostly authentic data has confirmed the view commonly accepted in cognitive linguistics (see Figure 2 in Chapter 1) that the boundary between semantics and pragmatics is somewhat fuzzy. The following chapter focuses on yet another type of pragmatic inference known as *implicature,* a term introduced by the philosopher of language H. Paul Grice (see e.g. Grice 1975).[26]

---

26. About the same time as Grice was developing his theory, the French linguist Oswald Ducrot (1969, 1972) coined the term *sous-entendu* (literally 'understood', but not said), which is equivalent to Grice's term *implicature.*

CHAPTER 4

Principles guiding communication
The role of implicature

1. Introduction

In Chapter 3 it was shown that entailment and presupposition are inferential relations that play an important role in the construction of language meaning. For example, understanding the meaning of a sentence includes knowledge about what the sentence entails, and what it presupposes. Presuppositions can also be linked to *background* or *old* information that is presumed to be shared by the interactants in a communicative exchange; nevertheless, as we have seen, occasionally, presuppositions are also used for other discursive and conversational purposes, including even the conveyance of *new* information.

In this chapter the conceptual and pragmatic mechanisms of communication are examined in more detail. To this end, in Section 2, a basic distinction is made between two models of communication, the code model and the inferential model of communication, and, following Sperber and Wilson (1995), it is argued that of these alternatives only the second may realistically be considered a good candidate for an adequate theory of linguistic communication.

In Section 3, following the philosopher of language Paul Grice, a related crucial distinction is introduced, i.e. the contrast between what is *said* in an utterance and what is *implicated* by it. The pragmatic notion of *implicature* has to be carefully distinguished from entailment and presupposition (see Chapter 3). In Section 4, various efforts to improve Grice's theory of conversation are discussed, more specifically, the work of Neo-Gricean scholars, such as Stephen Levinson and Laurence Horn, and that of Dan Sperber and Deirdre Wilson, two eminent scholars working in a framework known as *relevance theory*. Section 5 concludes this chapter with criticism that has been leveled against the Gricean model of conversation as being restricted to a Western perspective of what constitutes "rational" communicative behavior.

2. Two models of communication

According to Sperber and Wilson (1995: Chapter 1), the originators of a pragmatic paradigm known as *Relevance Theory*, two models of communication can be distinguished. The first model considers linguistic communication as based on a *code*, i.e. a set of phonological, morphosyntactic, lexical, and semantic rules shared by the members of a language community. Sperber and Wilson call this framework the *semiotic* model of communication (see in Figure 1).

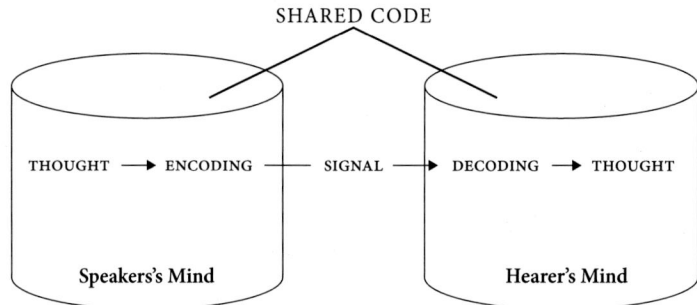

Figure 1. The code model of communication (adopted from Panther 2016a: 108)

According to Figure 1, communication involves a speaker who intends to communicate a thought to a hearer. The speaker *encodes* this thought according to the rules of the code, e.g. the lexicogrammatical system of English, and, in the case of oral communication, transfers it via an acoustic *signal* to the hearer or addressee. The hearer *decodes* the signal on the basis of her knowledge of the code, and as a result has the same thought in her mind as the speaker. Obviously, this description of the communication process is a gross simplification, because a language is not a uniform code. Within a language community, we find regional differences (dialects), socially conditioned variation (sociolects), and even linguistic differences among individual speakers (idiolects). But even if these additional dialectal, sociolectal, and idiolectal parameters were taken into account, the basic idea that communication is merely a matter of encoding and decoding of thoughts is, Sperber and Wilson argue, fundamentally flawed.

Sperber and Wilson (1995) do not deny that the encoding and decoding of thoughts are essential components in the overall picture of communication. However, they contend that, in addition to having mastered a linguistic code, native speakers normally *imply* more than they convey *explicitly*; and, for a full understanding of a communicative act, hearers are required to work out what these implied meanings actually are. Consequently, the code model has to be supplemented by an *inferential* model of communication, as represented in Figure 2.

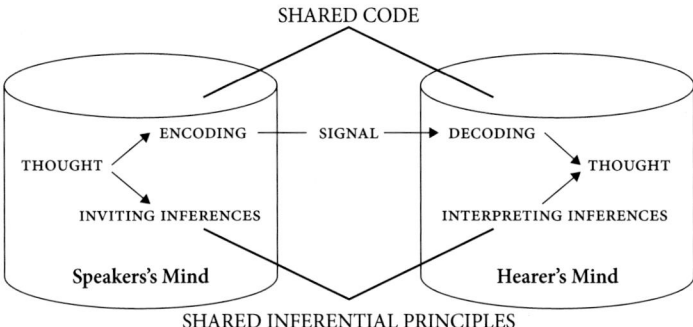

Figure 2. The inferential model of communication
(adopted from Panther and Thornburg (2017a: 3))

In what follows, the cognitive processes of 'inviting inferences' and 'interpreting inferences' are generically referred to as *pragmatic inferencing*, which, under normal circumstances, is a kind of fast and spontaneous mental operation. Language users are largely unaware of the reasoning processes they perform in the construction of pragmatic meaning. In other words, the kind of reasoning that takes place in ordinary communication is unlike the conscious and deliberate reasoning of experts about the intended senses of written texts that constitute the object of inquiry in hermeneutic disciplines such as literary criticism, theology, and the historical sciences (see Panther & Thornburg 2018).

In this chapter, the focus is on a type of pragmatic inferencing known as *conversational implicature*, a term coined by Grice (1975, 1989). Before providing a more technical characterization of this notion, it will be helpful to demonstrate the importance of pragmatic inferencing or conversational implicature in the construction of meaning by means of a dialogue between two fictitious characters, Farmer Brown and Sam. The dialogue is totally unrealistic, representing, in a humorous way, an extreme case of misunderstanding between the two interactants:

(1) FARMER BROWN: Hey, Sam, my mule's got distemper. What'd you give yours when he had it? SAM: Turpentine. *A week later*: FARMER BROWN: Sam, I gave my mule turpentine like you said and it killed him. SAM: Did mine, too.

The reliance on the code model of communication will not lead to an adequate understanding of what goes communicatively wrong in the conversational exchange (1). The two interlocutors share the same linguistic code, i.e. some variety/dialect of English (though not necessarily Standard English). The humorous effect of (1) largely rests on meanings that are *not coded*, i.e. on the inferences (presumably) invited by the speaker and the inferences drawn by the hearer regarding the meanings the speaker intends to convey.

There are two layers of meaning to be distinguished in (1): in Grice's (1975) terms, the layer of what is *said* and the layer of what is *implicated*, i.e. not overtly coded but contextually implied. Let us look at these layers in turn. In (1), Farmer Brown informs Sam that his mule has got "distemper", and he asks Sam what he gave his mule when it suffered from the same condition. This characterization of the content of (1) falls intuitively under the rubric of what Farmer Brown is saying, i.e. the *explicit* content of his message. But beyond this explicit content, Farmer Brown conveys some additional meaning not coded in his utterance: He gives to understand that he is seeking advice about what remedy or medication to use to treat his mule's distemper. And he interprets Sam's answer *Turpentine* not only as information about what Sam gave his mule but also as implying that turpentine restored Sam's mule's health. This interpretation sadly turns out to be the wrong inference, as Sam's utterance (1) reveals.

In the above piece of conversational interaction, Farmer Brown represents the "normal", i.e. pragmatically competent speaker – although he appears to be strikingly ignorant regarding the adequate remedy for his mule's viral disease. His interlocutor Sam is the kind of language user one would not like to meet in real life. Sam, a pragmatically incompetent speaker, invites inference-based interpretations in the minds of pragmatically competent language users, here Farmer Brown, which turn out to be completely wrong.

The two Gricean layers of saying and implicating with regard to the conversational exchange (1) are diagrammed in Figure 3.

To summarize, the dialogue in (1) illustrates the important distinction between what is said and what remains unsaid but is implicitly conveyed by the speaker. Furthermore, the dialogue between the two interactants shows that communication is not simply an exchange of coded utterances – encoded by the speaker and decoded by the hearer – but it is a *collaborative* effort that involves not only linguistic but also inferential competence on the on the part of language users. Interlocutors are required to read each other's minds, and Grice (1975) argues that they do not go about this task in a random fashion but abide by a relatively small set of conversational principles. These principles guide both the *production* and the *comprehension* of utterances. This is exactly the idea that Grice developed systematically and has rightly been praised for in the pragma-linguistic community.

There are different kinds of implicature that can be represented in a tree diagram, as in Figure 4.

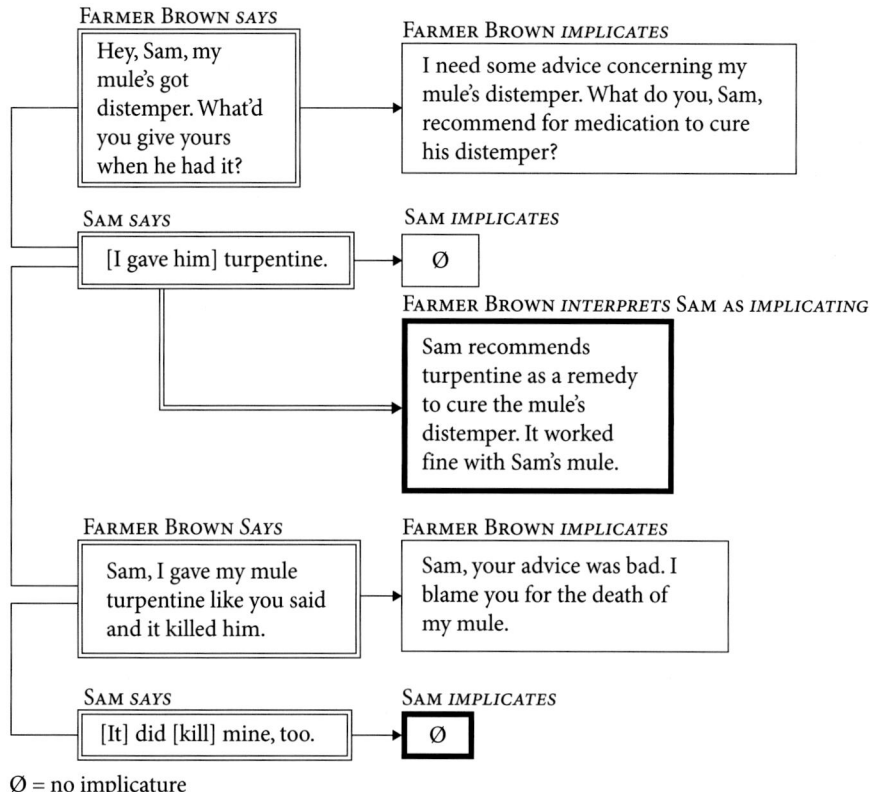

Ø = no implicature

Figure 3. Saying and implicating: Misunderstandings

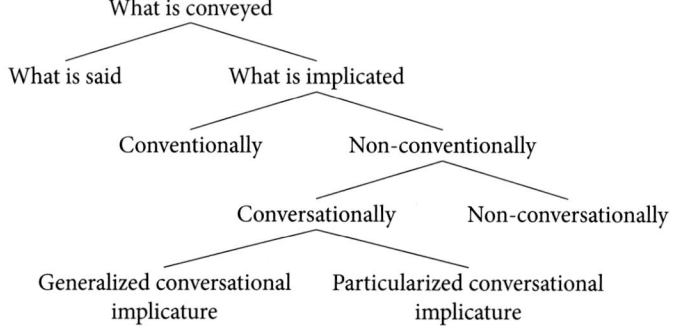

Figure 4. What is said vs. what is implicated (adopted from Horn 1988: 121)

As already pointed out above, essential for an adequate understanding of Grice's model of conversation is the notion of *conversational implicature*.[27] Conversational implicature comes in two kinds: *generalized conversational implicature* (GCI) and *particularized conversational implicature* (PCI). According to e.g. Levinson (2000), a GCI is a context-independent default inference, as in (2), whereas a PCI is triggered in specific contexts, as in (3). The symbols '+>' and '++>' are used to represent the GCI and PCI relation between what is said and what is implicated, respectively.[28]

(2) Some of the athletes look exhausted. +> Not all of the athletes look exhausted.

(3) You look exhausted. ++> You need to rest / I am worried about your health / You should not overexert yourself /…

An important property of conversational implicatures (of both kinds) is that that they are *cancelable* or *defeasible* (these two terms are used synonymously in pragmatics). This means that, in principle, speakers may withdraw conversational implicatures without contradicting themselves, as in (4) and (5):

(4) Some athletes look exhausted, in fact, all of them.

(5) You look exhausted; but I don't mean to imply that you need to rest / that I am worried about your health / that you have over-exerted yourself /…

In (4), the GCI *some* +> 'not all' is canceled, and in (5) an indefinite number of context-sensitive PCIs are explicitly revoked by the speaker.

3. Gricean principles guiding communication

3.1 The Cooperative Principle and the maxims of conversation

The made-up jocular dialogue in (1) illustrates one of Grice's important insights: Efficient communication is a collaborative or cooperative effort (see Tomasello 2009, who reaches the same conclusion from a bio-cognitive perspective). Grice (1975: 45) formulates his *Cooperative Principle,* which he regards as a prerequisite for successful communication, as follows:

> Make your conversational contribution such as is required, at the stage at which it occurs, by the accepted purpose or direction of the talk exchange in which you are engaged.

---

27. A more detailed discussion of the properties of implicature, including conventional and conversational implicature, is undertaken in Chapter 5, in which implicature is also compared and contrasted with entailment and presupposition.

28. Note that all the implicatures listed in the right column of Figure 3 are PCIs, i.e. highly context-dependent.

Grice regards the Cooperative Principle as a *rational* principle. In order for communication to function smoothly, it is reasonable to abide by it. This overarching principle is specified by various subprinciples that are called *maxims*, which in turn may comprise various submaxims. These Gricean maxims and submaxims read *verbatim* as follows:

Quantity (Grice 1975: 45)
1. Make your contribution as informative as is required (for the current purposes of the exchange.
2. Do not make your contribution more informative than is required.

Quality (Grice 1975: 46)
1. Do not say what you believe to be false.
2. Do not say that for which you lack adequate evidence.

Relation (Grice 1975: 46)
1. Be relevant.

Manner (Grice 1975: 46)
1. Avoid obscurity of expression.
2. Avoid ambiguity.
3. Be brief (avoid unnecessary prolixity).
4. Be orderly.

Before discussing and illustrating some of these maxims by way of example, a *caveat* is in order. Although the Cooperative Principle and the maxims are formulated as *imperatives* (see above), they are not to be understood as instructions about how people *should* communicate; i.e., they are not normative in the same sense as the recommendations for "correct" language use in prescriptive grammars. The maxims are, at least usually, *expected* to be complied with by interlocutors, because, according to Grice, it is *reasonable* to abide by them for the purpose of efficient and successful communication. A second point worth mentioning in this connection is that the Cooperative Principle and the maxims operate on a more or less subconscious level.[29] Most of the time, language users do not consciously think about the maxims – they just follow them. This does not preclude the occurrence of communicative situations in which it becomes necessary for interlocutors to reason and argue explicitly about implicated meanings.

A second important property of Grice's conversational model is that the Cooperative Principle and the maxims trigger (default) conversational implicatures – on

---

29. In the sense of Kahneman (2011), the presumed abidance by the Cooperative Principle and the manners in the construction of inferential meanings are examples of fast and spontaneous thinking (System 1). As long as communication runs smoothly, there is no need for them to be moved to the level of consciousness. Things will however be different when meanings are negotiated explicitly.

the presumption that interlocutors normally abide by them. However, the Cooperative Principle and maxims may also intentionally and recognizably be *flouted* by conversational interactants (Grice 1975: 49), and as a result, additional conversational implicatures are created. The options of abiding by the conversational principles and recognizably flouting them both further the goal of optimizing communicative efficiency. But there is also a third option for conversational interactants, namely that of "opting out", i.e. choosing to be uncommunicative, in which case, the Cooperative Principle and the maxims are "switched off."[30] In the following sections some of the Gricean maxims are discussed in more detail and illustrated with examples.

3.2 The Maxims of Quantity

Grice's Maxim of Quantity comprises two submaxims (see Section 3.1). The first (henceforth *Q1*) postulates that a speaker should provide as much information as possible (Grice 1975: 45). Assuming that the speaker abides by this submaxim, a conversational implicature arises, namely, that the speaker has indeed given the maximum amount of information that she is able to provide and that additional relevant information cannot be given. To illustrate, suppose that Mary, a witness to a bank robbery, is questioned by the police about the robber and she says:

(6) The robber was male, wore a mask, was about six feet tall, and had blond hair.

Suppose that these four conjoined descriptions of the bank robber are accurate, but assume in addition that Mary has recognized the bank robber: shockingly, it is her brother, but she is silent about this fact because she does not want her brother to be arrested, tried, and go to jail. The description of the bank robber Mary has given to the police is factually correct; however, she has suppressed *relevant* additional information. In uttering (6), Mary has automatically invited the inference that she does not know more than what she has said; in particular, she implicitly suggests that she does not know the identity of the robber. Although Mary *says* nothing wrong, what she *implicates* (or better pretends to be implicating) is definitely false. Example (6) illustrates an important point about maxims and the implicatures they induce: A speaker may *say* something *true*, but *implicate*, i.e. invite an inference, which is *false*.

The workings of Q1 can also be illustrated with *conceptual scales*. Such scales have been insightfully analyzed by Neo-Gricean scholars such as Horn (1989, 2006) and Levinson (2000: 79–98), in particular, the ones known as *Horn Scales* (named after the just-mentioned scholar), such as in (7):

---

30. For a more complete list of violations of the Cooperative Principle and the maxims, see Grice (1975: 49).

(7) *Quantifiers*: <all, most, many, some>

(8) *Epistemic modality/attitude*: <certain, likely, possible>, <know, believe>

(9) *Temperature*: <hot, warm>, <cold, cool>

(10) *Emotion*: <love, like>, <hate, dislike>, <ecstatic, happy, content>

By way of example, consider a Horn scale <X, Y>, where X is the "stronger" member and Y the "weaker" member. Note that the stronger member entails the weaker member, and the weaker member implicates the negation of the stronger member:

Scale <X, Y>, where X is stronger than Y

(11) *Entailment*: X entails Y

(12) *Implicature*: Y implicates not-X

Let us focus on cases that illustrate the implicature (12). The interpretation of a sentence such as (13) involves a quantification scale:

(13) Some people have severely damaged skin as a result of burns or ulcers […].
(COCA 2012)

The use of the noun phrase *some people* in (13) conversationally implicates that *not all* people who have suffered burns or ulcers have severely damaged skin.

The following sentence expresses a mental attitude (also called 'propositional attitude'), i.e. of what the speaker believes:

(14) I believe that no materials exist for a full and satisfactory biography of this man.
(COCA 2017)

Given an epistemic scale <*know, believe*>, with *know* as the stronger member, statement (14) will normally trigger an implicature that the speaker does not know for sure that *no materials exist for a full and satisfactory biography* of the man in question.

A somewhat longer piece of conversational discourse from the television show *Larry King Live* on CNN also nicely illustrates the workings of an epistemic scale:

(15) KING: Hey, a great pleasure to welcome to *LARRY KING LIVE* one of my favorite people, Chris Rock, the Emmy and Grammy winning comic; the star of the C.W. television sitcom, "Everybody Hates Chris," star of the new film, "I Think I Love My Wife." He also directed it and co-wrote it. Thanks so much for coming in, Chris. ROCK: Well, thanks so much for having me here, Larry. KING: What do you mean by I THINK I love my wife? ROCK: Well, I mean, I know I love my real wife. But in my – my movie wife, you know, sometimes you have to go through trials and tribulations and you realize, you know what? I think I love her.
(COCA 2007)

Example (15) transcribes an interview conducted by Larry King with the actor, director, and writer Chris Rock about his film *I Think I Love my Wife*, which came out in 2007. The title of the movie already evokes a scale, i.e. a contrast between thinking and knowing. *Knowing* conveys 'certainty', whereas *thinking*, here used in the sense of 'believing', occupies a lower value on the epistemic scale of certainty and leaves room for some doubt – in other words, in the fictitious world of the film, the character enacted by Chris Rock is not certain that he loves his *movie wife*, an interpretation that is supported by references to *trials* and *tribulations* in his final conversational turn in (15).

Next, consider the following statement about the weather, which involves a reference to a temperature scale:

(16) Even though it was overcast and cool today in the City of Angels, lots of volunteer turnout including a steady stream of walk-ins for all shifts!
(GloWbE 2012)

In (16), the meaning of the adjective *cool* is understood against the background of a *temperature scale* such as <*cold, cool*> (see (9)). Given Q1, the use of *cool* implicates that a stronger term or expression on the temperature scale such as *cold* or *freezing cold* does not hold.

Finally, terms that denote emotions are also conceived by language users as being ranked in terms of their intensity. A good example is what might be called the 'affection scale' <*love, like*> that is at work in the following dialogue from the American television show, *Oprah Winfrey*:

(17) Ms-KEATON: [...] And I really like Warren. WINFREY: OK. And just "like", though? Ms-KEATON: I'm not in love with Warren anymore. [...]
(COCA 2006)

Given the context, it becomes clear that Diane Keaton's first utterance in (17) conveys the implicature that she does *not love* Warren Beatty. In the next conversational turn, Oprah Winfrey wants to make sure that this is the intended implicature, which Ms. Keaton explicitly confirms in her reply (although she also conveys that she once loved Warren).

The following example highlights two central properties of implicature, i.e. its suspendability and its defeasibility (see Chapter 5 for more details):

(18) Tom is content, if not happy, in his new life as a would-be novelist.
(WebCorp)

Sentence (18) exhibits the constructional schema *X if not Y* with the reading 'X and perhaps even Y', which, in this case, conveys a progression from a "weaker" emotion to a "stronger" emotion, i.e. from *content* to *happy*. The adjective *content* triggers the implicature 'but not necessarily happy', which is immediately suspended by *if not happy*. Note that this inference can be *canceled* very easily if, instead of *if*, the conjunction *but* is used, as in (19):

(19) Tom is content, but not happy, in his new life as a would-be novelist.

Let us now turn to submaxim Q2, which requires that not more information than needed should be provided by the speaker, because the non-coded content can be inferred by the hearer. Consider a situation in which John wants to know the truth about how Mary feels about him and the following short dialogue unfolds:

(20) JOHN: Do you still like me? MARY: Oh yes, I do.

In (20), John could implicitly convey the question whether Mary still loves him, and he possibly interprets her answer as implicating that she does indeed love him, although neither of them explicitly uses the verb *love*. The wording ("oh yes") and prosodic features, such as intonation, may well be sufficient to evoke a more intense emotion than 'like', i.e. 'love', on the affection scale. In terms of traditional rhetoric, the trope used by John's question and Mary's response in (20) is an understatement, more specifically a case of *meiosis*, the opposite of *hyperbole*.

The conclusion to be drawn from the examples in this section is that interlocutors have to assess which of the two Maxims of Quantity is at work in a particular conversational exchange. Language users have to take both the linguistic context and the extralinguistic situation (including sociocultural parameters) into account in order to determine whether the application of Q1 or that of Q2 yields the most plausible interpretation.

3.3 The Maxims of Quality

At first sight, the first quality maxim looks like an ethical or moral principle: Make your contribution one that is truthful. What does ethics or morality have to do with communication? One answer is that communication would break down if everybody always lied, i.e. were intentionally untruthful.[31] From a Gricean perspective, it is thus rational to comply with this maxim – notwithstanding "social lies" that are tolerated by most people for reasons of politeness or considerateness.

In Grice's conversational model, the second maxim of quality is also regarded as being motivated by rationality. Language users are expected to be willing to provide reasons for their claims. In contrast to the two Maxims of Quantity described

---

[31]. The first quality maxim corresponds to what is termed 'sincerity condition' in speech act theory (see Chapter 6).

in Section 3.2, abidance by the maxims of quality does not seem to trigger any particular implicatures.

But what happens when a quality maxim is flouted? By way of example, let us consider the first quality maxim. According to Grice (1975: 53), the flouting of this maxim gives rise to rhetorical tropes like irony, metaphor, meiosis, and hyperbole. What these figures have in common is that they are literally false, as in the following examples:

(21) Did not you give your word you would be standing by, ever ready to serve the need of the Lady Lucent? A fine friend you are to her.
(https://books.google.co.uk/books?isbn=14391 70835)

(22) But soft, what light through yonder window breaks? It is the east, and Juliet is the sun. (Shakespeare, *Romeo and Juliet*, Act 2, Scene 2)

(23) He was a little intoxicated. (Grice 1975: 53)

(24) DONALD TRUMP: I've said it a million times, I'll make that decision at the right time. (COCA 2016)

In utterance (21), in the given discourse context, the exclamation *A fine friend you are to her!* functions as an ironic speech act. In a situation in which (21) is obviously false, the utterance triggers the implicature 'You are not a good friend to her'. In (22), Juliet is characterized as the *sun* by Romeo. In Gricean terms, on a literal interpretation, the sentence is patently false; hence a figurative interpretation, here a metaphorical one, is the most plausible one. The statement in (23) functions as a meiosis. For example, it could be predicated of a man who is blind drunk and has "broken up all the furniture" (Grice 1975: 53). Finally, (24) is a hyperbolic claim, which is literally untrue, because Donald Trump certainly did not say "a million times" that he would make the decision in question at the right time.

3.4 The Maxim of Relation (Relevance)

The Maxim of Relation, which is instantiated by the Maxim of Relevance, is intuitively easy to grasp, but its precise content is hard to pin down. The rationale for this maxim is the presumption that the interlocutors in a conversation mutually expect their contributions to be relevant in a particular conversational context. For example, a question requires an answer that is "relevant" with regard to the question:

(25) JOHN: Where is the newspaper? MARY: On the living room table.

Mary's response in (25) is a relevant answer to John's question. Suppose now that Mary's answer to John's question is:

(26) MARY: Where do you think it is? [slightly enervated tone of voice]

In this case, Mary does not provide the requested piece of information, i.e., she violates the maxim of relation. However, her response (26) may implicate, among other things, the following:

(27) John, you are asking a stupid question because
   a. it is obvious where the newspaper is, namely on the living room table/on the desk/on your bedside table, etc.
   b. you know that we canceled our subscription and therefore we didn't receive a newspaper this morning.
   c. the paper didn't appear this morning because of a strike (as you should know).
   d. [...]

The dots in (27) indicate that the list of implicatures associated with (26) does not have to stop here. The main point is, however, that even when a conversational turn seems irrelevant, the hearer usually assumes that, at some level, the speaker abides by the Cooperative Principle. The bottom line is that an utterance whose explicit content, on the face of it, is irrelevant may become relevant if the implicatures that the speaker intends to convey are taken into account.

3.5 The Maxims of Manner

According to Grice (1975: 46), *manner* refers "not [...] to what is said but, rather HOW what is said is to be said." The way something is said triggers certain implicatures. To see this, consider the following literary example from the nineteenth century novel *In the House of a Friend* by Fanny E. M. Notley (1881: 52):

(28) [...] I am alone and defenceless in the house of this man, who calls himself my friend [...].

The relative clause *who calls himself my friend* is "wordier" than necessary, i.e., the narrator flouts the submaxim 'Be brief', which, together with other clues such as the use of *this man* and of *calls himself* instead of the simple copula *is*, invite the inference that the man in question is *not* the narrator's friend. This implicature is immediately confirmed by the passage that follows (28), i.e. (29), where the narrator describes the man as her *direst enemy*:

(29) [...] but who is in truth my direst enemy – the one from whose hand I dread all cruelties, tyrannies, and wrongs. (Notley 1881: 52)

Next, consider the submaxim 'Be orderly', which is at work in the following fictional example (slightly adapted):

(30) She tripped and fell but got quickly back on her feet. (COCA 2013)

In (30), a series of three events is described: the protagonist tripped, fell, and got back on her feet. Let us focus on the first two events. Grice's submaxim 'Be orderly' postulates that the *temporal* order of the events described in the sentence be reflected in the *linear* order of the verbs denoting these events. Since the event of tripping occurs before the event of falling, the former event should be coded before the second event.

Note that the Gricean analysis of examples like (30) presumes that the coordinating conjunction *and* is to be interpreted in a strictly *truth-conditional* way, i.e. like the logical connective '∧' (see Chapter 1 for its truth-functional meaning). On the level of what is said, *and* does not convey any information about the temporal order of conjuncts. According to Grice, the reading 'and *then*' comes about through an implicature, given the context (a short narrative) and our world knowledge about likely sequences of events. In semiotic terms, the relationship between the linguistic coding of the events depicted in (30) is *iconically* motivated (see Chapter 2).

In the case of (30), the implicature 'and then' seems virtually non-cancelable because it is strengthened by a second implicature: the events of tripping and falling are conceived of as one event, i.e., the second event is an immediate consequence of the first. It is however not impossible to imagine a scenario in which the tripping event and the falling event are not immediately adjacent in time.

In the following example *and* does not necessarily implicate the reading 'and then', i.e., this implicature can be canceled:

(31) Becky smiled and nodded as the crowd offered another round of applause.
 (COCA 2015)

On one reading of (31), Becky smiled and *then* nodded, i.e., the implicature 'and then' is triggered. However, it is also possible to interpret the two actions of smiling and nodding as occurring simultaneously.

4. Reducing the number of maxims: Neo-Gricean approaches and Relevance Theory

There have been various efforts by pragmaticists to improve the Gricean model, especially, by reducing the number of conversational maxims. Two major representatives of this "Neo-Gricean" approach to communication – Stephen Levinson and Laurence Horn – are introduced in Section 4.1. In Section 4.2, a theory of communication is briefly described, i.e. Relevance Theory, which rejects the Gricean conversational principles *in toto*.

4.1 A sketch of Levinson's and Horn's models

Levinson (2000) reduces the Gricean maxims to three conversational principles: (i) the *Q(uantity)-principle*, (ii) the *I(nformativeness)-principle*, and (iii) the *M(anner)-principle*, which are briefly described and illustrated below.[32] In what follows, I rely on Huang's (2007: 40–54) excellent introduction to Levinson's work. The conversational principles take the perspectives of both the speaker and the addressee into account.

Levinson's Q-principle is formulated as follows in Huang (2007: 41):

i. Speaker: Do not say less than is required […].
ii. Addressee: What is not said is not the case.

The Q-principle is obviously based on Grice's First Maxim of Quantity and can be illustrated with entailment scales (Horn scales), as already demonstrated in Section 3.2. Here is another example that involves the Horn scale <*manage, try*>:

(32) But I do think that whoever is president next – in January of 2013 – is going to have to deal with immigration. First of all, it's been a problem that's been out there for too long. George W. Bush tried to solve it. His own party didn't let him. Barack Obama tried to solve it. He couldn't find a partner on the Republican side. (COCA 2012)

In (32), the speaker reports that two U.S. presidents, George W. Bush and Barack Obama, tried to solve the immigration problem. The phrase *tried to solve it* conversationally implicates that the presidents *did not manage* to solve it. The speaker does not say less than is required; and the addressee infers that, since the phrase *managed to solve it* has not been used, it is not the case that the problem of immigration was solved.

---

32. The Maxim of Quality is not integrated in Levinson's system.

The I-principle is based on the assumption that language users often resort to semantically more general expressions to implicate more specific meanings. The I-principle can be formulated as follows (Huang 2007: 46):

i. Speaker: Do not say more than is required […].
ii. Addressee: What is generally said is stereotypically and specifically exemplified.

To a large extent, the I-principle overlaps with Grice's Second Maxim of Quantity. The following example illustrates what is referred to as "conjunction buttressing" by Neo-Griceans (Huang 2007: 47):

(33) The door opened and an old couple stepped inside.   (COCA 2015)

In (33), the narrator conversationally implicates an interpretation of *and* as 'and then', and a pragmatically competent addressee is supposed to be able to infer the temporal interpretation of *and*. The hypothesis underlying this analysis is that *and* is often, if not most of the time, more than just a conjunction that loosely coordinates contents, but, via implicature, conveys specific senses, such as temporal sequentiality or causality. In sentence (34) (from Huang 2007: 47), which is again a case of conjunction buttressing, a causal relationship between the content of the first and the second clause is implicated:

(34) John pressed the spring and the drawer opened.

Finally, the Gricean Maxim of Manner – in Levinson's terms, the M-principle – is characterized as follows (Huang 2007: 50):

i. Speaker: Do not use a marked expression without reason.
ii. Addressee: What is said in a marked way is not unmarked.

As an example, consider the pair *likely* vs. *not unlikely*. The two expressions are logically equivalent, but *not unlikely* is "marked" in comparison to the former. The following piece of academic writing illustrates this contrast:

(35) While the precise identity of the book is not known for certain, it is not unlikely that Fuller possessed a text of the Grimm's fairy tales since she had a major interest in German literature and read German fluently.   (COCA 2017)

In using the double negation *not unlikely* instead of the unmarked option *likely*, the author of (35) gives to understand that it is possible, but less than (fully) likely, that Fuller possessed a text of Grimm's fairy tales; i.e., the following implicature is operative in (35): *not unlikely* +> 'less than fully likely'.

Laurence Horn (2006) proposes a further reduction of the number of Gricean maxims to two contrasting principles, *Q(uantity)* and *R(elation)*. Horn's Q-principle is a hearer-oriented "guarantee of the sufficiency of informative content" (ibid.: 14) and includes Grice's First Maxim of Quantity and the first two Maxims of Manner ('Avoid obscurity of expression' and 'Avoid ambiguity'). In contrast, the R-principle, which is a speaker-oriented maxim, requires "minimization of form"; i.e., it is an instance of the "Law of Least Effort" (Horn 2006: 13). It subsumes Grice's Second Maxim of Quantity, the Maxim of Relation, and the Third and Fourth Maxims of Manner ('Be brief' and 'Be orderly', respectively).

Typical examples illustrating the workings of the Q-principle are again Horn scales such as <*excellent, good*>. Consider (36):

(36) Despite lacking a control group, "it was a good paper", says Richard Cawthon, MD, Ph.D. [...]. (COCA 2013)

The assertion that the article in question was a *good* paper induces the implicature that it was not necessarily an excellent or brilliant publication, although this inference is defeasible.

An example of a speaker-based R-based implicature is the minimization of form in what speech act theorists call *indirect illocutionary acts* (see Searle 1975, and Chapters 9 and 10). Consider the contrast between (37) and (38):

(37) Can you turn off the radiator?

(38) Are you able to turn off the radiator? / Do you have the ability to turn off the radiator?

Utterance (37) is literally a *question* about the hearer's ability to turn off the radiator, but it routinely functions as an indirect *request* to turn off the appliance. In contrast, as already observed by Searle (1975), utterances such as (38) with the "wordier" *Are you able to [...]?* or *Do you have the ability to [...]?*, instead of *Can you [...]?*, are not conventionally used as requests, but they are interpreted as questions (see Horn 2006; Panther 1981; Panther & Thornburg 2014). The use of the modal *can* is obviously a more economical coding device for a request than longer expressions such as *be able to* or *have the ability to*. The Gricean maxim that motivates the use of *can* is the Maxim of Manner 'Be brief', which in Horn's system is subsumed under his R-principle.

4.2 The Principle of Relevance

The main competitor of Gricean and Neo-Gricean pragmatics is *Relevance Theory*, a theoretical paradigm developed by Dan Sperber and Deirdre Wilson (1995), which is briefly sketched in this section. The authors, like other pragmaticists (Grice 1975; Bach & Harnish 1979; Leech 1983; Green 1989), stress the importance of inference in an adequate model of communication. Sperber and Wilson postulate only one fundamental principle, which, they claim, underlies both cognition and communication, i.e. *relevance*. As repeatedly mentioned in this chapter, Grice regards his cooperative principle as rationally motivated, whereas Sperber and Wilson see their principle of relevance as a biologically rooted instinct.

Wilson (2005) distinguishes between two principles of relevance, the first of these is called the *Cognitive Principle of Relevance* and the second the *Communicative Principle of Relevance*. The first principle is formulated as follows in Wilson (2005: 387): "Cognitive Principle of Relevance: Human cognition tends to be geared to the maximisation of relevance." Wilson assumes that the search for relevance is not a matter of "choice" but a result "of the way our human cognitive systems have evolved" (ibid: 387). The Cognitive Principle of Relevance is supplemented by the Communicative Principle of Relevance, in which *overt communication* and *optimal relevance* are the key concepts (Wilson 2005: 388): "Every utterance (or other act of overt communication) communicates a presumption of its own optimal relevance."

The term *relevance* is reminiscent of Grice's Maxim of Relation whose only instantiation is the imperative 'Be relevant'. It is important to see, however, that the concept of relevance has a radically different status in Sperber and Wilson's theory. The first difference is that these authors regard communication as *exclusively* guided by the principle of (optimal) relevance; no maxims and no superordinate cooperative principle are needed. Furthermore, Sperber and Wilson try to give more substance to the notion of relevance itself, which is used in a rather pre-theoretical albeit intuitively appealing way by Grice. Sperber and Wilson define *relevant information* as information that together with *old* or *known* information serves as the basis for the derivation of *new information*.

According to Sperber and Wilson, the presumption of optimal relevance, which is evoked by every utterance, has two aspects to it: On the one hand, it creates the presumption of *maximal contextual effects*; on the other hand, it creates the presumption that the *cognitive effort* to process the utterance will be minimal. Thus, in interpreting utterances, interlocutors automatically and subconsciously process information in such a way that they are able to achieve a *maximal contextual effect* for a *minimum cost of processing effort*. The presumption of minimization of processing effort is comparable to, if not equivalent with, Horn's R-principle of minimization of form (see Section 4.1).

A peculiarity of Relevance Theory is that it postulates a "dedicated module" of pragmatic inferencing that is conceived of as being separate from other non-linguistic mind reading abilities of humans regarding the beliefs, intentions, and goals of other interactants (Sperber & Wilson 2002; Wilson 2005: 386). For example, Wilson (2005: 386) postulates a pragmatic module "with its own special-purpose inferential principles or procedures", which is assumed to be distinct from non-linguistic cognitive devices of "mind reading." In contrast, the philosopher of language Marco Mazzone argues against the existence of such a special-purpose inferential module. According to Mazzone (2018: 177), the recognition of communicative intentions cannot not be separated from the recognition of "general purposes or goals" of interactants. Mazzone's position is adopted in this book.

5. In lieu of a conclusion: The influence of cultural practices on maxims of conversation

The models presented in Sections 3 and 4 convey an overall picture of linguistic communication as a rationally motivated and/or biologically based activity. It has to be noted, however, that especially Gricean and Neo-Gricean approaches to communication have been criticized by scholars working from an anthropological and ethnological perspective (see e.g. Senft 2014: 37–39).

For example, the linguistic anthropologist Elinor Ochs Keenan (1976) contends that in Malagasy society speakers systematically do not abide by Grice's First Maxim of Quantity, which requires conversational interactants to be as informative as required. Ochs Keenan finds that Malagasy speakers "regularly violate this maxim" and gives two reasons for this violation: (i) "[n]ew information is a rare commodity", and (ii) Malagasy people live in small communities and their daily activities are "under public gaze", i.e., they are generally known (Ochs Keenan 1976: 70). Villagers who succeed in acquiring new information are therefore reluctant to share it with others.

Ochs Keenan surmises that a second and even more important reason for Malagasy speakers to violate Q1 is their fear that revealing information about the activities of community members "may have unforeseen unpleasant consequences" (Ochs Keenan 1976: 70) for the speaker and the speaker's family. There are thus strong sociocultural motivations for not abiding unreservedly by a Gricean "rational" maxim such as Q1.

Furthermore, intentional non-compliance with Q1, motivated by the value of information as a valuable commodity, is certainly more common in Western societies than the Gricean and Neo-Gricean models would suggest. Senft (2014: 39) points out that "Gricean maxims are based on a rather uni-dimensional understanding of language and conversation." This criticism is justified in the sense that Grice ignores sociocultural beliefs and their impact on communicative behavior. Still, despite his neglect of sociocultural and anthropological factors in his theory of conversation, Grice has contributed significantly to contemporary pragmatics in demonstrating the importance of inferencing in the construction of natural language meaning.

CHAPTER 5

Implicature, entailment, and presupposition
Differences and commonalities

1. Introduction

In this chapter, the notion of implicature (see Chapter 4) is taken up again. After a relatively brief characterization and discussion of what Grice (1975, 1989) calls *conventional implicature* in Section 2, Section 3 focuses on the notion of *conversational implicature* and its properties in comparison with and in contrast to entailment and presupposition, which were already introduced in Chapter 3. It turns out that implicature, on the one hand, and entailment and presupposition, on the other, differ markedly in various respects, but there are also some properties that these types of inference have in common. Section 4 concludes this chapter with a brief summary.

2. Conventional implicature

As pointed out in Chapter 4 (see Figure 4), Grice assumes a basic distinction between what is (literally) *said* and what is conveyed via pragmatic inference, i.e. *implicature*. On the level of what is implicated, Grice differentiates between *conventional* and *non-conventional* implicatures. The concept of conventional implicature was already introduced in Chapter 1 (Section 2.2.6) in connection with the contrast between truth-conditional and non-truth-conditional aspects of meaning of the coordinating conjunction *but* (in contrast to *and*). As a reminder, consider example (1) retrieved from the academic journal *The Tax Lawyer*, in which two propositions are connected by the coordinating conjunction *but*, and compare it with statement (2), in which, instead of *but*, the connective *and* is used:

(1) Jamie is a citizen of State A, but commutes to work each day to work in State B.
(COCA 2017)

(2) Jamie is a citizen of State A and commutes to work each day to work in State B.

Recall that according to Grice, from a logical perspective, the complex propositions *p but q* and *p and q* have exactly the same truth conditions, i.e., they are true if the component individual propositions *p* and *q* are true.

Informally, the conceptual-pragmatic difference between (1) and (2) can be described as follows. Example (1) conveys an element of surprise or unexpectedness: given that Jamie is a resident of State A, one would expect him to earn his living in that same State A, but, unexpectedly, Jamie has a job in State B, which raises the question where he should pay his taxes. In contrast to (1), sentence (2) does not convey this conventional implicature.

Grice maintains that, different from the kinds of non-conventional implicatures to be discussed below, conventional implicatures are not cancelable or defeasible, a property that they share with entailments. Grice's contention that the meaning conveyed by examples such as (1) is an implicature, i.e. does not belong to the level of what is said, is however debatable. One could argue that the *relation* of contrastiveness between two propositions p and q is actually *truth-conditionally* relevant, i.e., if this relation between the two propositions does not hold, then p *but* q as a *whole* could be considered false – even if the propositions p and q are *individually* true.

While the theoretical usefulness of the notion of conventional implicature remains controversial, *conversational implicature* is generally regarded as an essential cognitive mechanism in the construction of implicit meaning. Beyond the properties that were already described and illustrated in Chapters 3 and 4, this chapter introduces additional features of this important pragmatic concept.

3. Conversational implicature

The kinds of non-conventional implicature especially relevant for our purposes are known as *Generalized Conversational Implicatures* (CGIs) and *Particularized Conversational Implicatures* (PCIs) (Grice 1975, 1989; Levinson 2000) (see Chapter 4, Figure 4). Levinson (2000) assumes that GCIs are good candidates for *universals*, i.e., they are supposed to hold cross-linguistically, while PCIs are described as context-dependent, and may also be based on specific cultural beliefs and practices of a language community.

The following is a slightly adapted list of properties that, according to Levinson (1983: 119) and Levinson (2000: 14), GCIs and PCIs share:

i. *Suspendability* and *cancelability/defeasibility*: The implicature can be suspended or even be withdrawn, i.e. canceled, on the basis of additional assumptions. This property was already mentioned in Chapter 4 and illustrated with examples.
ii. *Non-detachability*: The same content would (usually) trigger the same implicatures.
iii. *Calculability*: The inferential structure of implicature can be rationally reconstructed.

iv. *Non-codability*: The implicature is not part of the coded content of an utterance.
v. *Reinforceability*: The implicature can be added to what is said without creating an effect of redundancy or tautology.

Let us now discuss and illustrate properties (i)–(v) in turn. Some of them turn out to be unproblematic, but others have to be taken with a grain of salt and will have to be reanalyzed and modified somewhat.

3.1 Suspendability and cancelability

What GCIs and PCIs have in common is that they are suspendable or even cancelable, which means that the speaker can retract an implicature without *contradiction*. According to Levinson (2000: 16), the difference between the two kinds of conversational implicature is that GCIs license context-independent *default* interpretations, whereas PCIs are inferences that are sensitive to specific contexts.

To begin with, let us again illustrate the suspendability and defeasibility of GCIs with a few examples. Consider the authentic piece of discourse in (3) that contains the quantifier *most*:

(3) We found that most countries used ad hoc priority-setting and planning methods, with little to no underlying systematic risk analysis. (COCA 2012)

Utterance (3) has the preferred or default interpretation, i.e. conveys the GCI formulated in (4):

(4) We found that not all countries used ad hoc priority-setting and planning methods, with little to no underlying systematic risk analysis.

Using the symbol '+>' for GCIs, the relevant implicature associated with the quantifier *most* can be notated as in (5):

(5) most +> 'not all'

The implicature (5) is very strong, but it can be *suspended* or even *canceled*. For example, the writer of (4) may say without contradiction:

(6) We found that most if not all countries used ad hoc priority-setting and planning methods, with little to no underlying systematic risk analysis.
(*suspension* of GCI)

(7) We found that most, in fact, all countries used ad hoc priority-setting and planning methods, with little to no underlying systematic risk analysis.
(*cancelation* of GCI)

In (6), the speaker or writer suspends the implicature (5) by inserting after *most* the conditional qualification *if not all countries*, which weakens the default inference 'not all countries' without explicitly canceling it. The cancelation of implicature (5) is explicitly achieved in (6) by means of an expression of the type *in fact, all x*. Notice that, as predicted in point (i), the cancelation of the implicature does not result in a logical contradiction.

As an example of a defeasible PCI, recall part of the dialogue (1) in Chapter 4, repeated here as (8):

(8) FARMER BROWN: Hey, Sam, my mule's got distemper. What'd you give yours when he had it? SAM: Turpentine.

As diagrammed in Figure 3 of Chapter 4, Farmer Brown's second sentence in (8) is not just a neutral question about what Sam gave his mule when it was sick. Farmer Brown wants some advice about what he should give his mule so that the animal recovers from its distemper. This context-dependent implicature is given in (9) (where the symbol '++>' is used to represent the PCI relation):

(9) Hey, Sam, my mule's got distemper. What'd you give yours when he had it?
++> Sam, what medication did you use to cure your mule's distemper?

Accordingly, Farmer Brown takes Sam's reply in (8) as PCI-implicating that the ingestion of turpentine cured Sam's mule:

(10) (Sam gave his mule) turpentine. ++> Turpentine cured Sam's mule.

Sam's answer to Farmer Brown's question is straightforward, but it is highly misleading because, in the given context, it strongly suggests the inferential relation (10), an inference that turns out to be totally wrong.

As demonstrated in the preceding paragraphs, conversational implicatures are suspendable and cancelable. The defeasibility of conversational implicature gives a speaker a definitive communicative advantage over the hearer. The speaker can always cancel an implicature by saying, 'I didn't mean it that way; I did not imply what you assume I implied'. This discursive strategy is however not available to the speaker in cases of entailment and (semantic) presupposition because these inferences cannot be canceled without contradiction (see Chapter 4). To see this, consider the following entailment relationship:

(11) [S]he remembered to keep her back straight.
(COCA 2001) ⊩ She kept her back straight.

It is not possible to deny the entailed proposition in (11), because this move would lead to the contradictory statement (12):

(12) #She remembered to keep her back straight, but she didn't keep it straight.

In some cases, the distinction between conversational implicature and entailment is more difficult to draw. Here is an example that illustrates the problem of defining a clear boundary between the two inferential mechanisms:

(13) The detectives ordered him [the suspect] out of his vehicle [...].
(COCA 2014)

Does (13) entail or implicate (14)?

(14) The suspect stepped out of his vehicle.

In this particular case, there is contextual evidence that (14) is a strong implicature rather than an entailment, because (13) is followed by a *but* clause that explicitly cancels the inference:

(15) [...] but instead he sped away.

From utterance (15) the conclusion can be drawn that the suspect did not abide by the detectives' order, i.e. did not move out of the car.
But now consider the following piece of narrative fiction:

(16) That week Jeffrey asked Rudy into his office for coffee, but they didn't drink coffee. Instead Jeffrey pounded a fist at his desk and wept into his other hand.
(COCA 2006)

Does (16) entail or implicate the proposition 'Rudy entered the office'? Given the linguistic context, the reader can conclude that, at Jeffrey's request, Rudy did indeed step into the office. This inference is not an intrinsic conceptual property, i.e. an entailment, of the phrase *ask s.o. into a LOCATION*, but it is a strong implicature, whose truth is confirmed, i.e. *reinforced* contextually (see Section 3.5).
Examples like (13) and (16) demonstrate that entailments and generalized conversational implicatures sometimes look virtually indistinguishable, but, on closer inspection of the context, evidence can often be found for the former or the latter kind of implication as the correct interpretation.
Regarding the difference between cases of presupposition and generalized conversational implicature, consider example (17):

(17) Hamilton is surprised that the price for the land is so low [...].
(COCA 1998) ~> The price for the land is so low.

Sentence (17) presupposes the truth of the complement clause following the predicate *is surprised*. As (18) shows, it is contradictory to assert that some person is surprised that *p* and, at the same time, to deny that *p* holds; i.e., the complement clause in (17) conveys a factive presupposition that is not defeasible:

(18) #Hamilton is surprised that the price for the land is so low, but in fact it is not so low.

In conclusion then, the linguistic data considered in this section confirm the thesis that, in contrast to entailments and presuppositions, which cannot be denied without contradiction, even very strong conversational implicatures are cancelable.

3.2 Non-detachability

Grice (1975) and Levinson (2000) contend that conversational implicatures, i.e. both GCIs and PCIs, are non-detachable. The intuitively plausible idea behind this postulate is that utterances with the same meaning trigger the same conversational implicatures.

Suppose the quantifier phrase *most countries* in (3) is changed into the longer synonymous expression *the majority of countries*. The principle of non-detachability predicts that the latter expression has the same implicature as *most countries*, and this is indeed the case:

(19) the majority of countries +> 'not all countries'

The GCI 'not all x' is associated with the noun phrase *the majority of x*, as in (20), and it can be suspended, as in (21), or even be canceled, as in (22):

(20) The majority of patients with allergic disorders can be safely managed within primary care [...]. (COCA 2012)

(21) The majority of patients, if not all patients with allergic disorders, can be safely managed within primary care. (*suspension* of GCI)

(22) The majority of patients, in fact, all patients with allergic disorders can be safely managed within primary care. (*cancelation* of GCI)

Nevertheless, the principle of detachability does not hold unconditionally. As already noticed by Grice (1975), the *way* or the *manner of speaking* may also influence the kind of implicature conveyed by an utterance (see Chapter 4, Section 3.5).

In principle, the non-detachability criterion also holds for entailments. Compare e.g. the near-synonymous verbs *make* and *have* in their causative use:

(23) He made them come to his office.

(24) He had them come to his office.

Both (23) and (24) entail (25):

(25) They came to his office.

Presuppositions are also non-detachable, as the following virtually synonymous examples show:

(26) Both girls were very pleased with their new hairstyles.

(27) Both girls were very happy with their new hairstyles.

Sentences (26) and (27) share the presupposition (28):[33]

(28) Both girls had new hairstyles.

3.3 Calculability

Grice (1989: 31) emphasizes that "[t]he presence of a conversational implicature must be capable of being worked out" and refers to this property as 'calculability'. In normal communicative interaction, conversational implicatures are created spontaneously and their content is immediately grasped by addressees without any noticeable cognitive effort; i.e., as already pointed out in Chapter 4 (footnote 3), the production and comprehension of implicatures are instances of what Kahneman (2011) calls "fast" thinking and Mazzone (2018: Chapter 3) refers to as "automatic" processing. However, there exist communicative situations in which interlocutors *reflect* on what might be pragmatically implied by an utterance; i.e., not infrequently interactants make a conscious effort to figure out what a speaker might have implicated with his or her utterance in a particular context or situation. An example that illustrates a deliberate effort to figure out what is meant, i.e. implicated, by an utterance is an article published in the *New York Times* on October 6, 2017, that was headlined *What Did President Trump Mean by 'Calm Before the Storm'?*, an excerpt of which is given in (29):

(29) Gesturing to his guests, [Trump] said, "You guys know what this represents? Maybe it's the calm before the storm." "What's the storm?" asked one reporter. "Could be the calm before the storm," Mr. Trump repeated, stretching out the phrase, a sly smile playing across his face. "What storm, Mr. President?" asked a third journalist, a hint of impatience creeping into her voice. "From Iran?" ventured another reporter. "On ISIS? On what?"

---

33. The negation test, and, in fact, the other NECI criteria (see Chapter 3) show that (28) is a presupposition of (26): e.g. *Both girls were not very pleased/happy with their new hairstyles* leads to the non-defeasible inference (28).

Apart from being familiar with the conventional meaning of the metaphorical expression *calm before the storm* as 'a period of unusual tranquility or stability likely to presage difficult times' (NOAD), journalists were not able to *work out* the context-dependent implicatures (PCIs) of President Trump's utterances.

Calculability also holds for entailments and presuppositions. For example, an entailment can be reconstructed and made explicit in the format of a simple deductive *modus ponens* argument (see Chapter 3). For example, the sentence *She succeeded in fixing the software* entails 'She fixed the software', and *He regrets that he missed the deadline* presupposes 'He missed the deadline'. The respective *modus ponens* deductions are given in (30) and (31):

(30) *Premise 1*: If she succeeded in fixing the software, then she fixed the software. (If p, then q)
Premise 2: She succeeded in fixing the software. (p)
Conclusion: She fixed the software. (q)

(31) *Premise 1*: If he regrets that he missed the deadline, then he missed the deadline. (If p, then q)
Premise 2: He regrets that he missed the deadline. (p)
Conclusion: He missed the deadline. (q)

3.4   Non-codability of conversational implicatures

By definition, conversational implicatures are not explicitly coded, but they are inferentially derived *on the basis* of what is coded. In this sense, conversational implicatures can be called *non-conventional* (Levinson 2000: 14; see also Figure 4 in Chapter 4). In contrast, entailments and presuppositions are intrinsic parts of what is coded. For example, the implicative verb *manage (to do s.th.)* has as the intrinsic meaning component 'agent performs an action', and part of the meaning of *regret (that p)* is the presupposition that *p* is a fact.

3.5   Reinforceability

The notion of reinforcement refers to the possibility of making inferences explicit without creating an effect of redundancy. Reinforceability is a salient discourse-pragmatic property of conversational implicatures (see Section 3.5.1), but it remains to be determined whether, as e.g. Levinson (2000) seems to assume, reinforceability is restricted to implicatures. In what follows, it is argued that entailments and presuppositions can also be reinforced under certain conditions (Sections 3.5.2 and 3.5.3).

3.5.1 Reinforceability of implicature

It has been observed (e.g. Sadock 1978; Horn 1991; Levinson 2000) that implicatures can be explicitly asserted without producing an effect of redundancy or tautology. The reinforceability of implicature can be demonstrated in examples that involve Horn scales, which were already introduced in Chapter 4. Recall that in a Horn scale the "stronger" term entails the "weaker" term, and the weaker term conversationally implicates the negation of the stronger term.

Consider scales of emotivity again, such as <happy, content> and <love, like>.[34] The semantic and pragmatic relations between the scalar terms are given in (32)–(33) and (34)–(35), respectively.

(32) X is happy. ⊩ X is content.

(33) X is content. +> X is not happy.

(34) X loves Y. ⊩ X likes Y.

(35) X likes Y. +> X does not love Y.

Examples (36) and (37) show that it is possible to reinforce the conversational implicatures (33) and (35), respectively, without an effect of redundancy:

(36) He had been content, but not happy, in that position for five years. Because of reorganization he was transferred to a nonmanufacturing division, where he was again content but not happy for another five years.
(https://books.google.co.uk/books?id= pSAUAQAAMAAJ)

(37) I liked him but did not love him, not just yet.
(https://books.google.co.uk/books?isbn=1483680797)

As a further example illustrating the property of implicature reinforcement, consider the default inference triggered by the noun *drink*, i.e. 'alcoholic beverage', in (38) (see Levinson 2000: 116):

(38) We had a drink at the Fairmont hotel [...]. (COCA 2011)

A brief glance at additional corpus data shows that *drink* often appears in the context of words such as *inebriate*, *drunk*, *booze*, and *alcohol*:

(39) [...] people on Twitter know I'm not drunk, I'm not inebriated, I haven't had a drink. (COCA 2012)

(40) Charles hasn't had a drink in five years. (COCA 2011)

---

34. This is of course an oversimplified conceptual picture. The scales in question may contain more than two members.

(41) "I think I need a drink," she said. "Do you have anything with alcohol in it?" (COCA 1993)

(42) How I need a drink, alcoholic of course, after the heavy lectures involving quantum mechanics. (WebCorp)

The speaker's claim in (39) that he is not drunk and has not had a drink and the statement in (40) that Charles has not had a drink in five years, are clear indications that *drink* implicates 'alcoholic drink'. Also, the use of *drink* in connection with *alcohol* and *alcoholic* in examples (41) and (42), respectively, is evidence that *drink* triggers the default inference 'alcoholic beverage'. Indeed, the expression *alcoholic drink* appears 59 times in the COCA; i.e., it is obviously not felt to be tautological by native speakers of American English.

The examples discussed so far are evidence that the reading 'alcoholic beverage' is very strongly associated with *drink*. Notwithstanding, 'alcoholic' is not an intrinsic conceptual feature of the noun *drink*; it is cancelable, as evidenced by examples like (43) and (44):

(43) I need a drink.

(44) I need a drink of water. (COCA 2005)

While (43) implicates that the speaker desires an alcoholic beverage, this inference is obviously not warranted in the case of (44). In conclusion then, the interpretation 'alcoholic drink' of *drink* is a GCI, i.e. a *default* implicature in Levinson's (2000) terms.[35]

There is however a thin line between strong default implicatures and entailments, as evidenced by the existence of compound expressions such as *drink problem* that could be argued to entail, rather than merely implicate, the interpretation 'alcohol problem':

(45) It was obvious that Tate had a drink problem […]. (COCA 2011)

The term *drink problem* is not applied to cases of excessive consumption of milk, grape juice or soft drinks. The same holds for nominal expressions such as *heavy drinker*, which can only refer to a person who consumes alcohol to excess (cf. the German equivalent *Trinker*).[36]

---

35. In cognitive linguistics, the default inference 'alcoholic drink' associated with *drink* would be regarded as a *metonymic* inference or, in Lakoff's (1987: 77–99) terms, as part of a *metonymic model* (for more on metonymy, see Chapter 8).

36. Note however that the 'alcohol' implication is not triggered in compounds like *coffee* drinker or *tea drinker*.

3.5.2 *Reinforceability of entailment*

Given that, unlike implicatures, entailments are not defeasible, it is tempting to hypothesize that language users avoid the reinforcement of entailments because of the redundancy effect this would produce. The same constraint would hold for presuppositions (to be discussed in Section 3.5.3). Moreover, the repetition of entailments and presuppositions is a violation of one of Grice's Maxims of Manner, namely, the maxim 'Avoid prolixity' (see Chapter 4).

Regarding the (possible or blocked) reinforceability of entailment, it is important to have a closer look at the relative sequencing of the *entailing* and the *entailed* unit. There are two possible linear orders:

i. The entailed linguistic unit *precedes* the entailing unit.
ii. The entailed linguistic unit *follows* the entailing unit.

Configuration (i) is instantiated by the following excerpt from the novel *Murder after Death* (2007) by Eva Robberts-Vankova:

(46) "Why?" "My sister is dead." "What?" I panic. "She was killed in the Savoy hotel here in Huddinge last night," answers Mary Bjorn, sounding as if she is trying to suppress her emotions.
 (https://books.google.co.uk/books?isbn=0595422306)

In (46), one of the interactants, Mary Bjorn, informs the first person narrator that her sister is *dead*. The sad news is followed by the additional information that *she was killed*, i.e., the entailed unit *dead* precedes the entailing unit *was killed*. This order is not felt to be redundant because the entailing unit *was killed* includes the attribute 'dead' as already *given* information, but, importantly, it also provides *new* information: Mary Bjorn's sister was killed, presumably murdered; i.e., she did not die of natural causes.

Better candidates for redundancy effects are cases in which the entailing unit precedes the entailed unit. Consider some examples exhibiting this configuration.

(47) [...] President Washington made Hamilton defend himself against a number of charges made by then-Secretary of State Thomas Jefferson, including the allegation that he was a monarchist.   (COCA 1993) ⊩ Hamilton defended himself against a number of charges made by then-Secretary of State Thomas Jefferson, including the allegation that he was a monarchist.

In (47), the causative construction with the verb *made* entails the proposition 'Hamilton defended himself'. The truth of this proposition cannot be denied without contradiction. The explicit repetition of this entailed proposition in (47) as a separate assertion would produce a strong tautological effect, which would render an utterance like (48) pragmatically infelicitous (see e.g. Sadock 1978 and Horn 1991 for additional examples of the same kind):

(48) #President Washington made Hamilton defend himself against a number of charges [...] and Hamilton defended himself against a number of charges [...].

The pragmatic oddity of (48) suggests that, for the sequencing *entailing-entailed*, non-reinforceability holds unconditionally. However, this generalization turns out to be untenable on closer inspection of further data. Consider, for example, the use of adverbials like *as well*, *also*, and *too*, and combinations thereof. The meanings assigned to these lexemes in a standard dictionary such as the NOAD are as follows: *as well* 'in addition, too', *also* 'in addition, too', *too* 'in addition, also'. The three lexical items share the reading 'in addition'. Moreover, *as well* and *also* are assigned the sense 'too', and, in a circular manner, *too* is defined as 'also', and *also* as 'too'. Thus, it is safe to assume that the three lexemes are synonyms, or at least, near-synonyms. The following examples illustrate the use of these items in actual discourse (italics have been added):

as well vs. *also* as well vs. *as well too* vs. *also [...] too*

(49) The comparative perspective highlights other problems in cooperative purchasing *as well*. (COCA 2017)

(50) I want to bring in our panelists right now, Donna Brazile, CNN political commentator, Democratic strategist and vice chair of the DNC voter project, *also*, former Reagan White House political director, Jeffrey Lord, contributing editor for "American Spectator", now a CNN commentator, *also as well*, CNN political commentator Ana Navarro, a Jeb Bush supporter and friend of Marco Rubio. (COCA 2015, CNN)

(51) We thank you very much for joining us, and we thank all of our guests for joining us *as well too*. (COCA 2000, CNN)

(52) The health care system has *also* collapsed *too*. (COCA 2000, CNN)

For the first example (49), a piece of academic writing, the issue of redundancy does not arise since it contains only the adverbial *as well*. In contrast, the subsequent data (50)–(52) exhibit the chaining of the three adverbs; i.e., these combinations should produce an effect of redundancy because *also*, *too*, and *as well* mutually entail one another. But do these chains really produce an effect of redundancy in the minds of language users?

The first point to note is that (50)–(52) are instances of *oral* language retrieved from broadcasts of the American television network CNN. Viewers of the CNN programs in question would (unless they are linguists!), most likely not even notice redundancies of the sort one finds in these examples. Oral communication is more spontaneous, less planned and less controlled than written discourse. Furthermore, in contrast to spoken language, written discourse can be revised; i.e., it allows authors to reread their texts, correct errors, and reduce or eliminate redundancy.

There is however another aspect to examples like (50)–(52). What, on the face of it, looks like an instance of redundancy may have a specific pragmatic function, such as to emphasize the *importance* of some piece of information. For example, the adverbial sequence *also as well* in (50) can be seen as a discursive device for conveying the new and perhaps important information that the panelist Jeffrey Lord, in addition to his work for the monthly magazine *The American Spectator*, is *now* a commentator for CNN. Similarly, the use of *as well too* in (51) and *also [...] too* in (52) can be seen as a means of putting special emphasis on the act of thanking *all of our guests* and on the news that the health care system *has collapsed*, respectively.[37]

In the following examples (53) and (54), the redundant lexical elements also have an emphatic function. Furthermore, they signal a strong emotional involvement of some conceptualizer, e.g. the narrator.[38] Example (53) is a passage from Danielle Steele's novel *Message from Nam*, and (54) is a case of spoken American English retrieved from the American television network CBS:

(53) Martin Luther King, Jr. had been killed in Memphis. Killed. Dead. Shot.
(COCA 1990)

(54) [A] lot of the opponents just want to see this industry killed, dead, no development [...].
(COCA 2000)

A proposition of the form *x kills y* obviously entails 'y is dead'. It is exactly this entailment that is explicitly verbalized in (53) and (54). From a perspective of economical coding, the information that Martin Luther King was dead (i.e. (53)) and that the opponents to the production of genetically modified food want this industry "dead" (i.e. (54)) is superfluous because this information is already entailed by the verb *kill*. Nevertheless, (53) and (54) sound entirely coherent and natural because the redundancy is discourse-pragmatically relevant in these examples. As pointed out above, both utterances convey a strong evaluative and emotional attitude toward some state-of-affairs: (53) expresses the conceptualizer's feeling of shock at the

---

[37.] I am grateful to Carita Paradis (p.c.) for pointing out that *also* and *as well* express slightly different meanings: when *as well* is added on to *also*, it signifies something like 'on top of' (similar to German *außerdem* (literally 'apart from this'). As a consequence, the juxtaposition of *also* and *as well* would not be felt to be repetitive. Nevertheless, a check of the search engine *Google Books* reveals that *also as well* hardly ever appears in written language. I found only two clear examples of this usage.

[38.] The conceptualizer is often, but not necessarily, the speaker or the author (see e.g. Langacker 2013 for this term).

news of Martin Luther's assassination, and (54) conveys anger and indignation directed at *opponents* who want the industry in question to be (metaphorically) *killed*. In this context, it is also worth mentioning that Broccias (2003: 210) finds literary examples of the resultative constructions *kill s.o./s.th. dead* such as *killed him dead* or the metaphorical use *killed the game dead*, in which *dead*, he claims, has an intensifying function with the meaning 'completely'.

But what about the contrast between example (55), which is non-redundant, and the seemingly unwarranted use of *down* in (56)?

descend vs. *descend down*

(55) Eleanor descended the last three steps and stopped in front of Nancy […].

(COCA 2017)

(56) Then Vernon descended down through strata of pallid light trying to imagine this man wielding a knife. (COCA 2007)[39]

The lexeme *descend* is defined as 'move down (a slope or stairs)' (NOAD), i.e., downward motion is an intrinsic meaning component of this verb. In other words, there is an entailment relation between *descend* and 'downward motion', as in (57):

(57) Eleanor descended the last three steps […]. ⊩ Eleanor moved down the three last steps.

The explicit coding of downward motion by means of *down*, as in (55), is *prima facie* redundant, and prescriptive grammarians and teachers of English as a foreign language would probably mark it as incorrect or as bad usage. Nevertheless, this usage occurs and it is not felt to be tautological by many native speakers. In expressing downward movement by means of an independent lexeme, i.e. coding it as an autonomous linguistic *sign*, the meaning component of downward motion is conceptually foregrounded and thus treated as important new information, although, strictly speaking, it is given information, i.e. already conceptually included in the meaning of *descend*.

Upward movement may also be coded redundantly as in (59), which contrasts with (58):

ascend vs. *ascend up*

(58) Having secured the lock to his satisfaction, Jones ascended the stair to the upper gallery. (COCA 2017)

(59) He ascended up that passageway, growing more and more distant, until he disappeared. (COCA 1990)

---

39. The original spelling *palid* has been corrected.

The dictionary meaning of *ascend* is 'go up or climb' (NOAD); i.e., upward movement of some entity, e.g. of a human agent, is entailed and thus non-cancelable. Consequently, additional explicit coding of upward movement, as in (59), is not necessary, and, again, is most likely regarded as incorrect by prescriptive grammarians. Nevertheless, the explicit coding of upward motion as a separate sign may have the pragmatic effect of foregrounding and emphasizing this meaning component.

The foregrounding function of a redundant element is quite marked in the case of the intransitive verb *gather*, which frequently co-occurs with *together*:

gather vs. *gather together*

(60) A few hundred people gathered outside Vice President-elect Mike Pence's temporary house [...]. (COCA 2017)

(61) The next day, a number of our folks from Wisconsin gathered together in the office of the chief of staff [...]. (COCA 2017)

The meaning of intransitively used *gather* is 'come together; assemble or accumulate' (NOAD). In contrast to (60), which does not code 'together' as a separate lexical item, in (61), retrieved from a broadcast of the U.S. television channel *Fox News*, the entailed feature of *gather*, i.e. 'together', is overtly expressed, and thereby foregrounded and presented as important information.

The same contrast between a non-reinforced and a reinforced usage involving *together* is manifest in (62) and (63), respectively:

merge vs. *merge together*

(62) In July, Random House and Penguin merged to form a corporate colossus that controls a quarter of world book publishing. (COCA 2013)

(63) The gigantic galaxies formed when smaller proto-galaxies merged together to create ever larger and larger structures [...]. (COCA 2012)

The verb *merge* has the meaning 'combine or cause to combine to form a single entity' (NOAD). This sense is instantiated in (62) where the process of combining two publishing houses (Random House and Penguin) is reported, resulting in a new entity, which is metaphorically characterized as a *corporate colossus*. Example (63) describes the emergence of larger galactic structures from smaller proto-galaxies. From a semantic perspective, the adverb *together* is redundant, because its sense is already entailed by the use of *merge*. Still, the overtly and separately coded concept 'together' has the effect of emphasizing the merging process of *separate* entities into *one* new structure.

An especially interesting contrast, which, in one important respect, differs from the ones that have been considered so far in this section, is the opposition between the transitive verb *enter* and the prepositional verb *enter into*. Notice first that both *enter* and *enter into* can be used literally, as in (64) and (65), and metaphorically, as in (66) and (67):

enter vs. enter into

(64) A female uniformed officer entered the room and whispered something into the detective's ear. (COCA 2017)

(65) And just as that was decided on, the young count entered into the church, and suddenly two snow-white doves flew on his shoulders and remained sitting there. (COCA 2006)

(66) Maine: Portland – The city's school system entered an agreement with the U.S. Department of Education that requires better educational opportunities for students. (COCA 2000)

(67) Montgomery County has entered into an agreement with the US Education Department's Office of Civil Rights [...]. (COCA 1999)

The relationship between *enter NP* and *enter into NP* is not merely one of contrast between a non-redundant sense (*enter NP*) and a redundant one (*enter into NP*), but it is, moreover, one of (partially overlapping) *complementarity*. The redundant element *into* has developed a distinctive conceptual function, which is elaborated below.

But first, some empirical evidence has to be provided in support of the hypothesis that the two constructions *enter NP* and *enter into NP* tend to fulfill complementary semantic functions. In Table 1, the patterns *entered a/the building* vs. *entered into a/the building* and *entered an/the agreement* vs. *entered into an/the agreement* are compared in terms of their frequency in the NOW corpus.[40]

Table 1. Distribution of *entered a/the building/agreement* vs. *entered into a/the building/agreement* in the NOW corpus

	SPATIAL: N: *building*	METAPHORICAL: N: *agreement*
entered a/the N	1173 (99.2%)	413 (7.8%)
entered into a/the N	9 (0.8%)	4931 (92.2%)
TOTAL	1182 (100%)	5344 (100%)

---

40. The NOW (*News on the Web*) corpus contains "5.6 billion words of data from newspapers and magazines from 2010 to the present time" (accessed January 2, 2018 at: https://www.english-corpora.org/now/).

Table 1 has two interesting numerical properties. The first is that *a/the building*, which denotes a concrete three-dimensional location, is overwhelmingly (99.2%) instantiated in the transitive pattern *entered a/the N*, whereas the prepositional pattern *entered into a/the building* is restricted to a mere 0.8% of the corpus data. Second, the inverse tendency can be observed in the case of an abstract concept in the noun slot, such as *agreement*, which is rarely used in the transitive pattern *entered a/the agreement* (7.8%) but typically occurs in the pattern *entered into a/the agreement* (92.2%). According to the Fisher Exact Test, the numerical distribution found in Table 1 is significant at the .01 level.

Given these empirical results, it is reasonable to assume a conceptual division of labor between the constructional patterns *enter NP* and *enter into NP*: the former tends to occur with nouns that denote concrete locations, and the latter is more likely to be used figuratively, i.e. metaphorically, with abstract nouns such as *agreement, lease, contract*, and the like. Of course, at this point, this generalization is only a working hypothesis, i.e., it is a tentative model, which has to supported and confirmed by more extensive empirical work.

The cognitive-semiotic principle on which this complementarity is based is well known in functional and cognitive linguistics: *one form* corresponds to *one meaning*, and vice versa. It is known as the principle of *isomorphism* (see e.g. Radden & Panther 2004: 18, and references therein). From the principle of isomorphism another principle can be derived: *distinctness in form* is reflected in *distinctness in meaning*. Although this principle does not *predict* with absolute certainty that the verb phrase *enter NP* should have a different meaning from *enter into NP*, the principle *motivates* the difference in meaning between the transitive and the prepositional verb (see Chapter 2 for the concept of motivation).

As a final example of the use of entailed, i.e. redundant information for *rhetorical* purposes, let us look at an excerpt from an interview conducted with former American president Donald Trump during his electoral campaign in 2015. In contrast to the examples discussed so far, in which usually single lexemes such as the prepositions *down, up, into*, or adverbials like *also, too, as well*, and *together*, are redundantly used, in the following interview certain key sentences are more or less *verbatim* repeated:[41]

---

[41]. Accessed at: Donald Trump's repetitive rhetoric. *Language Log* http://languagelog.ldc.upenn.edu/nll/?p=22691. December 5, 2015 @ 4:35 pm. Filed by Mark Liberman under *Language and politics, Rhetoric*.

(68) QUESTION: Let me ask you about women voters – why should they vote for you? TRUMP: Because I'm very much into the whole thing of helping people and helping women. Women's health uh issues are such a big thing to me and so important and you know I have many women that work for me. I was one of the first persons uh people in the construction industry in New York to put women in charge of projects, I mean I have it even today, and I have many women at high positions. I you know I've gotten a lot of credit for that, I mean I have so many women working for me and so many women in high positions working for me and I've gotten great credit for it.

Technically, the repetition of a statement constitutes a relation of entailment between the original statement and its copy. Notice however that, in (68), Trump does not use verbatim repetitions in the strict sense. For example, his claim *I have many women that work for me* is taken up again in *I have so many women working for me*. In the latter utterance, by means of the intensifier *so*, the content of the affirmation is emphasized. Likewise, Trump's contention *I have many women in high positions* is resumed and emphasized in *[I have] so many women in high positions working for me*, where, moreover, Trump repeats his claim that women are working for him. This repetitive rhetorical style is not very sophisticated, but maybe an efficient way of drumming some political message into the heads of voters.

The conclusion to be drawn from the data discussed so far is that reinforceability is a property of implicatures, which, by definition, are defeasible, but, as we have seen, there is some empirical evidence that entailments, which are non-defeasible, are reinforcable as well, if the redundant elements fulfill additional discourse-pragmatic functions.

3.5.3 *Reinforceability of presuppositions*
This section addresses the question of whether presuppositions can be reinforced without creating unacceptable redundancy effects. As a first example, consider the following headline published in an online news network in 2014:

(69) The King of Spain Steps Down, and Some Twitterati Call for Abolition of the Monarchy   (Bloomberg Businessweek, http://www.businessweek.com/articles/2014-06-02)

In (69), the definite noun phrase *the King of Spain*, which refers to King Juan Carlos, conveys an existential presupposition ('There exists a King of Spain') and a uniqueness presupposition ('There is only one King of Spain (at a given time period)'). Under normal circumstances, neither the first nor the second of these two presuppositions can be reinforced. Thus (70) is conceptually and pragmatically infelicitous:

(70) #The King of Spain steps down and the King of Spain exists.

Nevertheless, I contend that presuppositions are reinforceable and are acceptable if they produce pragmatic effects such as emphasis or signal emotional involvement. As in the case of entailments, the relative ordering of the presupposing unit and the presupposed unit is relevant. Thus, there are again two ordering options to take into consideration:

i. The autonomously coded (subsequently) presupposed unit *precedes* the presupposing unit.
ii. The autonomously coded presupposed unit *follows* the presupposing unit.

Analogously to what holds for entailments, one would expect the order *presupposed – presupposing* to feel less redundant than the order *presupposing – presupposed*, because, in the latter case, already presupposed, i.e. normally given information is coded again, whereas, in the former case, some new information is introduced that subsequently becomes a presupposition, i.e. given and backgrounded information.

To begin with, consider cases of ordering, as formulated in (i). The following pieces of discourse in (71)–(75) all involve the use of the verb *manage (to do s.th.)*. On the one hand, this verb is implicative; i.e., it entails the truth of the proposition expressed in the subsequent infinitival complement clause. On the other hand, this verb *presupposes*, among other things, that some agent *tries* to perform some action, i.e., some *effort* is applied to accomplish the intended action:

(71) With some effort he managed to pull himself to his feet, his head spinning slightly with the effort. (https://books.google.co.uk/books?isbn=1907230610)

(72) With some effort and a good sense of balance I managed to get dressed without getting down off the bunk.
(https://books.google.co.uk/books?isbn=1291583114)

(73) With some effort she managed to stammer out the words, "He-Hey, you're scaring me now. I thought I was alone with Lyn."
(https://books.google.co. uk/books?isbn=1465329218)

(74) With some effort, he finally managed to pry the hood of the car up and got the radiator filled with water.
(https://books.google.co.uk/books?isbn=1605988529)

(75) He works as an engineer for a large company, but despite his efforts, he didn't manage to climb the ladder to a better position (and a better income).
(www.imdb.com/title/tt0629550/reviews)

In examples (71)–(74), the explicit coding of the presupposition that a certain degree of effort is necessary in order to manage to perform the action in question does not produce an effect of redundancy. The same holds for sentence (75), in which *managed* is negated. Note that the presupposition that some effort was deployed to perform the action is not affected. In conclusion, the order *presupposed – presupposing* is, analogously to the order *entailed – entailing*, is not perceived as redundant.

But what happens in cases in which the presupposing unit precedes the presupposed one? One made-up example has already been briefly discussed, i.e. (70), in which the presupposed and following explicitly asserted existence of the King of Spain results in a pragmatic oddity. But if some linguistic material is added that goes beyond the mere repetition of the existence of the monarch, the utterance becomes more acceptable. Consider the following examples:

(76) The King of Spain steps down. Yes, Spain is a monarchy – believe it or not!

(77) He regrets that he said it, but he did say it.   (Horn 1991: 322)

From second sentence in (76) the existence of the King of Spain follows; but this sentence conveys additional implicated content such as 'You may be surprised that there is a King of Spain'. In (77), the factive presupposition associated with the verb *regret* is emphatically repeated in the following *but* clause: i.e., there is an additional implicature conveying the speaker's emotive and evaluative attitude towards the presupposed content. The example is adopted from an article authored by Laurence R. Horn, whose title aptly describes how (77) functions pragmatically: *Given as new: When redundant affirmation isn't*. What is given is the presupposition, but when repeated explicitly, it may convey, i.e. conversationally implicate, new information.

To summarize, analogously to what can be observed with regard to redundant entailments, additional pragmatic functions, such as emphasis and the expression of emotional attitude, allow already presupposed linguistic material to be repeated in the subsequent discourse. A further example retrieved from a search in Google Books nicely illustrates this important point:

(78) Occasionally I got the belt, but I have to admit I didn't get it as much as my four older brothers got it. Yes, I have FOUR older brothers.
(https://books.google.co.uk/ books?isbn=1496917170)

The noun phrase in the *but* clause of (78), i.e. *my four older brothers*, presupposes 'I have four older brothers', and it is exactly this proposition – with emphatic stress on the number *FOUR* – that is explicitly asserted in the following sentence. What the speaker conveys in this sentence is something like 'You may be surprised, but I have four older brothers'.

To conclude this section, here are two additional examples involving the verb *manage* that attest to the possibility of repeating presupposed information overtly after the presupposing unit:

(79) I didn't manage, although I tried.   (https://forum.us.forgeofempires.com)

(80) "The door's really heavy," I observed, "but I managed to get it open by applying some effort.   (https://books.google.co.uk/books?isbn=1901864197)

In (79), the presuppositions 'trying' and 'applying effort' associated with *manage* are coded overtly after *didn't manage* and *managed*, respectively, without creating a redundancy effect. The reason why the presupposed content can be coded overtly is that (79) *implicates* that the first person agent tried *harder* than usual to accomplish some unnamed action (but without success). Similarly, in (80), the first person narrator implicates he applied more *strenuous* effort than usual to (successfully) get the door open.

3.5.4 Conclusion: Reinforced implicature, entailment, and presupposition

We have seen that the reinforcement of conversational implicatures is generally permissible because such implicatures are, by definition, not an intrinsic part of the meaning of the linguistic unit that triggers the implicature. Hence, it is to be expected that the explicit coding of an implicature does not result in redundancy effects.

In the case of entailments and presuppositions, the situation is different. Since entailed and presupposed content is *inherent* in the meaning of the entailing or presupposing linguistic unit, the explicit repetition of entailed or presupposed content will result in redundancy effects that, especially in written discourse, may be felt to be pragmatically deviant. However, it has also been shown that entailed or presupposed content *is* reinforcable if its overt coding triggers additional implicatures that convey important new information or express some mental or emotional attitude that is not already conveyed by the entailing or presupposing unit itself.

Just like repeated entailments and presuppositions, reinforced implicatures may be enriched by additional implicated conceptual material, as in the following example :

(81) The writer asks the swineherd if he is indeed happy. He replies, "I am indeed, serene and also content, but I'm not happy. Oh, if only I were a fairy-tale prince!   (https://books.google co.uk/books?isbn=1490800476)

In (81), in saying *but I'm not happy*, the swineherd appears to convey an emotionally-laden implicature that he is, beyond serenity and contentment, really longing for happiness, as becomes clear from the following reinforcing conditional *Oh, if only I were a fairy-tale prince!* which expresses a strong wish.

In conclusion, the behavior of the inferential relations of implicature, entailment, and presupposition regarding their defeasibility and reinforceability can be summarized as in Table 2.

Table 2. Defeasibility and reinforceability of three inferential relations

INFERENTIAL RELATION	Defeasibility	Reinforceability	Reinforceability *with* additional *implicated* content
Implicature	yes	yes	yes
Entailment	no	no	yes
Presupposition	no	no	yes

On a final note, redundantly used entailments and presuppositions often appear to be motivated by the iconic principle *more form – more content*. In repeating already entailed or presupposed information, speakers intend to create the impression that they have more meaning to convey than with non-repetitive verbalization of entailments or presuppositions. There is however a thin line between genuine new information expressed through reinforced entailments and presuppositions, and mere *verbiage* – the latter constituting a violation of Grice's submaxim 'Avoid prolixity' (see Chapter 4).

3.6 Universality vs. culture-specificity of conversational implicatures

In this section, let us briefly consider the question whether a distinction can be established on empirical grounds between implicatures that hold universally across languages and implicatures that are restricted to specific languages and cultures. It has been claimed that universal implicatures exist, but much more research is needed to confirm this hypothesis (see Section 3.6.1); there is much stronger empirical evidence for language- and culture-specific implicatures (see 3.6.2).

3.6.1 *Scalar conversational implicatures: A possible universal*

Huang (2007: 35) hypothesizes that if a language has lexical items for the quantifiers 'all' and 'some', then its speakers will make use of a conversational implicature (GCI) *some* +> 'not all'. Thus, according to Huang, the translational equivalents of the assertion *Some young people like pop music* in Arabic, Catalan, Chinese, Modern Greek, Kashmiri, and Malagasy all trigger the GCI 'Not all young people like pop music'. For all we know then, this scalar implicature might be a universal.

In a similar vein, consider the following Italian sentence retrieved from a European Parliament session, which contains the quantifying phrase *molti firmatari* 'many signatories' (italics added):[42]

---

42. *European Parliament Proceedings Parallel Corpus 1996-2011* [http://www.statmt.org/europarl].

(82) Su richiesta di un deputato francese, l'onorevole Zimeray, è già stata presentata una petizione, che ha avuto molti firmatari tra cui il sottoscritto [...].

The quantifying phrase *molti firmatari* 'many signatories' in (82) triggers the GCI 'not all signatories'. The official translations of (82) into some other languages of member states of the European Union are given in (83)–(88):

English

(83) At the request of a French Member, Mr Zimeray, a petition has already been presented, which *many* people signed, including myself.

French

(84) À la demande d'un député français, Monsieur Zimeray, une pétition a déjà été introduite; elle a récolté de *nombreuses* signatures dont la mienne.

German

(85) Auf Wunsch eines französischen Mitglieds, Herrn Zimeray, wurde bereits eine Petition eingereicht, die von *vielen*, auch von mir selbst, unterzeichnet worden ist.

Portuguese

(86) A pedido de um deputado francês, o senhor deputado Zimeray, já foi apresentada uma petição, que teve *muitos* signatários, entre os quais o abaixo assinado [...].

Spanish

(87) A petición de un diputado francés, el Sr. Zimeray, se ha presentado una solicitud, cuyos firmantes han sido *numerosos* y entre los cuales me cuento, [...].

Swedish

(88) På uppmaning av en fransk parlamentsledamot, Zimeray, har redan en framställning gjorts, undertecknad av *många*, bland annat jag själv [...].

All of the above contain a quantifier with the sense 'many, numerous' (printed in italics), and the conversational implicature 'not all' appears to hold for all of them. To conclude, it seems a plausible hypothesis that the GCI 'a large number of x +> not all x' holds cross-linguistically and is perhaps a candidate for a universal.

3.6.2 Language- and culture-specific implicatures

In contrast to what has been claimed for quantifying lexemes, such as 'many', implicatures often also appear to be determined by specific sociocultural norms of a language community. As noted by e.g. Wierzbicka (1985: 148), at an English social event, it is polite to *offer* a guest a drink by saying:

(89) Would you like a beer?

Literally, the host's utterance (89) is a question that makes reference to the possible desires of the guest. In an Anglo-cultural context, via conversational implicature, this question is conventionally understood as a polite offer to serve the guest a drink. In Polish, Wierzbicka contends, the literal translation of (89), i.e. (90), would be understood as a question rather than as an offer:

(90) Miałbyś ochotę na piwo? (Wierzbicka 1985: 148)
'Would you like a beer?'

According to Wierzbicka (1985: 148), in the context of a Polish dinner party,

> the social convention requires the host to prevail upon the guest, to behave as if he or she was forcing the guest to eat and drink, regardless of the guest's desires, and certainly regardless of the guest's *expressed desires*, which would simply be dismissed.

A similar contrast between English culture and Polish culture holds for invitations. In an English-speaking sociocultural context, it is polite to invite somebody to go see a film by saying:

(91) Would you like to go to the movies with me?

Wierzbicka (1985: 149) claims that the literal equivalent of (91) would not be appropriate in Polish, but instead a speech act such as (92) would be performed, which does not address the potential desire of the hearer, but the speaker would intend to convey that "he would like to go out with, and see [the hearer's] consent":

(92) Może byśmy poszli do kina?
'Perhaps we would go to the cinema?' (implied: if I asked you)
  (Wierzbicka 1985: 149)

The gist of examples such as (89)–(92) is that implicatures are partially motivated by cultural norms, e.g. based on what counts as polite behavior in the language community in question.

4. Conclusion

In this chapter, the focus has been on the role of a pervasive inferential mechanism in the construction of meaning, which the British philosopher of language Paul Grice (1975, 1989) calls *conversational implicature* and the French linguist Oswald Ducrot (1969, 1972) refers to as *sous-entendu* ('what is (implicitly) understood'). Neo-Gricean pragmaticists, such as e.g. Levinson (2000), contrast conversational implicature with other modes of inference like entailment and presupposition, in terms of parameters such as suspendability and cancelability/defeasibility, detachability, calculability, non-codability and reinforceability. We have seen that suspendability and defeasibility are indeed distinctive properties of conversational implicature, but that other attributes are shared by implicature, entailment, and presupposition. A closer look at authentic examples has revealed that reinforceability is not a unique property of implicatures, but there is evidence that entailments and presuppositions may be reinforced under certain conditions as well, e.g., if the repeated entailment/presupposition implicates new information, an epistemic stance or an emotional attitude.

CHAPTER 6

Talking as action
Speech act theory

1. Introduction

Speech act theory and cognitive linguistics share a theoretical and methodological commitment to *use-* and *usage*-based models of language, respectively.[43] The terms 'use' and 'usage' can be considered roughly equivalent in the sense that they both refer to linguistic habits or practices. The most influential representative of the use theory of meaning was probably the Austrian philosopher Ludwig Wittgenstein (2009: 25e), who maintained that

> [f]or a large class of cases of the employment of the word 'meaning' – though not for all – this word can be explained in this way: the meaning of a word is its use in the language.

More generally, according to Wittgenstein, the meaning of linguistic units of any complexity, e.g. phrases or sentences, is constituted by their use in language.

Wittgenstein's use theory of meaning was adopted and further developed by philosophers such as John L. Austin (1962) and his student John R. Searle (1969). Austin's best-known work *How to Do Things with Words* (1962) has had a deep impact on theorizing in linguistic semantics and pragmatics. As can be gleaned from the title of Austin's book, its author contends that the use of language involves the performance of verbal actions, in particular, so-called *illocutionary acts*, such as affirming, promising, requesting, recommending, thanking, resigning (from an office), etc.[44] Much of what follows is based on the pioneering research on illocutionary acts by the afore-mentioned philosophers of language Austin and Searle.

In Section 2, a folk model of verbal communication as "mere talk" is contrasted with the notion of linguistic action as developed in *speech act theory*. Section 3, following Austin, focuses on how a speech act can go wrong, i.e. be infelicitous. Section 4 briefly characterizes some aspects of Searle's theory that are relevant to the cognitive linguistic approach to speech acts developed in this

---

43. This introduction is based on Panther (2016b).
44. See Burkhardt (1986) for some predecessors of speech act theory.

book. Section 5 illustrates the various ways that illocutionary acts are lexically and grammatically coded.

In Section 6, a model of illocution is presented which is based on the idea that the meaning of linguistic units can be modeled in terms of semantic or conceptual *frames*, as they are usually called in cognitive linguistics (see Ziem 2014). The frames that are relevant to a deeper understanding of speech acts are referred to as *illocutionary scenarios* in this book. Illocutionary scenarios are knowledge structures that guide the production and the understanding of illocutionary acts. I argue that illocutionary scenarios, first postulated by Thornburg and Panther (1997) and Panther and Thornburg (1998) are crucial for an understanding of the cognitive mechanisms involved in the performance and comprehension of *indirect speech acts*, which are discussed in Chapters 9 and 10.

2. Folk and expert models of action

2.1 Talk as deficient action

Speaking or talking is, of course, a kind of action. However, there exists a folk model, at least in the western world, that distinguishes talking from "real" action. The contrast between the two is reflected in the way people talk about events in their daily lives. For example, there is a common stereotype that politicians promise all kinds of things (talk), but allegedly they often do not keep their promises, i.e., according to this folk model, their words are often not matched by corresponding deeds.

Here are some English-language examples illustrating the conceptualization of *talk* as 'non-action' or, at least, 'not real action':

(1) He tweeted: All talk, talk, talk – no action or results. Sad!   (COCA 2017)

(2) "[…] Talk, talk, talk, but no action!" he exclaimed.   (COCA 2002)

(3) He can't do anything. It's just talk, blah, blah.   (COCA 2017)

Utterances (1) and (2) demonstrate that people tend to regard speaking and acting as separate, and, in fact, even antonymous categories. The two distinguishing features of talk and extra-linguistic action in this cultural model are that talking, in contrast to acting, is not a prototypical type of action and that, contrary to action, it does not change the world (see Panther 2016b: 181). Talk is, as the speaker of utterance (3), puts it, just "blah, blah."

2.2 An expert model of linguistic action: Speech act theory

In one branch of the philosophy of language, in contrast to the folk model of talk and action sketched in Section 2.1, TALK is conceptualized as a hyponym (subordinate sense) of the hyperonym (superordinate sense) ACTION. In other words, there are linguistic acts and non-linguistic acts, the latter including physical actions like running, grasping, or swimming, and mental actions such as thinking, reasoning, or drawing inferences. That the uttering of words constitutes deeds is a simple but ingenious idea, which has important consequences for the analysis of natural language. One crucial property of this "expert model", known as *speech act theory*, is that talking *is* a kind of action – on a par with non-verbal actions. The idea that the utterance of words are deeds, i.e. that people can "do things with words", opens up new avenues of research into the nature of human communication.

The term *speech act* subsumes various subtypes of linguistic actions performed in communication. Table 1 names the component acts proposed by Austin (left column), which are contrasted with Searle's taxonomy of linguistic actions (right column).

Table 1. Component acts of speech acts

Austin (1962)	Searle (1969)
Locutionary Act:	*Utterance Act*: Uttering sounds, morphemes, words, sentences
Phonetic Act: Uttering sounds	
Phatic Act: Producing morphemes, words in grammatical constructions	*Propositional Act*:
Rhetic Act: Reference & Sense	*Referring*
	Predicating
Illocutionary Act: Asserting, requesting, promising, apologizing, appointing, etc.	
Perlocutionary Act: Persuading, surprising, intimidating, boring, etc.	

Austin distinguishes between locutionary, illocutionary and perlocutionary acts. In a speech act, all of these activities usually occur at once. The locutionary act is simply the act of "saying" something. It involves the sub-acts of sound production (phonetic act) and of morpheme/words in grammatical constructions (phatic act). The rhetic act is supposed to capture the property of language as a system of signs that speakers can use to denote entities in extralinguistic reality (reference) and to signify conceptual content (sense).[45] According to Austin (1962: 93), reference and

---

[45]. The latter two terms go back to the distinction drawn by the mathematician and logician Gottlob Frege (1892), who differentiates between what he calls *Bedeutung* ('reference') and *Sinn* ('sense'). Instead of 'reference' and 'sense', especially in formal (logical) semantics, the terms *extension* and *intension*, respectively, are also used.

sense "together are equivalent to 'meaning'." Most importantly, Austin's speech act theory is concerned with the elucidation of what he calls *illocutionary acts*, i.e. acts that language users perform "in speaking", such as *asserting* something, *vowing* to do something, *ordering* somebody to do something, *thanking* somebody, *resigning* from office, etc. Locutionary and illocutionary acts are performed according to certain rules, e.g. phonological and morphosyntactic rules for the former, and rules of felicitous performance for the latter. Finally, illocutionary acts may also have an effect, which Austin calls *perlocutionary*. For example, by means of an act of *threatening*, the speaker may accomplish the perlocutionary act of *intimidating* the hearer.

Searle (1969: 24) uses the term *utterance act* for the production of sounds, morphemes, words and sentences, which is roughly equivalent to Austin's phonetic and phatic act. However, Searle's concept of *propositional act*, which comprises the sub-acts of *referring* and *predicating*, does not seem to have a counterpart in Austin's model, nor is Austin's conception of *rhetic act* part of Searle's model of linguistic actions. In both Austinian and Searlean speech act theory, the notion of *illocutionary act*, i.e. linguistic acts like the ones listed in Table 1, is of central importance, and it is this type of communicative act that the present chapter focuses upon.

To illustrate the notion of illocutionary act, consider first the following example that might be heard at an airport:

(4) Passengers are requested to proceed for their security check. (COCA 1995)

Every competent speaker of English knows that the utterance of sentence (4), under appropriate circumstances, will be understood as a polite instruction to passengers to move to the area in an airport where they and their luggage are screened for items that they are not allowed to take aboard an airplane. A request is a linguistic action. For the hearer to figure out what kind of linguistic act is performed by the speaker is obviously an essential part of utterance comprehension. In the case of (4), the utterance is overtly coded as a request (by means of a passivized form of the verb *request*) and therefore requires hardly any inferential effort on the part of addressees to be understood as such. Quite often, however, the hearer has to take the extralinguistic situation and/or the linguistic context of the speaker's utterance into account in order make a reasonable guess about the intended meaning of a speech act. To see the role of situation and context in speech act interpretation consider the following example:

(5) The door is over there.

The utterance of sentence (5) will induce varying interpretations as to what kind of act has been performed by the speaker. For example, it may be used as an answer to the question *Where is the door?* In this case, it functions as an act of *informing* the hearer about something. In another context, the speaker may use sentence (5) to *ask* or even *order* the hearer to leave the room, and one can imagine various other context- and situation-dependent uses of utterance (5).

Here is a third example that allows more than one interpretation as to what kind of speech act has been performed:

(6) I'll be there tomorrow.

Literally, the utterance of (6) functions as a *prediction* about the location where the speaker will be located "tomorrow." Note first that in (6) *there* is a deictic adverb, i.e. in semiotic terms, an index, whose interpretation relies on the linguistic context and/or extralinguistic situation, in which the sentence is uttered. Moreover, the reference of the first pronoun *I* and that of the temporal adverb *tomorrow* is determined situationally and/or contextually. As to the illocutionary meaning of (6), again depending on the context and the intention of the speaker, in addition to being a prediction, it could function as a *promise*, a *threat*, or a *warning*. Thus, the conclusion is warranted that communicating by means of natural language involves the performance of (verbal) actions. Furthermore, in using the same words speakers may perform different linguistic acts, depending on the context and on their communicative intentions. In order to figure out the intended interpretation of a speech act, hearers must be endowed with *inferential* skills, such as the ability to understand a conversational implicature – as well as skills to interpret metonymies and metaphors (see Chapters 7 and 8, respectively).

3. Some examples of infelicitous illocutionary acts (Austin)

One of Austin's insights, which *mutatis mutandis* has inspired Searle's work, is that speech acts succeed or are deficient (if not completely void) in various respects – in the same way that non-linguistic actions may be performed more or less successfully. If the illocutionary act is appropriately performed, it is called *felicitous* (or *happy*); in cases of deficiency or failure, the illocutionary act is termed *infelicitous* (or *unhappy*). Austin focuses his attention on situations in which an illocutionary act is infelicitous. He distinguishes between two kinds of infelicity: *misfires* and *abuses* (see e.g. Austin 1971).

Here are some examples illustrating these types of infelicity. Suppose a student says (7) to a professor:

(7) I appoint you chair of the Linguistics Department.

Although utterance (7) is morphosyntactically correct and semantically transparent, as a speech act it is most likely inappropriate. What makes it pragmatically infelicitous is that students are usually not entitled to appoint a professor head of a university department. In legal terms, the act performed in uttering (7) is *null and void*. Austin (1962) refers to such cases as *misfires*. In jurisdiction, an act, e.g. a contract that is categorized as null and void, is considered as not having come into existence. It is as if the act had never been performed. An additional example of an illocutionary act that is potentially null and void is (8):

(8) I hereby bequeath all my stock in Astro Corporation to my friend and local employee, Priscilla Lane [..]. (COCA 2001)

Sentence (8) conveys the *presupposition* that the stock referred to by the speaker actually exists (see Chapter 3 for the notion of presupposition). Now assume a situation in which it turns out that the utterer or writer of (8) does not own any stock. Then the act of bequeathing it to the addressee is again null and void. In the terminology of Chapter 3, it is a case of *existential presupposition failure*.

There are other circumstances under which a linguistic action does come about, i.e., it is not null and void, but it is deficient in some respect(s). Illocutionary acts instantiating this category are called *abuses* by Austin. Suppose that John meets a fellow student, who has just completed his master's degree. John does not like that person too much, but politeness requires that he mumbles something like (9):

(9) Congratulations!

The speech act verb *congratulate* has the meaning 'give (someone) one's good wishes when something special or pleasant has happened to them' (NOAD) and its (pluralized) nominal form can be used to perform an act of congratulating the addressee. But because of John's antipathy to his fellow student, his congratulatory act is not genuine. In this case, the act of congratulation comes about, but the speaker does not have the appropriate mental attitude, i.e. a positive evaluation and/or feeling of joy, that is normally conveyed with congratulations. The speech act is not felicitous because it is *insincere*.

A second type of abuse is constituted by what Austin calls a *breach of commitment*. Suppose Mary lends her fellow student John a book on metaphor over the weekend, but she needs the book back on Monday because she has to write a paper on conceptual metaphor theory. John utters (10):

(10) Mary, I promise I'll return the book to you on Monday.

Let us suppose that John intends to keep his promise, i.e., he is sincere. However, during the weekend some other more urgent business he has to attend to intervenes so that he is not able to keep his promise. In this case, John does not fulfill his self-imposed commitment, but it would not be correct to characterize his linguistic action as deceitful and his mental attitude as insincere.

4. Searle's speech act theory

4.1 Introduction

Austin's speech act theory has been revised and refined by John Searle, and, in this book, the latter philosopher's conception of illocutionary acts is adopted and elaborated, with the aim in mind of integrating it into a cognitive linguistic framework of pragmatics.

Searle does not define the notion of illocutionary act as such, but he contends that if his "analysis of a particular illocutionary act succeeds it may provide the basis for a definition" (Searle 1971: 39). Like Austin, he conjectures that there are thousands of expressions in English – and, one might add, in other languages as well – that denote illocutionary acts.

For Searle, an illocutionary act is "the minimal unit of linguistic communication", and he assumes that there is (roughly) a one-to-one correspondence between simple (one-clause) sentences as grammatical units and their pragmatic function as illocutionary acts. An illocutionary act comes about, i.e. is constituted, by means of "the production of [a] sentence token under certain conditions […]" (Searle 1971: 39). Illocutionary acts are characterized by sets of *necessary* and *sufficient* conditions, from which semantic rules for their felicitous performance can be derived (Searle 1971: 40).

Given that linguistic communication involves the performance of acts, it is reasonable to assume that illocutionary acts are produced with certain *intentions* and that they abide by certain *rules*. Searle (1971) postulates two kinds of rules: *regulative rules* and *constitutive rules* that are operative in both non-linguistic and linguistic actions. Regulative rules guide and constrain pre-existing kinds of behavior. They can be formulated as conditional imperatives of the form *If X, do Y*. The existence of the activity that is regulated by the rules is logically independent of the rules themselves. For example, the ingestion of food is a pre-existing activity of humans that is regulated by culture-specific norms, such as the proper use of cutlery in Western culture or chopsticks in Asian countries like China and Japan. Similarly, rules of etiquette and politeness can be regarded as norms that regulate pre-existent types of behavior.

In contrast to regulative rules, constitutive rules *define* an activity. For example, the game of chess is defined, i.e. constituted, by its rules. According to Searle, constitutive rules have the form *X counts as Y*. If chess players do not abide by the rules of the game, they are not playing chess. The felicitous performance of a chess game is thus "logically dependent on the rules" that define it (Searle 1971: 41). Regarding the use of language, Searle (1971: 44) concludes that "illocutionary acts are acts performed in accordance with […] sets of constitutive rules."

How do we know that speech acts, in particular, illocutionary acts, are significant elements of communication? One piece of evidence is that, in verbal exchanges or in narrative discourse, speakers or authors often make reference to illocutionary acts that have been performed, are being performed, or will (may, can, must) be performed in the future. Consider, for example, the following piece of academic writing in (11), which reports a recommendation:

(11) Donovan recommended that administrative and judicial functions be separated and that a federal bankruptcy commissioner be established in the executive branch to oversee bankruptcy administration. (COCA 2017)

Regarding narrative discourse, consider two excerpts from Eric Ambler's spy novel *Background to Danger* (Ambler 2001 [1937]). In (12) and (13), the illocutionary acts performed by the main protagonist are characterized as an *objection* to a prior statement and a piece of *advice*, respectively:

(12) "But then," objected Kenton evenly, "you would not get your photographs and I should almost certainly go free." (Ambler 2001: 87)

(13) "Go to bed when you are tired," he advised. (Ambler 2001: 67)

Often the nature of the illocutionary act performed is a matter of (occasionally controversial) negotiation in a talk exchange, as illustrated with the dialogue in (14) (italics added):

(14) "Are you *threatening* me?" I asked. "No, just *warning* you," she replied. (iWeb, xenu.net)

To conclude, speech act descriptions abound in written and oral discourse and support the thesis that interlocutors rely on their knowledge of illocutionary act concepts in utterance interpretation. But how is this knowledge conceptually structured? An answer to this question, which blends speech act theoretic approaches and cognitive linguistic conceptions of meaning, is proposed in Chapters 9 and 10.

4.2 Felicity conditions and illocutionary types according to Searle

In contrast to Austin, who, as mentioned and illustrated with examples in Section 3, characterizes illocutionary acts in terms of how they can go "wrong", Searle defines illocutionary acts "positively" in terms of their felicity conditions. As can be seen in Table 1, he draws a distinction between the illocutionary force F and the propositional content p of an illocutionary act (for more details and the way F and p are coded, see Section 4.5). What is the evidence for such a distinction? Searle points out that different illocutionary acts may have the same propositional content, as in the following examples that share the propositional content 'John will leave the room' (Searle 1971: 42):

(15) Will John leave the room?

(16) John will leave the room.

(17) John, leave the room!

(18) Would that John leave the room.

(19) If John leaves the room, I will also.

Utterance (15) has the illocutionary force of a *yes-no* question, (16) is a prediction, (17) is an order or a command, (18) expresses a wish, and in (19) the propositional content 'John will leave the room' is hypothetical, i.e. functions as part of a conditional assertion.

Simplifying Searle's (1969: 66) account somewhat, by way of example, the crucial felicity conditions and corresponding rules for the acts of asserting, promising, requesting, and thanking are formulated in (20)–(23), respectively.[46] The felicity conditions specified include the kind of the propositional content expressed (if there is one), preparatory conditions, the sincerity condition, which specifies the mental attitude associated with the illocutionary act, and, most importantly, the essential condition, which has the status of a *constitutive* rule, i.e., if it is not fulfilled, the illocutionary act does not come about. The other conditions can be regarded as *regulative* rules, i.e., they are necessary, but not sufficient, for a felicitous performance of the illocutionary act in question.[47]

(20) Assertion
Propositional content: Any proposition p.
Preparatory: S has evidence (reasons, etc.) for the truth of p.
Sincerity: S believes that p.
Essential: Counts as an undertaking to the effect that p represents an actual state of affairs.

(21) Promise
Propositional content: Future act A carried out by S.
Preparatory: S can do A & A benefits H.
Sincerity: S intends to do A.
Essential: Counts as a commitment to do A.

---

[46] Note that the felicity conditions proposed in (20)–(23) are skeletal; they have to be fleshed out in a more adequate account. For example, the felicity conditions formulated in (22) are not sufficiently elaborated to distinguish between e.g. requests and commands.

[47] The following abbreviations are used: S = speaker, H = hearer, p = proposition or propositional content, A = action.

(22) Request
Propositional content: Future act A carried out by H.
Preparatory: H is able to do A.
Sincerity: S wants H to do A.
Essential: Counts as an attempt to get H to do A.

(23) Thanking
Propositional content: Past act A done by H.
Preparatory: A benefits S.
Sincerity: S feel grateful for A.
Essential: Counts as an expression of gratitude.

4.3 Illocutionary types

Searle (1976) proposes a classification of illocutionary acts into five illocutionary categories, a taxonomy that, up to the present day, has been highly influential in the development of speech act theory:

1. *Representatives* (also called Assertives): e.g. claim, assert, tell (that), report, describe.
2. *Commissives*: e.g. promise, pledge, vow, swear, guarantee.
3. *Directives*: e.g. ask (to), tell (to), order, command, implore, entreat, beg, request, urge, advise, recommend.
4. *Expressives*: e.g. apologize, congratulate, thank, express condolences, blame, forgive.
5. *Declarations*: e.g. appoint, declare (war, a meeting open, etc.), baptize, marry (act and ceremony performed by a judge, priest), sentence (in a court).[48]

Searle's (1976) characterization of illocutionary categories is based on the following three criteria:

i. *Illocutionary point*: This term is synonymous with what Searle (1969) calls the 'essential condition' of an illocutionary act.
ii. *Direction of fit*: This criterion characterizes the relation between the propositional content and reality (or with the "world"). According to Searle, the direction of fit can go from the words to the world, from the world to the words, or there is not direction of fit at all.

---

48. Declarations are also frequently called 'declaratives' in the literature (see e.g. Searle & Vanderveken 1985: 205–211), but this usage is unfortunate given that the term *declarative* is usually reserved to a sentence type or grammatical mood (contrasting e.g. with the imperative and the interrogative sentence types).

iii. *Psychological state*: This term is equivalent to what Searle (1969) calls the 'sincerity condition' of the illocutionary act.

On the basis of criteria (i)–(iii), Searle defines illocutionary types as presented in a slightly simplified and adapted way in Tables 2–6.

Table 2. Representatives (e.g. *assert*)

Criteria of classification	Representatives
Illocutionary point	S commits self to the truth of *p*
Direction of fit	WORDs to WORLD: Words are chosen in such a way that they fit reality
Psychological state	S believes that *p*

In the case of a representative act, the content of *p* is not constrained and it is purported to be true. Thus, the propositional content has a truth value, i.e., it has to be coded linguistically in such a way that it fits reality. The words are intended to correspond to the world.

Table 3. Commissives (e.g. *promise*)

Criteria of classification	Commissives
Illocutionary point	S commits self to a future act *A*
Direction of fit	WORLD to WORDs: Reality is changed by S in such a way that it fits the propositional content *S does A*
Psychological state	S intends to do *A*

Table 4. Directives (e.g. *request*)

Criteria of classification	Directives
Illocutionary point	S places H under some (more or less strong) obligation to do *A*
Direction of fit	WORLD to WORDs: The world is changed by H in such a way that it fits the propositional content *H does A*
Psychological state	S wants H to do *A*

Commissives (Table 3) and directives (Table 4) differ from representatives in that their propositional content is constrained and the direction of fit between words and reality is the reverse of that of representatives, i.e., it moves from the world to the words. The propositional content of commissives and directives expresses a future action of the speaker and of the hearer, respectively. In this sense, commissives and directives have no truth value *per se*. When uttering a commissive, the speaker places herself or himself under an obligation to perform some future action whereas, by means of a directive speech act, the speaker aims at placing the hearer under a (more or less strong) obligation to carry out some action.[49] In other words, it is up to the speaker (commissives) or up to the hearer (directives) to make the propositional content true.

In expressive illocutionary acts, the propositional content has yet another semantic and pragmatic status (see Table 5).

Table 5. Expressives (e.g. *congratulate, apologize*)

Criteria of classification	Expressives
Illocutionary point	S expresses an emotional attitude towards *p*
Direction of fit	Ø: Factuality of *p* is presupposed
Psychological state	S has an emotional attitude towards *p*

Searle (1976) claims that expressives do not exhibit any direction of fit (hence the use of the empty set symbol 'Ø') because *p* is presupposed. One might however object that a presupposed propositional content, e.g. a factive presupposition, could be regarded as an implicit assertion. One could thus argue that the direction of fit moves from the words to the world. Consider an apology such as (24):

(24) I apologize for hurting your [...] feelings. (COCA 2012)

The propositional content *p* of (24) can be informally rendered as 'I hurt your feelings', and *p* is assumed to be true by the speaker. It could be regarded as a backgrounded assertion, which, accordingly, has a direction of fit from the words to the world. The hearer might actually dispute the truth of *p* by responding with (25):

(25) Don't worry. You haven't hurt my feelings.

The fifth illocutionary category – declarations – comprises speech acts that are embedded in institutional frameworks, e.g. political, administrative or religious (Table 6). In uttering or writing a declaration, an authorized or legitimized agent causes a propositional content to become true. In this sense, the direction of fit is both ways: from the words to the world, and vice versa. Searle assumes that declarations are not associated with a psychological state (sincerity condition). Here is an example from a letter of resignation:

(26) I hereby resign as CEO of Apple. (COCA 2011)

---

49. I follow Wunderlich (1976) in assuming that the *hearer's* obligation (which may be more or less strong) to carry out the action in question characterizes the illocutionary point of directives more adequately than Searle's formulation that, by means of a directive speech act, the speaker tries to get the hearer to perform some action (see also Thornburg & Panther 1997: 211).

In writing (26), the chief executor officer (CEO) of the computer company Apple, Steve Jobs, tendered his resignation from his post. This declaration made the propositional content 'I am no longer the CEO of Apple' true. Declarations are generally characterized by the formula 'Saying it makes it so'.

Table 6. Declarations (e.g. *appoint, baptize*)

Criteria of classification	Declarations
Illocutionary point	S brings about correspondence between *p* and reality
Direction of fit	WORDs to WORLD & WORLD to WORDs: The words correspond to the world ("it is so") and the world is changed so that it fits the words ("it be so")
Psychological state	Ø: There is no particular psychological state associated with declarations

4.4 Distinguishing between illocutionary force and illocutionary verbs

In his introductory textbook to pragmatics, Geoffrey Leech (1983: 174–175) emphasizes that a distinction has to be drawn between illocutionary acts and the lexical means (e.g. verbs) that are used to code illocutionary acts. According to Leech (1983: 174), the study of illocutionary verbs pertains to the domain of grammar, whereas the analysis of the illocutionary acts and their force is the object of inquiry of pragmatics. That such a distinction is necessary can be seen from the different meanings of illocutionary verbs like e.g. *promise, ask,* or *insist*.

Consider first the use of *promise* in the following examples:

(27) I promise to give you a sterling letter of recommendation. (COCA 2016)

(28) I promise that we will communicate with all of you guys. (COCA 2013)

(29) I promise that I haven't been running away. (COCA 2007)

(30) I promise I didn't see a single tumbleweed. (COCA 2014)

Utterances (27) and (28) are cases of commissive speech acts. In uttering (27) the speaker commits herself to providing the hearer with a *sterling letter of recommendation*, an act that benefits the hearer. An analogous interpretation holds for (28). The speaker commits himself to the future action *we will communicate with all of you guys*, which, in the given context, is also intended to benefit the addressees of the speech act, i.e. *you guys*.

But what about examples (29) and (30)? The first point to note is that in both sentences the propositional content refers to past events, a property that is not compatible with the felicity conditions of a commissive speech act of promising. The illocutionary force of the two utterances is an emphatic assurance that some past state-of-affairs holds. In other words, this use of *promise* constitutes a representative or assertive speech act. Nevertheless, the two uses of *promise* are conceptually related, i.e., *promise* is a polysemous verb. The commissive *promise* expresses or implies a future action performed by the speaker. The propositional content is made true by the speaker at some time after the time of the utterance. In the case of an assertive use of *promise*, the speaker commits herself to the truth of the propositional content. Interestingly, in German the verb corresponding to *promise*, i.e. *versprechen*, can be used only in the commissive sense. Thus, literal translations of (29) and (30), i.e. (31) and (32), respectively, are pragmatically infelicitous (if not ungrammatical):[50]

(31) *Ich verspreche, dass ich nicht weggerannt bin.
     I   promise   that I   not   away.run   am

(32) *Ich verspreche, dass ich keinen einzigen Steppenläufer sah.
     I   promise   that I   not.a   single   tumbleweed   saw

Idiomatic translations of (29) and (30) are (33) and (34), respectively, both of which convey a strong commitment to the truth of the *past* event expressed in the complement clause (introduced by the complementizer *dass* 'that'):

(33) Ich versichere Ihnen, dass ich nicht weggerannt bin.
     I   assure   you   that I   not   away.run   am
     'I assure you that I didn't run away'

(34) Ich schwöre, dass ich keinen einzigen Steppenläufer sah.
     I   swear   that I   not   a   single   tumbleweed saw
     'I swear I didn't see a single tumbleweed'

A final point to note is that the boundary between the commissive and the assertive uses of *promise* is fuzzy. A promise regarding a future action of the speaker is often not clearly distinguishable from a speaker's prediction that he or she will perform the action in question. Consider the following example from the novel *Dead Broke* by Trista Russell:

(35) I promise that you'll wake up in the morning.   (COCA 2008)

Utterance (35) is preceded by (36) (uttered by the same speaker):

---

50. A tumbleweed is a 'plant of dry regions that breaks off near the ground in late summer and is tumbled about by the wind, thereby dispersing its seeds' (NOAD). The corresponding German lexeme *Steppenläufer* literally translates as 'steppe runner'.

(36) Tiredness is a natural stage of recovery, get some rest. (COCA 2008)

The context given in (36) can be seen as lending support to two illocutionary interpretations of (35). On the one hand, it could be a seen as mere *prediction* that the hearer will wake up in the morning, an event that may or may not happen. On the other hand, (35) could also function as a *promise* in the sense that the speaker will see to it, i.e. act in such a way, e.g. knock on the door of the bedroom in the morning so that the hearer will wake up. This commissive interpretation is strengthened by the presumption that waking up in the morning is an event that is in the hearer's interest.

As a second example that illustrates the distinction between illocutionary force as such and illocutionary verbs that code the force, compare the use of *insist* in (37) and in (38):

(37) I insist that you apologize for violating my trust and leave my office.
(COCA 2016)

(38) [...] I insist that the historic barriers to black participation in the political, social, and economic life of the nation have been lowered dramatically over the past four decades, especially for the wealthiest 20 percent of the black population.
(COCA 1997)

The illocutionary force of (37) is clearly directive; in contrast, in the academic piece of discourse (38), the use of *insist* signals a representative or assertive speech act. Note that both uses of *insist* have something in common: the directive use of *insist* evokes a context of potential refusal on the hearer's part to comply with the demand, whereas the assertive use conveys that the speaker strongly rejects any objections to the propositional content of his or her assertion. Thus, the verb *insist* has (at least) two related meanings, i.e., it is a polysemous lexical item.

Finally, consider two illocutionary uses of the verb *ask*:

(39) I ask you to judge my father by his results. (COCA 2016)

(40) I ask you whether, the world over or in past history, there is anything like it?
(COCA 1991)

In (39), *ask* heads an infinitival complement clause and conveys a directive illocutionary force, whereas, in (40), *ask* is followed by a finite clause introduced by *whether*, i.e. has the force of a question. Note that these two uses appear in different constructions. The respective illocutionary meanings are, as in the case of *promise* and *insist*, conceptually related. While (39) is a request to perform a certain *extralinguistic* action, the question (40), as questions in general, can be seen as a request for *information*. Thus, the two illocutionary meanings of *ask* are semantically related.

In conclusion, the linguistic data that have been presented in this section provide evidence for Leech's (1983) claim that *illocutionary acts* have to be carefully distinguished from *verbs* that denote illocutionary meanings and are potentially polysemous.

5. Coding illocutionary force and propositional content

5.1 Introduction

From the preceding sections it has already become evident that there exist various ways of coding the illocutionary force and the propositional content of illocutionary acts (see e.g. Searle 1979: 20–27; Panther 2016b). Figure 1 lists (non-exhaustively) some coding devices for illocutionary force and propositional content in English. Illocutionary acts can be signaled by grammatical and lexical means. Furthermore, prosodic means (e.g. intonation) play an important role in the coding of illocutionary force in oral communication, but will be not discussed in what follows.

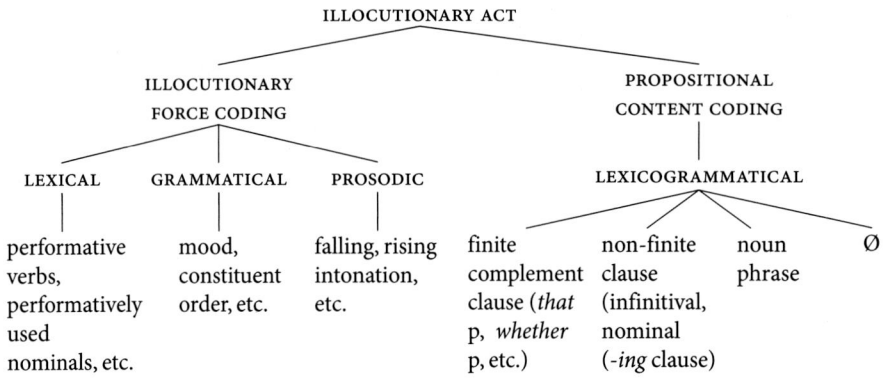

Figure 1. Illocutionary force and propositional content indicators
(slightly adapted from Panther 2016b: 183)

In the following subsections, some lexical and grammatical coding devices are illustrated with authentic examples from English-language corpora (for a more detailed description of illocutionary and propositional coding devices, see Panther 2016b). In Section 5.2, the focus is on the role of mood and constituent order as formal devices to code illocutionary types. The coding of specific illocutionary force is taken up in Section 5.3; in particular, by means of performative verbs (Section 5.3.1) and performatively used nominals (Section 5.3.2). Finally, in Section 5.4, it is shown how the propositional content of illocutionary acts is coded by means of clausal and complement constructions.

5.2 Illocutionary force and propositional content coding: Mood and constituent order

Illocutionary force and propositional content can be signaled by grammatical mood, word order, and intonation. For example, in Huddleston and Pullum (2002: 853), the following clause types are distinguished and illustrated (my numbering):

(41) You are generous. [declarative]

(42) Are you generous? [closed interrogative]

(43) How generous are you? [open interrogative]

(44) How generous you are! [exclamative]

(45) Be generous. [imperative]

The respective illocutionary potentials of these sentences are characterized as follows in Huddleston and Pullum (2002: 853):[51] Sentence (41) functions as a statement; (42) and (43) are categorized as a closed question and an open question, respectively; (44) is as an exclamatory statement; and (45) has the force of a directive speech act.[52] As can be seen from Huddleston and Pullum's (2002) examples, these sentence types are characterized by specific syntactic features, such as differing word order and, in oral communication, by specific intonational patterns, e.g. final falling pitch for declaratives sentences, i.e. assertive speech acts, and rising pitch for *yes-no* interrogatives, i.e. questions.

5.3 Illocutionary force coding

5.3.1 *Performative verbs*

The force of an illocutionary act can be coded lexically, e.g. by a verb, which (in the present tense) explicitly names the illocutionary act performed by the speaker. Examples have already been presented in (24), (26)–(30), (33)–(35), and (37)–(40). Typically, in such utterances, the speaker refers to herself or himself, sometimes also to the hearer, and explicitly names the illocutionary act performed. Hence, such

---

51. See also Huddleston and Pullum's (2005: 159) grammar, in which the same clause type distinctions are drawn.

52. It should be noted that these illocutionary functions do not coincide in all respects with Searle's (1976) illocutionary categories. In Searle (1976: 11), questions are treated as directives, i.e. *requests* for information – more precisely as attempts by the speaker to get the hearer to give an answer. Exclamatives have both assertive and expressive functions, but they are not expressives of the same type as in Searle's categorization.

speech acts are known as *explicit performative utterances*. Utterances (46)–(48) are additional examples that count as acts of promising, advising, and apologizing, respectively:

(46) I promise you that I shall never set anything before you that I haven't subjected to rigorous chemical analysis. (COCA 2002)

(47) I advise you to keep an eye on this woman. (COCA 2014)

(48) I apologize. (COCA 2017)

While in (46) and (47) the propositional content *p* is expressed by means of a finite and a non-finite complement clause, respectively, in (48), *p* has to be inferred from the extralinguistic situation and/or the linguistic context.

Illocutionary force can also be more indirectly marked by means of so-called *hedged performatives* (see Fraser 1975; Panther & Thornburg 2019) (italics added):

(49) I *can promise* you we will follow the facts wherever they lead. (COCA 2017)

(50) Once again, I *must ask* you to lower your voice. (COCA 2011)

(51) I'm *afraid* I *must ask* you to leave within the next seven days. (COCA 2012)

In (49), the illocutionary verb *promise* is hedged by the modal auxiliary *can*. Although this modal literally expresses 'possibility' or 'ability', utterance (49) functions as a commissive speech act, i.e., it counts as an actual promise. In the same vein, utterance (50) is interpreted as a directive speech act despite the fact that the performative verb *ask* is hedged by the modal *must*, which *per se* expresses 'obligation', not 'actuality'. Moreover, it is even possible for language users, as evidenced by example (51), to construct chains of hedges. In this sentence, the emotive predicate *be afraid* and the modal *must* include the directive verb *ask* within their scope.[53] Despite these hedges, the illocutionary force of (51) is directive; i.e., it is determined by the illocutionary meaning of *ask*.

5.3.2 Performatively used nominal expressions

Illocutionary force can also be explicitly coded by means of a noun or a noun phrase (often in the plural), as in examples (52)–(55), all of which function as expressive illocutionary acts. The propositional content may be coded or remain implicit, i.e. retrievable from context.

(52) Thanks!

---

53. From a cognitive linguistic perspective, a more detailed discussion of the conceptual-pragmatic properties of hedged performative that preserve the force denoted by the illocutionary verb can be found in Panther and Thornburg (2019).

(53) Thanks to the anonymous [...] reviewer who pointed out these parallels.
(COCA 2017)

(54) Apologies. (COCA 2017)

(55) My apologies for any discomfort it caused you. (COCA 2017)

Nominal expressions coding illocutionary force are also common in other languages. For example in French an act of congratulation can be expressed by means of a pluralized noun corresponding to English *Congratulations!*, i.e. *Félicitations!* The corresponding nominal performative for *Apologies!* in German is the singular noun *Entschuldigung!* ('apology').

5.4 Propositional content coding

It has already become clear from the examples given in Section 5.3 that the propositional content p of illocutionary acts can be coded by various syntactic means (including the "null" option notated as 'Ø'). Possible constructions that convey propositional contents are finite and non-finite complement clauses and nominal expressions. In the following examples coded propositional content has been italicized:

p = finite complement clause

(56) I promise you *that America will get stronger and more united, more prosperous, more secure.* (COCA 2009)

p = non-finite gerund clause

(57) I thank you *for responding to my message.* (COCA 2011)

p = infinitival complement clause

(58) I ask you *to judge my father by his results.* (COCA 2016)

p = nominal complement

(59) I thank you *for all your hospitality.* (COCA 2017)

p = Ø

(60) I apologize. (COCA 2017)

The coding devices for illocutionary acts that have been presented in Section 5 are by no means exhaustive, but they demonstrate that natural languages like English have a rich array of *morphosyntactic* and *lexical* means at their disposal to express illocutionary force and propositional content. This situation is not too surprising, given that one, if not the main, function of human language is communication. Illocutionary acts are the basic units to serve this purpose.

6. Illocutionary scenarios and their components

6.1 Introduction

Illocutionary meanings can be described in terms of conceptual-pragmatic *frames*, which, in what follows, are called *illocutionary scenarios* (for this notion, see Thornburg & Panther 1997; Panther & Thornburg 1998). In Sections 6.2 and 6.3, the notion of illocutionary scenario is worked out in more detail and scenarios are presented for instances of the five illocutionary categories proposed by Searle (1976) and Searle and Vanderveken (1985), i.e. assertives, commissives, directives, expressives, and declarations. These five illocutionary categories are regarded as subtypes of a schematic (linguistic) *action scenario* as diagrammed in Figure 2 (see Thornburg & Panther 1997; Panther & Thornburg 1998).

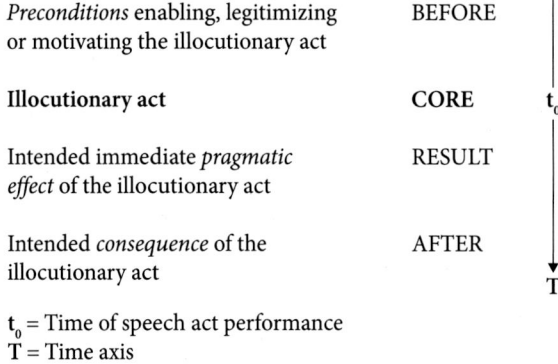

t_0 = Time of speech act performance
T = Time axis

Figure 2. Illocutionary scenario schema

The schema in Figure 2 diverges from Searle's set of felicity conditions in some respects. It proposes a template for the analysis of illocutionary acts in terms of scenario components that hold at certain *temporal* stages on a time axis *T*, relative to the time t_0 of the actual performance of the illocutionary act, i.e. the CORE. The BEFORE refers to various prerequisites that must obtain before the illocutionary act can be produced felicitously. Among them are Searle's preparatory conditions and mental attitudes, such as what he calls the 'sincerity condition'. The felicitous performance of the illocutionary act has an immediate (intended) pragmatic RESULT and possible further (intended) consequences (AFTER) that occur after the utterance time t_0.

6.2 Assertives

Figure 3 outlines a schematic illocutionary scenario for assertive speech acts.[54]

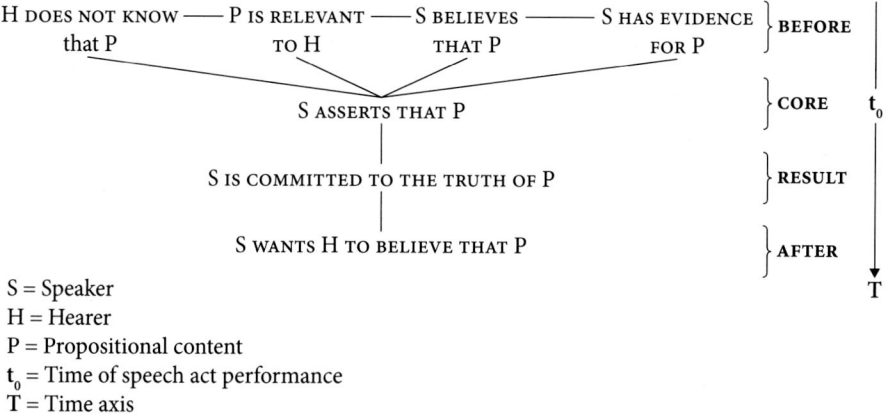

S = Speaker
H = Hearer
P = Propositional content
t_0 = Time of speech act performance
T = Time axis

Figure 3. Scenario for assertives

At the BEFORE stage, there appear several speaker-oriented and/or hearer-oriented components that relate to the propositional content *p* of an assertive. The speaker should only assert, claim, report, etc., a propositional content *p* that he or she believes to be true. This component is known as the sincerity condition in Searle's terminology. Furthermore, an assertive act should also, under normal circumstances, provide information *p* that the hearer does not know yet and that is relevant to her or him in the communicative situation.

Finally, I postulate a BEFORE condition that the speaker should have evidence for the truth of *p* or, alternatively, should be able to provide good reasons for his or her claim. This requirement might look a bit unrealistic at first sight. After all, people assert all kinds of things for which they have insufficient or perhaps no evidence at all. Despite this reservation, even in informal conversations or chats, there is an expectation that participants, if asked to do so, should make an effort and be able to provide reasons for the validity of their claims. There is certainly a difference between what ordinary people consider as sufficient evidence and what counts as evidence in e.g. an academic or legal context. Regarding the latter, in criminal proceedings, evidence from hearsay is in general not admissible (Garner 2009, s.v. *hearsay*), but in ordinary life hearsay is more readily accepted as sufficient evidence for the truth of an assertion if the source of information is considered to be trustworthy or authoritative. Keeping these *caveats* in mind, it is justified to integrate the EVIDENCE requirement into the illocutionary scenario of assertives.

---

54. Assertive speech acts are also called *representatives*.

The CORE of assertives, i.e. what Searle calls the essential condition, in the model presented here is simply the performance of the act itself. The performance of an assertive act has the immediate pragmatic RESULT that the speaker is viewed by the addressee(s) as being *committed* to the truth of the assertion.

Finally, the intended consequence of an assertive act, i.e. the AFTER, is usually to induce the hearer to believe that the propositional content *p* is true. This condition has to be taken with a grain of salt. There are situations, e.g. in a televised discussion between politicians and/or journalists with different political allegiances, in which the main goal of the discussants might be not so much to convince the political adversary as to propagate one's own political views in a forceful way.

6.3 Commissives

A typical instantiation of the commissive illocutionary type is the act of promising, which was already discussed in some detail in Chapter 6 in connection with Austin's and Searle's theory of speech acts (see Figure 4).

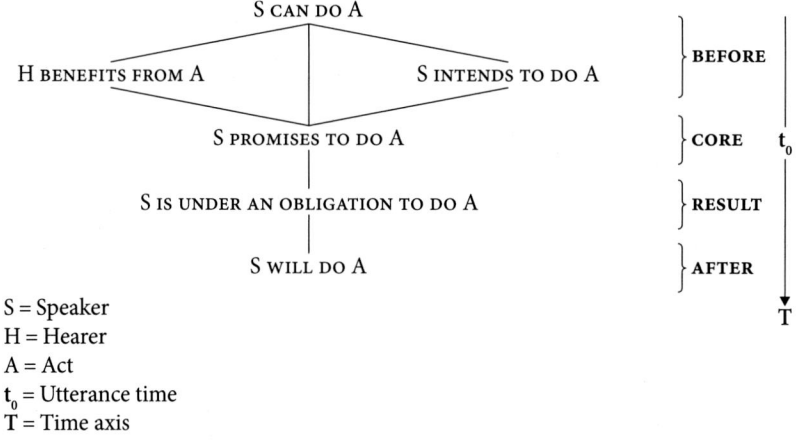

S = Speaker
H = Hearer
A = Act
t_0 = Utterance time
T = Time axis

Figure 4. Commissives (promise)

As can be gleaned from Figure 4, the BEFORE stage of the scenario comprises components that refer to the speaker's ability to carry out the action in question, to a specific mental attitude, i.e. the speaker's intention to perform the action, and to the speaker's belief that the hearer will benefit from the promised action.

The RESULT of a felicitous promise is the speaker's self-imposed obligation or commitment to carry out the action in question, and the promise is *satisfied* (AFTER), if it is fulfilled, i.e., the promised action is actually carried out by the speaker.[55] As

---

55. For the notion of satisfaction of illocutionary acts, see e.g. Vanderveken (2004).

in the case of directives, the propositional content of commissives is constrained – here, to future actions of the speaker. Notice, however, that, as already pointed out in Section 4.4, the verb *promise* can be used performatively in the sense of 'assure' with a propositional content that includes past events (which are not necessarily actions performed by the speaker). Such cases do not count as instances of commissive speech acts, but they have to be categorized as assertives.

As a second commissive speech act let us briefly consider the conceptual-pragmatic make-up of an *offer*. An offer has the same BEFORE, RESULT, and AFTER components as a promise, but an additional component of conditionality. The speaker commits herself to carrying out a specific action "conditional on hearer's acceptance" (Searle and Vanderveken 1985: 196). Consider the following explicit performative:

(61) We offer an opportunity to work with retail stores and consumers in your own area. (COCA 2012)

In case readers of (61) *accept* the offer, they will presume that the offerer is (legally) obligated to satisfy the propositional content 'We will give you an opportunity to work with retail stores and consumers in your own area'.

6.4 Directives

The next illocutionary scenario to be considered is the illocutionary type of directive speech acts whose schematic conceptual organization is diagrammed in Figure 5.

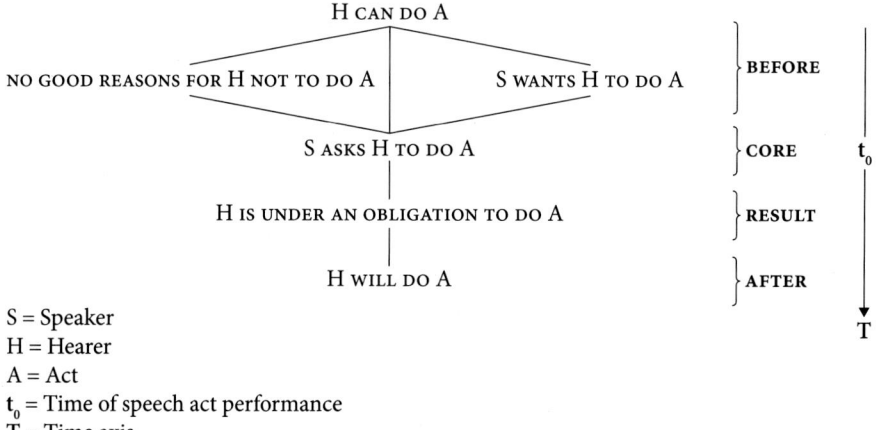

S = Speaker
H = Hearer
A = Act
t_0 = Time of speech act performance
T = Time axis

Figure 5. Directives

On the BEFORE level, a felicitous directive act, such as a request, order, command, or an act of begging or urging, conveys the speaker's presumption that the hearer is able to perform the requested action and that there are no good reasons why the hearer should not perform the action. Moreover, directives convey the speaker's wish that the hearer carry out the requested action. This analysis predicts that the following utterances (62)–(64) are pragmatically odd because the validity of one of these scenario components is explicitly denied in the *but* clause following the directive act (here, the imperative):

(62) #Open the window, but you are not strong enough to open it.

(63) #Open the window, but I don't see a reason for opening it.

(64) #Open the window, but I don't really want you to open the window.

Utterance (62) is infelicitous because it is incongruent with the BEFORE component that the addressee of directive speech act should be able to carry out the requested action. Example (63) is pragmatically incongruent because the BEFORE condition that there are no good reasons for not carrying out the action is explicitly canceled in the *but* clause, and (64) is not compatible with the mental attitude conventionally associated with directives that the speaker wants the hearer to carry out the action of opening the window.

The intended RESULT of an act of asking somebody to do something (CORE) is that the hearer is under some pressure or obligation to comply with the directive speech act. The obligation varies in strength as a function of the kind of directive uttered. A polite request exerts a relatively low degree of pressure on the hearer, whereas a military order issued by a commanding officer places a common soldier under a very strong obligation to comply with it. In the case of an order or command, the speaker is or pretends to be in a more powerful social position than the hearer, and the directive is more likely to be complied with (AFTER). In contrast, in the case of directive acts like entreating, imploring, beseeching or begging, the speaker occupies, at least, temporarily, a lower rank on the power hierarchy.

Note that the AFTER in Figure 5 corresponds to what Searle (1969) calls the 'propositional content condition' of directives. In contrast to many assertive illocutionary acts, which do not place any constraints on the propositional content, in directive acts, *p* must conform to the schema 'H will do A', i.e., the propositional content expresses a future action of the hearer.[56]

---

56. Some subtypes of assertive acts pose constraints on their propositional content, e.g. predictions or forecasts, which, by definition, refer to *future* states of affairs.

Figure 5 is highly schematic in the sense that it does not specify idiosyncratic features of individual directive acts. For example, for requests, one might postulate an additional scenario component: as a consequence of being put under a certain amount of pressure, the hearer forms the intention or willingness to carry out the requested action. In contrast, in the case of orders or commands, compliance with the speech act can be enforced *against* the addressee's will. As to acts of advising or recommending, which, in Searle's classification, figure as directive acts, the degree of obligation to comply with the such consultative acts is relatively low and, furthermore, these speech acts have the additional component that the recommended or advised course of action is beneficial to the hearer. Thus, acts of recommending and advising are not prototypical exemplars of directives (see Panther & Köpcke 2008: 100). Table 7 lists some commonalities and differences between stronger directives like orders, commands, and requests, on the one hand, and weaker consultative speech acts like recommendations and advice, on the other.

Table 7. Prototypical directives vs. consultatives

Scenario components	order/command/ request	recommendation/ advice
H CAN DO A	yes	yes
S WANTS H to DO A	yes	not necessarily
H BENEFITS from A	not necessarily	yes
S places H under an OBLIGATION to DO A	yes	not necessarily
H WILL DO A	yes	yes

6.5 Expressives

Figure 6 diagrams a schematic conceptual-pragmatic scenario for expressive speech acts (in the sense of Searle 1976).

The BEFORE component of an expressive comprises a (factive) presupposition that some event E occurred before the time of utterance t_0. This event triggers an emotional and/or evaluative response in the speaker's mind. The illocutionary act itself, i.e. the CORE, verbalizes the emotional and evaluative stance of the speaker, and, regarding the (intended) pragmatic RESULT, the speaker is understood as truly experiencing the emotional response and as having a corresponding evaluative attitude towards the presupposed event. In contrast to assertives, directives, and commissives, the AFTER component of expressives is not specified, i.e., it is variable (see below).

134 Introduction to Cognitive Pragmatics

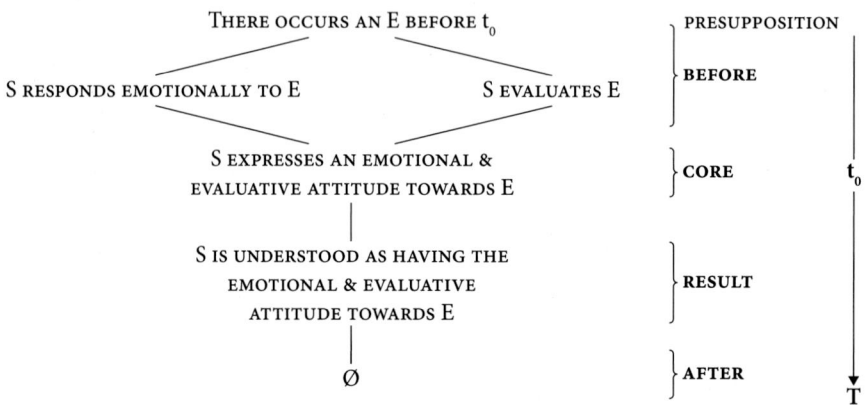

E = Event
S = Speaker
H = Hearer
P = Propositional content
t_0 = Time of speech act performance
T = Time axis
Ø = unspecified/variable

Figure 6. Expressives

Three typical instantiations of expressive speech acts are apologies, congratulations, and acts of thanking, whose conceptual-pragmatic structures are diagrammed in Figures 7, 8, and 9, respectively.

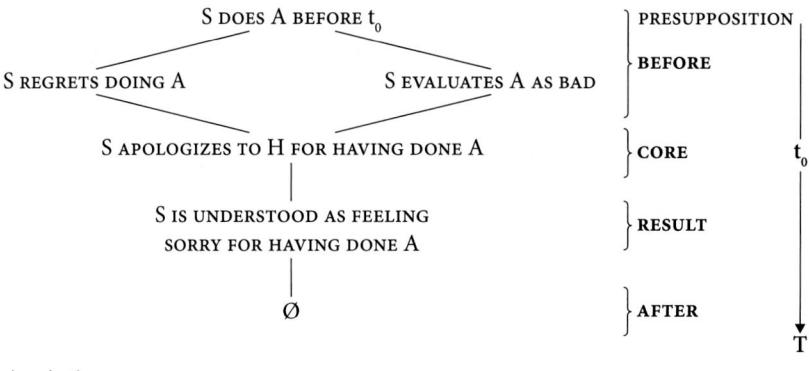

A = Action
S = Speaker
H = Hearer
t_0 = Time of speech act performance
T = Time axis
Ø = unspecified/variable

Figure 7. Apologizing

The BEFORE component of an apology describes an event, in this case an action performed by the speaker, which is presupposed as having actually occurred. Furthermore, the BEFORE also displays a mental state of regret (emotional response) on the part of the speaker, who, at the same time, evaluates his or her action as bad, inappropriate, immoral, etc.

The CORE of an apology is, as in the previous figures, the illocutionary act itself, here an expression of regret and contrition regarding the speaker's bad behavior towards the hearer at some time prior to the utterance. The immediate pragmatic RESULT of the performance of an apology is that the speaker is understood as feeling sincerely sorry for his or her inappropriate behavior. The AFTER component is, as pointed out above, unspecified. One intended goal, i.e. the AFTER, of an apology could be that the hearer accepts the apology or even forgives the speaker.

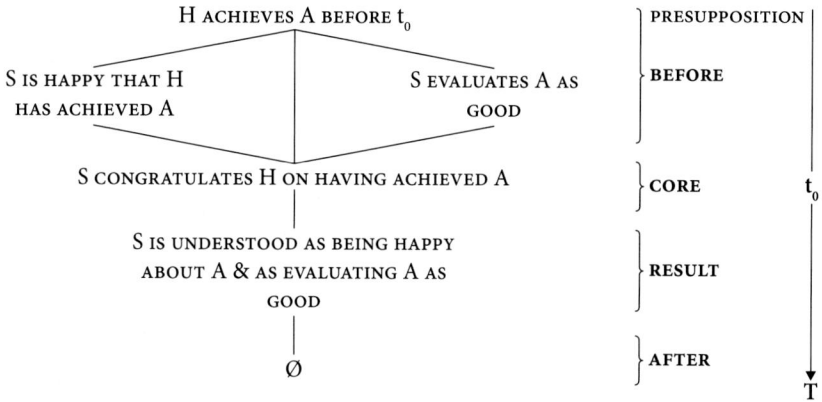

A = Action
S = Speaker
H = Hearer
t_0 = Time of speech act performance
T = Time axis

Figure 8. Congratulating

Congratulations presuppose an action performed by the hearer (before the time of speaking), such as e.g. successfully passing an exam, which causes positive emotions, such as joy, in the speaker's mind and which he evaluates as good (BEFORE). The CORE triggers the pragmatic RESULT that the speaker is now understood as having the mental states of happiness/joy and positive evaluation regarding the hearer's achievement. The intended AFTER may be a verbal response from the hearer, e.g. an utterance that expresses gratitude or appreciation. Depending on circumstances and the cultural background of the interactional situation, an appropriate response from the hearer may also be just an appreciative nod or equivalent facial expression.

As a third instance of an expressive speech act, consider the act of thanking somebody for something (see Figure 9).

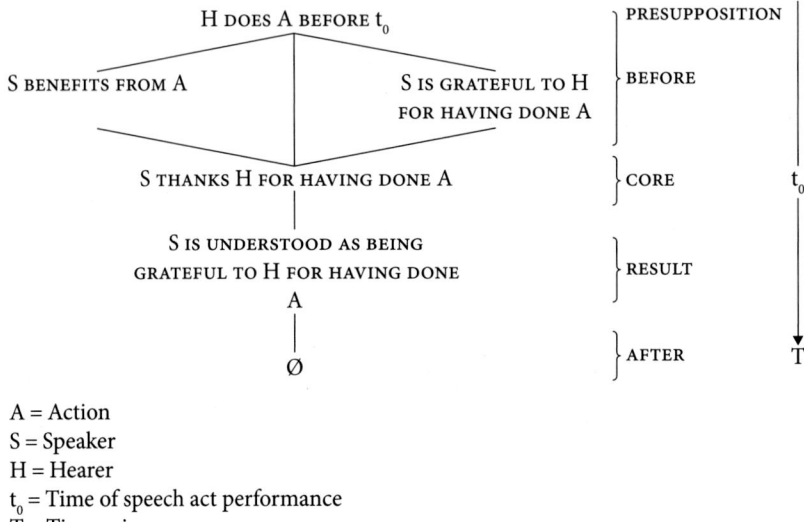

A = Action
S = Speaker
H = Hearer
t_0 = Time of speech act performance
T = Time axis

Figure 9. Thanking

When performing an act of thanking, the speaker presupposes that the hearer performed an action that benefits the speaker, and the speaker expresses his or her feelings of appreciation or gratitude for the hearer's action. Just as in the case of congratulatory acts, there is no specific AFTER associated with thanking. A possible anticipated reaction from the person thanked might be a response such as *No problem* or *You're welcome*.

6.6 Declarations

The fifth illocutionary type is named 'declaration' in e.g. Searle (1976: 13), but in a later publication (Searle & Vanderveken 1985: 205), the term 'declarative' is used.[57] The schematic conceptual-pragmatic structure of declarations is represented in Figure 10.

In a nutshell, for their successful performance, declarations require some extralinguistic political, legal, or religious, i.e. institutional framework. According to Searle (1976: 13), the "successful performance [of a declaration] guarantees that the propositional content corresponds to the world […]." Declarations are however not

---

57. In his book, the term *declaration* is preferred (see footnote 48).

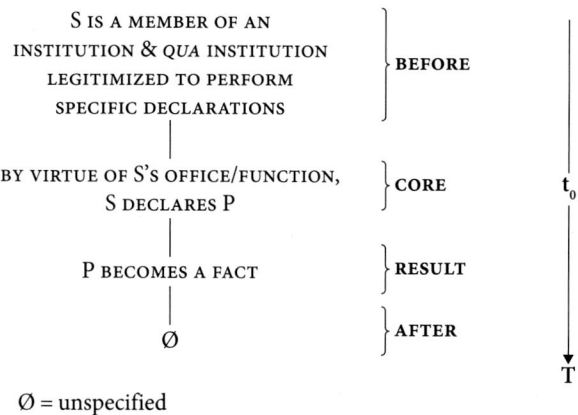

Figure 10. Declarations

necessarily definitive; for example, in the legal domain, there often exists a right to appeal a decision, such as a conviction, in a higher court of justice.

The power of words to create "facts", i.e. of "Saying so makes it so", is nicely illustrated by the following declaration, issued on November 26, 2000 by Katherine Harris, Secretary of State of Florida, regarding the contested outcome of the U.S. presidential election:

(65) In accordance with the laws of the State of Florida, I hereby declare George W. Bush the winner of Florida's 25 electoral votes for the President of the United States.
(Accessed May 1, 2018 at: http://www.nndb.com/people/067/000038950)

Harris' certification that Bush won the electoral votes in Florida (and thereby the presidential election) against the Democrat candidate Al Gore was ultimately confirmed by the U.S. Supreme Court (another declaration).[58]

Declarations are also common in the domain of sports, where they are known as *referee's decisions*. For example, in soccer (association football), a referee has "full authority to enforce the Laws of the Game in connection with the match to which he has been appointed (Law 5)."[59] Thus, the referee's decision that a goal has been scored by one team is irreversible, even if there is objective video proof that the ball did not cross the goal line.

As a final example, in Figure 11, the illocutionary scenario of an act of resignation from some office or position is diagrammed.

---

58. Whether Bush really won the majority of the votes is an open question.

59. Source: https://en.wikipedia.org/wiki/Referee#Football_(association).

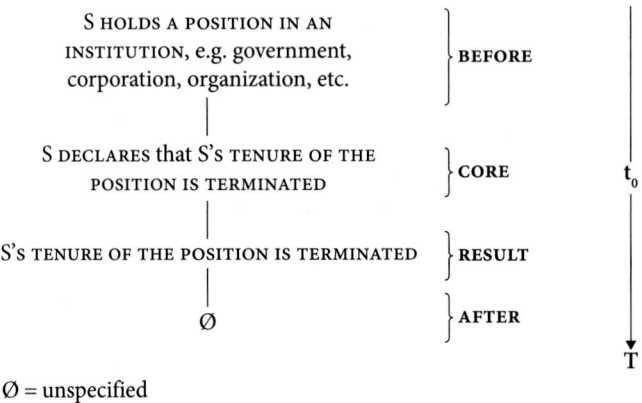

Ø = unspecified

Figure 11. Resigning

If the act of resigning, which usually has to be submitted as a written document, is performed according to the laws or regulations of the institution from which the writer resigns, it has the effect (RESULT) that the writer's tenure of the office or position in question is terminated, i.e., it is a fact that the writer of the letter of resignation is not employed any longer.

7. Conclusion

In this chapter, some of the basic meaning components of illocutionary acts have been identified and it has been proposed that Searle's felicity conditions can be modeled in a cognitive linguistic framework in terms of conceptual frames. Following e.g. Thornburg and Panther (1997), Panther und Thornburg (1998, 2007), these frames can be called speech act scenarios or more, narrowly, illocutionary scenarios.

In Chapters 9 and 10, it is shown that the notion of illocutionary scenario provides the basis for analyzing *indirect speech acts* or *indirect illocutionary acts*.[60] For example, a case can be made that an indirect speech act such as *Can you turn down the radiator?*, which is literally a question but conventionally used as an implicit request, can be accounted for in terms of metonymic inferencing. The concept of metonymy as an inferential figure of thought and language is introduced in Chapter 8.

---

60. These two terms are used synonymously in this book.

CHAPTER 7

Metaphor

A figure of iconic and analogical reasoning

1. Introduction

In Chapters 3–5, various kinds of inferential mechanisms, i.e. entailment, presupposition, and implicature, were presented and their properties illustrated with examples. In this chapter, a figure of thought and language is introduced, i.e. metaphor, whose nature has been discussed since antiquity, most famously by the Greek philosopher Aristotle (384–322 BCE) in his works *Poetics* and *Rhetoric*.

Traditionally, metaphor is regarded as an implicit comparison (see Lausberg 1990: 78) that, at least in cases that have the structure *X is Y*, can be made explicit (into a *simile*) by adding the preposition *like* between the two units *X* and *Y*, as exemplified in (1) and (2), respectively:

(1) Achilles is a lion.

(2) Achilles is like a lion.

Furthermore, in traditional rhetoric, metaphor is usually regarded as a *trope*, i.e. a figure of speech that is used to render discourse more effective and to embellish prose and poetry.

This chapter starts with a brief summary and critique of contemporary theories of metaphor (Section 2), especially some approaches put forward by philosophers of language. Section 3 introduces the conception of metaphor in cognitive linguistics, in particular the one developed by the George Lakoff and Mark Johnson, which is adopted (with some additonal theoretical ingredients) in this book. There is agreement in cognitive linguistics that metaphors are not just ways of speaking (*façons de parler*), of embellishment and of rendering discourse rhetorically more effective, but that they reflect ways of *thinking*. Although this idea is generally presented in the cognitive linguistics literature as having originated in the early 1980s, it is, as has been shown in various publications by Olaf Jäkel, much older (for more details, see Section 3.1). In Section 4, the inferential properties of metaphor are considered in more detail. Section 5, by way of one example, briefly makes a case for metaphor as a linguistic device that can shape thinking. Section 6 concludes the chapter with a short summary and paves the way for the treatment of another central figure of language and thought in Chapter 8, i.e. metonymy.

2. Some contemporary approaches to metaphor

In contemporary metaphor theory, it is generally assumed that a metaphor has two senses: a literal meaning and a distinct figurative one, which is derived from the literal sense via various cognitive mechanisms, such as implicature (Gricean pragmatics) or conceptual mappings (cognitive linguistics).

Davidson (1978: 32) attributes the view that metaphors have two meanings to literary critics like I. A. Richards, philosophers "from Aristotle to Max Black", psychologists such as Freud and Skinner, and "linguists from Plato [sic] to Uriel Weinreich and Lakoff." Davidson challenges this approach to metaphor, claiming that metaphorical meaning does not exist: the words in a metaphorical expression have their ordinary literal meaning – and there is no additional figurative sense. For Davidson (1978: 31), metaphor is "the dreamwork of language", a matter of language *use*. More precisely, according to this author (ibid.: 33), metaphor is "the imaginative employment of words and sentences and depends entirely on the ordinary meaning of these words and hence on the ordinary meanings of the sentences they comprise."

From a cognitive linguistic and pragmatic vantage point (see e.g. Chapter 1; in particular, Langacker 2013), Donaldson's denial of the reality of metaphorical meanings and his binary distinction between meaning (the domain of truth-conditional semantics) and use (pragmatics) is highly problematic. There is evidence that metaphors range from more or less *entrenched* or *conventional* to *novel* poetic or other creative instantiations. A well-known instance of a completely conventional metaphor is the conceptualization of TIME in terms of SPACE. For example, the adjective *long*, whose literal meaning is spatial ('measuring a great distance'), also has a conventional metaphorical sense 'lasting a great amount of time'. Hence, in English, and equivalently in other languages, one finds non-metaphorical spatial uses of *long* such as *a **long** line in front of the departure gate*, in contrast to metaphorical meanings of *long* in the phrase *a **long** career in the diplomatic service*. Another example of an entrenched metaphor, which is discussed in more detail below, is the conceptualization of human LIFE as a JOURNEY, as e.g. in the noun phrase *her intellectual journey towards cognitive linguistics*, where *intellectual journey* is immediately understood in the sense of 'intellectual development'.

In contrast to Davidson, Grice (1975) (see Chapter 4) maintains that metaphor *does* involve two meanings. In his view, a metaphorical utterance like (3) flouts the first maxim of quality "Do not say what you believe to be false" (ibid.: 46).

(3) You are the cream in my coffee. (Grice 1975: 53)

Grice claims that the assertion in (3) is literally "a categorial falsity" (ibid.: 53), but, given the presumption that the speaker is rational and cooperative, a coherent interpretation such as 'You are my pride and joy' (Grice's paraphrase) can be inferentially derived via conversational implicature.

Searle (1979: 77), whose conception of metaphor is not essentially different from the Gricean model, distinguishes between what he calls "*word, or sentence, meaning*" from "*speaker's utterance meaning.*" He claims that "[m]etaphorical meaning is always speaker's utterance meaning" (ibid.: 77). In a simple metaphorical utterance, the speaker says *S is P* but metaphorically means 'S is R', where *P* and 'R' are different in meaning (ibid.: 115). As an example of how Searle analyzes metaphor, consider (4):

(4) Sam is a giant. (Searle 1979: 107)

The lexical meaning of *giant* is 'an imaginary being of human form but superhuman size' (NOAD). If Sam is a human being (i.e. not a mythical or fairy tale character), then the grammatical subject *Sam* and the predicate *is a giant* are not semantically compatible. One possible solution to overcome this semantic anomaly is to interpret (4) as meaning as 'Sam is big' (Searle 1979: 107) or 'Sam is an abnormally large person', etc. Of course, this metaphorical sense is neither novel nor poetic, but highly conventionalized.[61]

The problem with Davidson's, Grice's, and Searle's approaches is that, more or less explicitly, these authors appear to regard metaphor as a kind of deviant language use. Of course, especially poetic metaphors can be somewhat unusual, novel, and creative, but in ordinary language conventional metaphors abound of which speakers are hardly aware and which they certainly do not feel to be deviant. Moreover, the above-mentioned scholars consider literal meaning as the basis of imaginative language use (Davidson) or implicated or pragmatically derived figurative meaning (Grice and Searle). From a psycholinguistic perspective, these accounts suggest that literal meaning is processed by language users *before* an imaginative or implicated metaphorical sense is derived from the literal meaning of the metaphorical expression. But as argued in Section 3, this assumption is problematic.

The Gricean approach to metaphor has also been criticized by pragmaticists working in the framework of Relevance Theory (see Chapter 4, Section 4). According to Carston (2012: 478), "metaphorically used words and phrases are cases of pragmatic broadening of the linguistically encoded concepts [...]." Carston rejects Grice's conception, which relies on the intentional and recognizable violation

---

61. In certain contexts, utterance (4) could also be interpreted as meaning metaphorically that Sam is 'a person of exceptional talent of qualities' (NOAD), another conventionalized metaphor.

of the maxim of truthfulness. She proposes that metaphors involve cognitive mechanisms of pragmatic enrichment, i.e. *explicature*, of what is lexically coded. For example, according to Carston (2012: 479), the metaphorical interpretation of an utterance like *Sally is a chameleon* is based on the "lexically encoded concept" of the *chameleon* as a species of lizard. The discourse context and "the addressee's search for an optimally relevant interpretation of the utterance" (ibid.: 479) are crucial in the derivation of the metaphorical sense of *chameleon* as a human being with a specific character and behavioral traits. The lizard is known for its 'highly developed ability to change [skin] color' (NOAD), and this ability is likened to that of 'a person who changes their opinions or behavior according to the situation' (NOAD). Furthermore, Carston points out that this metaphorical explicature, depending on the context, "gives strongly inferential warrant" to implicatures such as 'Sally changes her stated views to mesh with whoever she talking to' and 'she is unreliable, fickle, untrustworthy' (ibid.: 479). According to Relevance Theory, broadening (or, alternatively, loosening) is not only a feature of metaphor, but it holds for other pieces of figurative language, such as hyperbole, as well.

As mentioned above, Gricean and Searlean approaches to metaphor suggest that language users process metaphorical meaning on the basis of, i.e. *after*, literal word and/or sentence meaning. There is however experimental evidence presented by e.g. Giora (2002) that this assumption is incorrect. Giora postulates a *Graded Salience Hypothesis*, which predicts that salient meanings, i.e. conventional, highly frequent, and prototypical meanings, are accessed before non-salient or less salient meanings, which may be retained and reactivated at later stages if required by context. The Graded Salience Hypothesis predicts that unfamiliar metaphors are indeed interpreted via their literal meaning before their figurative meaning is inferentially derived. However, highly conventionalized metaphors are often more salient than their literal counterparts; and, consequently, in such cases, figurative meaning is mentally accessed straight away, i.e. not via the detour of literal meaning. Giora's model is supported by research reported in Ariel (2010: 48), according to which there is neurophysiological evidence that

> the right [brain] hemisphere [...] is involved in interpreting novel metaphors (pragmatically mediated meanings), a slower process than that of interpreting conventional metaphors, where we rely on left-hemisphere brain regions, as befits lexically encoded meanings.

The conventionalization of metaphors thus involves a shift of neuronal activation from the right to the left brain hemisphere (Faust & Mashal 2007; Mashal & Faust 2008; cited in Ariel 2010: 48).

Furthermore, the linguistic and extra-linguistic context plays an important role in the interpretation of figurative meaning. As a simple example, consider the literal and metaphorical meaning of the lexical item *grasp*, both as a verb and as a noun:

(5) The child grasped the bottle. (NOAD)

(6) The child slipped from her grasp. (NOAD)

(7) The child grasped complex ideas at an early age.

(8) These ideas are beyond my grasp.

In (5), the concrete referent of the direct object *the bottle* strongly evokes the concrete meaning of *grasp*, viz. 'seize firmly with one's hands'. In sentence (6), the noun *grasp* also instantiates the idea of a 'firm hold or grip'(NOAD), i.e. physical action. However, regarding (7), the abstract direct object *complex ideas* strongly invites a metaphorical interpretation of *grasp* as a mental process. It is highly implausible that the hearer of (7) would first consider this utterance as "deviant" and then, on the assumption that the Gricean submaxim of truthfulness has been intentionally flouted, draw the inference that (7) is meant as a metaphorical statement. Analogously, utterance (8) would not initially be interpreted as denoting the physical action of grasping but, given that the subject of the sentence is *these ideas*, it would immediately be assigned a metaphorical interpretation.

Another good example of a metaphorical meaning that is more salient than its literal counterpart is the transitive verb *begreifen* in German, which, following the *Oxford German Dictionary* (OGD) can be translated as 'grasp mentally, comprehend, understand'. This metaphorical meaning is the first entry in the OGD and also in the German, while the literal haptic meaning 'feel, touch, grasp' is listed as a secondary sense and characterized as *informal* in the OGD and as *regional* in the *Duden* dictionary. It is therefore plausible to assume that the metaphorical meaning of *begreifen* is accessed by language users as the intended interpretation before the haptic meaning is considered as an interpretive option – all the more so, since in German a verb exists without the transitivizing prefix *be-*, i.e. *greifen* 'take hold of, grasp [...], grab, seize' (OGD), which has a basic haptic sense. Presumably, for many native speakers of German, the literal sense of *begreifen* is not even part of their semantic competence, although, because of the existence of the verb *greifen*, the metaphorically motivated relationship between the concepts GRASP and UNDERSTAND is most likely transparent for these speakers. Interestingly, the distinction between a literal (physical) (*greifen*) and a metaphorical (*begreifen*) reading is reflected morphologically in the absence vs. the presence of the prefix *be-*.

3. Metaphor in cognitive linguistics

3.1 Precursors of conceptual metaphor theory

It has been known since the works of 19th century philologists that many lexical items with abstract meanings originate from words with a concrete sense (see e.g. Sweetser 1990; Geeraerts 2010). For example, the present-day English speech act verb *affirm* 'state emphatically or publicly' (NOAD) entered English via Old French and goes back to Latin *affirmare*, which originally signified 'to make firm' (from *ad-* 'to' and *firmus* 'strong'). A metaphorical root can also be identified for the mental verb *comprehend* 'understand', which was first attested in English during the Middle English period; it goes back to Old French and ultimately to Latin *comprehendere*, which morphologically consists of the prefix *com-* 'together' and the verb *prehendere* 'grasp'. In cognitive science and cognitive linguistics, the historical philological insight that a large part of vocabulary is metaphorically-based has been revived and reformulated as the claim that much of linguistic meaning is *embodied*. In Vyvyan Evans' (2007: 66) formulation, the basic tenet of the embodied cognition hypothesis is that "the human mind and conceptual organisation are a function of the way in which our species-specific bodies interact with the environment we inhabit." The concept of embodied cognition is especially relevant to an adequate understanding of metaphor and metonymy, two basic tropes of thought and language (see also Chapter 2, Section 5.1). Relying on experimental evidence, Raymond Gibbs has shown that the interpretation of metaphorical expressions involves mental simulation of bodily action, which facilitates the understanding of expressions such as *get over something* or *grasp a concept* (see Gibbs 2005, 2006).

The assumption that metaphorical meaning is typically embodied is also propounded by George Lakoff and Mark Johnson (1980) in their book *Metaphors We Live By*, which is generally considered as a milestone in the history of cognitive linguistics. Lakoff and Johnson offer what seems to be a radically new conception of metaphor as not merely a rhetorical or ornamental trope, but as a fundamental figure of thought. For reasons of fairness, it should however be kept in mind, as shown in much detail by Olaf Jäkel (1997, 1999), that there exists a rich philosophical and linguistic tradition of metaphor research, which, in many ways, prefigures central ideas of Lakoff and Johnson's conceptual metaphor theory. In this regard, Jäkel (1999) cites thinkers such as the 18th philosopher Immanuel Kant, and 20th century scholars like Hans Blumenberg and Harald Weinrich.

3.2 Lakoff and Johnson's metaphor theory[62]

Although Lakoff and Johnson have not acknowledged the above-mentioned contributions to metaphor theory, there is no doubt that they have contributed new and important insights into the nature of metaphor – not least because they discuss a myriad of new English-language examples in their book, providing fresh evidence that metaphor is pervasive in ordinary language.[63] Furthermore, they make a strong case against the view that metaphor is solely an ornamental figure of style, emphasizing that there are good reasons to assume that thought can be influenced by conceptual metaphor. Last but not least, they also demonstrate that metaphors are organized in complex systems that underlie much of the semantics of natural languages.

Lakoff and Johnson (1999), following Grady (1997), distinguish between *primary* and *complex* metaphors. Primary metaphors are directly related to experience, often bodily experience, and, according to Lakoff and Johnson (1999: 50), they constitute basic conceptual correlations that form the building blocks of complex metaphors. In what follows, instead of the usual notation x_{TARGET} IS y_{SOURCE} for metaphors, which names the target x of the metaphor first and then the source y that conceptually structures it, the reverse order is used here: the double-lined arrow $x_{SOURCE} \Rightarrow y_{TARGET}$ symbolizes the metaphorical relation between the source x and target y (the arrow head always points to the target meaning).[64]

Primary metaphors postulated by Lakoff and Johnson include the following:[65]

(9) CLOSENESS ⇒ INTIMACY

(10) DESTINATIONS ⇒ PURPOSES

(11) WARMTH ⇒ AFFECTION

For example, (9) is to be interpreted as meaning 'emotional intimacy (target meaning) and is conceptualized in terms of spatial closeness (source meaning)'. Lakoff (2008: 27) describes the experiential basis of the primary metaphor (9) as follows: "The people you are most intimate with are typically the people you have spent time physically close to: your family, lover, and so on."

---

62. Part of this section is based on Panther and Thornburg (2017b).

63. It should be noted, however, that Lakoff and Johnson often do not provide sources (e.g. from corpora) for their examples.

64. The present author prefers this notational practice because in his experience the notation x_{TARGET} IS y_{SOURCE} relatively frequently leads to unintentional errors.

65. In the following examples, the subscripts SOURCE and TARGET are omitted.

Thus in English, expressions such as (12) and (13) are common:

(12) Those two women are such close friends. (COCA 2017)

(13) That was the beginning of their even deeper closeness. (COCA 2016)

The primary metaphor DESTINATIONS ⇒ PURPOSES is exemplified by expressions such as (14) and (15):

(14) Her goal is to open her own store and to sell her products in Macy's. (COCA 2014)

(15) I really believed we were on our way getting married. (COCA 2017)

The underlying image schema in sentences such as (14) and (15) is a path on which people move towards a destination, and it is this image that is metaphorically likened to the pursuit of purposes in life.

Finally, here are two examples of the primary metaphor that correlates WARMTH with AFFECTION:

(16) She had [...] a very, sweet, warm, caring personality. (COCA 2017)

(17) I thrive on personal relationships, *warm* ones if possible. (COCA 2017)

In Lakoff's metaphor theory primary metaphors are the elementary building blocks of *complex metaphors,* which are the focus of the present chapter.[66] The conceptual organization of complex metaphors is diagrammed in Figure 1.

A metaphorical expression occurs in a certain extralinguistic situation and a (linguistic) context. In this book, the metaphorical word or expression is called the *linguistic vehicle,* which conveys a conventional ("literal") meaning, called the *source* meaning. This meaning is represented by means of a *conceptual frame,* a knowledge structure consisting of meaning components that entertain various conceptual and encyclopedic relations with one another (see Ziem 2014 for further reference and for an in-depth introduction to and discussion of frame semantics). The conceptual components of the source frame $X_1, X_2, \ldots X_n$ are mapped onto, or correspond to, the components $Y_1, Y_2, \ldots Y_n$ of a distinct conceptual frame, the *target* frame. The target frame is ideally homomorphic to the source frame, i.e., it is a kind of analogical replica of the relational structure of the source frame. The overall relationship between source and target is thus one of *structural resemblance* and, in this sense,

---

[66]. In Chapter 9, I argue that "primary metaphors" are better regarded as metonymies, i.e. indexical relations (see Chapter 3 for the semiotic notion of index).

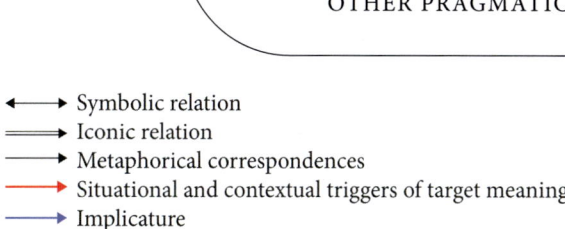

→ Symbolic relation
⇒ Iconic relation
→ Metaphorical correspondences
→ Situational and contextual triggers of target meaning
→ Implicature

Figure 1. Conceptual-pragmatic structure of metaphor

it can also be called *iconic*.[67] Finally, as we have already seen in connection with the example discussed by Carston (2012: 479) (see Section 1), repeated here as (18), metaphors may give rise to additional pragmatic effects, i.e. implicatures:

(18) Mary is a chameleon.

A simplified representation of the metaphorical sense of (18), in which only two mappings are represented, is diagrammed in Figure 2.

---

67. The American philosopher Charles Sanders Peirce regarded metaphor as a kind of icon (*hypoicon*) (see Bergman & Paavola 2014).

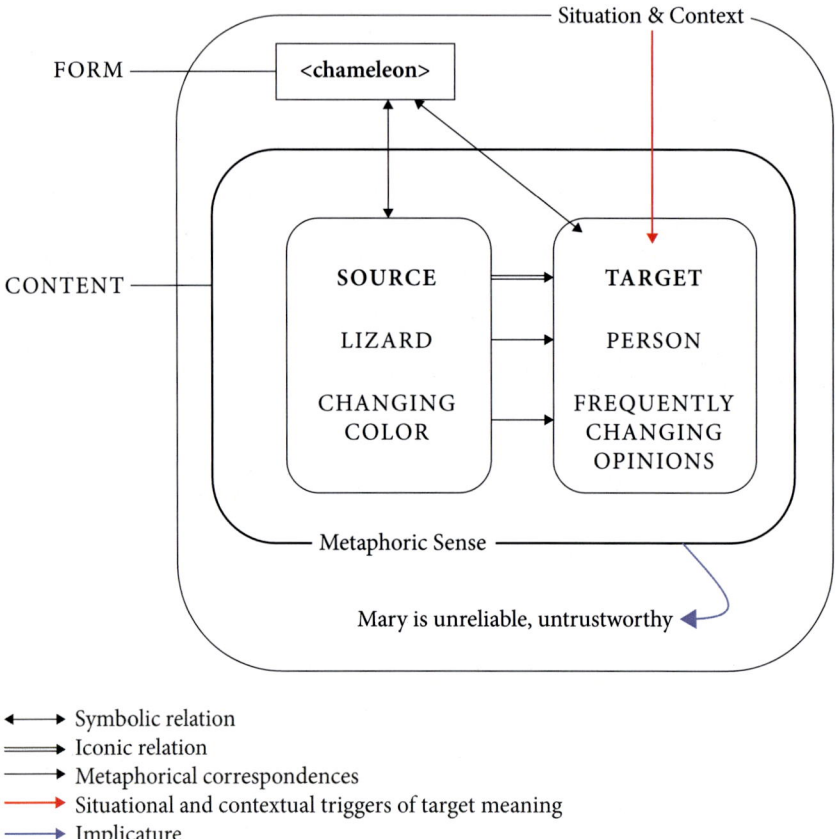

Symbolic relation
Iconic relation
Metaphorical correspondences
Situational and contextual triggers of target meaning
Implicature

Figure 2. The metaphor CHAMELEON ⇒ PERSON (adapted from Carston 2012: 479)

The implicature that Mary is an unreliable and untrustworthy person is triggered by the metaphorical target sense that Mary tends to change her opinions opportunistically, depending on what serves her own advancement best.

A famous and often cited poetic metaphor is found in the monologue performed by Jaques in William Shakespeare's comedy *As You Like It*, Act II, Scene VII:

(19) All the world's a stage,
And all the men and women merely players;
They have their exits and their entrances,
And one man in his time plays many parts,
His acts being seven ages. […]

The metaphorical structure of (19) is represented, again in a simplified way, in Figure 3.

The first line in (19) expresses the overarching metaphor STAGE ⇒ WORLD (printed in bold in Figure 3), which is elaborated in more detail in the subsequent

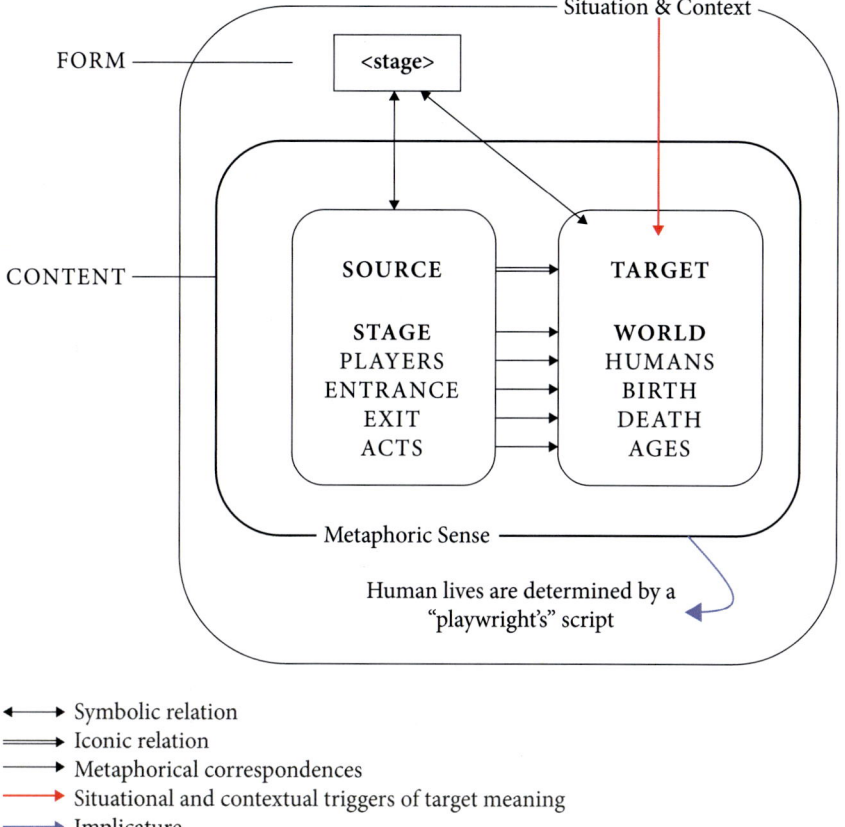

Figure 3. The Shakespearean metaphor STAGE ⇒ WORLD
(adapted from Panther and Thornburg 2017b: 277)

lines by means of concepts (in normal print in Figure 3) that are components of the STAGE frame. In terms of traditional rhetoric, Shakespeare's STAGE metaphor is a (short) *allegory*, i.e., the metaphorical theme introduced in the first line is sustained throughout the subsequent lines (cf. Lausberg 1990: 139). In addition to the metaphorical mappings, there are various implicatures that might be conveyed by Jaques' melancholy monologue. By way of example, one of them is given in Figure 3: It is the message that humans are completely controlled in their actions by extraneous forces, i.e. by a "playwright" who determines what happens to the characters of the play (comedy or tragedy). Another implicature triggered by the STAGE ⇒ WORLD metaphor might be that people assume roles (like actors) that do not necessarily reflect their real nature (essence), i.e., they pretend to be what they are not in reality. The list of such pragmatic effects, i.e. implicatures, derivable from the metaphorical mappings in Figure 3 is open-ended.

The following metaphorical lines, which are extracted from Robert W. Service's (2008) *Quatrains*, paint an even more somber picture of human life:[68]

(20)   Blind fools of fate and slaves of circumstance,
Life is a fiddler, and we all must dance.
(https://www.poemhunter.com/poem/quatrains)

The lines in (20) contain several metaphorical expressions: (i) *blind fools of fate*, (ii) *slaves of circumstance*, and (iii) *Life is a fiddler*. Let us focus on the third metaphor, i.e. FIDDLER ⇒ LIFE. In the context of the poem, it conceptualizes the life of humans as being controlled by some external power that determines people's behavior and actions. These verses could be interpreted, among other things, as implicating that free will is an illusion (see Figure 4).

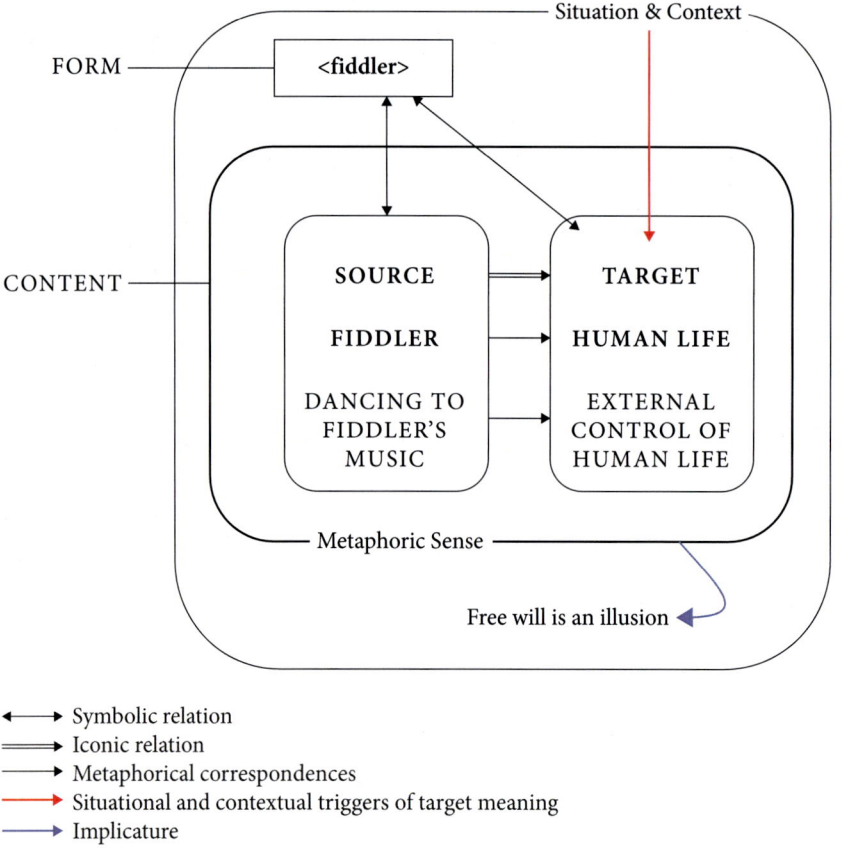

Figure 4. The metaphor FIDDLER ⇒ LIFE

---

68. Robert W. Service (1874–1958) was a British-born Canadian poet.

In this connection, it is worth mentioning that *fiddler*, at least in British English, in addition to its sense 'a person who plays the violin, especially one who plays folk music', is also used to refer to 'a person who cheats or swindles, especially one indulging in petty theft' (NOAD). In other words, given that the fiddler, i.e. the agent who influences or even controls the dancers, is a swindler, by metaphorical analogy, the inference is invited that the lives of humans may also be shaped by morally reprehensible forces. Finally note the existence of the idiomatic expression *to dance to someone's tune* (NOAD, s.v. *dance*), with the metaphorical meaning 'comply completely with someone's demands and wishes', which supports the interpretation proposed in Figure 4.

4. The role of inferencing in Lakoff and Johnson's conception of metaphor

In this section, additional theoretically relevant aspects of Lakoff and Johnson's conception of metaphor are discussed. In particular, I argue that, apart from relating components of a source frame in a one-to-one fashion to the components of a distinct target frame, an adequate theory of metaphor has to take the internal *inferential* organization of source and target frames into account. The inferential relations that are relevant in this respect have already been introduced in Chapters 3, 4, and 5: entailment, presupposition, and implicature.

4.1 Metaphorical entailments

Let us start with a clarification of the use of the term 'entailment' in Lakoff and Johnson's metaphor theory and the use of this notion in the present book. To see how Lakoff and Johnson understand the term it is helpful to have a closer look at a metaphor that these authors have analyzed in some depth, i.e. the conceptualization of human life as a journey. Lakoff and Johnson (1999: 60–62) suggest that JOURNEY ⇒ LIFE is a *complex* metaphor based on a *cultural model* that they formulate as follows: "People are supposed to have purposes in life, and they are supposed to act so as to achieve those purposes" (Lakoff & Johnson 1999: 61).

In Lakoff and Turner (1989: 3–4), what these authors call "metaphorical entailments" of this metaphor are elaborated in more detail, as in (21)–(29).[69]

(21) The person leading a life is a traveler.
(22) His purposes are destinations.

---

[69] The metaphorical correspondences in (21) are formulated, as usual in Lakoff and Johnson's work, as X IS Y, where X refers to the target and Y to the source.

(23) The means for achieving purposes are routes.
(24) Difficulties in life are impediments to travel.
(25) Counselors are guides.
(26) Progress is the distance traveled.
(27) Things you gauge your progress by are landmarks.
(28) Choices in life are crossroads.
(29) Material resources and talents are provisions.

Some of the mappings (21)–(29) that are operative in the complex metaphor JOURNEY ⇒ LIFE, are represented in Figure 5:

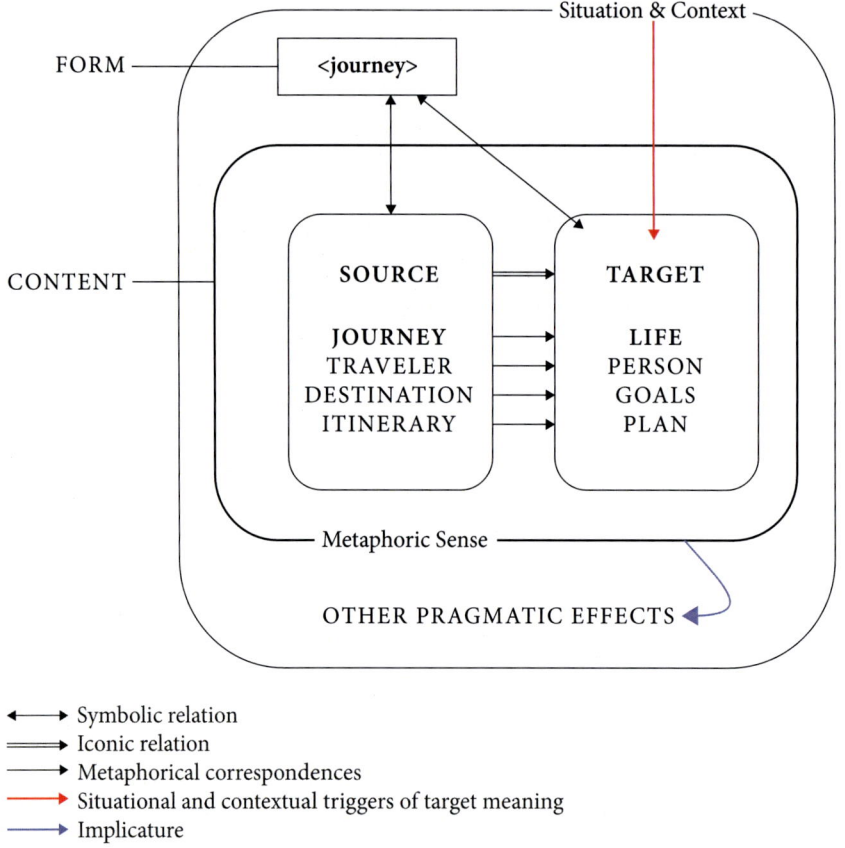

Figure 5. Some mappings of the metaphor JOURNEY ⇒ LIFE

The label *metaphorical entailments* is firmly established in cognitive linguistics, but it has to be emphasized that its use is problematic and should, in the present author's view, be avoided. Although submetaphors (21)–(29) can be *inferred* from the superordinate metaphor JOURNEY ⇒ LIFE, many of these inferences are *not* (semantic) *entailments*, i.e., they do not follow by necessity from the target concept LIFE or from the metaphorical source JOURNEY. For example, difficulties in life occur, but they are not necessarily components of, i.e. entailed by, the concept of life itself. In general, the submetaphors listed in (21)–(29) appear to be based on *world knowledge*, also called *encyclopedic knowledge*, about trips or journeys – in other words, by the JOURNEY frame.[70] When people travel by car, they will mostly likely, but not necessarily, encounter crossroads; but the same does not apply to train or air travel. Thus, the term 'metaphorical entailments' in the sense that it is used by Lakoff and Turner should be carefully distinguished from the notion of semantic entailment introduced and exemplified in Chapter 3.

4.2 The Invariance Principle

We have seen that metaphor is a mode of *reasoning* that relates two conceptual frames, a source frame and a target frame, where the former imposes its conceptual structure on the latter. The relationship between the source and the target is one of *structural resemblance*, i.e., the target frame is conceptually organized in the same way as the source frame. As noted above, in semiotic terms, the relationship between the source frame and the target frame is a special case of *iconicity* (cf. Chapter 2 for iconic signs).

Structural resemblance between source and target domain is, as we have seen, at the heart of Lakoff and Johnson's account of metaphor. Lakoff (1993: 215) proposes that metaphor is governed by what he calls the *Invariance Principle*, which stipulates that

> [m]etaphorical mappings preserve the cognitive topology (that is, the image-schematic structure) of the source domain, in a way consistent with the inherent structure of the target domain.

The Invariance Principle imposes constraints on fixed correspondences between the source and target domains of metaphors. According to Lakoff (1993: 215), a corollary of the Invariance Principle is that "the image-schematic structure inherent in the target domain cannot be violated […]." As already mentioned in Section 3.2,

---

70. Lakoff (1987: Chapter 4) uses the term *Idealized Cognitive Model* (ICM), which is roughly equivalent to the notion of conceptual frame used in this book.

image schemas are "schematic versions of images" (Croft & Cruse 2004: 44), which are based on perceptual schemas such as containers, forces, paths, etc., which play a crucial role in the construction of (embodied) meanings.

Lakoff contends that image schemas are frequently used as the source domain of abstract thought. To illustrate, Lakoff (1993: 214) postulates a metaphor PATH ⇒ LINEAR SCALES, which is at work in statements like the following (italics added):[71]

(30) What happened? No, actually I'm *way beyond* angry. I'm supremely pissed.
 (TV 2015)

(31) She [the Queen] was *far* more intelligent than the King, she had a *far* wider range of interests. (TV 2012)

According to Lakoff (1993: 214), the metaphor PATH ⇒ LINEAR SCALES "maps the starting point of path onto the bottom of the scale and maps distance traveled onto quantity in general." In (30), the first person narrator has traveled a considerable distance (*way beyond*) on some path, and the traveler's distant location from the beginning of the path is mapped onto a high value on an emotive scale of irritation, i.e., the narrator is *extremely* angry (see Figure 6).

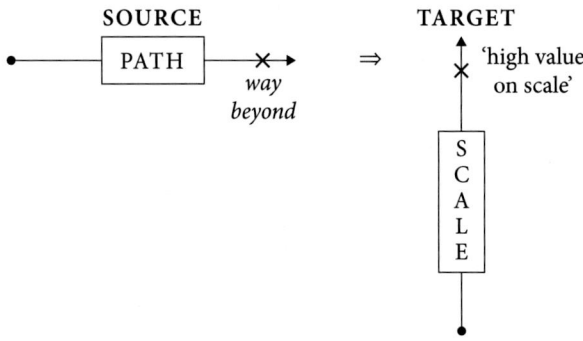

• BEGINNING OF PATH ⇒ LOWEST VALUE ON SCALE
✗ POINT REACHED ON PATH ⇒ VALUE ON SCALE

Figure 6. Metaphorical mapping of PATH topology onto SCALE topology: *way beyond* (adapted from Lakoff 1993: 2014)

---

71. The examples in (30) and (31) have been retrieved from the *TV Corpus*, which is based on 75,000 "very informal TV shows (e.g. comedies and dramas) from 1950–2018" (overview available at: https://corpus.byu.edu).

In (31), the *Queen* is located in a more advanced position on the path than the *King*; and this spatial configuration is mapped onto a scale of intelligence that ranks the Queen's intelligence "far" higher than the King's (see Figure 7).

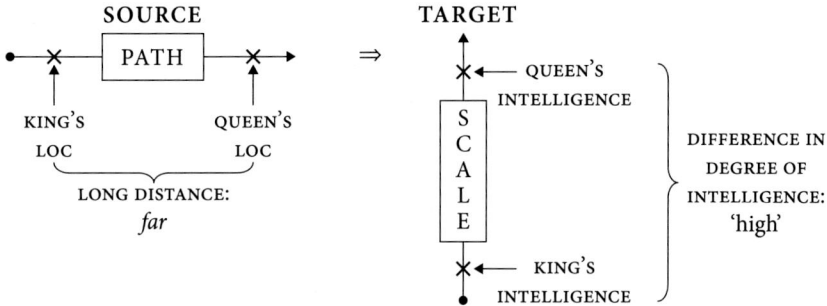

- BEGINNING OF PATH ⇒ LOWEST VALUE ON SCALE
- × POINT REACHED ON PATH ⇒ VALUE ON SCALE

Figure 7. Metaphorical mapping of PATH topology onto SCALE topology: *far more* (adapted from Lakoff 1993: 2014)

As Figures 6 and 7 show, the topological structure of the source domain is preserved in the target domain of the respective metaphors. Furthermore, via *analogical* reasoning, the conceptual structure of the target can be inferred from the conceptual structure of the source. As examples (30) and (31) show, the distance of some person's location from the beginning of a path corresponds to the degree of anger and of intelligence of that person, respectively.

4.3 Inferential structure of source and target domain

The Invariance Principle stipulates that the image-schematic (topological) structure of the source frame is preserved in the target frame, with the exception of image-schematic properties of the target frame that are not compatible with the source frame. In this section, the intriguing question is addressed: To what extent do metaphorical mappings preserve the *inferential* structure of the source frame in the target frame? Let us illustrate and try to answer this question by a closer look at the *ditransitive construction* as exemplified in (32) and (33):

(32) Mary gave Fred a red rose.

(33) Mary gave Fred a smile.

In sentence (32), *give* is used literally, i.e., it denotes the transfer of a THING (*a red rose*) from an AGENT (*Mary*) to a RECIPIENT or BENEFICIARY (*Fred*). In contrast, in sentence (33), the transfer is figurative, i.e. an instance of the conceptual metaphor ACTIONS ARE TRANSFERS (Lakoff 1993: 216), which Kövecses (2010: 130) reformulates as CAUSATION IS TRANSFER (OF AN OBJECT), i.e. in the notation used in this book, TRANSFER (of an OBJECT) ⇒ CAUSATION (of an ACTION). Here are a few more examples of this metaphor with the nouns *smile*, *kiss*, and *hug*, which denote actions performed by the subject referent. Notice the entailments associated with sentences such as (34)–(36):

(34) He gave Hannah a kiss. (TV 2012) ⊩ He kissed Hannah.

(35) He gave us a hug. (TV 2012) ⊩ He hugged us.

(36) She gave Molly a smile. (COCA 2004) ⊩ She smiled at Molly.

In what follows, further interesting inferential properties of literal transfers, in contrast to metaphorical ones, are considered and tabulated. In Table 1, the act of transferring a red rose (literal transfer), i.e. of a concrete object, as in (32), and the metaphorical transfer of a smile, i.e. of an action, such as in (33), are compared in terms of their respective presuppositions (preconditions) and entailed results of the transfer.

Table 1. Contrasting literal and metaphorical transfer I

SBJ GIVE OBJ₁ OBJ₂	Transfer of a THING	Transfer of an ACTION
Presupposition	~> Mary had a red rose	*~> Mary had a smile
	⋮	⋮
Ditransitive sentence	*Mary gave Fred a red rose*	*Mary gave Fred a smile*
Entailment	⊩ Fred had a red rose	*⊩ Fred had a smile

~> = presupposition; ⊩ = entailment; * = non-valid inferences; SBJ = subject; OBJ₁ = indirect object; OBJ₂ = direct object

Table 1 shows that, although it is possible for a human possessor to have a red rose and give it to another person with the result that the latter is in possession of this flower (see (32)), it is impossible to "have a smile" and transfer it like an object to a recipient with the result that the latter "has" it. It is however possible to use *have* as a *light* verb to express the *act* of smiling itself, see (37), and this act can be directed towards and have an effect on other interactants, as in (38)–(40):[72]

(37) She always had a smile on her face. (COCA 2017)

(38) She had a smile that could have melted the world […]. (COCA 2010)

---

72. Instances of light verbs are *have* in constructions such as *They had a swim*, or *make* in *They made a sign*, in which the meaning of the verb "is so unspecific that it needs a COMPLEMENT in order to function effectively as a PREDICATE " (Crystal 2008: 281).

(39) He had a smile that could melt any girl's heart. (COCA 2014)

(40) She always had a smile for kids [...]. (COCA 2017)

The verbal expression *had a smile* in examples (37)–(40) is construed as a permanent characteristic of a person, a symptom of the subject's inherent friendliness. However, a person does not *possess* a smile that she can then *give* to others, in the same sense that she can possess a box of Belgian truffles and give them as a present to another person. Hence, the examples in (37)–(40) are compatible with the analysis of *give somebody a smile* proposed in Table 1, which stipulates that (33) does not presuppose that Mary "had" a smile.

In conclusion, the metaphorical use of *give* as in (33) is not strictly analogous to its literal use in (32). The source and the target frames of the literal use and the metaphorical use are coded ditransitively as *SBJ give OBJ$_1$ OBJ$_2$*, but they differ in their respective inferential properties. Before returning to these differences, let us briefly consider an additional example that involves a metaphorical use of the ditransitive construction with *give*:

(41) Mary *gave* Fred a headache.

Example (41) expresses the metaphorical transfer of an experience of pain.[73] In Table 2 this metaphorical transfer scenario is again compared with the inferential properties of the non-figurative example (32).

Table 2. Contrasting literal and metaphorical transfer II

SBJ GIVE OBJ$_1$OBJ$_2$	Transfer of a THING	Transfer of a FEELING
Presupposition	~> Mary had a red rose	*~> Mary had a headache
	⋮	⋮
Ditransitive sentence	*Mary gave Fred a red rose*	*Mary gave Fred a headache*
Entailment	⊩ Fred had a red rose	⊩ Fred had a headache

~> = presupposition; ⊩ = entailment; * = non-valid inferences; SBJ = subject; OBJ$_1$ = indirect object; OBJ$_2$ = direct object

The first thing to notice is that, in contrast to (32), in example (41) the presupposition that the human CAUSER of the headache, i.e. *Mary*, "had" a headache does not hold. Notice that the crucial point argued here is that (41) does not mean that Mary transfers her own headache to Fred. This finding corresponds to the non-validity of the presupposition that Mary "had a smile" in (33). Furthermore, it is important to note that Mary, the cause(r) of the headache, is not necessarily acting with the

---

73. Note that, apart from its meaning of physical pain, *headache* can also be used metaphorically to convey the sense 'emotional distress, anxiety'.

intention of causing Fred to have a headache. Quite possibly, she causes Fred to have a headache inadvertently.[74] Differently from (32), sentence (41) entails that the experiencer, i.e. Fred, ends up having a headache, which is analogous to the entailment of sentence (32) that, as a result of Mary's action of giving him a rose, Fred has this flower.

As the metaphorical uses of *give* in (33) and (41) have shown, the inherent conceptual structure of the target frame, here its inferential properties, are not necessarily the same. Notwithstanding, I want to argue that, although the conceptual structure of metaphorical transfers coded by the ditransitive verb *give* does not result in "perfect" correspondences between the source and the target, it is possible to identify such correspondences between source and target on a more abstract conceptual level. These correspondences are fleshed out in Table 3 for THING transfers like *give s.o. a red rose/book/present* and ACTION transfers such as *give s.o. a smile/kiss/kick*; and in Table 4 for THING transfers, in contrast to FEELING transfers in expressions like *give s.o. a headache* (for a similar analytical approach, see Panther 1997).

Table 3. Ditransitive construction with *give*: THING transfer vs. ACTION transfer

SBJ GIVE OBJ$_1$OBJ$_2$	SOURCE: Transfer of a THING	⇒	TARGET: Transfer of an ACTION
Presupposition	~> X$_{POSS}$ has Z$_{THING}$	⇒	~> X has ability to do Z$_{ACT}$
Ditransitive construction meaning	X$_{AG}$ causes Y$_{REC}$ to have Z$_{THING}$	⇒	X$_{AG}$ causes Y$_{EXP}$ to experience Z$_{ACT}$
Entailment	⊩ Y$_{POSS}$ has Z$_{THING}$	⇒	+> Y$_{EXP}$ is affected by Z$_{ACT}$

~> = presupposition; ⊩ = entailment; +> = implicated result; SBJ = subject; OBJ$_1$ = indirect object; OBJ$_2$ = direct object; ACT = action; AG = agent; EXP = experiencer; POSS = possessor; REC = recipient; THING = concrete object; ⇒ = metaphorical mapping

The first row of Table 3, the presupposition, links 'having an object' metaphorically to 'having the ability to perform an action'. Having a THING means having control over it: the POSSESSOR can manipulate the thing in various ways, including giving it to somebody. As to the ability to perform an action, it also involves the notion of control. Having the ability to carry out a certain action normally implicates that the agent is in control of that action.

---

74. In other words, in (41), Mary, the person, *metonymically* stands for Mary's character or behavior (for metonymy, see Chapter 8). Notice also that Fred's headache might be not an instance of physical pain in the head, but could be (metaphorically) understood as an emotion such as 'worry, anxiety' caused by Mary's behavior.

The second row notates the source meaning of the ditransitive construction (literal sense), i.e. a human agent causing a concrete thing to be transferred to a recipient (source meaning). The corresponding metaphorical target sense specifies that an agent produces some experiential effect on the referent of the indirect object (mentally or physically) by means of an action, such as smiling, kicking, kissing, etc.

In the third row of Table 3, the result of the transfer of a concrete object is that the recipient has the object in question. This result is entailed in the case of a THING transfer. However, in the case of a metaphorical ACTION transfer, the result is not entailed, but it is merely expected that the action will have some impact on the experiencer. In other words, there is a (cancelable) implicature that the experiencer is affected in some (unspecified) way by the action in question. Thus, in the case of Mary giving Fred a smile, Fred might be emotionally touched, e.g. pleasantly surprised by Mary's smile.

Let us now reconsider the conceptual structure of sentences of type (41) and idioms such as *give s.o. the creeps, chills, pain* that convey bodily experiences and feelings. The overall organization of such ditransitives is summarized in Table 4.

Table 4. Ditransitive construction with *give*: THING transfer vs. FEELING transfer

SBJ GIVE OBJ$_1$OBJ$_2$	SOURCE: Transfer of a THING	⇒	TARGET: Transfer of a FEELING
Presupposition	~> X$_{POSS}$ has Z$_{THING}$ ⇒		~> X has certain character traits / behavioral dispositions
	⋮		⋮
Ditransitive construction meaning	X$_{AG}$ causes Y$_{REC}$ to have Z$_{THING}$	⇒	X's character/behavior causes Y$_{EXP}$ to experience Z$_{FEEL}$
	⋮		⋮
Entailment	⊩ Y$_{POSS}$ has Z$_{THING}$ ⇒		⊩ Y$_{EXP}$ experiences Z$_{FEEL}$

~> = presupposition; ⊩ = entailed result; SBJ = subject; OBJ$_1$ = indirect object; OBJ$_2$ = direct object; ACT = action; AG = agent; EXP = experiencer; FEEL = feeling/emotion; POSS = possessor; REC = recipient, THING = concrete thing

Table 4 is organized along the same lines as Table 3, i.e., it distinguishes between the presupposition (precondition) of an action, the transfer proper, and the result. The metaphorical target sense does not depict *X* as necessarily being an intentional human agent. Rather, it is *X*'s character or behavior that produces a certain feeling *Z*, such as pain, distress, discomfort, etc. in the mind of the experiencer *Y*. And in contrast to some (cancelable) *implicated* result of the ACTION transfer (Table 3), in the case of FEELING transfers, the result of the agent's action is *entailed*, i.e., *Y* actually experiences the feeling caused by the agent's character or behavior.

Notice also in this connection that the subject referent of the expression *give somebody a headache* does not have to be human or animate but can be inanimate and even denote an event:

(42) The thought gave him a headache. (COCA 2010)

(43) The lights gave him a headache. (COCA 2009)

(44) Reading in the sun gave him a headache [...]. (COCA 1995)

In sentences (42)–(44), the subject denotata *the thought, the lights,* and *reading in the sun,* respectively, *have* certain (presupposed) properties that cause the experiencer's headache. The thought mentioned in (42) is probably disagreeable or worrisome, the lights referred to in (43) are too bright or too dim, and the activity of reading in the sun described in (44) causes pain because the sun is blinding the reader.

The gist of the conceptual analysis proposed above is that even though, at first sight, the respective source and target frames in Tables 3 and 4 do not seem to be organized conceptually in the same way, on a more abstract level, analogies between source and target meanings can be detected. As to the presupposition or precondition, the concept HAVE applies to both the POSSESSION of THINGS as well as to the POSSESSION of ABILITIES (Table 3) and BEHAVIORAL DISPOSITIONS (Table 4). Regarding the result of the transfer, in Table 3, there is a structural parallelism between the RECIPIENT'S POSSESSION of a THING transferred (entailed result) and an EXPERIENCER affected by some ACTION (implicated result). In Table 4, the entailed result of the transfer of a THING in the source frame corresponds to the transfer of a FEELING in the target frame.

How do these findings square with the Invariance Principle proposed by Lakoff (see also Kövecses 2010: 130–131)? We have seen that mappings are indeed constrained, i.e., the image schema underlying the act of giving a person a concrete object cannot be mapped onto "giving actions" such as giving someone a smile/kiss/hug. However, with certain adjustments of the inferential mechanisms the overall analogical, i.e. iconic relationship between metaphorical source and target is preserved, albeit not always in a perfect fashion.

5. Metaphor and thought

Metaphor is not merely a *façon de parler* but it may reflect the ways language users think about the world, i.e., metaphors may "frame" people's thinking about moral, social, and political issues (see e.g. Burgers, Konijn & Steen 2016; Lakoff 2016; Musolff 2016; and Wehling 2016 on framing in German politics).

There is experimental evidence for the important role of metaphor as a figure of thought. By way of example, in what follows, the results of one psycholinguistic experiment conducted by cognitive psychologists Paul Thibodeau and Lera Boroditsky (2011) are summarized. Their work supports the Lakoffian claim that metaphor can indeed have an impact on cognition.[75]

In Thibodeau and Boroditsky's experiment, participants, who were divided into two groups, were given a text about the crime rate in a fictitious town named 'Addison'. The first group read a text that systematically conceptualizes crime as a virus whereas the second group received a text that conveyed the same content but metaphorized crime as a wild beast. Here are crucial excerpts from the two texts (Thibodeau & Boroditsky 2011: 3):

Group 1: VIRUS ⇒ CRIME
Crime is a virus infecting the city of Addison. The crime rate in the once peaceful city has steadily increased over the past three years. In fact, these days it seems that crime is plaguing every neighborhood […].

Group 2: WILD BEAST ⇒ CRIME
Crime is a wild beast preying on the city of Addison. The crime rate in the once peaceful city has steadily increased over the past three years. In fact, these days it seems that crime is lurking in every neighborhood […].

After the participants had read their respective texts, they were asked, among other things, the following question: "In your opinion, what does Addison need to do to reduce crime?" Thibodeau and Boroditsky found (ibid.: 4) that "[p]articipants given the crime-as-beast metaphorical framing were more likely to propose enforcement (74%) than participants given the crime-as-virus framing (56%)." In general, Group 1 participants, who were exposed to the metaphor VIRUS ⇒ CRIME, recommended better education, reduction of poverty, and social reform as effective measures to reduce the crime rate, whereas Group 2 participants, who had been subjected to the metaphor WILD BEAST ⇒ CRIME, were in favor of law enforcement, police force, and prison sentences to achieve the same objective.

To conclude, metaphorical framing may have an influence on how people think, and experiments like the one conducted by Thiboudeau and Boroditsky graphically illustrate the dangers of misuse, if not abuse, of metaphorical framing methods by populist politicians and demagogues.

---

75. This section is based on the description of Thibodeau's and Boroditsky's experiment in Panther and Thornburg (2017b: 278). I would like to thank the editors of the journal *Synthesis philosophica* and Linda Thornburg for granting permission to reproduce this text (with slight adaptations).

6. Conclusion

In this chapter, a cognitive linguistic model of metaphor has been introduced and illustrated with various examples from literature and everyday language. It has been shown that metaphor is a central linguistic and cognitive phenomenon, not merely a stylistic and rhetorical device, although it obviously also fulfills the latter functions. I have pointed out some problems that should be addressed in future research, especially in connection with Lakoff's invariance principle. Although the principle works well for many cases such as the metaphorical mappings from components of the PATH schema onto the target concept of SCALES, there are problems concerning the mapping of inferential properties from a source frame into a target frame. These problems have been demonstrated with various uses of *give* in the ditransitive construction. In the following chapter, another figure of thought and language is discussed that, arguably, is as fundamental as metaphor, namely, metonymy.

CHAPTER 8

Metonymy
A figure of indexical and associative reasoning

1. Introduction

In this chapter, a mode of reasoning or inferencing, which is pervasive in natural language and is well-known from traditional rhetoric – i.e. metonymy – is presented, analyzed, and illustrated with examples.[76] Metonymy as a rhetorical trope is defined as follows in the online OED (3rd ed.):

> (A figure of speech characterized by) the action of substituting for a word or phrase denoting an object, action, institution, etc., a word or phrase denoting a property or something associated with it; an instance of this.

In Gricean pragmatics, metonymy – like metaphor – is generally regarded as a kind of conversational implicature (see Chapter 4), or, as Davis (2014) phrases it in the online *Standford Encyclopedia of Philosophy Archive* (Fall 2014 Edition):

> The most widely recognized forms of implicature are the *Figures of speech (tropes)*. Irony, overstatement (hyperbole), understatement (meiosis and litotes), metonymy, synecdoche, and metaphor have been known at least since Aristotle.

In this book, metonymy is considered as a kind of pragmatic *inference* or mode of *reasoning*. Notwithstanding, in one respect, the conception of metonymy in the rhetorical tradition and in Gricean pragmatics differ from that of metonymy in cognitive linguistics (and hence cognitive pragmatics). In the latter framework, metonymy is regarded as both a figure of *speech* and a figure of *thought*. When the focus is on metonymy as a thought process, i.e. a reasoning or inferencing mode, the term *conceptual metonymy* is commonly used.[77] In pragmatic terms, metonymy is part and parcel of the human faculty to draw spontaneous inferences about what

---

76. For recent introductions to the conceptual structure and function of metonymy, see Bierwiaczonek (2013), Ruiz de Mendoza Ibáñez (2014), Barcelona (2015), Littlemore (2015), Denroche (2015), Tóth (2018), and Wachowski (2019).

77. In the same vein, the term *conceptual metaphor*, which evokes metaphor both as a figure of speech and a vehicle of thought, has been used since the publication of Lakoff and Johnson's (1980) pioneering monograph *Metaphors We Live By*.

are relevant interpretations of signs (simple and complex) in a given context and communicative situation.

In Section 2 of this chapter, two literary and various colloquial examples, including commercial messages (see Sobrino Pérez 2017 for the role of metonymy and metaphor in advertsing), are presented that demonstrate the ubiquity of metonymy. In Section 3, the main properties of metonymy are first represented in a diagram (Figure 1) and then further elaborated and illustrated with linguistic examples. In Section 4, it is argued that a large class of metonymic inferences can be described in terms of abductive reasoning (see also Panther & Thornburg 2018). Section 5, which relies on Paradis (2004), discusses the important theoretical problem of how metonymy can be constrained, i.e. be distinguished from other phenomena that involve meaning shifts, such as facetization and zone activation. Section 6 presents some types of metonymy that have effects on the propositional content and/or the illocutionary force of a speech act.

2. Metonymy in literary and ordinary language

2.1 Examples of metonymy in literary language

Let us begin with two examples of metonymy in literature. The first often-quoted example is drawn from William Shakespeare's drama *Julius Caesar* (Act III, Scene 2, 79–80), namely, Antony's speech to the Romans after Caesar has been brutally murdered by Brutus:[78]

(1) Friends, Romans, countrymen, lend me your ears;
    I come to bury Caesar not to praise him.

Lend me you ears in (1) stands for the appeal 'Listen to what I am going to say'. This is a typical example of metonymy whereby an association is established between *ear*, the organ of hearing, and one its major functions, the reception and processing of verbal information.[79]

The second example is from Robert Frost's poem *Out, Out* (1916), which is about a boy who cuts firewood with a buzz saw and severely injures his hand:[80]

---

78. Retrieved from http://shakespeare.mit.edu/julius_caesar/full.html.

79. Note in this connection that the verb *lend* in (1) is used metaphorically. The Romans are not literally expected to lend, i.e. grant Antony permission to "use" their ears temporarily, but they are urged to focus their attention on Antony's subsequent speech.

80. Retrieved from https://www.poetryfoundation.org/poems/53087/out-out.

(2) The boy's first outcry was a rueful laugh,
    As he swung toward them holding up the hand
    Half in appeal, but half as if to keep
    The life from spilling. [...]

The last two lines in (2) refer to the boy's attempt to *keep the life from spilling*, where *life* metonymically evokes 'blood'. There is an obvious (causal) connection between the loss of too much blood and the loss of life, which is metonymically exploited in the poem.

2.2 Examples of metonymy in ordinary language

In British supermarkets one can find egg cartons with the inscription:

(3) 6 British free range eggs.   (e.g. *Tesco* supermarket in Kendal, Cumbria)

The literal meaning of (3) does not make sense: eggs cannot have the property of being 'free range'. This attribute holds for the hens that lay the eggs. In order to obtain a coherent meaning of (3), customers will have to perform a conceptual, i.e. metonymic, "leap" from *free range eggs* to 'eggs laid by free range hens'.

An example which, at first sight, does not look like it involves metonymy is (4):

(4) Rippingille had a reckless reputation in his adopted city of Bristol.
                              (https://books.google.co.uk/books?id=YyoeAQAAIAAJ)

The characterization of Edward Rippingille, a nineteenth century English painter, as having a *reckless reputation*, is a metonymic shorthand for 'reputation of a person who shows reckless behavior'. And indeed metonymies are often (although not always) convenient coding shortcuts for longer expressions, as the following utterance demonstrates as well:

(5) Let me ask you this because you mentioned the middle class, you know, and it was something I remember we had during Clinton.   (COCA 2016)

In (5), on a literal reading, the prepositional phrase *during Clinton* is conceptually incoherent. The temporal preposition *during* requires a subsequent noun or noun phrase that denotes a time period; but the referent of the proper name *Clinton* is not compatible with this collocational constraint. Notwithstanding, the expression makes sense as soon as the denotatum of *Clinton* as a person is metonymically shifted to 'the period of Clinton's presidency'.

Let us consider additional examples illustrating incongruities between meanings as a trigger of a metonymic interpretation that resolves these incongruities. In the popular British television series *Doc Martin*, set in a small coastal village in Cornwall, a recurrent narrative theme is that people (locals or non-villagers) suddenly collapse and Doctor Ellingham (aka Doc Martin) rushes to the scene of the incident to provide life-saving medical assistance. Before leaving his surgery, the doctor produces utterances like the following:

(6) Cancel all my patients for the afternoon. (Season 8, Episode 5)

(7) Will it take long? Because I couldn't cancel all of my patients.
(Season 6, Episode 7)

(8) Shh! Cancel the ambulance. (Season 7, Episode 4)

In one of its meanings, the verb *cancel* requires a direct object that is interpreted as an event. However, in sentences (6) and (7), the direct object literally refers not to an event but to human beings (i.e. patients). There is thus a discrepancy between what is explicitly coded in these utterances and the intended meaning. Patients cannot be "canceled" – only events can, such as the envisaged or planned events of patients coming to the surgery at the appointed times and being examined by the doctor. It is this EVENT reading that is metonymically *coerced*, i.e. enforced, by the verb *cancel*. Similarly, in (8), what is canceled is not the ambulance car, i.e. the motor vehicle, but the planned event involving an ambulance picking up patients in need of urgent medical treatment in a hospital.

Another metonymic shortcut is exemplified by the following message:

(9) The weather sponsored by Qatar Airways …

This commercial appears every day with slight variations on various English-language television channels. What is is sponsored by Qatar Airways is of course not the weather as such, i.e., (9) instantiates a metonymy that links a natural phenomenon, the *weather*, to the 'weather report' or 'weather forecast'.

As a final example, consider an advertisement seen in the window of a hairdresser's shop in Northwestern England, which claims the following:

(10) Great hair doesn't happen by chance, it happens by appointement.

First, notice that in (10) *hair* is intended to mean 'hairdo', i.e., there is already a metonymic shortcut that links *hair* with a fashionable hairstyle (notice the use of the evaluative adjective *great* as a modifier of *hair*). On the basis of this metonymic meaning, a second metonymy is triggered: a hairdo *per se* is an artefact, a THING, and this meaning does not square with the sense of the negated EVENT predicate *doesn't happen by chance*. Given the conceptual discrepancy between subject and predicate, should this advertisement be rejected as non-sensical, i.e. meaningless? This would not be a linguistically satisfactory analysis since people apparently understand the commercial message without any difficulty, and many will find it attractive and flock to the hair salon. But how do customers make sense of this message? They interpret *great hair*, i.e. attractive hair or an attractive hairstyle, as the *result* or *effect* of an action. More generally, the metonymic inference from an effect to the action that brings about the effect is a very productive one in English (though not necessarily in other languages).

A pattern emerges from the examples considered so far. Metonymic interpretations (as other figurative meanings) are often triggered by some conceptual incongruity between meanings in a local (e.g. sentential), or wider discourse context and the extralinguistic situation. These properties of metonymy are taken up in more detail in Sections 3 and 4.

3. Properties of metonymy

From the examples given in Section 2, various attributes of metonymy can be abstracted that are diagrammed in Figure 1 (see e.g. Panther & Thornburg 2018), some of which are commented on in more detail in subsequent sections.

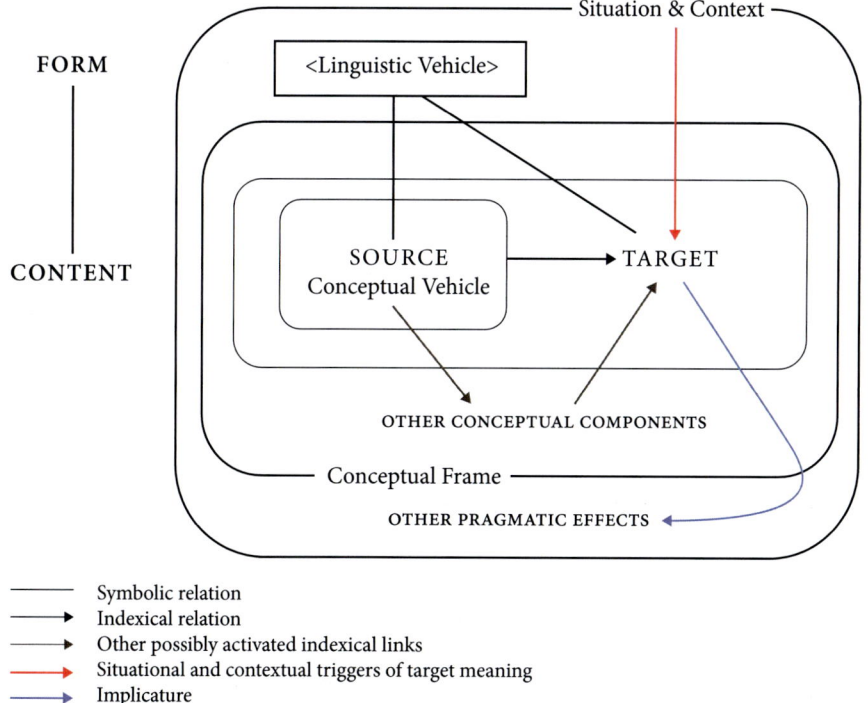

```
──────────    Symbolic relation
─────▶        Indexical relation
─ ─ ─▶        Other possibly activated indexical links
─────▶        Situational and contextual triggers of target meaning
─────▶        Implicature
```

Figure 1. Basic metonymic relation

Figure 1 represents the structure of natural language metonymy; but as noted aboved, metonymy is both a figure of speech and of thought. A widely accepted working definition of metonymy was first proposed by Kövecses and Radden (1998: 39) and Radden and Kövecses (1999: 21):[81]

> Metonymy is a cognitive process in which one conceptual entity, the vehicle, provides mental access to another conceptual entity, the target, within the same domain, or ICM.

Zoltán Kövecses and Günter Radden adopt the notion of ICM, an abbreviation for *Idealized Cognitive Model*, from Lakoff (1987: Chapter 4). An ICM is a knowledge structure that is equivalent to what is called *conceptual frame* in this book (see Figure 1). The characterization of metonymy proposed by Kövecses and Radden provides a good starting point, but it has to be elaborated and constrained in various respects in order to distinguish it from e.g. metaphor and inference types such as entailment and presupposition (see Chapter 3), and to elucidate how it relates to the Gricean notion of implicature (see Chapters 4 and 5).

In the following sections, the properties of metonymy as diagrammed in Figure 1 are commented on in more detail and illustrated with further examples. Notice that in this book the metonymic relation between source and target meaning is symbolized by means of an arrow '→'.

3.1 Situation and context

Like any other linguistic units, metonymies are embedded in an extralinguistic situation and a linguistic context (see the most inclusive rounded rectangle in Figure 1). In other words, whether some expression is interpreted metonymically or not may depend on situational and contextual factors, the latter including what is called 'other conceptual components' of the frame. Consider a statement like (11):

(11) Paul Auster is on the second floor.

Example (11) has at least two possible readings: one where *Paul Auster* literally refers to the well-known novelist, and one in which the referent of the proper name metonymically refers to Auster's books (e.g. in a library or in a bookstore). Regarding the literal interpretation, a possible extra-linguistic context could be a situation in which an avid Paul Auster reader wishes a new Auster novel to be autographed by the author and asks "Where does the Paul Auster reading take

---

[81]. Essentially the same definition is provided in a revised version of these two seminal papers (Radden & Kövecses 2007: 336).

place?", and this request for information might be answered by something like (11). In contrast, a metonymic interpretation AUTHOR → AUTHOR'S WORKS would be plausible in a context in which a student in a university library, who has to write a term paper on Paul Auster, asks a librarian where this author's books are located.

In the following example, no context outside the sentence itself is needed to induce a metonymic interpretation :

(12) The *Bay of Pigs* took place the year that I was born.
(https://obamawhitehouse. archives.gov/the-press-office/2016/03/22/remarks-president-obama-people-cuba)

Sentence (12) was uttered by U.S. President Obama in a speech delivered in Havana, Cuba, on March 22, 2016. The purpose of this state visit was to normalize diplomatic relations between the U.S. and Cuba that had been frozen for decades after Cuba had become a communist country under the leadership of Fidel Castro. Utterance (12) refers to the landing of a CIA-sponsored brigade of Cuban exiles in the Bay of Pigs (southern coast of Cuba) on April 17, 1961, with the aim to invade Cuba and replace the communist government with a U.S. friendly regime. In (12), there is conceptual incongruity between the subject of the sentence *The Bay of Pigs* and the predicate *took place*. A geographical location, the Bay of Pigs (in Spanish: Bahía de Cochinos), cannot happen, but there exists a productive metonymy in English and other languages that associates locations with important, e.g. historically significant, events that take place at these locations: LOCATION → IMPORTANT EVENT AT LOCATION. The target meaning of this metonymy yields a pragmatically coherent interpretation. How intricately events and locations are conceptually interwoven is also evidenced by the use of the verbal expression *took place* 'happened', which contains the noun *place*. Witness also the coding of events in other languages, such as French *avoir lieu*, Italian *avere luogo*, Spanish *tener lugar*, Portuguese *ter lugar* (all literally meaning 'have place'), or German *stattfinden* 'lit. place/location find'.

An example like (12) shows that the full understanding of a metonymy may require encyclopedic background knowledge – here historical knowledge about the political situation in Cuba and the United States during the Cold War. But what competent speakers of English, even if they do not know anything about the historical facts, will grasp immediately is that Obama's utterance does not merely refer to a geographical location but to an event or events that took place at that location.

3.2 Metonymy as an indexical and associative relation

In contrast to metaphor, which, in semiotic terms (see Chapter 7), can be regarded as an iconic relation between two conceptual frames, metonymy functions as a type of *indexical* relation. A non-linguistic example of an index is given in Figure 2.

Figure 2. Footprints in the desert as a visual index of the passage of camels
(Source: Author's photo)

The footprints in the desert sand in Figure 2 point to, i.e. are an index, of the recent passage of camels. One might call this case a *visual* metonymy that can be formulated as FOOTPRINTS → CAMEL(S) CAUSING THE FOOTPRINTS.

In the case of linguistic metonymy, one conceptual component in a conceptual frame, the source meaning, serves as a conceptual vehicle, i.e. a conceptual index that points to a target (meaning) within the same conceptual frame. The relation between source and target is *associative*.[82] To illustrate with a linguistic example, on July 26, 2012, the online newspaper Huffington Post published an article about a gold medalist at the 1968 Winter Olympic Games in Grenoble, France:

(13) Olympic gold medal winner Peggy Fleming […] has *tears in her eyes* as she is embraced by her mother, Doris, after winning the Women's Figure Skating competition in Grenoble, France, on Feb. 10, 1968. (GloWbE, US)

In (13), the meaning of the phrase *tears in her eyes* functions as a conceptual vehicle for a highly emotive target meaning – in the present context, a sense that conveys a strong feeling of joy and happiness.

---

82. See Mazzone (2018) for notion of association and its significance for a theory of pragmatic inferencing. The concept of frame is closely related to what Mazzone calls *schema*. For Mazzone (2018: 6) "mental concepts are schemata in associative memory", i.e. associations among frame elements that are activated in inferential processes.

At this point, it is important to note that the source meaning, i.e. the conceptual vehicle, as a result of the metonymic operation does not vanish, but is incorporated into the target meaning, a process that can be called, following Fauconnier and Turner (2002), *conceptual blending* or *conceptual integration*.[83] In Figure 1, this integration process is represented graphically by means of a rounded rectangle that properly contains the rectangle representing the source meaning. In example (13), the source meaning 'tears in her eyes' is thus a conceptual part of the target meaning, which can be paraphrased as 'feeling of joy/happiness causing tears', an instance of the metonymy SYMPTOM → CAUSE OF SYMPTOM, or more generally, EFFECT (tears) → CAUSE (happiness) (see Panther & Thornburg 2007: 257–258).

3.3 Metonymy as reasoning within a conceptual frame

As pointed out in Section 3.2, metonymy is a mode of indexical reasoning that makes use of associative relations among meaning components located *within* one *conceptual frame*. This property differentiates metonymy from metaphor, which, as has been argued in Chapter 7, is characterized by mappings *across* two conceptual frames. According to e.g. Cruse (2006: 66–67), the notion of (conceptual) frame encapsulates the idea "that word meanings can be properly understood and described only against the background of a particular body of knowledge and assumptions."

For purposes of illustration regarding the notion of conceptual frame, recall first examples (6)–(8). The vehicle of the metonymic operation is the human noun *patient*, which has as one of its the meanings 'a person receiving or registered to receive medical treatment' (NOAD). In a nutshell, this definition describes what native speakers know about patients, and, in fact, one could add other bits of knowledge about patients to the dictionary entry, such as, that, in general, they need to make an appointment in order to see and consult their doctor. Patients are thus participants in scheduled events; and such events can be canceled (i.e. will not take place, as planned). Utterances (6)–(8) are instances of the metonymy PATIENT → SCHEDULED EVENT INVOLVING PATIENT – and more generally, of the metonymy PARTICIPANT → EVENT INVOLVING PARTICIPANT.

As a second example, recall (9) above, which involves the relation between a natural phenomenon (real-world denotatum) and its linguistic representation – more

---

[83]. Ruiz de Mendoza Ibáñez (2000) advocates a distinction between source-in-target and target-in-source metonymies, contending that, in the first case, the target is an expansion of the source whereas, in the latter case, it is conceptually contained in the source. In contrast, in this book it is assumed that metonymy (like metaphor) is a type of meaning expansion or elaboration. In this sense, metonymies are (conceptually) always of the source-in-target type.

precisely, the relation between the weather and the weather forecast. This content-form relation is also exploited in expressions such as (14):

(14) I am Chuck Miller.

Sentence (14) metonymically implies 'I am the bearer of the name Chuck Miller' or 'My name is Chuck Miller'. Strictly speaking, a person cannot *be* his or her own name, but the association between a name and its bearer is tight and, in many cultures, people feel that their name is an essential attribute of their identity. The two components NAME and BEARER OF NAME are thus felt to belong to the same conceptual frame (or, alternatively, to the same *cognitive domain*, as some metonymy theorists prefer to call it). As a result of the tight associative bond between a name and its bearer, language users are hardly aware of the metonymy NAME → BEARER OF NAME. The metonymy has become completely conventionalized, and many present-day speakers might feel that the non-metonymic alternative of (14), i.e. *My name is Chuck Miller*, is unnecessarily wordy.

3.4 Conceptual distance between source and target

Two conceptual components that are linked by means of metonymy are preferably *immediate* or *close* conceptual "neighbors", i.e., they are perceived as being conceptually tightly connected. The shorter the conceptual distance between two frame components (measured as the number of conceptual links between them), the more likely they are exploited for metonymic purposes. As the *conceptual distance* between components increases, the probability of their metonymic use decreases (see Panther & Thornburg 1998).

To see the relevance of conceptual distance in the creation of metonymies, consider the contrast between (15) and (16):

(15) We have some new faces on our team.

(16) #We have some new noses/eyes/mouths/chins on our team.

Sentence (15) exemplifies the metonymy FACE OF PERSON → PERSON. It sounds perfectly normal because there is a tight link between a person's face and the person *per se*. Notice that conceptual contiguity between FACE and PERSON is also relevant in the visual domain: the photo on an identity card, passport, or driver's license shows the face of the owner of these documents. In contrast, the body parts listed in (16) are less strongly associated with a person as such, although it is not impossible to imagine a situation when it would make sense to have e.g. *some new noses* on the team. Imagine a perfume manufacturer who hires "noses" whose job is to check and evaluate the scents of some new brand of Eau de Cologne.

Similarly, it is probably not accidental that there exists a metonymically based idiomatic expression like (17) in English, but (18) is unlikely to be exploited for metonymic purposes:

(17) All hands on deck!

(18) #All fingers on deck!

(19) All men on deck!

The hands are more closely associated with hard work and thereby with workers (here: sailors) than the fingers, which are parts of the hand. Hence, it does not come as a surprise that the metonymic utterance (17) is virtually equivalent with the non-metonymic command (19).

As pointed out to me by Carita Paradis (p.c.), in the examples in this section, and, more generally, in many other cases of metonymy, *relevance* plays a role in the selection of a metonymic source concept to evoke a specific target. The significance of some notion of (communicative) relevance (see Chapter 4) becomes evident when the pragmatically appropriate command (17) is compared with the pragmatically odd order conveyed in (18). The hands are crucially important instruments for the kind of work performed on a ship (although lifting e.g. heavy objects also involves the use of fingers and arms).

3.5 Contingent relation between source and target

An intriguing problem is the nature of the conceptual relationship between the source and the target meaning of a metonymy. The position assumed here and defended in various publications (see e.g. Panther & Thornburg 2007, 2018) is that this relation is *contingent*, i.e., it is a "real-world" relation based on experience and/or cultural practices and beliefs. In other words, one would not expect to find metonymies than link source and target meaning by a relation of entailment.

Examples that illustrate the concept of contingency are (20) and (21) (see also Panther & Thornburg 2018: 132):

(20) As long as I breathe, I'll never accept what's been done to me, so I'm just stuck [..]. (COCA 2008)

(21) The kettle is boiling.

The expression *as long as I breathe* in (20) has the conventional metonymic interpretation 'as long as I live/am alive'. The relationship between breathing and being alive is based on world knowledge, i.e., it is a robust empirically supported correlation. Nevertheless, it is not a conceptually necessary relationship; i.e., the proposition that a person breathes does not entail that the person is alive, nor does the proposition that the person in question does not breathe entail the person is dead, although there is a high degree of likelihood that these inferences hold. As observed in Panther and Thornburg (2018: 132), breathing is a strong index of being alive; but respiration can also be artificially effectuated by appropriate medical equipment.

At first blush, sentence (21) also looks like an example in which the target meaning 'The fluid in the kettle is boiling' is entailed. But again, as pointed out by Panther and Thornburg (2018: 138), it is not impossible that the kettle itself is boiling – even though this interpretation is unlikely, given our world knowledge about kettles and their uses. The relation between the source and the target is contingent and the metonymic inference is in fact defeasible, which is a property that metonymy shares with implicature (see Chapters 3 and 4).

At this point, some readers might object that what is known as *type coercion* or *logical metonymy* (see e.g. Pustejovsky & Bouillon 1995) constitutes counterevidence to the hypothesis put forward in this book that the metonymic relation is based on world knowledge, i.e. not conceptually necessary. Consider the following corpus examples (italics added):

(22) As part of my creative work, I *began a new novel* [...]. (COCA 2012)

(23) Two years later, Ronald *began a new book*. (iWeb)

(24) As the Louvre was too small, [King Louis XIV] *began a new palace at Versailles* [...]. (GloWbE)

The verb *begin* in examples such as (22)–(24) requires a direct object that denotes an action carried out by an agent, i.e. the referent of the subject. However, in (22)–(24), the direct objects, i.e. the noun phrases *a new novel*, *a new book*, and *a new palace at Versailles*, literally do not code actions. The respective actions associated with these objects have to be inferred. A plausible interpretation of (22) is that the human agent 'began *writing* a new novel'. Similarly, (23) implies that Ronald 'began *writing* a new book' or perhaps 'began *reading* a new book', and it is even possible that he performed some action like '*binding* a new book'. However, the context makes it clear that the proper name *Ronald* refers to the author J. R. R. Tolkien, who began *writing* a new book. Finally, regarding (24), the understood action carried out by King Louis XIV is to effectuate the construction of a new royal palace outside Paris, i.e. in Versailles. These interpretations are based on world knowledge, such as that books/novels are written or read, etc., and that palaces are built.

In conclusion, I propose that the interpretation of examples of type coercion like (22)–(24) can be accounted for in two inferential steps. The first inference is an *entailment* and the second a *metonymic* inference. What is entailed is that the subject referent of *began* performs some (unspecified) action that involves the referent of the direct object; however, the determination of what kind of specific action is performed involving the referent of the direct object is a matter of metonymic inference (see (25)).

(25) SBJ$_{AG}$ *begin* NP$_{THING}$
⊩ SBJ$_{AG}$ *begin* generic ACTION that INVOLVES NP$_{THING}$
→ SBJ$_{AG}$ *begin* specified ACTION that INVOLVES NP$_{THING}$

Type coercion thus involves both entailment, i.e. a conceptually non-defeasible type of inference, and metonymic inference based on world or encyclopedic knowledge.

3.6 Pragmatic effects

Metonymic operations, in combination with the linguistic context and the communicative situation, trigger *pragmatic effects* (traditionally called *connotations*), e.g., they may implicate an emotional stance, signal social parameters (e.g. politeness/rudeness), and convey aesthetic values (poetic embellishment). These pragmatic effects can be related to Levinson's *M(anner) Heuristic* "What's said in an abnormal way isn't normal" (Levinson 2000: 38; cf. the Maxim of Manner postulated by Grice 1975).

The following examples illustrate some of the stylistic and pragmatic effects of metonymy:

(26) I was interviewed at the Consulate by the same exquisite suit.
(https://books.google.co.uk/books?id=5H8rAAAAYAAJ)

(27) That would mean the place would be raided by flatfoots at any moment.
(COCA 2015)

(28) JUDY-WOODRUFF: On the "NewsHour" online: Math geeks and sweet tooths alike are celebrating Pi Day today.   (COCA 2016)

Sentence (26) is drawn from Eric Ambler's spy novel *Cause for Alarm*, which takes place in Fascist Italy shortly before the Second World War. The fictitious narrator is the representative of a British firm in Milan, Nicholas Marlow, whose passport has been "mislaid" by the Italian authorities, and Mr. Marlow asks the British Consulate (in vain) for help to retrieve his passport. The use of the metonymy EXQUISITE SUIT → DIPLOMAT WEARING AN EXQUISITE SUIT is an instance of a more general, i.e. hyperonymic, metonymy ATTRIBUTE OF PERSON → PERSON. In the context of the novel, it has a somewhat *ironic* if not *sarcastic* effect on the reader. The consular official is elegantly clad and polite, but completely inefficient; he is no more than a "suit."

Example (27) exploits the metonymy ATTRIBUTE OF PERSON → PERSON as well. Police officers walking the streets of New York used to be called *flatfoots* by e.g. mafiosi and other criminals.[84] Literally, the compound noun *flatfoot* signifies 'a condition in which the foot has an arch that is lower than usual' (NOAD). Metonymically, *flatfoot* refers to a 'person with flat feet', and, more specifically, to a 'police officer' – who, quite possibly, might not even suffer from this anatomical anomaly. In example (27), the metonymy has a pejorative or derogatory effect. It is worth noting that the plural form *flatfoots* is used in (27) – not *flatfeet*. When *flatfoot* has a metonymic interpretation referring to a person, it is possible to attach the regular plural morpheme -*s* to the compound. This is an interesting case of metonymic meaning having an impact on morphological structure, i.e. more generally, on grammar (see Chapter 11 for examples of interaction between meaning and pragmatic function with grammatical structure).

Finally, in (28), the plural form of the nominal expression *sweet tooth*, which the NOAD defines as 'a great liking for sweet-tasting foods' (itself a fairly complex metonymy!), triggers, in turn, another metonymic target meaning, i.e. 'person with a liking for sweet-tasting foods'. This metonymy connotes a more friendly and understanding attitude than the metonymies in (26) and (27) – because many people like to indulge in the consumption of pastry, cakes, chocolates, desserts, etc. Moreover, note the humorous tone of (28), which is based on the homophony of *Pi*, the numerical value π, and *pie*, the pastry. Analogously to (27), the plural form of *sweet tooth* is not *sweet teeth*, but, with the metonymic reading 'person with a liking for sweet-tasting foods', it has been regularized to *sweet tooths* (for the interaction of metonymy and word-formation, see also Brdar 2017).

3.7 Experiential and sociocultural motivation of metonymy

In this section, metonymy is viewed from the perspective of how it relates to human experience and/or cultural beliefs and practices. Accordingly, three kinds of metonymy can be distinguished:

i. *experientially* motivated metonymies, i.e. metonymies motivated by universal human experiences, emotions, and feelings that have observable "bodily" effects;
ii. metonymies motivated by *sociocultural institutions, practices* and *beliefs* of language users;
iii. metonymies that are both *experientially* and *socioculturally* motivated.

An example that involves an experientially motivated metonymy is given in (29):

---

84. The term is characterized as informal and dated by the NOAD.

(29) His face flushed red with anger and he started accusing me of not wanting to be with him anymore. (NOW Corpus, GB 2011)

Sentence (29) describes the perceptually observable event of a person turning red in the face, which can be a symptom (index) of an underlying strong emotion. In fact, in this case, the emotional cause is even explicitly coded by means of the prepositional phrase *with anger*. On a more abstract level, (29) is another example of a metonymy that relates an effect to its cause (see Section 2.2). The metonymy in (29) can thus be formulated as EFFECT (flushed face) → CAUSE (anger).

A socioculturally motivated metonymy is at work in the following text that appeared in the British newspaper *The Guardian* :

(30) Northern Ireland exists as a unit for one reason alone: as a haven for a Protestant community that a century ago was traumatised by the prospect of being absorbed into a Catholic-dominated Ireland. Loyalist, it likes to call itself, though its loyalty to the *Crown* has always been more transactional than deferential. (NOW, GB 2017)

Literally, the noun *crown* denotes 'a circular ornamental headdress worn by a monarch as a symbol of authority, usually made of or decorated with precious metals and jewels' (ODE). Metonymically, in the context of (30), the noun phrase *the Crown* refers to the British monarchy, with the monarch as the head of state of the United Kingdom of Great Britain and Northern Ireland. More generally, this metonymy relates a ceremonial object to a form of government: OBJECT (crown) → INSTITUTION (monarchy).

The third category, metonymies that combine both experiential and cultural aspects, can be illustrated with the following idiomatic expression in German :

(31) Dem ist wohl eine Laus über die *Leber* gelaufen.
DEM.MASC.DAT is.PRF maybe a louse across the liver run.PTCP
Literally: 'Maybe a louse has run across this guy's *liver*'
Idiomatically: 'This guy got out of bed on the wrong side' or 'Something's eating this guy'

Sentence (31) is an idiomatic expression that relies on a cultural conception of the liver, which goes back to the Middle Ages or even Greek antiquity. But there is also an experiential dimension to this expression: a malfunction of the liver may have an effect on a person's feelings and emotions.[85] According to the German dictionary

---

85. Note that this conception of the liver is a pre-scientific one, which does not necessarily coincide with what is known about this organ and its effects on emotions and feelings in this day and age.

Duden Universalwörterbuch, expressions like (31) are historically motivated by a conception of the liver as the seat of negative emotions and feelings such as anger and irritability, and the bodily organ *Leber* 'liver' can stand for these emotions or feelings. The *Laus* 'louse', a tiny creature, was probably added for alliterative purposes, and it conveys the additional meaning that the experiencer in question is very *easily* angered or irritated.[86] Thus, a sentence like (31) makes use of a metonymy MALFUNCTION OF LIVER → FEELING OF IRRITATION.[87] Interestingly, in contrast to example (29) where the emotion of anger causes the redness of the face, in (31) the causal relation is reversed: the malfunction of the bodily organ causes the feeling of irritation and anger.

3.8 Transparency of metonymy motivation

Metonymies are more or less *transparent*, i.e. recognizably motivated by some associative or indexical relation, more or less *productive*, i.e. creatively exploited by speakers, and more or less *conventionalized*, i.e. more or less likely to be stored in the mental lexicon of language users. In cognitive linguistics, instead of 'conventionalization', the term *entrenchment* is often used to refer to the "establishment of a linguistic unit as a cognitive pattern or routine in the mind of an individual language user" (V. Evans 2007: 73). The term 'convention(alization)', which is used in this book, has a more sociocultural ring to it: it emphasizes the *mutually shared* tacit linguistic knowledge of the native speakers of a language. The focus of this section is on the notion of metonymic transparency, which, in what follows, is elaborated and illustrated with some examples.

Two highly productive metonymies in English are BODY PART OF PERSON → PERSON and ATTRIBUTE OF PERSON → PERSON. In animated cartoons, BODY PART or ATTRIBUTE metonymies are often used to refer to a person, and such metonymies even tend to become proper names. For example, two creatures in the animated cartoon *Tangled* (produced by Disney) are called 'Big Nose' and 'Hand Hook', respectively. These names are evidently motivated by salient body parts and attributes of the two characters in question.

A more complex case is the already mentioned compound noun *flatfoot* 'condition of having flat feet', which has a metonymic target sense 'person with flat feet'. This metonymic sense is completely transparent. However, the OED lists a

---

86. Accessed at: https://www-1munzinger-1de-100399e9g04d2.emedien3.sub.uni-hamburg.de/search/query?query.id=query-duden.

87. For more details on the conceptualization of body organs from a cross-linguistic and cultural perspective, see the contributions in Sharifian et al. (2008) and Maalej and Yu (2011).

number of additional metonymic meanings of *flatfoot* that are less transparent, i.e. readings like 'police officer' (see example (27)), 'foot soldier, infantryman', and 'sailor'. These three conventionalized senses have undergone meaning *specialization*, which makes them less transparent or even somewhat opaque to language users. Moreover, these examples exhibit metonymic chaining: LOWER FOOT ARCH (flat feet) → PERSON WITH LOWER FOOT ARCH THAN USUAL (flatfoot) → PERSON BELONGING TO A SPECIFIC PROFESSIONAL GROUP (e.g. police officer). The final link in this chain does not necessarily express the sense that the person in question has flat feet, but conveys a derogatory meaning, i.e. pragmatic effect (see Figure 1). The *flatfoot* example illustrates what has been called *post-metonymy* by Riemer (2002, 2005), i.e. cases in which the real-world denotatum of the metonymic vehicle is no longer conceptually present in the target meaning because it does not exist as a real-world referent.

A clear example of post-metonymy is the idiomatic expression *beat one's breast*, i.e. 'make an exaggerated show of sorrow, despair, or regret' (NOAD). According to Riemer (2002: 389), this expression is metonymically motivated. It was originally based on "the religious practice of beating one's breast while making a public confession [...]." However, since this religious practice does not exist anymore, from a present-day perspective, the metonymy is dead. Notwithstanding, the motivational link between the action of beating one's breast and the concomitant emotions of sorrow, despair or regret is probably still transparent to speakers of present-day English.

Another example of a post-metonymy is the noun *bluestocking* with the conventional meaning 'intellectual or literary woman'.[88] At first blush, the underlying metonymy seems to be ATTRIBUTE OF PERSON (clothing) → PERSON. But how are blue stockings associated with intellectual and literary women? On closer examination of the history of the expression, which can be found in the OED (s.v. *bluestocking*), it turns out that in the 18th century blue (worsted) stockings were originally worn by men (!) "as opposed to more expensive and formal white silk stockings." They were worn by males in literary salons characterized by their "social informality and intellectual exchange." Female intellectuals were encouraged to attend these events, and the term *bluestocking* was henceforth associated "specifically with the involvement of women in the intellectual world." Later, the OED concludes, this association was "reinforced further by the increasing identification of stockings as an item of female rather than male attire." In some contexts, there is also a negative

---

88. As observed by Verspoor and de Bie-Kerékjártó (2006: 91) in an article on "colorful bits of experience", the lexeme *bluestocking* has its equivalents in other languages, such as *Blaustrumpf* (German), *blauwkous* (Dutch), *blåstrumpa* (Swedish), *kékharisnya* (Hungarian), *sinisukka* (Finnish). Presumably, all of these are ultimately loan translations from English.

pragmatic effect (anti-feminism) associated with *bluestocking*, as in (32) from a piece of narrative fiction :

(32) She excelled at appearing bookish. Prim. A bluestocking with no sense of humor. (COCA 2011)

As a final example consider the verb *genuflect*, which has two religiously motivated metonymic senses derived from ecclesiastical Latin *genuflectere* (Latin *genu-* 'knee' and *flectere* 'to bend'). The first sense 'lower one's body briefly by bending one knee to the ground, typically in worship or as a sign of respect' (NOAD), is exemplified in (33):

(33) He genuflected each time he passed the figure of Christ.

The second sense of *genuflect* is 'show deference or servility' (NOAD). On this reading, the act of bending one's knee is no longer present. This is a genuine case of post-metonymy, as evidenced in (34) :

(34) Despite the fog of his something-for-everybody approach. Clinton managed to make a decent case for himself. He genuflected to the GOP, and even Ronald Reagan, at the right points […].
(https://books.google.co.uk/books?id=z5MqAQAAIAAJ)

4. Metonymy as abductive reasoning

What kind of inferential mechanism could best account for the associative relationship between source and target meaning of metonymy? In her monograph on the subject, Jeannette Littlemore (2015: 138) reports that traditional computational approaches to automatic metonymy detection rely on the assumption that metonymic meanings are triggered by violations of semantic *selection restrictions*. An example of such violations is the following headline published by the news agency Reuters on February 15, 2018:

(35) Russia denies British allegations that Moscow was behind cyber-attack.

The sentence exhibits two violations of selection restrictions. First, strictly speaking, a *country* cannot perform a communicative act, only a human spokesperson (for the country's government) can; i.e., under a non-figurative interpretation, there is semantic incompatibility between the subject of the sentence and the speech act verb *denies*. Second, the *city* of Moscow cannot be the alleged cyber-attacker. And third, strictly speaking, allegations do not have the property of being British, but they are speech acts that have presumably been performed by a spokesperson of the British government. These semantic incongruities trigger a metonymic interpretation, i.e.

something like 'Russian officials deny allegations by a spokesperson of the British government that Russian hackers were behind the cyber-attack'.

In this chapter, various examples have already been given that coerce metonymic readings because, literally, they exhibit conceptual conflicts. Recall cases like (3) where eggs are assigned the property 'free range', or (6), in which a doctor 'cancels' patients and ambulances.

However, as Markert and Hahn (2002) (see also Littlemore 2015: 138) have shown, one can easily find metonymies that do not seem to violate selection restrictions. As an example, consider (36):[89]

(36) Voltaire is in the French Department library.

Since every student of French literature knows that Voltaire lived in the 18th century (to be precise, 1694–1776), a metonymic interpretation suggests itself, namely, that not the author himself but his *works* can be found in the library of the French Department. In sentence (36), no selectional constraints are violated. How can such examples be accommodated in a framework that relies on the concept of violation of selection restrictions? Markert and Hahn (2002) provide an answer. They point out that, for the automatic identification of metonymies, the larger *discourse context* has to be taken into account and, one might add, the *extralinguistic situation*, including the *sociocultural* context (see Section 3.1 and Figure 1 for these notions). The discourse context includes not only selection restrictions within phrases and sentences but also conceptual clashes across sentences. The (extra-linguistic) situation includes the mental states, e.g. communicative intentions and the (world) knowledge of the interactants. In (36), a literal, i.e. non-figurative, interpretation of this example is not compatible with language users' world knowledge about Voltaire, and it is this incompatibility that triggers the metonymic reading 'Voltaire's works/books'.

To conclude, metonymic shifts often involve incompatibility of the literal sense of some linguistic vehicle (see Figure 1) with the discourse context and/or extra-linguistic situation. The metonymic meanings can be modeled as conclusions of spontaneous abductive reasoning, i.e. as everyday reasoning to the best explanation, or more narrowly, to the interpretation that is the most plausible one in a given context and/or situation (see Chapter 3, Section 2.4, for the notion of abduction). The American philosopher and semiotician C. S. Peirce coined the term "abductive instinct" for this kind of non-logical reasoning (see e.g. Paavola 2005: 150; Buchler 1955: 151). Table 1 schematically sketches the abductive reasoning process involved in metonymy resolution.

[89.] See also example (11) about Paul Auster.

Table 1. Correspondences between language-independent abductive reasoning (Peirce) and an abductively motivated interpretation strategy for metonymies (adapted from Panther & Thornburg 2018: 148–149)

	Abductive reasoning (Peirce)	Metonymic reasoning
Premise 1	Surprising fact C is observed.	A linguistic vehicle LV (vehicle) has a meaning S_1 (SOURCE) that is conceptually *incompatible* with the *context/situation* in which it is used.
Premise 2	If A is true, C is a "matter of course."	If meaning S_1 (SOURCE) is shifted to meaning S_2 (TARGET) within the same *conceptual frame*, LV becomes conceptually *compatible* with the *context/situation* in which it is used.
Conclusion	A is true.	S_2 (TARGET) is the intended interpretation.

According to Table 1, a metonymic reading is triggered when a conceptual-pragmatic conflict arises between the literal (source) meaning of a linguistic vehicle and the surrounding linguistic context and/or the extralinguistic situation. The metonymic operation that shifts the source sense S_1 to the target sense S_2 within the same conceptual frame serves as a means of conceptual-pragmatic *adjustment* that establishes compatibility between the sense of a linguistic unit and the context/situation in which it is used.

Interestingly, other rhetorical tropes can be accounted for in terms of metonymic reasoning. This holds for example for irony, which often involves the shift of one meaning to its opposite (see e.g Athanasiadou 2017; Panther & Thornburg 2012b).

(37) I love this elevator music. → 'I hate this elevator music'

As has been shown in psycholinguistic experiments (see e.g. Postman & Keppel 1970; Clark & Clark 1977), a given stimulus word most frequently evokes its antonym. No wonder that antonymy is productively exploited for metonymic purposes (see Voßhagen 1999; Panther & Thornburg 2012b, 2017a: Chapter 6). The abductive schema in Table 1 applies to cases like (37): there is a conceptual discrepancy between what is literally expressed and the context and/or situation in which the utterance in question occurs, and it is this incongruence that has to be adjusted metonymically.

The problem remains however to determine if *all* linguistic phenomena that intuitively look like metonymies can be accounted for by the abductive schema outlined in Table 1. Consider the following inferences, which would be regarded by many cognitive linguists (e.g. Lakoff 1987) as metonymic and by Levinson (2000) as default conversational implicatures:

(38) *drink* → / +> 'alcoholic drink' (Levinson)

(39) *road* → / +> 'paved road' (Levinson)

(40) *secretary* → / +> 'female secretary' (Levinson)

(41) *mother* → / +> 'housewife mother' (Lakoff)

In examples (38)–(41), the metonymic inference or implicature to the sociocultural stereotype is *not* triggered by an incongruence between the linguistic vehicle with the discourse context or extralinguistic situation (e.g. world knowledge). On the contrary, the target meaning represents the normal and expected case; i.e., it is a default implicature in Levinson's terms. What is idiosyncratic about the inferences in (38)–(41) is that they relate a *hyperonymic*, i.e. superordinate, source meaning to a *hyponymic* (i.e. subordinate) target sense. The target sense is not an inherent facet of the linguistic vehicle but it can be canceled, as shown in (42)–(45):

(42) I need a drink, but no alcohol please!

(43) Let's take the southern road, but it is not paved.

(44) John's boss hired a new secretary, but he is male.

(45) Louise is the mother of five daughters, but not your typical housewife mother.

Diachronically, meaning specialization may lead to the loss of the superordinate sense so that only the more specific meaning survives. This kind of development happened e.g. in American English with *corn*, which originally denoted any cereal, and is nowadays used with the specialized sense of what is called *maize* in British English.

As pointed out by Geeraerts (2010: 26–27), specialization is an important factor in meaning change, as already recognized by historical linguists in the late 19th and early 20th century – the other driving forces of semantic change being *generalization*, *metaphor*, and *metonymy*. Many cognitive linguists regard meaning specialization and generalization as subtypes of metonymy (e.g. Kövecses & Radden 1998; Radden & Kövecses 1999, 2007). The following examples illustrate meaning *generalization*:

(46) Next, get out your Kleenexes as we take a trip back to some of our most touching moments. (COCA 1991)

(47) We scrubbed their toilets, hoovered their carpets, polished their silver. (COCA 2003)

In (46) the brand name *Kleenexes* is most likely used generically for any paper tissues, and in (47) the verb form *hoovered* has, apart from its literal sense 'vacuum-cleaned with a hoover', the generalized default target sense 'vacuum-cleaned', i.e., a speaker can truthfully assert (47) even if some other vacuum cleaner was used than a

Hoover. Note that the proposition 'We hoovered their carpets' can be described in terms of metonymic chaining as in (48):

(48) PRODUCER (Hoover) → PRODUCT (Hoover vacuum cleaner) → PRODUCT (any vacuum cleaner) → ACTION PERFORMED WITH PRODUCT (vacuum-cleaning)

5. Constraining the scope of metonymy

An important issue in conceptual metonymy theory, as in fact in any theory, is the development of a definition that is sufficiently constrained. There is a certain tendency in contemporary metonymy research to overgeneralize the concept, with the result that it is in danger of losing its descriptive and explanatory power. As already mentioned, the widely accepted characterization of metonymy proposed by Günter Radden and Zoltán Kövecses (2007: 336) as a "cognitive process in which one conceptual entity, the vehicle, provides mental access to another another conceptual entity, the target, within the same idealized cognitive model", needs to be refined and constrained in various respects.

Carita Paradis (2004) maintains that the same desideratum holds for Langacker's (2000) definition of metonymy as a *reference point* and *activation phenomenon*, and, one might add, for his conception of metonymy as a cognitive device that effectuates a *profile shift* (Langacker 2013: 69):

> [W]e speak of metonymy when an expression that ordinarily profiles one entity is used instead to profile another entity associated with it in some domain.

Paradis (2004) argues that the conceptual processes of *metonymization* have to be distinguished from those of *facetization* and *zone activation*. Consider the following examples from her seminal article (Paradis 2004: 246):

(49) The red *shirts* won the match. (metonymization)

(50) The *court* had to assume that the statement of claim was true. (facetization)

(51) I have a really slow *car*. (zone activation)

Example (49) instantiates the already discussed metonymy ATTRIBUTE (red shirts) → PERSONS (wearing red shirts), which, in the given context, can be further metonymically elaborated into the target sense SPORTS TEAM (wearing red shirts). As Paradis (2004) shows, an important property of metonymy, which distinguishes it from facetization and zone activation, is its sensitivity to *zeugmatic* effects.[90]

---

90. A zeugma, also called *syllepsis*, in one of its meanings, is "a coordinate structure in which a verb, combining with NPs with different roles, has different interpretations" (Brown & Miller 2013: 429).

It is not possible for the source meaning, the red shirts as a piece of clothing, to co-occur with the target meaning, i.e. with the persons wearing these shirts, within the same syntactic unit, e.g. a sentence. Hence examples (52) and (53) are conceptually ill-formed:

(52) #The red shirts haven't been in the laundry for a while and won the match.

(53) #The red shirts won the match and haven't been in the laundry for a while.

The same kind of pragmatic oddity is observable in syntactic structures that do not exhibit coordination but subordination, as in (54) and (55):

(54) #The red shirts, which haven't been in the laundry for a while, won the match.

(55) #The red shirts, who won the match, haven't been in the laundry for a while.

In (54), the relative clause modifies the literal (source) meaning of *red shirts*, whereas the remainder of the main clause coerces a metonymic reading of *red shirts*, i.e. 'team wearing red shirts'. In (55), the relative clause modifies the metonymic target 'the team wearing red shirts', but the matrix clause ends in a non-metonymic reading. In both cases, the discrepancy between the source and the target meaning of *red shirts* is unbridgeable.

In contrast to (49), the different meaning components of *court* in (50) are not subject to metonymization. The semantic features that define this noun are called *facets*. Facets are different senses of a word, but they are "not distinct enough to count as completely separate readings and therefore as straight polysemy" (Brown & Miller 2013: 166). Hence, it is possible to switch from one facet to another within the same sentence, as can be demonstrated with example (56) from the *Irish Times* (June 17, 2016):

(56)　The court, which is based in Luxembourg, has initiated an inquiry into the use of European funding at the college in Templemore.　(NOW)

A court, in its judicial sense, has facets such as 'institution', 'location', 'building at location', and 'judicial staff' (see Paradis 2004 for a more detailed and sophisticated analysis). In (56), the relative clause refers to the geographical location of the court (notice the relative pronoun *which*). However, in the remainder of the main clause (following the relative clause), *the court* is conceptualized as an institution comprising judges and other administrative staff that initiate the inquiry in question. The link between these facets is felt to be so tight by language users that a switch from one facet to another within the same sentence is not felt to be conceptually deviant. From a semiotic perspective, which heeds the importance of both the form and the meaning and pragmatic use of linguistic signs, there is a clear difference between prototypical cases of metonymization and facetization.

Finally, Paradis (2004) also argues against Langacker's view that *active zone* phenomena are metonymies. Consider an example like the following (Langacker 2009b: 44):[91]

(57) The cigarette in her mouth was unlit.

The most likely interpretation of (57) is that not the entire cigarette was in the lady's mouth, but only a portion of the cigarette was in a portion of her mouth – more precisely, between her lips. Langacker (2009b: 43) calls these portions 'active zones', and he considers sentence (57) as an instance of *profile/active-zone discrepancy*. The phenomenon is pervasive in natural language and – to focus just on the semantics of the preposition *in* – profile/active-zone discrepancy is also observable in expressions like *the swan in the water*, *the axe in your hand*, *the arrow in the target*, etc., where the referent of the head noun, i.e. the *trajector*, is not entirely located *within* the region denoted by the prepositional phrase, i.e. the *landmark*, in Langacker's terminology.

The concept of profile/active-zone discrepancy is reminiscent of the abductive schema for metonymies formulated in Table 1, which relies on the notion of conceptual incompatibility/incongruence of the linguistic vehicle with the context/situation. For examples like *the axe in your hand*, world knowledge, which is part of the extralinguistic situation in the model assumed in this book (see Figure 1), tells us that the axe cannot be entirely *covered* by the hand of the person in question, but that, most likely, the person grips only part of the axe handle. Accordingly, the meaning of *in your hand* is adjusted so that it becomes compatible/congruent with language users' extralinguistic knowledge about axes and how they are gripped. Metonymy and zone activation differ however in that the former is, as shown in (52)–(55), subject to zeugmatic effects, whereas the latter, like facetization, is immune to them. For example, it is possible to say:

(58) I saw a pike and a swan *in* the water.

(59) John had a marble *in* his left hand and a hammer *in* his right hand.

Most likely, sentence (58) describes a situation in which the pike is totally immersed in the water while, in the case of the swan, it is only the lower part of its body that is positioned under the surface of the water. Despite the differing senses of *in* as 'totally immersed' (*pike*) versus 'partially immersed' (*swan*), the coordination of these slightly different meanings of *in* is perfectly acceptable. Analogously, in

---

91. Langacker's (2009b) Chapter 2 on metonymy is a revised version of Langacker (2009a), which was published in Panther, Thornburg, and Barcelona (2009).

(59), the marble is not visible because it is completely enclosed in John's left hand, whereas in the case of the hammer only a relatively small portion of it, i.e. part of the handle, is in John's hand.

To conclude, in Langacker's model, metonymy is regarded as a general property of grammar that is equated with *indeterminacy* of coded meaning. In this book, a more constrained conception of metonymy is proposed that, in accordance with Paradis (2004), does not regard facet switching (facetization) and active zone phenomena as instances of prototypical metonymy, although they involve modulations of meanings. Whether the boundary between active zone phenomena and metonymy is clear-cut or fuzzy, is an open question. Consider e.g. the use of the adjective *healthy* in *a healthy person* vs. *a healthy diet*. In the latter, *healthy* has a metonymic reading 'a diet whose purpose is to cause/preserve health', while in the former, the interpretation is non-metonymic, i.e. 'a person who is healthy'. Can these readings be coordinated without producing a zeugmatic effect, i.e., is e.g. *Mary and her diet are healthy* a pragmatically felicitously utterance? This sentence seems slightly odd but perhaps not impossible, although I have not been able to find empirical evidence for its use in corpora.

6. Types of metonymy

Viewed from the pragmatic perspective of "talking as action" (see Chapter 6), several types of metonymies can be distinguished. Relying on Searle's (1969) theory of speech acts, I distinguish between *referential* and *predicational* metonymies, both of which affect the *propositional content* of a speech act (see Panther & Thornburg 1998: 758). In addition, I briefly discuss two additional metonymic types, i.e. *modificational* and *grounding* metonymies. The former shape, like referential and predicational metonymies, the propositional content of a speech act; the latter may have some impact on both the propositional content and on the illocutionary force of a speech act. Finally, I introduce *illocutionary metonymies*, which are operative in the performance of *indirect speech acts* and are discussed in Chapters 9 and 10.

6.1 Referential metonymies

The vehicle of a referential metonymy is typically a nominal expression whose literal referent indexes another referent. Here are some examples of referential metonymy:

(60) All the black suits came back out, weapons now shouldered, leading a like number of handcuffed captives. (COCA 2016)

(61) Short of manpower and funds from the start, the blue helmets in Haiti have struggled for the upper hand over armed gangs since the mission began in June 2004. (COCA 2006)

In (60), the quantifier phrase *all the black suits* is metonymically used to refer to humans (wearing black suits), possibly secret agents. In the same vein, in (61), *the blue helmets* indirectly refers to U.N. soldiers. In both cases, a salient attribute, i.e. 'black suit' in (60) and 'blue helmet' in (61), metonymically evokes the persons themselves. Note that this reading is contextually triggered by the verb phrases *came back out* and *have struggled for the upper hand [...]*, which strongly suggest a metonymic interpretation of the *black suits* and *blue helmets*, respectively, as humans.

6.2 Predicational metonymies

Predicational metonymies operate within predicates on expressions such as the italicized ones in (62) and (63):

(62) Thomas Jefferson freed all of Sally Hemings's children: Beverly and Harriet *were allowed to* leave Monticello in 1822 [...]. (COCA 2012)

(63) I decided to just do the best as I could and *was able to* finish just in time [...]. (COCA 2012)

Examples (62) and (63) illustrate a productive metonymy in English, i.e. POTENTIALITY → ACTUALITY, which links a state-of-affairs that is virtual or potential to what happens in reality (see Panther & Thornburg 1999). Thus, the statement in (62) that the slaves Beverly and Harriet were allowed to leave Monticello metonymically suggests that they *actually* left Monticello in 1822; and (63) triggers the strong metonymic inference that the writer or speaker *managed* to finish, i.e. actually did finish the task that had to be completed. The expression *be able to do something* has the literal reading 'having the power, skill, means, or opportunity to do something' (NOAD). The link between POTENTIALITY – here more narrowly, ABILITY – and ACTUALITY is tight, i.e., the power, skill, or opportunity to do something is typically exercised. Nevertheless, as strong as the association between the source meaning and the target meaning may be, the metonymic inference does not constitute an entailment, but is, in principle, defeasible.

6.3 Modificational metonymies

Related to predicational metonymies, but not equivalent to them, are metonymies triggered by certain adjectival modifiers that exhibit a mismatch between morpho-syntactic structure and meaning. Consider the following news item from a British web source :

(64) She follows a healthy diet and makes sure she exercises regularly [...].
(NOW 2018, GB)

In (64), *healthy* syntactically modifies the noun *diet*. However, as already observed in Section 5, a diet does not have the intrinsic property of being healthy; being healthy is a property of persons (or other animate beings). The purpose of abiding by a *healthy diet* is to preserve a person's health or cause that person to become healthier. Thus, *healthy* functions as a conceptual modifier of the non-coded concept 'person'.[92] The meaning of noun phrase *a healthy diet* involves the metonymy EFFECT → CAUSE: the good health of the referent of the personal pronoun *she* results from or is preserved by the diet in question. Note that the first clause in (64), i.e. *She follows a healthy diet*, can also be coded with *healthy* as a predicate adjective: *She follows a diet that is healthy*. This also holds for the adjective *restless*, which can be used both as a modifier of a noun and as an adjective predicate, as in (65) and (66), respectively:

(65) What should she do? # Morning came too soon after a restless night.
(COCA 2017)

(66) Saturday night was restless. She was in pain, both physically and emotionally.
(COCA 2012)

The expression *restless night* in (65) exemplifies again a modificational metonymy. It is a metonymic shortcut for 'night period during which a person is unable to rest or sleep'. As (66) shows, *restless* can also trigger a predicational metonymy with the same target meaning as the modifier metonymy activated in (65).

Consider next two examples of modificational metonymy that have no predicational counterpart:

(67) We'd wake each morning at the same time, share a quiet cup of coffee as we listened to the news, and then leave for work. (COCA 2018)

(68) Nelyubov got himself into a drunken brawl for which he refused to apologize.
(COCA 2019)

---

92. The modifier *healthy* would however not apply to any kind of organism. One would not characterize a microbe or a virus as healthy.

In (67), the attribute of quietness is assigned to the fictional characters' behavior when they have their cup of coffee in the morning. The cup of coffee is metonymically conceptualized as an event characterized by little or no talking of the coffee drinkers. This situation cannot be coded predicationally; i.e., it is not possible to say something like *The cup of coffee we share is quiet*. The intended meaning of (68) is that Nelyubov is drunk and gets himself into a 'rough or noisy fight or quarrel' (NOAD).[93] It is not the brawl as such that is intoxicated, but this attribute is assigned metonymically to guests like Nelyubov – and most likely other drunken customers.

As a final, and, at first glance, non-metonymic example, consider the following:

(69) It's a hard question for me to answer. (COCA 2012)

In the case of (69), the incongruence resides in the fact that, in syntactic terms, *hard* modifies *question*, but conceptually it is an attribute of the *answer* to be given to the question.[94]

The data presented in (64)–(69) are usually characterized as instances of *hypallage*, i.e. a 'figure of speech in which there is an interchange of two elements of a proposition, the natural relations of these being reversed' (OED). Lausberg (1990: 102) regards hypallage as a grammatical figure.[95] Both characterizations are compatible with the conception presented in this section that there is a mismatch between syntactic form and conceptual-pragmatic content and that this mismatch is bridged and resolved via metonymic inference.

6.4 Grounding metonymies

Langacker (2013: vi) characterizes

> grounding units as grammatical indications of how entities described linguistically relate to the speaker, the hearer, and the speech event. Nominals are grounded by elements like articles and demonstratives, clauses by tense and modality.

Regarding nominal grounding, compare the differing functions of the definite article in the following two sentences:

---

93. Note that *drunken*, differently from *quiet*, can be used only in an attributive position: *a drunken customer* vs. **a customer who is drunken*.

94. Example (69) can also be coded with *hard* as a predicate adjective: *It is a question that is hard for me to answer*.

95. For the structure and meaning of premodifiers in English, in particular, hypallage, see Feist (2012).

(70) The tiger attacked a dog in the back yard of a residence before animal control could arrive. (COCA 2017)

(71) The tiger is India's national animal and is categorized as endangered under the Wildlife Protection Act (COCA 2019)

In (70), the definite article refers to a specific instance of the type 'tiger' that has already been introduced in the preceding discourse, i.e. is treated as a given discourse referent. The use of the noun phrase *the tiger* is non-metonymic in this example. In contrast, in (71), the definite article has a TYPE reading, i.e., it refers to the species *panthera tigris*. Radden (2009: 215) argues that in examples like (71), among other cognitive mechanisms, the metonymy INSTANCE → TYPE is operative, which could alternatively be formulated as INDIVIDUAL MEMBER OF A CATEGORY → CATEGORY.[96]

Clausal grounding may also be metonymically motivated. The use of the past tense in (72) is a possible example of the grounding metonymy PAST → PRESENT.

(72) I was wondering if it's possible to post a question about PCSX in this forum? (COCA 2012)

Under one interpretation, the writer of the blog (72) *is* actually wondering about the proposition formulated in the *if*-clause. In formulating his (indirect) request by means of the past tense verb form *I was wondering [...]*, the speech act becomes less aggressive or face-threatening (for the latter term, see Brown & Levinson 1987), and hence more polite than its counterpart in the present tense *I am wondering [...]*.

Modal auxiliaries can also be used as grounding devices, both literally and metonymically. To see this consider the following sentence from the academic journal *Hispanic Review*, which grounds a performatively used verb and hence the speech act (or 'speech event', as Langacker would put it):

(73) From this evidence we may conclude that, as a participial ending, *-udo* was indeed becoming extinct by the end of the thirteenth century in Castilian [...]. (COCA 1996)

The writer of (73), who uses the authorial *we* instead of *I*, literally characterizes his communicative act as a *possible* or *permissible* conclusion regarding the disappearance of the participial ending *-udo* in Castilian. However, despite the modal hedging of the performative verb *conclude* by means of *may*, the sentence is most likely intended to be understood as an actual act of drawing a well-supported inference. The metonymy at work is POTENTIALITY → ACTUALITY, which, in this example, is used to ground the whole utterance as an act of conclusion (see Panther & Thornburg 1999).

---

96. Radden (2009) integrates his metonymic approach to generic uses of nominals into an overall framework of conceptual blending theory (see e.g. Fauconnier & Turner 2002).

In conclusion, as the examples in this section show, grounding metonymies can affect propositional content, as in (71) and (72), but can also impact illocutionary force (see (73)), a topic that is briefly touched upon in Section 6.5 and is treated in more detail in Chapters 9 and 10, which focus on the role of metonymy in the production and interpretation of indirect illocutionary acts.

6.5   Illocutionary metonymies

Illocutionary metonymies have an impact on the illocutionary force of a speech act, and frequently also on its the propositional content. In Chapters 9 and 10, it is shown that the evocation of an illocutionary scenario component (see Chapter 6, for this concept) is a pragmatic means to create *indirect* illocutionary meanings. For example, by means of the utterance (74), the speaker may indirectly request the hearer to pass the salt:

(74)   Can you pass the salt?   (Searle 1975: 65)

Searle (1975) contends that an indirect speech act is a composite of two illocutionary acts: (i) the (intended indirect) illocutionary act, whose force has to be pragmatically inferred, is called *primary*, (ii) the illocutionary act that is signaled by means of the literal meaning of the utterance is called *secondary*. Thus, in example (74), the speaker performs the primary illocutionary act of requesting the hearer to pass the salt, which is achieved via the secondary illocutionary of asking the hearer whether she or he is able to pass the salt. The literal question addresses a BEFORE condition of directive speech acts, i.e. a preparatory condition in Searle's terminology.

It is worth noting at this point that indirect requests like (75) and (76) fulfill different sociopragmatic functions.

(75)   Can you lend me your sweater?

(76)   Would you mind lending me your sweater?

Gibbs (1994: 354–357) adduces psycholinguistic evidence that the speakers address different "obstacles" that may prevent hearers from complying with requests like (75) and (76). In (75), the utterer addresses the potential obstacle that the addressee might not be able to perform the requested action; whereas in (76) the potential obstacle to compliance is a mental attitude, i.e., the hearer might not be willing to lend the speaker his sweater. Brown and Levinson (1987) were among the first to discuss how sociocultural factors, such as face-saving strategies and politeness principles influence the lexicogrammatical form of indirect illocutionary acts. A detailed account of such sociocultural parameters goes however beyond the scope of this book because their presentation and discussion would require a monograph in its own right.

7. Conclusion

The objective of this chapter has been to make a case for metonymy as a figure of thought, in particular, an automatic and spontaneous process of inferencing within one conceptual frame, which can be modeled in terms of abductive reasoning. Metonymy is ubiquitous in language structure and use. A case in point are indirect speech acts, which are the focus of Chapters 9 and 10. To a large extent, the cognitive-inferential mechanisms at work in indirect illocutionary acts can be described in terms of conceptual metonymy, i.e. as instances of associative reasoning within illocutionary frames.

CHAPTER 9

Metonymic inferencing in indirect speech acts I
Assertives and commissives

1. Introduction

In this chapter, the thesis is put forward that the interpretation of indirect speech acts crucially relies on metonymic relations among illocutionary scenario components, of the kind that were introduced and illustrated in Chapter 6. If illocutionary scenarios are a specific type of conceptual frames, then it is only one step to the conclusion that they play an important role in the production of indirect speech acts, although they are possibly not the only sources of illocutionary indirectness. As in the case of other metonymies, the target meaning of an illocutionary scenario-based metonymy integrates the literal source meaning conveyed by the vehicle. The target meaning of the metonymy is more or less foregrounded. The more conventionalized the metonymic target, the more foregrounded or prominent it will be, and, consequently, the literal source meaning will be proportionately backgrounded. By way of example, consider:

(1) Can you open this window for me and prop it with something? (COCA 2018)

Utterance (1) can be intended as a literal question regarding the addressee's ability to open the window and prop it with something, but it can also serve as a vehicle (source) to ask the hearer to carry out the two actions coded in the respective infinitive clauses. In other words, its target illocutionary force is that of a request. This target meaning is foregrounded, although the literal question sense is not obliterated but backgrounded. Note that the directive interpretation is strengthened by the prepositional phrase *for me*, which indicates that the requested action benefits the speaker and thus signals the speaker's wish that the two actions be performed (see Chapter 6, Figure 4).

This chapter focuses on the *inferential* mechanisms at work in the production and comprehension of indirect speech acts, many of which, I argue, are metonymically motivated (see also Baicchi 2012 on the function of metonymy in indirect illocutionary acts). Given the ubiquity of indirectness in natural language, the discussion of indirect speech act types is by necessity non-exhaustive. Moreover, in what follows, the sociocultural function of indirect speech acts are only alluded to in passing.[97]

---

[97] The classical work that explores the politeness function of indirect speech acts – especially in terms of "face" (see Goffman 1967) – is Brown and Levinson (1987). See also Pérez-Hernández (2021), who deals with this subject from the perspective of teaching English as a foreign language.

2. The role of metonymic inferencing in indirect speech acts

In Chapter 6 (see Section 6), schematic illocutionary scenarios were developed for the five illocutionary categories proposed by Searle (1976). The following metonymic mechanisms that relate an illocutionary scenario component (source) to the CORE (target) can be exploited to generate indirect speech acts: (i) BEFORE → CORE, (ii) RESULT → CORE, and (iii) AFTER → CORE, all of which are instances of PART → WHOLE relations. There also exists a conceptually and pragmatically interesting category that is known as *hedged performatives*, i.e. performative utterances, in which the performatively used verb is specified by e.g. a modal auxiliary such as *can* or *must* (see Chapter 6, Section 5.3.1). This fourth mechanism is notated HEDGED CORE → CORE. In what follows, the focus is on these four options.[98] Using the classification of illocutionary acts into five illocutionary types proposed by Searle (1976), in Sections 2.2–2.6, I illustrate the four options of performing more or less *conventionalized* indirect speech acts with corpus data. The illocutionary scenario components that function as linguistic vehicles (see Chapter 6, Figure 2) of indirect speech acts are coded in various ways, e.g. as declarative, interrogative, or imperative sentences, but also by means of smaller phrases or words.

Following Searle (1969: 31), according to whom the "general form of (very many kinds of) illocutionary acts is $F(p)$", with F standing for 'illocutionary force' and p for 'propositional content', indirect speech acts can be described as a combination of illocutionary force shift and propositional content shift.

Before discussing linguistic data, some remarks on my use of the terms *direct speech act* vs. *indirect speech act* are in order. My assumption is that *direct* illocutionary acts are based on the *literal* meaning of the speech act in question, i.e., they evoke the CORE of the illocutionary scenario requiring no additional or, at most, minimal pragmatic inferencing regarding the meaning intended by the speaker. As a case in point, consider J. L. Austin's conception of an *explicit performative* utterance. Austin (1961: 222) assumes that when using an explicit performative utterance, such as (2), the speaker is "*doing* something rather than merely *saying* something"(see also Chapter 6, Section 5.3.1):

(2) I promise to be there.

In other words, in uttering (2), the speaker is not merely *describing* ("saying", in Austin's words) her communicative act (i.e. promising), but actually *performing* a promise.[99]

---

[98]. There are, as indicated by the lines, in the illocutionary scenario diagrams in Chapter 9, also potential metonymy links among scenario components, i.e. PART → PART relationships.

[99]. Austin here prefigures Searle's conception of explicit performative utterances as declarations (Searle 2002: 168–176.), i.e. as cases of "Saying so, makes it so."

In their introductory textbook to linguistics, Akmajian, Demers, Farmer, and Harnish (2010: 395) challenge Austin's account of explicit performatives claiming that their interpretation does involve inferencing. According to these authors, example (2) is literally a statement, i.e. an assertive speech act with a truth value, and that its intended performative, i.e. commissive, meaning is to be derived inferentially as follows:

i. The speaker is stating that she is promising to be there.
ii. If her statement is true, then she must be promising to be there.
iii. Presumably, the speaker is being truthful.
iv. So the speaker must be promising to be there in saying *I promise to be there*.

I assume explicit performative utterances to be of the most *direct* type, involving minimal pragmatic inferencing, as postulated by Akmajian et al. (2010). I also consider the standard illocutionary function of the major sentence types declaratives, imperatives, and interrogatives, i.e. assertives, directives, and questions (i.e. requests for information) as belonging to the category of direct illocutionary acts (on the relationship between speech acts and sentence types, see Siemund 2018). In the following sections a few examples of direct illocutionary acts are given first, followed by data that illustrate different types of indirect illocutionary acts in more detail.

2.1 Assertives

Assertive speech acts can be expressed directly by means of sentences such as (3) and (4):

(3) Postmodernism is imploding, collapsing inward with the weight of its own preposterousness. (COCA 1999)

(4) I claim that postmodernist theorists refrain from invalidating literary theory as establishing principles of knowledge. (COCA 1995)

Both sentences have been retrieved from academic works on literary theory. Example (3) is a *declarative* sentence with the illocutionary force of an assertive speech act, whereas (4), which, grammatically, is a declarative as well, instantiates an explicit performative utterance, i.e. marks its assertive force explicitly through the illocutionary verb *claim*.

Let us now turn to the types of metonymic inferences that motivate indirect assertive speech acts (see the corresponding illocutionary scenario in Chapter 6, Figure 2).

2.1.1 Inferences from BEFORE to CORE

As a first example consider assertions that are performed by means an of explicit assertion of the mental attitude associated with this illocutionary type:

S BELIEVES THAT P

(5) I believe that everyone can grow their own food and be self-sufficient.

(COCA 2017)

Depending on the discourse context, example (5) can be understood literally as a direct statement about the speaker's belief coded in the complement clause. It can however also be interpreted as evoking the illocutionary scenario component that, in speech act theory, is known as the *sincerity condition* of assertive speech acts, i.e. the speaker's belief that *p* is the case. In (5), the speaker, in addition to conveying the *belief* that *p*, will often (though not necessarily) be understood as indirectly *asserting* or *claiming* that *p*. The metonymic relationship between the source BEFORE and the target CORE can be formulated as follows:

(6) S ASSERTS that S BELIEVES that p → S ASSERTS that p

It is important to note that the relation between source meaning and the metonymic target meaning in (6) is *not* one of entailment. The relationship between the source meaning and the target meaning constitutes a strong pragmatic inference, but it does not hold by necessity. A speaker's assertion that she believes that *p* is weaker than her assertion that *p*. Support for this hypothesis comes from examples such as (7):

(7) I personally believe that books, journals, newspapers, etc., are much more efficient to read for the reader than online sources. (COCA 2012)

While 208 examples can be found in the American English corpus COCA for *I personally believe that p* (accessed: 17 August 2020), there is no attestation for e.g. *I personally claim/assert/contend/maintain/argue that p*. This finding can be seen as evidence that the expression of beliefs is felt by language users to be more subjective, i.e. less forceful, regarding their truth, than straightforward direct assertions. Thus one could imagine a situation in which a speaker asserts that he believes or thinks that something is the case, but admits the content of his belief may be wrong, as in (8):

(8) Many of these [centers] have clinics that provide assessments and I believe they are usually at no cost, but I may be wrong. (NOW, 19-10-26)

A second BEFORE component that may be invoked in indirect assertives is exemplified by (9) and (10):

S HAS ARGUMENTS FOR P / S HAS EVIDENCE FOR P

(9) The bust of Nefertiti has long been a bone of contention in the art world. Arguably, it belongs in Egypt, but German archaeologists took it from Amarna, Egypt over a century ago and have never given it back. (COCA 2016)

(10) There is evidence that travel and new environments are stimulating to children and their brains [...]. (COCA 2017)

An important feature of assertives is that, at the audience's request, the speaker is expected to provide evidence, i.e. reasons and arguments for the truth of the propositional content asserted. As illustrated by examples such as (9) and (10), this meaning component may be coded explicitly by a sentence adverb such as *arguably* or an existential construction such as *there is evidence (that)*.

If a speaker or writer asserts that that *p* is *arguably* true as in (9), it is only a short inferential leap to the conclusion that the writer *claims* that *p*. But what is the status of this inference? In pragmatic terms, it is a strong *implicature*, or, in the parlance of this book, an *illocutionary* metonymy, but, again, not an entailment. The arguments that bolster the assertion in (9) have been challenged and actually rejected (rightly or wrongly), as demonstrated by the history of ancient Egyptian archeological finds, many of which were removed (possibly illegally) from Egypt and are nowadays exhibited in European and American museums.

Evidence might also be merely *circumstantial*, as in many legal cases, and turn out to be insufficient to establish the truth of *p* without "reasonable doubt." What is considered as "evidence" for the truth of *p*, varies. In science, the criteria for what counts as evidence are more demanding than in ordinary discourse and conversation. In the latter, hearsay or other less reliable sources are often assumed to be sufficient for people to accept the truth of some assertion.

To conclude, as in the preceding cases, the claim that there is evidence that *p* implicates (but does not entail) the (defeasible) reading that the speaker claims that *p*:

(11) S ASSERTS that S has EVIDENCE that p → S ASSERTS that p

Another BEFORE presumption conveyed by an assertive speech act is that its propositional content *p* is relevant and/or of interest to the hearer.

P IS RELEVANT/OF INTEREST TO H

(12) It is also of interest that campaign skills do not affect ambition [...]. (COCA 2014)

(13) In this regard, it is of interest that the noradrenergic innervation of the neocortex may play a role in focusing the vascular response (Bekar et al., 2012), a concept that requires further exploration. (COCA 2017)

As (12) and (13) show, assertions that p can be indirectly conveyed by stating the BEFORE component that p is relevant or of interest. As argued in Chapter 6, relevance and interest are important meaning components of the assertive scenario. After all, if some proposition p is not of any interest or irrelevant in the communicative situation or context, the act of asserting p is superfluous, unless it is meant as a reminder. Examples like (12) and (13) instantiate the metonymic inference (14):

(14) S ASSERTS that p is of INTEREST / RELEVANT to H → S ASSERTS that p

An especially interesting illocutionary metonymy that relates a BEFORE component to the CORE as its illocutionary target, is the presumption that the hearer does not (yet) know p; i.e., p is news to the hearer.

H DOES NOT KNOW THAT P

(15) Did you know that water can still remain liquid below zero degrees Celsius? (COCA 2017)

(16) I case you didn't know, the 1960s didn't actually end in the 1960s. (COCA 2016)

(17) Why did you opt for a career in law? Didn't you know that girls in the 1960s were supposed to be nurses or teachers? (COCA 2006)

In what sense can (15)–(17) be considered as *indirect* assertives? All of them reference the addressee's knowledge state, and in doing so they indirectly function as assertives, i.e. as illocutionary acts whose primary function is to convey a *true* propositional content. In (15)–(17), the truth (of the content of) the complement clause embedded under *know* is *presupposed*, i.e. taken for granted, by the speaker (see Chapter 3).[100]

In (15), the speaker poses a *yes-no* question regarding the hearer's knowledge of some propositional content p. As pointed out in the preceding paragraph, the content of the complement clause introduced by *that* is *presupposed*. The presupposition p (indirectly) serves the communicative purpose to *inform* the hearer that

---

100. Kiparsky and Kiparsky (1970) classify *know* as a *factive* verb. There exist however uses of *know*, e.g. in the 1st person singular and present tense, that are not factive. As an example, consider: *Now, I don't know that I'm going to get along with Vladimir Putin.* (COCA 2017, SPOK). In this case, the complement clause is not presupposed but signals epistemic uncertainty, i.e., the complementizer *that* has the reading 'whether'. Because of such non-factive usages, *know* is classified as a semi-factive verb by Karttunen (1971).

p. The question about the hearer's knowledge state thus functions as a metonymic vehicle for the act of informing the hearer that *p*:

(18) S ASKS H whether H KNEW that *p* → S INFORMS H that *p*

An alternative way of representing the conceptual-pragmatic information in (18) is shown in Figure 1:

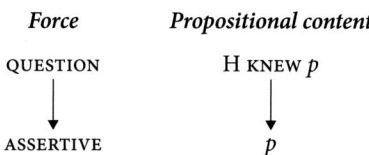

Figure 1. Metonymic shifts in illocutionary force and propositional content (example (15))

In (16), like in (15), the propositional content *p* is indirectly asserted – this time by means of the hypothetical assumption that the hearer is not familiar with *p*. Sentences such as (16) are known as *relevance conditionals*. The conditional clause introduced by *in case* does not formulate a sufficient condition for the truth of the content of the consequent clause, i.e., the truth value of the consequent clause is not dependent on whether the hearer knows or does not know that *p*. The subordinate clause hypothetically expresses a communicative condition, namely, that *p* could be newsworthy and relevant information.[101]

Finally, consider (17), which is drawn from an interview conducted by the *Saturday Evening Post* with "Judge Judy" (i.e. Judge Judy Sheindlin), the host of a reality court show in the U.S. The interviewer uses a negative question concerning Judge Judy's state of knowledge that *p* as a vehicle to convey the implicit assertion that in the 1960s girls were supposed to become teachers or nurses, rather than judges. In the given context, by means of the question *Didn't you know [...]?*, the interviewer also implicitly conveys that it was unusual for a girl in the 1960s to strive to become a lawyer. Simplifying somewhat, the metonymic inference chain from the literal question to the indirect assertion can be represented as in (19):

(19) S ASKS H whether H did NOT KNOW that *p* → S is SURPRISED that H did NOT (seem to) KNOW that *p* → S ASSERTS that *p*

More schematically, the metonymic inference pattern underlying (15)–(17) can be summarized as follows:

---

101. See Köpcke and Panther (1989) and Sweetser (1990) on different pragmatic types of conditional sentences.

(20) S PRESUPPOSES that *p* → S ASSERTS that *p*

The interesting feature about the inferential schema (20) is that a propositional content, which is presented as presupposed by the speaker, i.e. given information, is used as if it were new information of high interest and relevance.

2.1.2   Inference from HEDGED CORE to CORE

It is also possible, and actually not at all uncommon, that the illocutionary force coding device – if it is a performative verb – is grounded by a modal or attitudinal word or expression. Such cases are known as *hedged performatives* if the illocutionary force *F* denoted by the performative verb is not affected by the hedge. Consider the following examples, in which the assertive verb *inform* is hedged by the modals *must* and *can*, respectively:

S MUST/CAN ASSERT THAT P

(21) I must inform you that I have closed your credit account with us.
(iWeb, writeexpress.com)

(22) I can inform you there is no danger in utilizing iodine and salt (when diluted) to treat eye infections or inflammation.   (iWeb, trupanion.com)

Literally, in (21) the writer states his or her obligation to inform the addressee of some important piece of news, i.e. the closure of the addressee's credit account. There is a metonymically-based inference at work, which can be formulated as OBLIGATION TO ACT → ACTUAL ACTION, i.e., the obligation to inform the addressee of something counts as an act of actual informing the addressee. Thus, the hedge *must* does not affect the illocutionary force denoted by the verb *inform*. Nevertheless, it contributes to the overall meaning of the speech act in often (though not necessarily) inviting the metonymic inference that the news expressed in the propositional content is *bad*.

In contrast, in (22), the performative hedge *can* invites the inference that the propositional content of the assertive act conveys *good* news. The inference can be formulated again as a metonymy: ABILITY TO ACT → ACTUAL ACTION, a special case of the high-level metonymy POTENTIALITY → ACTUALITY (discussed at length in Panther & Thornburg 1999 and Panther 2016b).

2.1.3   Inferences from RESULT to CORE

The immediate pragmatic RESULT of an assertive act is that the speaker is regarded as being *committed* to the truth of the propositional content *p*; i.e., in principle, the speaker cannot assert some propositional content *q* that is conceptually or pragmatically incompatible with *p*. The RESULT component can be invoked by means of matrix clauses that explicitly express such a commitment to the proposition *p*:

S IS COMMITTED TO THE TRUTH OF P

(23) I am eternally committed to the truth that things could always be worse!
(NOW, 20-04-02)

(24) I am committed to the idea that everyone has a right to have an income [...].
(NOW, 17-01-16, GB)

(25) I am committed to the view that the more you fly, the faster you learn.
(NOW, 16-01-10, US)

In (23), the speaker overtly asserts his commitment to the truth of the propositional content that 'things could always be worse'. In doing so, he indirectly asserts this propositional content. The metonymic relation between the source and the target meaning is conceptually so tight that one could argue it is a case of entailment, which would contradict the constraint put forward in Chapter 8, Section 3.5, that the relationship between the source and the target meaning of a metonymy is contingent, i.e. does not hold by necessity. There are two ways of dealing with this problem: Either (23) is not an example of a metonymically motivated indirect speech act, or it is a borderline case where the metonymic relationship merges into one of semantic implication, i.e. entailment. The relationship between source and target is not one of entailment in (24) and (25), which express a commitment to an *idea* and a *view* that *p*, respectively. A speaker could be committed to the *idea* or *view* that *p* without explicitly going as far as to *assert* that *p*. Thus, the speaker of (24) or (25) might concede to be wrong about the truth of *p* (see (8) above).

The inferential relation between the speaker's claim that he or she is committed to the truth of *p* and the claim that *p* can be represented as in (26):

(26) S ASSERTS that S is committed to the TRUTH of *p* → S ASSERTS that *p*

2.1.4   Inferences from AFTER to CORE

Typically, in asserting some propositional content *p*, the speaker's intent is to make the hearer believe that *p*. Thus, one would expect that there are communicative situations or contexts in which speakers will make reference to this meaning component, as attested in the following examples:

H BELIEVES THAT P

(27) Believe me that quiet is rare in our current electronic culture. (COCA 2000)

(28) They work in, believe it or not, an old, converted dairy barn in Louisville, Ky.
(COCA 2017)

(29) Believe it or not, I am a romantic guy.[102]

(30) Can you believe that there were actually people during the design phase for Oriole Park who wanted to tear down the deteriorating B&O Warehouse and replace it with a view of the Convention Center and the Sheraton Hotel?
(COCA 2017)

(31) Unbelievably, about 70% of the heavy metals and 40% of the lead in U.S. landfills seeps out of dumped electronics, according to the Environmental Protection Agency. (COCA 2008)

In (27), the speaker invokes the AFTER component of assertives through an imperative sentence, i.e. directive speech act, asking the hearer to incorporate the propositional content 'quiet is rare in our current electronic culture' into his or her belief system. The scenario component syntagmatically *points* to a propositional content which is assumed to be asserted indirectly (see Figure 2).

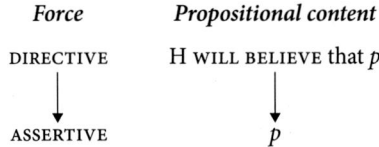

Figure 2. Asserting *p* by means of asking H to believe *p*

In (28) and (29), the appeal to the hearer's belief concerning *p* is coded by means of two truncated disjunctive imperatives. Via implicature, the truth of *p* is presented as not being conditional on whether the hearer believes or does not believe *p*. An additional pragmatic effect (implicature) of this kind of formulation is that the hearer's belief is *irrelevant*. In (30), the hearer's belief of *p* is formulated literally as a question *Can you believe that p?*, the implicature being that it is hard to believe that *p* – nevertheless, *p* is true. The implausibility of *p* is even more strongly conveyed in (31) where *p* is modified by the adverb *unbelievably*; but despite the implausibility of *p*, i.e. against all odds, *p* holds.

2.2 Commissives

In this section, indirect commissives are selectively illustrated with *promises* and *offers*. In the case of a promise, the speaker presumes that the hearer wishes the action in question to be carried out (hearer's benefit); in the case of offers, the

---

102. A quote from Donald Trump's book *Think like a Billionaire: Everything you Need to Know about Success, Real Estate, and Life* published in 2004 by Random House, New York (co-author: Meredith McIver).

speaker might not be so sure about whether the hearer feels that the offered action is in his/her best interest; i.e., offers are *conditional* on the hearer's acceptance of the propositional content of the offer.

Before illustrating the role of meaning components as metonymic sources for indirect commissives, it is useful to recall the important distinction between illocutionary *acts* and *verbs* that denote these acts (see e.g. Leech 1983). To keep these two levels apart is especially pertinent in the case of illocutionary verbs that are polysemous. A good example is the verb *promise*, which is used in English with varying (albeit) interconnected senses. The polysemy of *promise* can be illustrated with data from the English-language corpus *iWeb*:

(32) I promise to help spread kindness wherever and whenever possible.
 (iWeb, thenet24h.com)

(33) I promise I'll bring you lots of yummy yummy treats!
 (iWeb, tornadoughalli.com)

The examples in (32) and (33) are commissives: the performatively used verb *promise* evokes the whole illocutionary scenario represented in Chapter 6, Figure 4, i.e. the CORE.

However, quite commonly, one also finds examples in which *promise* does not signal a commissive function:

(34) I promise I did not use bad language! (nstperfume.com)

(35) I promise you Geometry was the only math in high school I excelled at.
 (iWeb, paperdaisydesign.com)

(36) It promises to be an interesting debate. (iWeb, corefiling.com)

Sentences (34) and (35) are explicit performative utterances; however, they are not acts of promising in the sense of Figure 4 in Chapter 6, but are understood as emphatic *assertives*. Their propositional content refers to *past* events or states-of-affairs – not to self-imposed *future* actions performed by the speaker, as in genuine commissives.

Utterance (36) instantiates an impersonal construction, in which *promise* is used non-performatively and does not involve a human promisor. In illocutionary terms, the construction functions as a prediction, i.e., its propositional content (coded by the infinitive clause) refers to a future event and, analogously to genuine commissive promises, such as (32), the propositional content is viewed as being of interest or beneficial to people who will witness the event in question (here, a debate).

In the following subsections genuine indirect commissives are presented and discussed that metonymically exploit components of commissive scenarios.

2.2.1 Inferences from BEFORE to CORE

Utterances (37) and (38) address the speaker's ability to perform the future actions of helping the addressee to find a way to get home and to get the hearer something to drink, respectively.

    S CAN DO A

(37) I can help you find a way to get home. (COCA 2017)

(38) Can I get you something to drink? Coffee or tea? Wine or soda? (COCA 2017)

Both (37) and (38) can be understood as offers. Interestingly, in the latter case, the ABILITY component is formulated as a question although, quite obviously, the speaker of (38) knows that he or she *is* able to get the hearer something to drink because, as an afterthought, the offerer lists some of the drinks available. The formulation as a question appears to be a less impositive and therefore more polite way of offering one's service than a statement, such as (37), of one's ability to help or serve the addressee. The coding of the offer by means of the construction *Can I VP$_{ACTION}$?* makes it easier for the hearer to decline the offer than if it is coded as an assertive of the form *I can VP$_{ACTION}$*.

Schematically, the metonymic pathways of examples like (37) and (38) can be represented as in Figure 3.

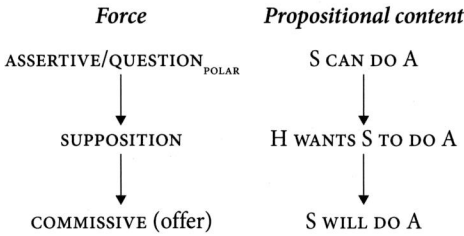

Figure 3. Offers by means of *I can VP / Can I VP?*

Note that the SUPPOSITION, i.e. the speaker's conditional assumption concerning the hearer's wish that the offered action be carried out has been integrated into Figure 3.

    H BENEFITS FROM A / H WANTS A

(39) Would you like me to get you some coffee? (COCA 2016)

(40) Do you want me to carry out your suitcase? (COCA 2017)

Utterances (39) and (40) invoke the scenario component that the offered action is in the hearer's best interest. This is conventionally done by means of interrogative vehicle constructions concerning the hearer's wish that the propositional content be fulfilled. In Figure 4, it is assumed that the speaker implicitly also conveys that he or she is able to perform the action in question.

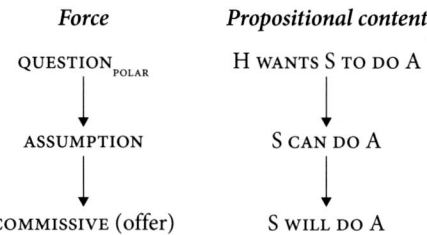

Figure 4. Offers by means of *Do you want/would you like me to do A?*

    S INTENDS TO DO A

(41) I intend to work with President Trump on those issues where he will, in fact, work for the middle class and working families in this country. (COCA 2016)

As (41) shows, a promise can be indirectly performed by asserting the mental attitude associated with promises, i.e. the *intention* to carry out an action that is in the interest of the hearer. Note that promises cannot be felicitously performed by means of the polar question *Do I intend to VP*_{ACTION}? The reason for this constraint seems to be that people are usually expected to be aware of their own mental states – here of their intention to act in a certain way. The metonymic inferences involved are diagrammed in Figure 5.

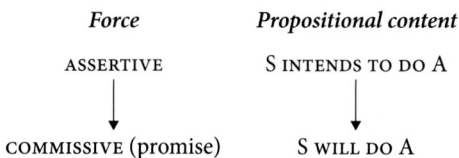

Figure 5. Promising by means of *I intend to VP*

2.2.2 Inferences from HEDGED CORE to CORE

Performatively used verbs like *promise* and *offer* can be hedged by the modal auxiliary *can* and still preserve the illocutionary force signaled by the verb.

    S CAN PROMISE/OFFER TO DO A

(42) I can promise we will follow the facts wherever they lead […]. (COCA 2017)

(43) I can offer you a position as a senior research associate […].   (COCA 2014)

Thus, (42) and (43) count as conventional indirect commissives. Interestingly, *I must promise [...]* or *I must offer [...]* are not understood as acts of promising and offering, respectively, and occur actually very rarely. In Panther (2016b) and Panther and Thornburg (2019), it is argued that the reason for this behavior is that *can* is conceptually and pragmatically *congruent* with *promise* and *offer* because it is associated with positive emotions and evaluations regarding some propositional content. Thus a promised action, as in (42), is conceived of as being beneficial to the hearer and therefore positively loaded. Analogously, being offered a senior research position as in (43) is considered an emotionally rewarding event for an academic. In contrast, the modal *must* often (though not necessarily) conveys negative feelings and evaluations. Figure 6 diagrams the illocutionary and propositional content shifts involved in examples like (42) and (43).

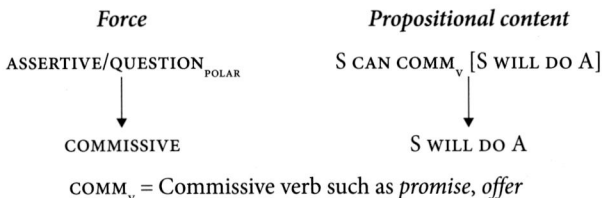

Figure 6. Hedged performative commissives: *I can promise/offer (you) to do A*

2.2.3 Inferences from RESULT to CORE

In performing a promise or an offer the speaker places herself under an obligation to carry out the promised or offered action. Alternatively, this self-imposed obligation, which is the immediate pragmatic result of a commissive speech act, can also be formulated as the speaker's *commitment* to perform the action in question.

S IS UNDER SELF-IMPOSED OBLIGATION TO DO A

(44) Shall I give you a ride, Miss Havisham? (iWeb, literature.org)

(45) Very good, sir. Shall I get your car for you? (COCA 2016)

(46) D. TRUMP: And, by the way, Ivanka Trump – everybody loves Ivanka. (CHEERING AND APPLAUSE). D. TRUMP: Come up, honey. Should I bring Ivanka up? (CHEERING AND APPLAUSE). D. TRUMP: Come up.
(COCA 2017)

In utterances (44) and (45), apart from signifying a future event, in using the construction *Shall I VP$_{ACTION}$?* the speaker conveys a deontic meaning, i.e., it invokes the illocutionary scenario component of self-imposed OBLIGATION, which is characteristic of commissives.[103] In (46), an extract from a speech given by U.S.

---

103. In German, as in English, offers can indirectly be conveyed by utterances such *Soll ich dich vom Flughafen abholen?* ('Shall I pick you up at the airport?').

President Trump, the *deontic* nature is explicitly coded by *should*. Examples (44)–(46) count as highly conventionalized indirect offers. In these examples, the speaker's obligation to perform the action in question is formulated as a polar question and the obligation to act becomes effective once it is accepted by the hearer. The inferential pathway from source to target meaning can be represented as in Figure 7.

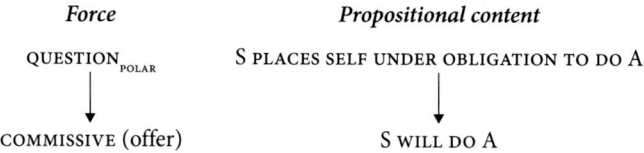

Figure 7. Indirect offers: *Shall I VP*$_{ACTION}$*?*

Speaker-oriented indirect offers coded as *Shall I VP*$_{ACTION}$*?* bear some resemblance to hearer-oriented offers of the type *Do you want me to VP*$_{ACTION}$ or *Would you like me to VP*$_{ACTION}$*?* The question *Shall I VP*$_{ACTION}$*?* solicits a response from the hearer regarding the latter's potential wish that some action be carried out that benefits him. While in polar questions of the type *Shall I VP*$_{ACTION}$*?* the modal *shall* conveys a deontic sense, for the corresponding declarative construction *I shall VP*$_{ACTION}$ the picture is less clear. There exists a normative rule in British English to the effect that *I shall VP* is the correct morphosyntactic form to express a future event, i.e., it is considered to be a future tense marker that applies to the 1st person pronominal subjects *I* and *we*. Thus (47), a letter of appreciation from a happy buyer of eye glasses, can be interpreted both as a prediction and as an indirect promise. In the latter function, which is strongly suggested by the adverbial expression *most definitely*, it invokes the AFTER component of commissives, i.e. S WILL DO A. Similarly, (48) is meant as a commitment to a future action, i.e. as a promise.

(47) I shall most definitely strongly recommend use of your services to all of my friends worldwide, and look forward to doing business with you again soon.
(iWeb, framesdirect.com)
(48) I shall most definitely be promoting The CV Store.   (iWeb, thecvstore.net)

But what about obligations that stem from some external source? An example of this type is (49):

(49) BILL CLINTON: Cigarette companies say they want to reduce teen smoking, but their lawyers rushed to the courthouse to seek an order blocking our actions. Well, that's their right, but it is my duty to safeguard the health and the safety of our children and I won't back down.   (COCA 1995)

Utterance (49), extracted from one of former U.S. President Bill Clinton's weekly radio addresses, can be interpreted as an indirect promise to safeguard the health and the safety of the nation's children. In the present context, the noun phrase *my duty* signals an ethically motivated commitment to the performance of future actions. Notice however that the interrogative pattern *Is it my duty to VP*$_{ACTION}$? cannot be used to convey a commissive speech act.

One of the intriguing puzzles regarding the coding of indirect commissives is that it is hard to find convincing data that illustrate the use of the modal *must*. While *must* quite commonly occurs in indirect directives (see Chapter 10), the constructional schema *I must VP*$_{ACTION}$ is not frequently used in a commissive sense. Here are two examples that could be interpreted as having an indirect commissive force:

(50) "Come, let's go to the bar. I must buy you a drink," he said as he wiped away the tear. (COCA 2007)

(51) Let him through. Jesse! Jesse! Hello, David. I must show you my new paintings sometime. (iWeb, script-o-rama.com)

In the fictional example (50), the male character literally asserts that he *must buy* the addressee a drink, and doing so *he* indirectly offers or promises to treat the addressee to a drink. Similarly, in (51), the speaker's self-imposed obligation (*I must [...]*) to show the hearers Jesse and David his new paintings can be interpreted as an indirect promise.

Finally, commitment, i.e. self-imposed obligation, can also be verbalized by means of *be committed (to)*, as in (52), which counts as a promise.

S IS COMMITTED TO DOING A

(52) I have personally apologized to anyone who I have upset, and I am committed to doing what is necessary to make up any damage that I may have caused. (COCA 2017)

Keeping in mind that the occurrence of promises of the form *I must VP*$_{ACTION}$ is somewhat restricted, the inferential pattern from the assertion of an obligation to perform some action to the promise to perform the action in question can be diagrammed as in Figure 8.

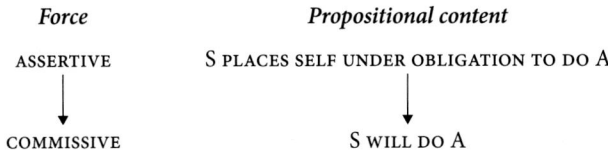

Figure 8. Indirect commissives via constructions that denote S's obligation to do A

2.2.4 Inferences from AFTER to CORE

The AFTER component of a commissive is the performance of the offered or promised action itself (Searle's propositional content condition). The promisor's future action can be coded by *will* or, with first person pronouns, following the rule of normative grammar, by means of *shall*, as in (53) and (54), respectively:

S WILL DO A

(53) I will buy you a drink next time we bar hop. (iWeb, dreamact.info)

(54) You're paying me a great deal of money. I shall return it all to you.
(COCA 2012)

Speech acts of the type illustrated by (53) and (54) involve a metonymic shift from a predictive assertion to a commissive, i.e. typically a promise (see Figure 9).

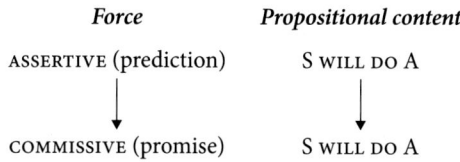

Figure 9. Indirect commissives: *I will/shall* VP_{ACTION}

Notice that the polar question construction *Will I VP*$_{ACTION}$? is not usable as a commissive speech act. The reason for this constraint seems to be that the conceptual gap from the literal polar question *Will I VP*$_{ACTION}$ to the target sense do 'I promise to do A', is hard if not impossible to bridge. The polar question construction conveys uncertainty about what the speaker will do in the future, and consequently it is not suitable or appropriate for conveying a promise by means of which the speaker commits herself unequivocally to a future action.

To finish this section, consider an "odd man out" example, which can be used conventionally as a commissive speech act, i.e. the imperative *Consider it done*. The online *Cambridge Dictionary* provides the reading "Used to say that you will do a particular task immediately."[104] Here is the example given by the dictionary (including some linguistic context):

(55) "Could you give me a copy of this page, please?" "Consider it done."

The promise *Consider it done* is often a reaction to an assumed wish or need of the addressee, which can actually be voiced as a request, as in the following discourse data in (56) and (57):

---

104. Retrieved from https://dictionary.cambridge.org/dictionary/english/consider-it-done.

(56) Need a certain encryption method? Want a dedicated database I? Consider it done. Our team specialists will help you build the solution you envision.
(iWeb, clicdata.com)

(57) "I hope you can help me, Mr. Baudouin … my car, a Renault Caravelle convertible, broke down some kilometer, outside of Antibes. I was lucky to get a ride into Cannes. Would you be kind enough to take care of it?" "No problem, Mademoiselle Xaubert, consider it done." "Thank you very much."
(https://books.google.co.uk/books?isbn=1491865687)

The dialogue in (57), which is drawn from the novel *It Began in Cannes* by Alpha de Monté is especially interesting because it contains a conversational sequence of three illocutionary acts: REQUESTING – PROMISING – THANKING; see (58):

(58) (i) Mademoiselle Xaubert indirectly REQUESTS Mr. Baudouin to DO A: "Would you be kind enough to take care of it?" (ii) Mr. Baudouin indirectly PROMISES to DO A: "Consider it done." (iii) Mlle Xaubert THANKS Mr. Baudouin (in advance) for DOING A: "Thank you very much."

Figure 10 diagrams the metonymical pathways from the literal directive source meaning to the commissive target meaning.

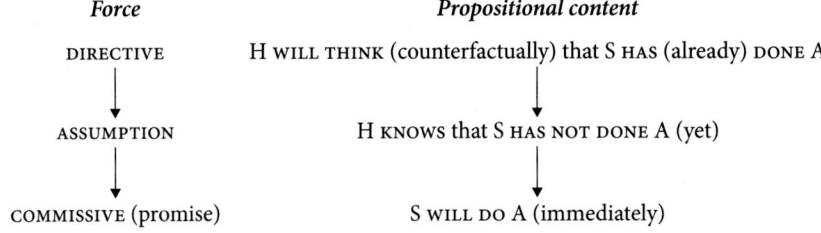

Figure 10. Inferential structure of *Consider it done*

On the face of it, the utterance *Consider it done* violates the propositional content condition, i.e. the AFTER, of promises, namely, that the speaker will perform the action expressed in the propositional content *after* the time of utterance t_0. The action is presented as already having been completed, although both speaker and hearer share the knowledge that its performance is merely an *imaginary* or *virtual* scenario, but one that will be implemented, i.e. made *actual* in the (near) future.

3. Conclusion

In this chapter, it has been argued that indirect speech acts can be accounted for, to a large extent, in terms of inferential schemas that operate within illocutionary scenarios. An illocutionary scenario is a kind of conceptual frame. The relevant inferential tool for deriving indirect illocutionary acts is "the metonymic relationship […] between parts of the same frame", i.e. what Dancygier and Sweetser (2014: 101) call *frame metonymy*. As shown in the chapter, the parts or components of illocutionary scenarios can be addressed in various ways, e.g. by means of statements, questions, or directives, which serve as metonymic sources, from which the target meaning, i.e. the intended illocutionary meaning, of the utterance in question can be derived. Indirect illocutionary uses of assertives and commissives, retrieved mostly from internet corpora of American English (e.g. COCA), were analyzed in terms of metonymic reasoning. In Chapter 10, three additional illocutionary categories are investigated in terms of their potential to be performed as indirect speech acts: directives, expressives, and declarations.

CHAPTER 10

Metonymic inferencing in indirect speech acts II
Directives, expressives, declarations

1. Introduction

This chapter resumes the topic of indirect illocutionary acts, focusing on directives, expressives, and declarations. I assume, as in Chapter 9, that the derivation of indirect speech acts involves associative links among illocutionary scenario components. It comes as no surprise that directives and expressives are often conveyed indirectly; but one would not expect that even declarations, which are embedded in official institutions such as government, church, the judiciary system, etc., can also be performed indirectly.

2. Directives, expressives, and declarations

2.1 Directives

Direct directive speech acts are schematically coded as imperatives (see (1)), or, more specifically, by means of performatively used verbs, i.e. *order*, *beg*, and *urge* in examples (2), (3), and (4), respectively:

(1) Lock the doors, and don't let anyone in until I get back. (COCA 2009)
(2) I order you to stay where you are. (COCA 2007)
(3) I beg you to help me, for only you are strong enough. (COCA 2010)
(4) Up next, a really fascinating documentary, you're really going to like it. I've seen it. I urge you to watch it. (COCA 2014)

In contrast to typical directives, such as (1)–(4), as pointed out in Chapter 6, Table 7, acts of recommendation and advice lack the scenario component S WANTS H to DO A, and they have an additional scenario component H BENEFITS FROM A.

2.1.1 Inferences from BEFORE to CORE
To begin with, consider a construction that is commonly used to code indirect directives: it makes reference to the hearer's ability to carry out the desired action.

H CAN DO A

(5) Can you close your eyes, please? (COCA 2011)
(6) 'Hey, could you be like a little more quiet,' Marchiafava said. (COCA 2017)
(7) If you can explain what you meant. (COCA 2017)
(8) If you could please follow me. (COCA 2011)
(9) You can set the table. (COCA 2016)
(10) Maybe you could be a little bit more precise. (COCA 1990)

Examples (5)–(10) function as highly conventionalized indirect requests (see Searle 1975). In utterances (5) and (6), the hearer is literally asked a *question* about his ability to perform some specific action (the secondary illocutionary act in Searle's terminology) and in doing so is actually *requested* to carry out the action (the primary illocutionary act, according to Searle). In (7) and (8), the hearer's ability is represented as a hypothetical state-of-affairs (a common coding strategy to render the request less impositive and more polite), while in (9) and (10) the hearer's ability to perform the action is *asserted*. Furthermore, in (10), the imposition is considerably softened down owing to the epistemic adverb *maybe* and the past tense form *could*, which signify possibility or hypotheticality, respectively. Schematically, the metonymic pathway for examples (5)–(10) from source to target can be diagrammed as in Figure 1.

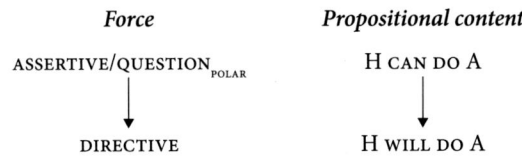

Figure 1. Directives by means of *You can/could VP*$_{ACTION}$ and *Can/could you VP*$_{ACTION}$?

Especially interesting, both from a syntactic and a conceptual-pragmatic perspective, are examples such as (7) and (8). These utterances instantiate the more general phenomenon of "insubordination", (N. Evans 2007; Evans & Watanabe 2016), i.e. clauses that look formally like subordinate clauses – in the case of (7) and (8), like conditional clauses – function as independent illocutionary acts, here conventional indirect requests (see e.g. Vallauri 2016 on "insubordinated" conditionals in Italian). In (7) and (8), only the antecedent clause (protasis) is coded; the consequent clause (apodosis) remains unexpressed. It is sometimes retrievable from the discourse context, but the elliptic apodosis is not essential to an adequate understanding of the directive construction *If you can/could VP* any longer, since it has acquired a conventionalized requestive meaning (see Figure 2).

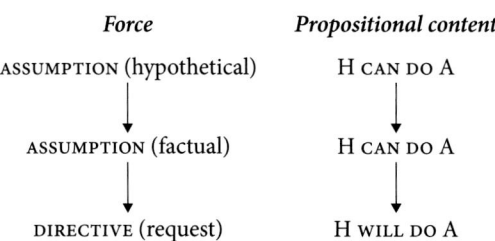

Figure 2. Indirect requests by means of *If you can/could VP*_{ACTION}

Figure 2 provides a somewhat simplified picture of the inferential structure of *if*-requests (see Panther & Thornburg 2005 for a more detailed analysis), but one crucial metonymy is represented: the switch from hypotheticality to factuality. The speaker of an *if*-request normally assumes that the hearer *is able* to perform the requested action, although, for politeness reasons, in order to decrease the impositive pressure on the hearer, the speaker formulates her or his request as a conditional antecedent clause. This strategy is also at work in the case of requests coded as *Can/could you VP?* (see Figure 1), where it is the interrogative form of the illocutionary construction that mitigates the degree of obligation imposed on the hearer to comply with the request.[105]

Let us now turn to a general property of directives that could be called a "reasonableness condition", i.e., the meaning component that the speaker sees no good reasons why the hearer should not comply with the directive (see Chapter 6, Figure 5). But in what sense is it "reasonable" to comply with a directive? The answer varies with the kind of directive performed and the social relationship between speaker and hearer. In the case of a directive with a strong degree of imposition or pressure on the hearer, such as an order or a command, reasonableness might simply amount to the consideration that it is not opportune or advisable for the addressee to challenge a socially superior speaker, such as the hearer's boss in a workplace or a commanding officer in the military.

NO GOOD REASONS FOR H NOT TO DO A

(11) […] you treat me like a big joke. You think I don't notice? Why don't you like me? (iWeb, desuarchive.org)

---

[105]. Notice that questions and conditionals are conceptually closely related. Historically, English *if* and German *ob* 'whether' are etymological cognates. The conjunction *if* can be used in conditional clauses but also head indirect questions. Like *if*-clauses, German *ob*-clauses can be used in an "insubordinate" way as requests, e.g., *Ob du mal eben das Fenster öffnen könntest?* 'If you could open the window'.

(12) Q. "Why don't you offer any WaterSense certified kitchen faucets?" A. Currently, the WaterSense program doesn't offer certification for kitchen faucets.
(iWeb, plumbings.supply.com)

(13) Why don't you go to the oil store and buy as much as you need?
(iWeb, logos.com)

(14) "Why don't you feed the hens and bring in some eggs." A command, not a question. (COCA 2017)

(15) Why not paint your kitchen cabinets glossy purple? (COCA 1996)

Examples (11)–(14) exhibit the construction *Why don't you VP?*, while in (15) a non-finite construction *Why not VP?* is used. In (11) and in (12), the *Why don't you VP* construction is used in its *literal* sense, i.e., it is a question *why* some state or event does *not* hold. Thus the speaker or writer of (11) wants to know why the addressee does not like him.[106] Likewise, the questioner in (12) wishes to be given reasons why the faucets in question are not offered on sale.

In contrast, (13) and (14) can be understood as directive speech acts. By means of invoking the "unreasonableness" of not carrying out the action expressed in the propositional content, the two utterances function as (more or less strong) suggestions to perform the action expressed in the propositional content. However, this does not mean that their literal meaning as *why*-questions has been completely supplanted by the directive meaning. The addressee could still answer (13) providing reasons why he does not go to the oil store. Likewise, evidence that the literal *why*-question interpretation is still accessible can be found in the fictional piece (14), in which the narrator categorizes the utterance *Why don't you feed the hens [...]?* as a command, i.e. a directive, rather than as a literal question. Figure 3 represents the conceptual-pragmatic mechanisms at work that lead from the source meaning 'Why don't you do VP?' (a negative *why*-question) to the target meaning 'I suggest that you do VP'.

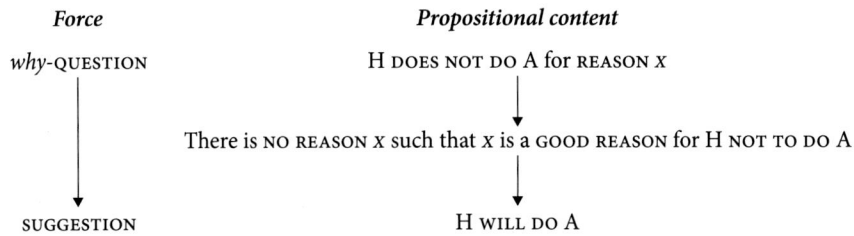

Figure 3. Directives (suggestions) by means of *Why don't you VP*$_{ACTION}$*?*

---

106. Note that the *why*-question interpretation is strengthened by the verb *like*, which is not an action verb, but refers to an emotional *state*. Prototypical directives usually require predicates that are interpretable as actions.

Finally, consider (15), which exemplifies the non-finite *Why not VP?* construction, discussed e.g. in Gordon and Lakoff (1975). According to these authors, there is no inferential pathway from a "literal" interpretation as a question to the interpretation as a suggestion – the strongly suggestive illocutionary force of the construction has been completely conventionalized in this case.

Next, consider a few examples that address the mental attitude, i.e. the speaker's wish or desire that the hearer carry out a certain action:

S WANTS H TO DO A

(16) I want you to keep your eyes and ears open, and your mouth shut.
(COCA 2017)

(17) I would like you to go over our papers and make whatever comments seem appropriate.
(COCA 2017)

In both (16) and (17), the speaker *asserts* his *wish* that the hearer perform the respective action, and in doing so, indirectly *asks* the hearer to act accordingly. The inferential pathway from a mental attitude (sincerity condition) to the corresponding illocutionary act can be formulated as in Figure 4.

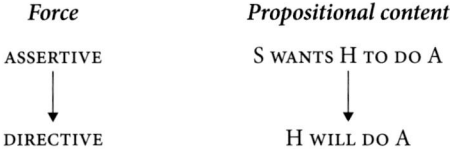

Figure 4. Directives by means of *I want you to VP*_{ACTION}

2.1.2 Inferences from HEDGED CORE to CORE

It is not uncommon to find directives, in which a performatively used directive verb is hedged by a modal such as *must* (e.g. (18) and (19)) or even two hedges such as *afraid* [...] *must* (e.g. (20) and (21)):

(18) Once again, I must ask you to lower your voice. (COCA 2011)

(19) General Stanton, I must insist that you listen to me. (COCA 2009)

(20) I'm afraid I must ask you to leave within the next seven days. (COCA 2012)

(21) I'm afraid I must insist that you stay at least a day. (COCA 2017)

By way of example, the inferences involved in an indirect directive like (18) can be represented as in Figure 5 (where DIR_V denotes a directive verb).

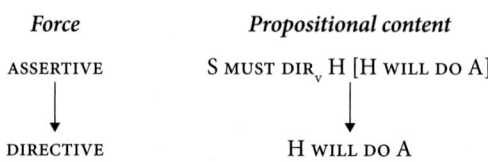

Figure 5. Hedged directive performatives: *I must ask you to VP*_ACTION

Modals like *must* that hedge a performatively used directive verb *ask (to)* or *order* co-occur with propositional contents that connote a negative emotion or evaluation. For example, (18) could be uttered in a situation when the speaker feels it is inappropriate to talk in a loud voice; furthermore, in using the modal *must*, the speaker signals that he is reluctant to perform the directive speech act, i.e. would rather not to have to perform it, because it contains a negative message. The interesting property of such hedged performative utterances is that the directive force of the speech act is not affected by the modal *must*. Double hedges like *afraid [...] must*, as in (20), convey an even stronger effect of negative emotivity and evaluation, which is signaled by the emotive predicate *(be) afraid*.

It is important to note that when a directive verb such as *ask (to)* or *order* is hedged by the modal *can*, its directive illocutionary force is not necessarily preserved:

(22) Your stay here is a very temporary one. I can ask you to leave at any time.
(iWeb, parahumans.wordpress.com)

(23) All I can ask you is to trust me on that issue and to watch me.
(iWeb, murderpedia.org)

In utterance (22), the speaker is not asking the hearer to leave at any time – rather he *warns* him or *threatens* him that he may have to leave in the future. In contrast, utterance (22) can be interpreted as an appeal to trust the speaker on the issue in question. However, the wording *all I can ask you* suggests that the speaker might not have high expectations regarding the addressee's willingness to comply with the request.

2.1.3   *Inferences from* RESULT *to* CORE

The immediate pragmatic result of a felicitous directive is that the hearer is understood as being under an obligation to comply with the directive. The strength of the obligation, or degree of imposition, varies from directive to directive. It is relatively low in the case of a polite request where the hearer is at liberty not to comply. It is very strong in the case of an order by a superior addressed to a subordinate person, e.g. an order given by a commanding officer to a common soldier. Strong obligations can be expressed by *must*, while the weaker modal *should* is used in acts of suggesting, recommending and advising. Thus (24) and (25) function as impositive indirect directives, such as ordering, commanding but also, possibly, urging or entreating, all of which signal a very strong desire on the part of the speaker that a certain action be carried out. In contrast, (26) and (27) signal a weaker obligation, which is not binding and leaves the addressee the option of following or disregarding the respective suggestion, advice or recommendation.

H IS UNDER OBLIGATION TO DO A

(24) You must come to Lyonsgate at once. (COCA 2017)

(25) You must leave tonight and go – elsewhere. (COCA 2017)

(26) You should plan ahead and prepare for important events in your business, too. (COCA 2017)

(27) You should read this, Barton. (COCA 1991)

The underlying metonymic schema for examples like (24)–(27) is represented in Figure 6.

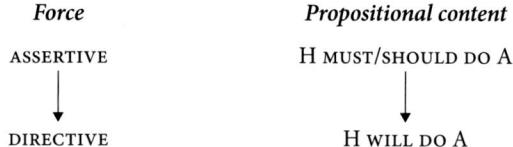

Figure 6. Directives by means of *You must/should* VP$_{ACTION}$

2.1.4 Inferences from AFTER to CORE

The AFTER component of the directive scenario is what Searle's (1969, 1976) calls the propositional content condition. Different from assertives whose propositional content is unconstrained, in a directive speech act the propositional content must directly signify or indirectly point to a *future action* of the hearer, i.e. an action that takes place after the utterance time, which in this book is notated H WILL DO A.

H WILL DO A

(28) Jim, you clean up this mess. (iWeb, dailyscript.com)

(29) Silence, mortal. You will leave my realm immediately. (COCA 2010)

(30) You will leave the air base and proceed to a rented fishing boat and head out. (COCA 2017)

(31) Will you please define essentialism for me? (COCA 2012)

(32) Will you please calm down? You're making me nervous. (COCA 2009)

(33) Would you please get out of the car? (COCA 2015)

As can be seen in (28), the hearer's future action can be coded in the present tense, but the action of cleaning up "this mess" is supposed to occur *after* the time of the utterance. Furthermore, the reference to the component H WILL DO A can be coded as an assertive speech act, i.e., more narrowly as a prediction, as in (29) and (30), or more politely as a question, as in (31) and (32). It is also noteworthy that, in the latter two examples, the adverb *please* signals that they are not to be interpreted as questions, i.e., *please* (placed before the verb) marks them as completely *conventionalized* indirect requests. Finally, polite requests can also be performed by means of the past tense form *would*, as in (33), but this illocutionary function is coded only by interrogative structures like *Would you VP$_{ACTION}$?*; i.e., declaratives sentences of the form *You would VP$_{ACTION}$* do not seem to be usable in a directive function.

Figure 7 shows the inferential illocutionary and propositional content shifts involved in indirect directives of the form *You will VP$_{ACTION}$* and *Will you VP$_{ACTION}$?*

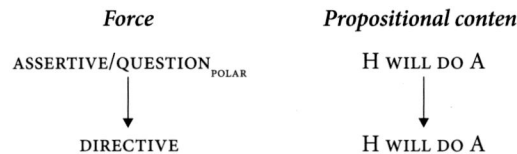

Figure 7. Directives by means of *You will VP$_{ACTION}$* or *Will you VP$_{ACTION}$?*

2.2 Expressives

In this section, indirect expressives such as acts of thanking, praising, congratulating, apologizing, and combinations of these, are presented and analyzed (see Chapter 6, Figures 6–9, for illocutionary scenarios of expressives). The following corpus data again illustrate the important role of context in the interpretation of indirect speech acts. In a conversational exchange, the interactants, as it were, "move" within scenarios, and in doing so, strengthen or reinforce the interpretation of linguistic units, e.g. sentences or clauses, as metonymically pointing to certain illocutionary acts.

2.2.1 Inferences from BEFORE to CORE

BEFORE components are addressed in the narrative excerpts (34) and (35):

(34) "You did an excellent job on this case, Eric, and you really helped me out. I'm sorry I ever doubted you. I'm very glad that Leslie encouraged me to trust you – even if you did risk your life." "Thanks. I'm just happy I was able to contribute [...]."   (https://books.google.co.uk/books?isbn=1411658086)

(35) "You really helped me back there." "You're welcome, young man. Be careful out there," he said.   (https://books.google.co.uk/books?isbn=1449752349)

The first sentence in (34) refers to two illocutionary scenario components of acts of *congratulation* or *praise* at the same time: an action performed by the addressee Eric combined with an evaluation of this event as GOOD, i.e. *You did an excellent job [...]*. This positively evaluated action can be linked to the *presupposition* of the congratulation scenario. Moreover, the subsequent clause *[...] you really helped me out* can be understood as a metonymic index of thanking Eric – it invokes a BEFORE component, again a factive presupposition, of the illocutionary frame of thanking. The speaker continues with an *apology*, in naming the mental attitude (a.k.a. sincerity condition) associated with apologies (*I am sorry [...]*), which is a BEFORE component of this speech act type.

In example (35), the first speaker refers to an event that can be linked to the factive presupposition of the *thanking* scenario, and in doing so invites the interpretation that he thanks his interlocutor. This interpretation is strengthened by the normally positive evaluation of acts of support and help, i.e. by the scenario component S BENEFITS FROM A, and the reaction of the person being thanked, who responds with *You are welcome, young man*, a conversational turn that is a normal follow-up of an act of thanking.

Consider next a piece of discourse that consists of a series of (asyndetic) sentences every one of which can be interpreted as invoking BEFORE components of the apology scenario:

(36) I know I made you feel uncomfortable. I behaved badly. I'm sorry.
(iWeb, www.brisbanetimes.com.au)

The speaker of (36) starts out with the proposition that he (knew he) made the hearer feel *uncomfortable*, which sets the scene for the evaluation *I behaved badly*. These propositions can be linked to the BEFORE component of the apology scenario: the speaker did something (factive presupposition) and his action is evaluated as BAD for the hearer. The interpretation that the speaker is apologizing to the hearer is strengthened, i.e. reinforced, in the third sentence, which expresses the mental attitude associated with apologies, i.e. *I am sorry*. Although neither the verb *apologize* nor the noun *apology* is used, given these contextual clues, it is clear that the speaker apologizes for his behavior.

Finally, as another good example in which BEFORE components of the apology scenario are addressed, consider an excerpt from the song *Lonely* composed by the Senegalese-American singer Akon:

(37) Can't believe I had a girl like you and I just let you walk right outta my life, //
After all I put you through you still stuck around and stayed by my side. // What really hurt me is I broke your heart, // Baby you were a good girl and I had no right, // I really wanna make things right, [...]. (iWeb, links2love.com)

The lyrics of the song quoted in (37) make reference to a number of the first person narrator's actions that he evaluates as BAD, such as *[…] I let just let you walk right outta my life, After all I put you through […], […] I broke your heart*, or *[…] I had no right*, which he contrasts with the *good* and loyal behavior of the girl. These propositions are clear indicators of an act of apology, an interpretation that is further strengthened by the (indirect!) promise *I really wanna make things right […]*.

2.2.2   Inferences from HEDGED CORE to CORE

Expressives are also often construed as hedged performatives. Hedges can be modals such as *must*, as in (38) and (42), and *may*, as in (43); as well as mental attitude expressions like *want (to)* in (40) and *would like (to)* in (39) and (41):

Apologizing

(38)   I must apologize for the errors in my previous post.
                                                             (iWeb, bestsaxophonewebsiteever)

(39)   I would like to apologize for the unfortunate incident that took place at the Booz Allen Classic, Sabbatini said in a statement Monday.   (COCA 2005)

Thanking

(40)   I want to thank you for your country's support for the UN Security Council efforts […].   (iWeb, humanrights.gov)

(41)   I would like to thank you for your clear, easy to understand, well explained text and diagrams.   (iWeb, mathopenref.com)

Congratulating

(42)   I must congratulate you on a business well run.   (iWeb, kennedyviolins.com)

(43)   May I congratulate you on your recent marriage, Lord Greenleigh? I wish you and your intrepid lady the best.   (COCA 2006)

While in utterances (38)–(42) the speaker *asserts* that he or she *must*, *wants* to or *would like* to perform the speech act named by the illocutionary verb, example (43) differs from the former in interesting ways. It involves *double hedging*: there is a shift in grammatical mood from declarative (assertion) to interrogative (question), and the illocutionary verb *congratulate* is hedged by the modal auxiliary *may*. Literally, the speaker *asks* Lord Greenleigh for *permission* to congratulate him on his recent marriage, but the intended target meaning is obviously to congratulate the addressee on his recent marriage (in a polite way).

2.2.3 Inferences from RESULT to CORE

The immediate RESULT of the performance of an expressive act is that the speaker is taken to have a certain mental attitude or feeling. For example, expressions such as *(be) grateful* or *appreciate* are routinely used in acts of thanking as in (44) and (45):

(44) I am grateful for your dedication to helping your fellow Floridians and rebuilding our beautiful communities. (iWeb, harris.com)

(45) Wow! Very nice work of yours, I really appreciate it! Thanks [...]. (iWeb, owlcation.com)

Example (45) is especially interesting. It is a brief comment on an Internet article titled *Did you Know that "Spicy" is not a Taste?* by Mushtahid Salam.[107] The commenter starts with an expression of admiration, i.e. *Wow!*, and continues with a proposition that points to the presupposition (BEFORE) of the scenarios of congratulation and/or thanking, followed by the positive mental attitude predication *I really appreciate it* (RESULT) and concludes with the nominal performative *Thanks*, i.e. with an explicit reference to the CORE. The writer moves sequentially through various components of the thanking scenario, which mutually reinforce each other, i.e. intensify the force of the act of thanking.

2.3 Declarations

Declarations are illocutionary acts that are used in institutional, legal, or religious contexts. Within such institutions, certain formulaic ways of speaking and writing are common, which are associated with precise meanings that do not require (much or any) pragmatic inferencing for their correct interpretation. The role of individual language users in the construction of meaning is thus minimized; the utterance of the right words in the right situation by an institutionally authorized speaker or author is sufficient to guarantee successful performance. Hence, one would expect that *indirect* declarations are rare or even non-existent. Moreover, since the illocutionary force of declarations has to be crystal-clear, one would also expect that they be formulated as *explicit performative* utterances.

To test the assumptions formulated in the previous paragraph, in the following sections various types of declaration are presented and analyzed, such as (i) declarations of war, (ii) verdicts and sentences assigned by a jury and judge to a defendant in a court of justice; (iii) acts performed by authorized clergy, such as baptizing and marrying; and (iv) acts of resignation from some official function or employment.

---

107. Retrieved August 1, 2018 from https://owlcation.com/stem/Did-you-know-that-spicy-is-not-a-taste.

As will become evident in what follows, the working hypothesis that declarations are maximally explicit will be confirmed to some extent, but, interestingly, indirect declarations can also be found.

2.3.1   Declarations of war

In June 18, 1812, the Senate and House of Representatives of the United States enacted a declaration of war on the United Kingdom. Here is an excerpt of that resolution:

(46)   *Be it enacted by the Senate and House of Representatives of the United States of America in Congress assembled*, That war be and is hereby declared to exist between the United Kingdom of Great Britain and Ireland and the dependencies thereof, and the United States of America and their territories […].
(http://avalon.law.yale.edu/19th_century/1812-01.asp)

In December 8, 1941, one day after the Japanese attack on Pearl Harbor, the United States' declaration of war on Japan ran as follows:

(47)   [B]e it *Resolved by the Senate and House of Representatives of the United States of America in Congress assembled*, That the state of war between the United States and the Imperial Government of Japan […] is hereby formally declared […]. (https://govtrackus.s3.amazonaws.com/legislink/pdf/stat/55/STATUTE-55-Pg795.pdf)

Both texts (46) and (47) confirm the hypothesis that official declarations are conveyed (here, coded in the passive voice) by explicit performatives such as *war is hereby [formally] declared*, i.e., they are typical examples of "saying it, makes it so."[108]

On December 8, 1941, Japan declared war on the United States of America and the British Empire. The official English translation of the "imperial rescript" uses an explicit performative formula, this time in the active voice (italics added):

(48)   *We hereby declare War* on the United States of America and the British Empire.
(https://en.wikipedia.org/wiki/Japanese_declaration_of_war_on_the_United_States_and_the_British_Empire)

In contrast to (46)–(48), consider an excerpt of the British Declaration of War on Japan, which was transmitted by Winston Churchill to the Japanese ambassador on December 8, 1941 (italics added):

---

108. It is noteworthy that many military interventions by the U.S. military, such as the "Iraq War" of 2002, was not sanctioned by the U.S. Congress as a war but as an act of "Authorization for the use of Military Force against Iraq Resolution of 2002" (https://www.gpo.gov/fdsys/pkg/PLAW-107publ243/PLAW-107publ243.pdf). Thus, technically, a state of war did not exist between the United States and Iraq.

(49) His Majesty's Ambassador at Tokyo has been instructed to inform the Imperial Japanese Government in the name of His Majesty's Government in the United Kingdom that *a state of war exists between our two countries*.
(https://en.wikipedia.org/wiki/United_Kingdom_declaration_of_war_on_Japan)

The text in (49) does not contain a performative formula that characterizes it explicitly as a declaration of war. Although its communicative intention in the given historic situation is clear, it is an indirect way of declaring war that requires pragmatic inferencing from a somewhat wordy source meaning to the target meaning that this letter counts as a declaration of war. The inferential steps from source to target can be informally sketched as in (50):

(50) Britain's Prime Minister Churchill *informs* the Japanese ambassador in London that he has *instructed* the British ambassador in Tokyo to *inform* the Japanese Government that *a state of war exists* between the United Kingdom and Japan. → A *state of war exists* between the United Kingdom and Japan. → The United Kingdom *declares war on* Japan.

Interestingly, the statement of the existence of a state of war , which itself is implied by (50), functions as the premise for the inference that the United Kingdom actually *declares* the existence of a state of war between the two countries. In other words, this inference is an example of the metonymy RESULT → CORE. The RESULT component of the declaration-of-war scenario, i.e. the existence of a state of war, stands for the declaration of war (CORE) itself.

In conclusion, even declarations of war, occasionally at least, are not necessarily performed in the most explicit performative way. In the subsequent sections, additional examples of indirect declarations are presented and discussed.

2.3.2 Verdicts and sentences

To begin with, consider specific uses of a verb that, at first sight, does not seem to have anything "communicative" in its meaning, i.e. *find*. Notwithstanding, apart from its basic senses, such as 'discover' or 'recognize', *find* is used as a speech act verb in legal contexts with the reading 'officially declare to be the case' (NOAD). This sense is exemplified by sentences such as (51) and (52), which describe declarations performed in the courtroom:

(51) The court found that he aided her in the murders.   (COCA 2017)

(52) The court found him guilty of committing domestic violence […].
(COCA 2015)

Explicit performative uses of *find* in courts of justice are also common. The following verdict was broadcast by the U.S. television channel NBC on December 1, 2017:[109]

(53) JUDGE (in court): The record will reflect that the jury has reentered the courtroom indicating that they have reached a verdict. UNIDENTIFIED WOMAN (in court): Murder in the second degree, how do you find the defendant? Guilty or not guilty? UNIDENTIFIED WOMAN (in court): Not guilty.
(COCA 2017)

Example (53) is an instance of a verdict reached by a jury in a criminal case. In speech-act terms, such verdicts are declarations because, apart from their claim to truth, a property that they share with assertives, their successful performance *creates* new facts. The decision of a jury to *find* a defendant *guilty* or *not guilty* has important personal and social consequences for the defendant's future life.

That expressions like *find guilty* can be used as explicit performatives is supported by the observation that they collocate with the instrumental adverb *hereby*, which is an indicator of the verb's performativity (see Chapter 6). An example of this usage is (54):

(54) We the jury, do hereby find the defendant, Thomas Barton Whitaker, guilty of the offense of capital murder as charged by the indictment. (COCA 2008)

The explicit performative use of *find* as a declaration is also common in legislative acts. Here are two examples of legislation enacted in the states of California and Colorado, i.e. (55) and (56), respectively:

(55) The people of the State of California hereby find and declare that the purposes of the Compassionate Use Act of 1996 are as follows: […] To ensure that seriously ill Californians have the right to obtain and use marijuana for medical purposes […]. (iWeb, canorml.org)

(56) The people of the state of Colorado hereby find that tobacco addiction is the leading cause of preventable death in Colorado, that Colorado should deter children and youth from starting smoking […]. (iWeb, state.co.us)

Interestingly, in (55) the performative reading of *find* is not only reinforced by *hereby* (see also (56)), but, in addition, by its syntactic conjunction with the (performatively used) verb *declare*.

Another type of declaration occurring in courtrooms is the act of *sentencing*, which is accomplished by a judge through an explicit performative formula *I sentence you to […]*, as in (57):

---

109. The transcript has been edited slightly for the reader's convenience. For example, voiceover comments and times have been omitted.

(57) I sentence you to life imprisonment for the offence of second-degree murder [...]. (www.calgarysun.com)

Indirect speech acts of sentencing appear to be non-existent, i.e., it would be legally incorrect, and therefore unlikely, for a judge to sentence a defendant to life imprisonment by uttering e.g. (58):

(58) You will spend the rest of your life in jail.

2.3.3 Religious ceremonies

Speech acts performed in religious ceremonies are, like illocutionary acts in the judiciary, regulated, i.e., religious authorities usually do not tolerate deviations from the "correct" wording. Consider an act of baptizing in a Catholic church reported in a magazine:

(59) On Palm Sunday 2007 Father Joseph Kraker poured water over the head of a baby boy in St. Vincent's Church in Akron, Ohio. "I baptize you in the name of the Father, and of the Son, and of the Holy Spirit," he said, grinning as the baby sent forth a mighty howl. (COCA 2007)

The act of baptizing is a declaration *par excellence* in that its performance has the effect that the child or person baptized is henceforth admitted into the religious community.

In the Catholic Church, the act of absolution is another example of an ecclesiastically sanctioned declaration – this time an act that results in the forgiveness of sins. The intended effect is typically achieved by the explicit performative formula *I absolve you from your sins [...]*, as in (60) and (61):

(60) [...] I absolve you from your sins in the name of the Father, and of the Son and of the Holy Spirit. (http://www.catholicplanet.com/catechism.htm)

(61) I absolve you from your sins in the name of the Father and of the Son and of the Holy Ghost. (iWeb, cathololictradition.org)

Finally, explicit performatives are commonly used in church wedding ceremonies, as in the two following examples:

(62) As your pastor, I pronounce you man and wife. (COCA 1991)

(63) I now pronounce you man and wife.
(Royal wedding: Prince Harry and Meghan Markle, May 19, 2018, officiated by the Archbishop of Canterbury, Justin Welby)

The performative formula *I pronounce you man and wife* is also used in civil marriage ceremonies officiated by e.g. a justice of peace.

To conclude, indirect ways of baptizing a child, pronouncing a couple husband and wife, absolving the sinner from his or her sins seem to be non-existent; at least, the present author has not been able to find any empirical evidence for indirect illocutionary declarations of this type.

2.3.4 Resigning from a post

In this section, a type of declaration is presented and illustrated with authentic data that occurs in all walks of secular life, e.g. the resignation from an employment or a government position. Such acts of resignation can be accomplished by means of explicit performative sentences like the following:

(64) I hereby resign from Roswell City Council Post 4 […].
(iWeb, www.myajc.com)

(65) As agreed with the national associations, I resign from my role as president of UEFA in order to be able to continue my fight before the Swiss courts to prove my integrity in this case. (iWeb, espnfc.us)[110]

While (64) and (65) are straightforwardly performative, i.e. exhibit the standard explicit performative formula *I (hereby) resign from p*, there is some rhetorical leeway of how letters of resignation may be composed. In what follows, examples are presented and discussed that involve more or less elaborate hedging of the performative expression of resignation.

On July 8, 2018, David Davis, Secretary of State for Exiting the European Union, wrote an official letter to British Prime Minister Theresa May, which concludes with the following sentence:

(66) While I have been grateful to you for the opportunity to serve, it is with great regret that I tender my resignation from the Cabinet with immediate effect.
(*The Sun*, July 9, 2018)

In (66), the performative phrase *tender my resignation* is hedged by the emotive expression *with great regret*. Note that in this case the performative interpretation is *entailed* by the hedged performative, i.e., with or without regret, this is an act of resignation (see (67) (italics added):

(67) It is *with great regret* that I *tender* my *resignation* from the Cabinet with immediate effect. ⊩ I *tender* my *resignation* from the Cabinet with immediate effect.

---

110. The author of this letter is Michel Platini, who resigned from his post as President of the Union of European Football Associations (UEFA) on May 9, 2016.

Examples that exhibit more or less elaborate emotive and modal hedging can also be found on a website that offers sample letters of how to resign from a job, office or other function:[111]

(68) Regretfully I inform you that I must resign from my position as a counselor, effective immediately.

(69) Please accept this letter as official notification of my intent to resign from my position as a counselor, effective two weeks from today.

The somewhat flowery letter (68) contains three hedges, i.e. the sentence adverb *regretfully*, a performative use of *inform*, and the deontic modal *must*, before the legally relevant verb of declaration *resign* enters the scene. On a strictly literal reading, (68) does not entail that the writer actually resigns – although this is of course the intended and understood target sense, i.e. the primary illocutionary act in Searle's terminology. The inferential chain leading from the literal source meaning to this target sense can be informally described as follows (italics added):

(70) *Regretfully* I *inform* you that I *must resign* from my position as a counselor, effective immediately. ⊩ I *inform* you that I *must resign* from my position as a counselor, effective *immediately*. → I *must resign from my position as a counselor, effective immediately.* → I *resign* from my position as a counselor, effective immediately.

Note that the inferential chain in (70) involves one entailment and two metonymically motivated inferences that are not entailments.

As regards (69), the inferential chain that leads to the conclusion that the writer of the letter resigns from his or her position exhibits the metonymic chaining in (71) (italics added):

(71) Please *accept* this letter as official *notification* of my *intent* to *resign* from my position as a counselor [...]. → This letter is the official *notification* of my *intent* to *resign* from my position as a counselor [...]. → My *intent* is to *resign* from my position as a counselor [...]. → I *resign* from my position as a counselor, effective two weeks from today.

As can be seen from (71), the metonymic vehicle of the source is an imperative sentence, i.e. a *directive* in speech-act terms, but its target meaning is a *declaration* (resigning) that establishes the *fact* that the writer's tenure as counselor is terminated.

The final example of an indirect act of resignation has Boris Johnson as its author, who withdrew in July 2018 from his office as Secretary of State for Foreign

---

111. Retrieved July 26, 2018, from: https://www.writeexpress.com/resign06.html.

and Commonwealth Affairs over disagreements with Prime Minister Theresa May's Brexit policy. The two-page letter mostly focuses on these disagreements and about what Johnson considers to be his own foreign policy achievements during his tenure. In (72)–(74), only those sentences in the letter are listed that make more or less direct or indirect reference to the official illocutionary purpose of Johnson's letter, i.e. his resignation from the British cabinet (italics added):[112]

(72) Since I cannot in all conscience champion these proposals, I have sadly concluded that I *must go*.

(73) As I *step down*, I would like to thank the patient officers of the Metropolitan Police […].

(74) As I *leave office*, the FCO now has the largest and by far the most effective diplomatic network of any country in Europe […].

(Source of (72)–(74): https://www.theguardian.com/politics /2018/ jul/09/ full-text-of-boris-johnsons-resignation-letter-to-the-pm)

The first remarkable property of the three sentences (72)–(74) is that the vehicle conveying the act of resignation is a clause that is itself part of a complex sentence. In (72), it is the main clause following the reason clause headed by the conjunction *since*. More specifically, sentence (72) alludes to reasons that led Boris Johnson to the conclusion that he was obligated to *go*, where the latter verb literally denotes movement from some location to or towards another (undefined) location. There is also an emotional component, coded by the adverb *sadly*. When a person resigns from some job or office, characteristically, as a result, she or he literally moves out of the location of the workplace – in the case of Boris Johnson's resignation – out of the Foreign Commonwealth Office Headquarters on King Charles Street, London SW 1. There is thus a metonymy at work that can be formulated as MOTION OUT OF A WORKPLACE → LEAVING A JOB. The inferential chain that links source and target meaning can be described as follows:

(75) I have *sadly concluded* that I *must* go. ⊩ I have *concluded* that I *must* go. → I *must* go. → I *will* go → I *will* leave my office. → I *resign* from my office. (CORE)

In (73), the act of resignation is figuratively expressed by means of *I step down* in the initial temporal subordinate *as*-clause, which is combined with a simultaneous act of thanking the Metropolitan Police (a hedged performative) that is coded in the main clause. Stepping down involves movement from a higher location to a lower one. And since it is not unlikely that Secretary Johnson occupied an office on the upper floors of the FOC building, as a consequence of his resignation, he literally

---

112. The abbreviation *FOC* in (28) stands for 'Foreign & Commonwealth Office'.

moved down from a higher to a lower location when he left his workplace. This is the metonymic basis of the metaphor STEPPING DOWN ⇒ RESIGNING. Some of the mappings of this metaphor are represented Table 1.

Table 1. The metonymy-based metaphor STEPPING DOWN ⇒ LEAVING OFFICE

SOURCE	⇒	TARGET
STEPPING DOWN	⇒	RESIGNING (with the RESULT of LEAVING OFFICE)
DOWNWARD MOTION	⇒	CHANGE OF PROFESSIONAL STATUS
HIGHER LOCATION	⇒	PROFESSIONAL STATUS PRIOR TO RESIGNATION
LOWER LOCATION	⇒	PROFESSIONAL STATUS AFTER RESIGNATION

Finally, in (74), the vehicle of the (indirect) act of resignation is again coded in a subordinate temporal *as*-clause, i.e. *As I leave office [...]*. This involves another metonymy that links the source meaning LEAVING JOB to the target RESIGNING FROM JOB. Leaving a job is the RESULT of an act of resigning and as such it can stand for the illocutionary act of resigning itself. Thus, the subordinate clause in (74) can be viewed as a vehicle for the illocutionary metonymy formulated in (76):

(76) I leave office (RESULT) → I resign from my office (CORE)

3. Conclusion

It comes as no surprise that directive and expressive speech acts, as shown in this chapter, like assertives and commissives discussed in Chapter 9, can be performed as indirect illocutionary acts. The basic idea advocated in both chapters is that the inferential mechanisms linking literal source meanings to target senses, to a large extent, can be accounted for by means of conceptual metonymy, i.e. reasoning processes within illocutionary frames (called 'scenarios' in this book). The focus of both chapters has been on the inferential mechanisms involved, and sociocultural factors that motivate indirectness, an important topic in their own right, have only been mentioned in passing.

An interesting object of inquiry that deserves further attention is the pragmatic nature of declarations. I have provided some preliminary empirical evidence that although declarations, at least in judicial proceedings and religious ceremonies, tend to be coded by means of explicit performative utterances, certain types of declaration might be (felicitously) performed in an indirect way. Examples are acts of resignation from a job or an office, which, as shown in this chapter, may be formulated indirectly, i.e. involve metonymic inferencing and even metaphor, as in the case of "stepping down" from an official office or position.

CHAPTER 11

Cognitive pragmatics and grammar

1. Introduction

This chapter deals with a central issue in modern linguistics, i.e. the *interface* between grammatical structure, in particular, morphology and syntax, and meaning and pragmatic function. The main thesis advocated in this chapter is that conceptual structure and pragmatic function often (though not necessarily) have an impact on grammatical structure, and that the explicit and precise formulation of this influence is part and parcel of an adequate theory of language.

This chapter is thematically related to Section 4.1 in Chapter 2, where the topic of how pragmatics relates to grammar was introduced and illustrated with the phenomenon of Auxiliary-Subject Inversion triggered by certain sentence-initial negative adverbials in English (Brugman & Lakoff 1986), and the main clause syntax in the apodosis of certain conditional sentences in German (Köpcke & Panther 1989).

Formalist theories of language, e.g. generative grammar, appear to view motivational relations between form and conceptual structure and/or pragmatic function as more or less irrelevant to an explanatory theory of language. In a standard textbook on generative syntax we read the postulate that "[n]o syntactic rule can make reference to pragmatic, phonological, or semantic information." (Radford 1988: 31). This postulate is known as the *Autonomy of Syntax Principle*. However, Newmeyer (1992) contends that e.g. motivational relations between form and meaning do not present a challenge to generative grammar. According to this author, they are compatible with the generative framework, in particular, with the thesis that "grammatical structure is a reflection of conceptual structure" (Newmeyer 1992: 756). In a later publication, Newmeyer (1994) repeats this assessment and points out that the founder of generative grammar, Noam Chomsky, rejects the position attributed to him by the philosopher of language John Searle (1972) that there exist no correlations between grammatical structure and the communicative function of language. On the contrary, Chomsky (1975: 245) emphasizes that "[s]urely there are significant connections between structure and function; this is and has never been in doubt." Thus, as again pointed out by Newmeyer (1994: 245), Chomsky agrees with Searle's thesis that communicative "needs" have an influence on language structure.

Nevertheless, many linguists consider the doctrine of autonomous syntax as not being in line – if not incompatible – with the position that syntactic structure is often conceptually and/or pragmatically motivated. Bernard Comrie (1988: 266) formulates this conception as a research heuristic:

> [A]utonomous syntax [is] a fallback position, the null hypothesis, to be accepted only if we fail in valiant attempts to explain syntax in pragmatic and/or semantic terms.

In cognitive linguistics, the conceptual-pragmatic motivation of morphosyntactic structure has been advocated by e.g. Lakoff (1987), Lakoff and Johnson (1999), Langacker (2009b, 2013), Köpcke and Panther (1989), and the contributions in Panther, Thornburg, and Barcelona (2009), to name just a few. Ariel (2008) presents evidence that at least parts of grammar are not arbitrary but shaped by pragmatic factors. More recently, Brdar (2017) has published a monograph that deals with the role of metonymic motivation in word-formation processes in various languages. The interaction of metonymy and grammar has also been investigated by Ruiz de Mendoza Ibáñez and Pérez-Hernández (2001) and Ruiz de Mendoza Ibáñez and Otal Campo (2002), to cite just a few studies.

In this chapter, the impact of function and meaning on grammatical structure is exemplified by way of three kinds of grammatical phenomena in English. In Section 2, inspired by an article by Brugman and Lakoff (1986) the conceptual motivation of *subject auxiliary inversion*, i.e. the inversion of the grammatical subject and auxiliary verb, is examined, a change in word order that is triggered by certain sentence-initial negative adverbials.

Sections 3 and 4 consider two coordinate constructions with the connective *and*. At first sight, the syntactic form of these constructions clashes with their conceptual content and pragmatic function. This mismatch between form and content and/or function seems to provide support for the Autonomy of Syntax Principle. However, it is argued in this chapter that a motivational relationship between the semantics and/or pragmatics of these coordinative constructions and their syntactic realization can be established.

Section 3 discusses what was originally believed to be a purely formal constraint on syntactic structure, known as the *Coordinate Structure Constraint*. Violation of this constraint usually results in ungrammaticality, but it turns out that in English this constraint can be violated under certain circumstances and that these "violations" are conceptually and pragmatically motivated.

In Section 4, based on work by Panther and Thornburg (2009b), another type of coordinative construction is analyzed, i.e. the pattern *nice and Adj*, which again exhibits an apparent mismatch between syntactic structure and conceptual content/pragmatic function. Notwithstanding, the meaning and the pragmatic function of the *nice (and)* as a kind of conceptual modifier of the following adjective is inferentially derivable, in part, via metonymy, from the literal coordinative meaning of the construction.

Section 5 concludes this chapter with a few remarks on other motivated relationships between morphosyntactic form and meaning/function.

2. Preposed negative adverbials and auxiliary inversion

The phenomenon of *subject-auxiliary inversion* has been controversially discussed in the linguistic literature. While Goldberg (2009: 110–114) argues that auxiliary-subject inversion patterns constitute a family of polysemous constructions whose formal properties are conceptually motivated, Borsley and Newmeyer (2009), in conformity with generative approaches to syntax, claim that subject-auxiliary inversion is a purely formal word-order pattern that cannot be accounted for in semantic or functional terms.

In this section, I do not discuss the whole range of syntactic patterns that exhibit subject-auxiliary inversion, but restrict myself to a special case of inversion which occurs after sentence-initially placed negative adverbials. Following Brugman and Lakoff (1986) and Goldberg (2009), I argue the constituent order AUX-SBJ is conceptually motivated in these cases.

Consider first the sentences from Brugman and Lakoff (1986: 1) with the preposed negative adverbials *never* and *under no circumstances*, respectively:

(1) Never have I seen such behavior.

(2) Under no circumstances will he be admitted.

In sentences (1) and (2), the sentence-initial negative adverbials trigger the change of the default word order SBJ-AUX to AUX-SBJ. However, Brugman and Lakoff (1986: 1) observe that "not all preposed negative adverbs trigger aux-inversion", as shown by the ungrammatical examples in (5) and (6) (slightly adapted from Brugman and Lakoff 1986: 1–2):

(3) With no help, he will move the piano upstairs.

(4) With no hat, he went out into the cold.

(5) *With no help will he move the piano upstairs.

(6) *With no hat did he go out into the cold.

The difference between the examples in (1)–(2) and (3)–(4) is that the former *entail* (i.e. semantically imply) a *negative* proposition, whereas, in the latter, the negative adverbial does not enforce a negative polarity of the subsequent proposition.[113] Thus, (1) and (2) entail the negative propositions (7) and (8), respectively.

---

113. For a more detailed discussion of the notion of entailment, see Chapter 4.

In contrast, sentences (3) and (4) entail the affirmative propositions (9) and (10), respectively:

(7) I have not seen such behavior.
(8) He will not be admitted.
(9) He will move the piano upstairs.
(10) He went out into the cold.

The preliminary generalization following from these data is that sentences with preposed negative adverbials trigger AUX SBJ order if they entail the negation of the proposition coded by what follows the negative adverbial. In contrast, sentences with preposed negative adverbials that do not exhibit AUX-inversion do not involve any change in polarity – the adverbial does not have any polarity effect on the subsequent propositional content. Thus, the sentence pairs (1)–(2) and (3)–(4) nicely illustrate content-form motivation: their syntactic form, i.e. their constituent order, is shaped by their conceptual structure (see Chapter 2, Section 4.1).

Brugman and Lakoff (1986: 3) also consider preposed adverbs and adverbial expressions that are not strictly negative but have a *negative orientation*, such as *rarely*. Consider the following example:

(11) Rarely did he accept an invitation to dinner.

Brugman and Lakoff (1986: 3) claim that (11) *entails* "the occurrence of the event in question", in this case, that the referent of *he* (sometimes) accepted an invitation to dinner. However, this implication is arguably pragmatic rather than semantic; i.e., it is of the type that Grice (1975) calls *conversational implicature* (see Chapter 4). In contrast to entailments, conversational implicatures can be either suspended if their truth is in doubt, or they may even be overtly canceled. The authentic data in (12)–(13) and (14)–(15) illustrate the workings of implicature suspension and cancelation, respectively.

Suspension

(12) Rarely if ever has a plaintiff sued on so many points. (COCA 1990)
(13) Rarely if ever is the teacher supposed to color the opinions of his pupils. (COCA 1995)

Cancelation

(14) Very rarely, in fact never, do men treat me like you have. (https://books.google.com/books?isbn=1908090367)
(15) Rarely, in fact never, can we compute things exactly [...]. (https://books.google.com/books?isbn=981238149X)

Examples (12) and (13) induce an implicature that some event occasionally happens; the occurrence of the expression *if ever* suspends this inference as possibly not valid. More specifically, utterance (12) suggests that one occasionally finds plaintiffs who *sued on so many points*, like the plaintiff referred to in the sentence, but possibly there exists no plaintiff who behaves like the plaintiff in question. Analogously, (13) does not totally exclude situations in which the teacher is *supposed to color the opinions of his pupils*, but this inference is not enforced, i.e. may be invalid. In contrast, in (14), the implicature that occasionally men treat the narrator *like you have* is not just suspended, but canceled explicitly by *in fact never*; and the latter expression also defeats the implicature triggered in (15) that occasionally the persons referred to by *we* can *compute things exactly*.

In conclusion, the determining factor of subject-auxiliary inversion in the examples discussed in this section appears to be the *negative orientation* of the preposed adverbial (on a temporal scale). While initial *Never p* or *Under no circumstances p* entails *not-p*, *Rarely p* implicates 'Sometimes p', but this inference can be suspended or even be canceled. The adverb *rarely* behaves like the quantifier *few* (in contrast to *a few*) in signifying a negative orientation, but not negativity *per se*.

3. Felicitous constraint violations: The Coordinate Structure Constraint

3.1 Introduction

In his influential doctoral dissertation *Constraints on Variables in Syntax*, John R. Ross (1967: 161) postulates, among other syntactic principles, the *Coordinate Structure Constraint* (CSC). The CSC restricts the movement of conjuncts or of elements within conjuncts: "In a coordinate structure, no conjunct may be moved, nor may any element in a conjunct be moved out of that conjunct." Lakoff and Johnson (1999: 485) rephrase the CSC as follows: "No constituent can be moved out of a coordinate structure unless it is moved out of all conjuncts."

In generative grammar, the supposedly universal CSC is conceived of as a well-formedness condition on syntactic form, i.e., it is not conceptually and/or pragmatically motivated. Consider e.g. the interrogative sentence following the dash in (16):

(16) The big question that came to mind while watching *The Crossing* short film was – what did Shaw eat and drink on her voyage?   (iWeb, film-book.com)

The relevant syntactic structure of the *wh*-question is (16) can be represented as in (17):[114]

(17)   What$_{i/j}$ did Shaw [[eat Ø$_i$] and [drink Ø$_j$]]?

For the sake of clarity, bracketing, subscripts, and the null symbol Ø have been added to indicate the sites from which linguistic material is extracted and moved. The direction of movement is symbolized by means of an arrow. The question clause in (16) abides by the CSC as formulated above, i.e., the interrogative pronoun *what* has been extracted from both conjuncts and moved to the front of the sentence.

Now consider the declarative sentence in (18) and the two ill-formed corresponding (starred) *wh*-interrogatives in (19) and (20):

(18)   Shaw ate a piece of cake and drank two cups of coffee.

(19)   *What$_i$ did Shaw [[eat Ø$_i$] and [drink two cups of coffee]]?

(20)   *What$_i$ did Shaw [eat a piece of cake] and [drink Ø$_i$]]?

Both (19) and (20) violate the CSC, given that extraction has taken place from only one of the conjuncts – not, as required, from both conjuncts.

As already pointed out above, in generative grammar, the CSC has been regarded as a purely formal constraint on the syntactic structure of English (and probably many other languages). The fact that its violation (often) leads to ungrammaticality has been considered as evidence for the hypothesis that syntax is an autonomous component within the overall architecture of grammar, i.e. a module supposedly functioning according to its own formal rules and principles, which are immune to being shaped by conceptual structure and/or pragmatic function.

However, acceptable violations of the CSC can be found. Consider the following literary examples (21) and (22):

(21)   This is a less attractive scene and not without a few rusty tins and broken bottles which I must one day climb down and remove.   (Murdoch 1999: 12)

(22)   It doesn't matter how special we are, David, there are certain things we all have to sit down and learn.   (Quoted by Peter Craven at https://meanjin.com.au/essays/taking-the-name-of-jesus)

In example (21), from Iris Murdoch's novel *The Sea, the Sea*, the direct object of *remove*, i.e. *a few rusty tins and bottles*, is extracted and moved out of the relative

---

114. I continue to use the terms 'extraction' and 'movement', with the caveat that they represent theoretical terms within the paradigm of generative grammar. I do not want to suggest that movement and extraction really take place in language processing, in the sense that they are psychologically and cognitively real phenomena, but I consider these terms as didactically useful metaphors.

clause. Analogously in (22), a quote from John M. Coetzee's (2016)novel *The Schooldays of Jesus*, it is the direct object of *learn*, i.e. *certain things*, that has undergone movement. The CSC predicts that these movements are illicit, i.e. result in ungrammatically. However, both (21) and (22) are perfectly acceptable to native speakers (with the possible exception of prescriptively oriented language users).

In Sections 3.2–3.5, further examples are presented that contain two verb phrases conjoined by *and*, i.e. exhibit the structure VP_1 *and* VP_2. What the data illustrating these syntactic patterns have in common is that he first conjunct (VP_1) conveys a preparatory action that is interpreted as an enabling, facilitating, or even necessary condition for the action denoted by the second conjunct (VP_2). The latter codes what I call the *main action*. As is shown in these sections, under certain conditions, the CSC can be violated without resulting in unacceptability, and this fact is in need of explanation (see also Deane 1992: 18–22; Goldsmith 1985).

3.2 The pattern *go [...] and VP*

The constructional schema with a form of *go* plus an optional directional expression, e.g. a prepositional phrase or an adverbial in the first conjunct, and a VP that expresses an action in the second conjunct, is very common in English. Some American English examples retrieved from COCA are:

(23) He loves to go to the store and buy those instant rice packages [...]. (COCA 2011)

(24) Then I went to the library and did some reading. (COCA 2002)

(25) Kiana went to the library and found some of Gandhi's essays. (COCA 2015)

(26) He went to the refrigerator and took out a bottle of white wine. (COCA 2009)

In (23)–(26), the first conjunct denotes goal-directed motion of an agent. The conjunct functions as a real-world precondition or preparatory action that enables or facilitates the agent's subsequent action. The connective *and* implicates the temporal meaning 'and then'. In addition to pragmatically implying temporal subsequence, *and* becomes a component of the complex *aspectual* marker *go [...] and* with the meaning 'preparatory action for subsequent main action', with the subsequent action being coded by the second conjunct.[115]

Sentences (23)–(26) exemplify a process of emergent grammaticalization. Thus, in (23), the action of going to the store is a precondition for the subsequent action of buying instant rice packages; in (24) and (25), walking to the library enables

---

115. Note that there is an apparent *mismatch* between syntactic and conceptual structure: *go [...] and* does not belong to any phrasal syntactic category, but, has a specific aspectual meaning.

the first person narrator and Kiana to do some reading and find Gandhi's essays, respectively. Finally, in (26), the fictional character's movement to the refrigerator is construed as a precondition for retrieving a bottle of wine from it.

The temporal and aspectual structure of the pattern *go [...] and VP* can be diagrammed as in Figure 1.

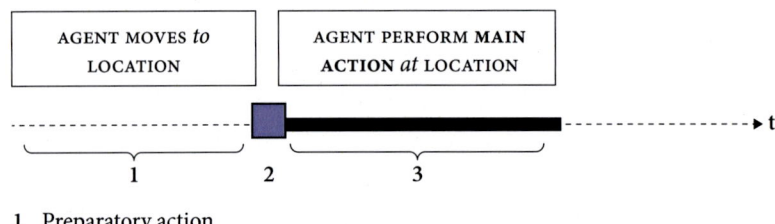

1   Preparatory action
2   Onset
3   Main action
t   Time axis

Figure 1. Temporal-aspectual structure of *go [...] and VP*[116]

Examples (23)–(26) do not violate the CSC; they are perfectly grammatical. But now consider the *wh*-question in (27):

(27)   What$_i$ did John [[go to the store] and [buy Ø$_i$]]?

In (27), the CSC is violated since movement (of the interrogative pronoun) takes place only out of the second conjunct; nevertheless, the sentence is, at least in colloquial English, fully acceptable.[117] Lakoff and Johnson (1999: 493) report that Ross himself already observed that the violation of the CSC does not necessarily result in non-acceptability, as (27) demonstrates. Likewise, in the following authentic example, the CSC is not abided by, but again this violation does not result in unacceptability.

(28)   There's nothing$_i$ he won't [[go to the store] and [purchase Ø$_i$ for me]] if I need it.   (COCA 1995)

---

116.   See also Panther and Thornburg (2003c; revised in Panther and Thornburg 2017a) for the aspectual properties of ingressive verbs like *start* and *begin*, and the ingressive uses of the French simple past (*passé simple*).

117.   Sentences like (27) are most likely rejected by normative grammarians and language teachers, but they occur and have to be considered in a usage-based approach to linguistic analysis.

Example (28) instantiates an existential construction that involves extraction of a direct object from a relative clause.[118] The negative quantifying expression *nothing* is moved out of Ø into the main clause, leaving, as generative grammarians put it, a "trace" behind. More precisely, (28) exhibits double negation: it entails that there is *nothing* that the male person referred to (*he*) would *not* purchase for the speaker – in other words, he would buy anything the speaker wishes to acquire.

Examples (27) and (28) contain tokens of *go to the store* and *won't go to the store*, respectively, as their first conjuncts. Perhaps more common are uses of *go* without any goal-oriented prepositional or adverbial complementation, as in (29)–(33):[119]

(29) MR KEMP: Was he driving the same car in which you had gone to the house? MR KOK: I can't recall. MR KEMP: He left you somewhere along the road and what$_i$ did he [[go] and [do Ø$_i$ then]]?
(http://www.justice.gov.za/trc/amntrans/pe/mother6.htm)

(30) What$_i$ did he [[go] and [do Ø$_i$]]? (COCA 1992)

(31) Ah, what$_i$ did he [[go] and [look down for Ø$_i$]]?
(https://books.google.co.uk/books?isbn=1444905481)

(32) What$_i$ did he [[go] and [do that for $_i$]]?
(https://books.google.co.uk/books?isbn=0857908790)

(33) "I bought bakery this morning from Vesecky's," Father says. "What$_i$ did you [[go] and [buy bakery for Ø$_i$]]?" (COCA 1990)

Examples (27)–(33) exhibit the following pattern:

(34) What$_i$ did NP [[go (…)] and [V (…) Ø$_i$]]?

In constructions of type (34), two presupposed ACTIONS are coded: the first denotes MOVEMENT of an AGENT (lexicalized as *go*) to a certain LOCATION (the latter is not explicitly coded, but understood), and the second is another ACTION performed by the same AGENT. As to the first action *go*, it is construed as a real-world *precondition* for a subsequent action; i.e., it *enables* the action coded in second conjunct to take place. The conjunction *and* implicates both a temporal sense of SUBSEQUENCE ('and then') and also that the subsequent action has been made possible by the action denoted by the first conjunct (ENABLEMENT). The implicated meaning of (34) can thus be paraphrased informally as in (35):

---

118. Note that the relative pronoun (*that* or *which*) is not overtly coded.

119. Example (29) is an excerpt from an Amnesty Hearing after the end of apartheid in South Africa in 1997.

(35) AGENT_i MOVES to some LOCATION that enables AGENT_i to subsequently DO A.

The schema (34), with the reading (35), appears to be fairly conventionalized, i.e., it is a partially lexicalized construction. No corpus data have been found by the present author that involve a violation of the CSC with other (more specific) motion verbs than *go*, such as *drive, run, rush*, etc. Thus, questions like (36) appear to be more marginal although they are not necessarily totally unacceptable:[120]

(36) ?What_i did Mary [[drive (to the shopping mall)] and [buy Ø_i]]?

In (36), the CSC is violated, given that movement occurs only out of the second conjunct, but not out of both conjuncts. However, in analogy to the cases with the motion verb *go*, in principle, the action of driving to the shopping mall could be interpreted as a preparatory or an enablement condition for doing some shopping – still it seems to be less acceptable (albeit certainly interpretable) than the use of *go*. The generic motion verb *go*, in contrast to hyponyms such as *rush, run*, and *hurry*, appears to be the most felicitous filler in the first conjunct slot of construction (34).

To conclude, construction (34) is a good example of a mismatch between syntactic form (coordination) and its conceptual content/pragmatic function in which *go (and)* arguably serves as an *aspectual* specifier or grounding element. To repeat the main point: it denotes an action, i.e. motion of some agent, which constitutes an enabling condition for the subsequent main action (coded in the second conjunct) to take place.

In the following sections, other examples of coordinative constructions are considered, in which, again, the first conjunct expresses a kind of enabling, preparatory, or facilitatory condition for the action denoted by the second conjunct to take place.

3.3   The pattern *sit down and VP*

The coordinative pattern *sit down and VP* is attested in examples like the following:

(37) I sit down and take off my running shoes.   (COCA 2016)

(38) The cat sat down and stared at him.   (COCA 2017)

(39) "On the house," he said. He sat down and slid his own straw into the beer.
                                                                   (COCA 2017)

(40) Do you think that Donald Trump and Colin Kaepernick should get together and sit down and talk?   (COCA 2017)

---

120. See e.g. for the literary example (6), which contains the motion verb *climb (down)*.

(41) Paul Ryan, Republican from Wisconsin, Patty Murray, Democratic senate budget committee chair, sat down and hammered out a budget and then Barbara Mikulski and Congressman Rogers sat down and put together the spending bill. (COCA 2014)

(42) If they were able to sit down and have a conference, they would have done it by now. (COCA 2017)

The first question arising in connection with the pattern *sit down and VP* regards the meaning of the initial conjunct, i.e. a finite or non-finite form of *sit down*. Is the speaker or writer committed to a literal interpretation of *sit down*, i.e. the occurrence of a real or imagined act of sitting down? In (37), (38), and (39), the first conjunct is alleged to be true, i.e., the reporter or narrator asserts that the subject referent actually changes from a standing position to a sitting one as a prerequisite for the occurrence of the main action coded in the second conjunct. This literal interpretation of *sit down and VP* is diagrammed in Figure 2.

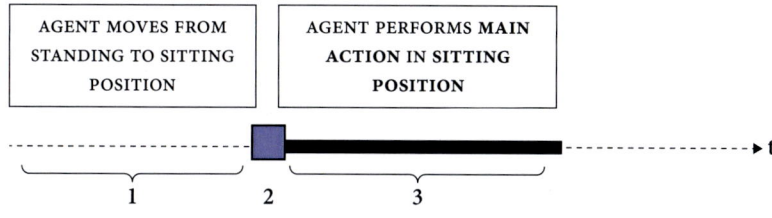

1 Preparatory action
2 Onset
3 Main action
t Time axis

Figure 2. Temporal-aspectual structure of *sit down and VP*

However, in (40)–(42), it does not really seem to matter whether an act of sitting down actually occurs; what matters is the truth value of the action expressed in the second conjunct. For example, in (41), a situation is described in which the relevant actions described are coded in the second conjuncts, i.e. *hammered out a budget* and *put together the spending bill*, respectively. It does not matter whether these actions are preceded by an act of literally sitting down. What is metonymically conveyed by *sit down* is a preliminary action that facilitates or enables the action described by the second conjunct.

What do the data involving verb phrase conjunctions of the type *sit down and VP* and *go and VP* have in common? In both patterns (see Section 3.2), the first conjunct formulates a prerequisite action that facilitates or enables the implementation of the action expressed in the second conjunct. However, it has to be emphasized that *sit down and VP* exhibits an event structure that differs in some respects from that of *go and VP*. The latter involves a sequence of two separate events: motion to a destination *followed* temporally by a second event. In contrast to *go*, the phrasal verb *sit down* denotes an accomplishment (in terms of Vendler 1957), i.e. a bounded event that literally involves change from an upright position to a sitting position, which is followed by the second event. It is important to note that the sitting position is, at least in its literal interpretation, *maintained* by the participant(s) for the duration of the activity coded by the second conjunct. The period of sitting provides the time frame within which the event denoted by verb phrase in the second conjunct takes place.

The pattern *sit down and VP* implicates that the interactants take their time to *think* or *talk* leisurely about some issue. Typically, the VP expresses certain verbal and cognitive activities.[121] Furthermore, the meaning of the construction is associated with connotations such as 'relaxation', and 'calming down', and, as the writer of (43) explicitly points out, *sit down and rest* may even have a good effect on people's blood pressure:[122]

(43) [...] the only manner for lower blood pressure is to sit down and rest, until it goes well again. (iWeb, authorityremedies.com)

To conclude, the construction *sit down and VP* has become so conventionalized in English that it does not even necessitate the physical action of sitting down in order to be used truthfully. *Sit down (and)* simply functions as an index of a subsequent action, of the type discussed above. In other words, the meaning of *sit down (and)* has been bleached, i.e. generalized, as already pointed out above, to the sense 'preparatory action for a subsequent action'. Again, as argued in Section 3.2, the conjunction *and* conveys that, after the condition of 'sitting down' has been fulfilled literally or metonymically, a subsequent action *can* begin. As to the conjunction *and*, in addition to its truth-conditional meaning, it functions both as an index of temporal subsequence ('and then'), and it also contributes to the enablement or facilitation of the action expressed in the second conjunct (see Figure 3).

Consider now the question of how the pattern *sit down and VP* fares when it is subjected to extraction and movement out of the second conjunct. Ross's CSC predicts that the result should be an ungrammatical structure. However, remarkably,

---

121. A perusal of the first 100 examples of *sit down and VP* in the *iWeb* corpus shows that what follows *and* are typically expressions of verbal and mental activities and/or processes – notwithstanding examples like "sit down and eat" with somebody "in a fancy restaurant" (iWeb, www.salon.com).

122. Of course, as the reader will have noticed, (43) does not violate the CSC, but it nicely illustrates the conceptual properties associated with *sit down (and)*.

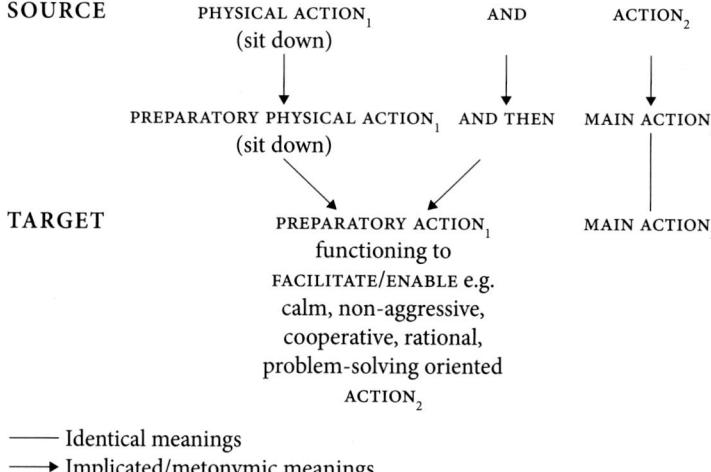

Figure 3. Literal *sit down (and)* as aspectualizer signaling a facilitating/enabling action

just as in the case of *go[...] and VP*, the CSC can be violated without resulting in grammatical ill-formedness.

To begin with, recall example (22), repeated here as (44) (bracketing and subscripts have been added):

(44) It doesn't matter how special we are, David, there are certain things$_i$ we all [[have to sit down] and [learn $\emptyset_i$]].

Although the CSC has been violated in (44), since extraction has only taken place out of the second conjunct, as already pointed out above, it sounds perfectly normal and acceptable in colloquial English. The same holds for the following corpus examples:

(45) [T]here are a lot of things$_i$ we need to [[sit down] and [talk about $\emptyset_i$]].
(https://books.google.co.uk/books?isbn=1311416404)

(46) These are the things$_i$ we should [[sit down] and [consider $\emptyset_i$]] [...].
(http://www.washingtonubf.org/BibleMaterials/Luke2005/luke14b_msg.html)

(47) One of the questions$_i$ that [[we sat down] and [we asked ourselves $\emptyset_i$]] was, why Twitter? (mitadmissions.org › blogs)

(48) It's a huge distraction. And it's definitely something$_i$ we need to [[sit down] and [talk about $\emptyset_i$]]. (COCA 2012)

Examples (45)–(47) illustrate extraction of material from a relative clause (without overt relative pronouns) into the matrix clause. The extracted constituents are *a lot of things*, *the things*, and *one of the questions*, respectively. In example (48), which occurs in the context of a warning about the risks of using an electronic device while driving, the empty slot Ø is the site of the pronoun *something* before movement – the latter, in turn, refers back to the preceding sentence *It's a huge distraction*. Although these examples violate the CSC, given that extraction occurs from only one of the two conjuncts in question, the resultant structures are perfectly acceptable to many speakers (although in written discourse the violation of the CSC is not considered to be "good usage").

As a final example of CSC violation, consider (49), in which the relevant antecedent of the empty slot Ø is *what*, which is here used as a nominal relative pronoun. Again, the outcome of the extraction from the second conjunct is acceptable in colloquial English:

(49) He'd want to talk about T-shirt designs, what$_i$ we should [[sit down] and [plan Ø$_i$ in future meetings]]. (http://chicagosmma.com/2013/11/the-brief-but-destructive-wake-of-praetorian-fighting-championships/5/)

To summarize, the pattern *sit down and VP* formally exhibits a coordinative structure, but conceptually *sit down (and)* is on its way of developing the grammatical function of an *aspectualizer* that designates the preparatory phase of a subsequent action expressed in the second conjunct. Because of this process of (on-going) grammaticalization, extraction out of the second conjunct is licensed, i.e., it is not felt to be deviant by language users. Furthermore, pragmatically, *sit down (and)* triggers a rich array of metonymic associations, such as that the ensuing activity can be characterized as 'relaxed', 'calm', 'cooperative', 'rational', i.e. 'not overly emotional and aggressive'. These metonymically induced meanings are more or less conventionalized target meanings of *sit down (and)*, although, like conversational implicatures, they are cancelable.

3.4 The pattern *stand up and VP*

The constructional schema *stand up and VP* is in an antonymic, more precisely, reverse relationship to the schema *sit down and VP*. The chunk *stand up (and)* is, like *sit up (and)*, developing an aspectual meaning with the general sense 'preparatory action to subsequent main action', which is derivable from its literal meaning.

Consider first two literal uses of *stand up*, i.e. cases that involve an agent's act of rising from a e.g. sitting or lying position to a standing one :

(50) He stood up and reached for his coffee mug full of pens. (COCA 2017)
(51) I stood up and walked to the bookcase. (COCA 2017)

The next example is ambiguous between a literal and a figurative interpretation (derivable from the literal meaning):

(52) They stood up and spoke for all of us. (COCA 2016)

Sentence (52) describes a situation, which, literally, could denote the act of rising from a sitting to a standing position, but in addition, it strongly suggests a reading where *stood up* figuratively denotes an action that is preparatory to verbally *supporting* the persons referred to by *us*. On this reading of (52), it does not matter whether an act of (literal) standing up actually happened or not.

There are also cases in which the likelihood of the agent's literally standing up is low if not zero. An example is (53):

(53) And the only way he could get through this, if he stood up and took full accountability for it and admitted what happened. (COCA 2017)

The meaning of the situation described in the subordinate clause *if he stood up* does not necessarily describe a hypothetical event in which the male participant gets on his feet (although, this is not impossible), but, more importantly, the first conjunct refers to a hypothetical decision, i.e. a preparatory mental action of the agent *he*, to take full responsibility for whatever happened. The same holds for other corpus examples like the following:

(54) "Every generation has to confront its own demagogues, and every generation has stood up and kept them away from the White House," Bloomberg said. (COCA 2016)

(55) The citizens of this community need to stand up and take action. (iWeb, theoaklandpress.com)

(56) We must stand up and say we can no longer accept these monstrosities. (iWeb, humanrights.gov)

Again, as in the case of *go [...] (and)* and *sit down (and)*, the CSC can be violated in constructions of the form *stand up and VP* without causing ill-formedness and pragmatic infelicity, as attested in the following examples:

(57) What$_i$ I will [[stand up] and [scream $\emptyset_i$]] is that newborn without intact immune systems and detoxification systems are being over-burdened with PRESERVATIVES AND ADJUVANTS IN THE VACCINES. (COCA 2017)

(58) What$_i$ would you [[stand up] and [fight for $\emptyset_i$]]? (https://books.google.co.uk/books?isbn=1471841642)

In stark contrast to the calming effect of *sit down (and)*, the unit *stand up (and)* conveys more dynamic and even sometimes aggressive metonymically based implicatures, which can be sketched as in Figure 4.

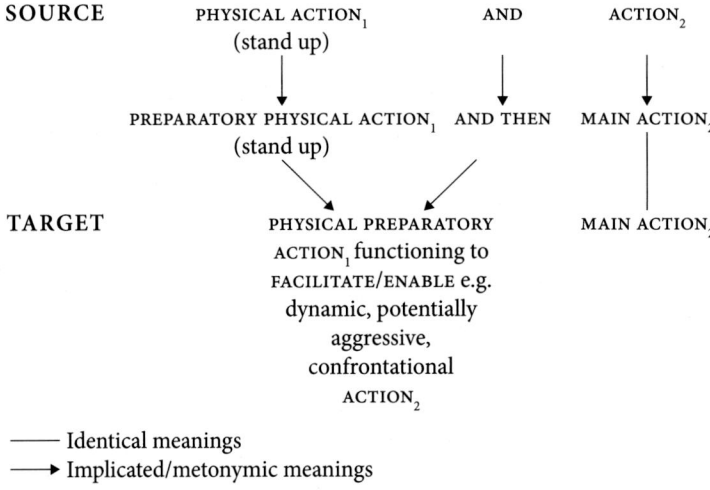

── Identical meanings
──▶ Implicated/metonymic meanings

Figure 4. Literal *stand up (and)* as aspectualizer signaling a facilitating/enabling action

To conclude, in Table 1, the shared and contrastive properties of the two patterns *sit down and VP* and *stand up and VP* are summarized according to the conceptual and pragmatic parameters of iconicity, lexical aspect, emergent grammaticalization, information structure, and metonymy.

Table 1. Conceptual and pragmatic properties of *sit down and VP* and *stand up and VP*

Conceptual & pragmatic & properties	Sit down and VP	Stand up and VP
ICONICITY	TEMPORAL SEQUENCE OF EVENTS ⇔ ORDER OF CONJUNCTS	
1st CONJUNCT: ASPECTUAL CLASS	ACCOMPLISHMENT	
1st CONJUNCT: EMERGENT GRAMMATICALIZATION	PREPARATORY ACTION	
1st CONJUNCT: INFORMATION STRUCTURE	BACKGROUNDED ACTION	
2nd CONJUNCT: INFORMATION STRUCTURE	FOREGROUNDED MAIN ACTION	
METONYMY: EFFECT → CAUSE	SITTING → RELAXED BODY POSTURE	STANDING → TENSED BODY POSTURE
METONYMY: EFFECT → CAUSE	RELAXED BODY POSTURE → CALM MENTAL ATTITUDE	TENSED BODY POSTURE → DYNAMIC MENTAL ATTITUDE

Some comments are in order on how the parameters named in Table 1 are to be understood. The term *iconicity* refers to the default assumption of language users that the sequential ordering of conjuncts reflects the temporal sequence of the events described. This is definitely the case in the three coordinative constructions *sit down and VP* and *stand up and VP*, as well as for *go (...) and VP*. The thesis that the first conjunct in *sit down and VP* and *stand up and VP* denotes an accomplishment, which undergoes a process of grammaticalization has also already been discussed in some detail. The grammaticalization process has some impact on *information structure*, i.e. the "encoding of the relative salience of the elements of a message" (Crystal 2008: 245). The first conjunct is less salient, i.e. more backgrounded, than the second conjunct, which conveys the main message.

Finally, the important role of metonymic inferencing in the two constructions is noteworthy. As to *sit down and VP*, moving from a standing to a sitting position results in a (more) relaxed body posture, and the relaxed body posture can be interpreted as an index of a calm mental attitude. In contrast, regarding *stand up and VP*, the motion from a sitting (or lying) position to a standing one results in a relatively tense body posture that indicates a dynamic and, sometimes, aggressive mental attitude. Some cognitive linguists have suggested (e.g. Lakoff & Johnson 1999: 45–73; Grady 2005) that correlations between body posture and mental attitude should be called *primary metaphors*. However, it is assumed here that these correlations are basically metonymies that link an effect, a body posture, to an underlying psychological cause (see Panther 2006: 163–165), i.e., they are instantiations of the pervasive metonymy EFFECT → CAUSE.

3.5   The pattern *take a step back and VP*

As a fourth type of the schema VP_1 and VP_2, consider the partially lexicalized coordinative construction *take a step back and VP*, whose conceptual-pragmatic properties are close to those of *go (...) and VP*, *sit down and VP*, and *stand up and VP*, in the sense that *take a step back (and)* indexes a preliminary action that is construed as preparatory to the ensuing main action.

Here are some corpus examples in which the action of stepping back is described as actually taking place :

(59)   His face horrified, he took a step back and raised his revolver to correct his aim.   (COCA 2014)

(60)   Mrs. Quince now adjusted Lucy's posture in the mirror and took a step back and examined what she saw [...].   (COCA 2011)

(61)   The man took a step back and blinked.   (COCA 2014)

(62)   Momentarily startled, Stead took a step back and fell into his swimming pool.   (COCA 2014)

In three of the above sentences, i.e. in (59)–(61), the agent deliberately steps back in space. However, stepping back may also occur as a non-intentional spontaneous reaction to some possibly "startling" event, as illustrated by (62), where the protagonist Stead most likely does not step back with the intention to fall into his swimming pool.

In contrast to (59)–(62), the following examples do not (necessarily) designate actually occurring actions of stepping back:

(63) [T]his began with them saying there were no contacts with Russians. So take a step back and ask yourself why have they consistently been lying?
(COCA 2017)

(64) [...] Ainsley, you have got to slow down. You have to take a step back and start looking at life through her eyes. (COCA 2017)

(65) [W]e need to take a step back and look at the larger dynamics of the streaming market. (COCA 2017)

(66) The coaching turnover has forced Cota to take a step back and consider his options across the country. (COCA 2017)

The underlying experiential basis of these figurative uses is metonymic and metaphoric. The preparatory *physical* action of stepping back (source) often functions as a metaphor for a preparatory *mental* action (target). Figure 5 diagrams the metonymic and metaphoric processes that link the literal source meaning of *take a step back and VP* to its figurative target sense.

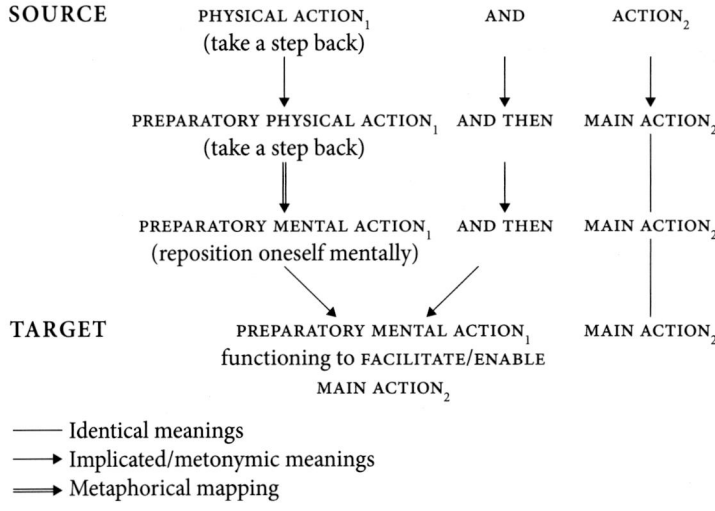

Figure 5. Metonymic and metaphoric structure of *take a step back and VP*

The metaphor PREPARATORY PHYSICAL ACTION ⇒ PREPARATORY MENTAL ACTION involves a number of additional metaphorical mappings, as shown in Table 2, where the central metaphorical mapping – printed in bold – is spelled out in more detail.

Table 2. Additional metaphorical mappings triggered by *take a step back*

SOURCE	⇒	TARGET
CONCRETE OBJECT	⇒	MENTAL OBJECT
BEING TOO CLOSE TO THE CONCRETE OBJECT	⇒	FOCUSING TOO MUCH ON THE DETAILS OF THE MENTAL OBJECT
INABILITY TO SEE THE CONCRETE OBJECT AS A WHOLE	⇒	INABILITY TO COGNIZE THE MENTAL OBJECT FROM A HOLISTIC PERSPECTIVE
STEPPING BACK FROM THE CONCRETE OBJECT IN ORDER TO HAVE A BETTER VIEW OF IT	⇒	**REMOVING ONESELF FROM THE DETAILS OF THE MENTAL OBJECT IN ORDER TO THINK ABOUT IT FROM A FRESH / BROADER PERSPECTIVE**

While examples that violate the CSC are easy to find for the constructional schemas *go (…) and VP*, *sit down and VP*, and *stand up and VP*, they appear to be less frequent in the case of *take a step back and VP*. An instance illustrating the acceptable violation of the CSC is (67), from an interview conducted by CNN journalist Christiane Amanpour with the "whistleblower" Christopher Wylie, who revealed the allegedly unauthorized use of private Facebook data by some British political consulting firm (April 11, 2018). Bracketing and subscripts have been added:

(67) WYLIE: Yes. Well – and I think one of the – one of the things$_i$ that I think we really need to sort of [[take a step back] and [look at Ø$_i$]] is that you know when – when – when we look at things like building standards or safety standards for automobiles, right?
(http://edition.cnn.com/TRANSCRIPTS/1804/11/ampr.01.html)

The verbal expression *take a step back (and)* is used metaphorically (PHYSICAL ACTION ⇒ MENTAL ACTION) in (67) and exhibits a number of metaphorical correspondences, as listed in Table 2. Whistleblower Wylie suggests that unauthorized use of private data by Facebook be viewed from a broader perspective, i.e., people should "step back" in a figurative sense, and compare the lack of safety standards for Facebook customers with the safety standard usually assumed for buildings and automobiles. This broader perspective helps viewers to understand the extent to which certain Internet providers encroach on the privacy rights of their customers.

4. Syntactic and conceptual mismatches: More on the pragmatics of *and*

4.1 Introduction

As demonstrated in Section 3, the connective *and* frequently displays senses that go beyond its basic coordinative sense. In what follows, further evidence is given that this conjunction is a versatile linguistic device allowing speakers to code complex meanings without too much cognitive effort; and given that the pathways of pragmatic, in particular, metonymic inferencing, at work in the elaboration of the intended meaning of this connective, are fairly entrenched, these target meanings can be grasped by hearers with relative ease. The pragmatic motivation of linguistic form can be illustrated with a specific coordinative construction, i.e. the pattern *nice and Adj*, instantiated by locutions such as *nice and cozy* and *nice and comfortable*.

The *nice and Adj* construction exhibits a mismatch between syntactic structure and conceptual content and/or pragmatic function. At first blush, this lack of isomorphism between form and content/function seems to lend support to the thesis that syntactic structure is not motivated by conceptual-pragmatic factors, but it turns out that there is an inferential relationship (metonymic and/or metaphorical) between what is *literally* expressed and what is *conventionally meant* by the construction in question. In other words, the relationship between syntactic form and semantic content/pragmatic function of the *nice and Adj* construction is not arbitrary, but motivated.

4.2 From coordination to evaluation: The *nice and Adj* construction

The syntactic form of the *nice and Adj* construction is *coordinative*, but on the conceptual-pragmatic level *nice (and)* frequently functions like an *evaluative operator* of the adjective in the second conjunct.[123] This evaluative sense is based on and derivable from the literal coordinative sense. Examples that allow *only* a literal coordinative interpretation are rare, an example being (68):

(68) Babies can spot nice and nasty characters
 (WebCorp, Nature News, November 21, 2007)

Sentence (68) has a purely coordinative, i.e. in logical terms, conjunctive meaning. Evidence for this claim is that the two conjuncts *nice* and *nasty* can be commuted without any change of meaning, as (69) shows:

---

[123]. The *nice and Adj* construction is analyzed in more detail in Panther and Thornburg (2009b, 2017a: Chapter 9). Much of what follows, is based on these two publications.

(69) Babies can spot nasty and nice characters.

Sentences (68) and (69) are truth-conditionally equivalent. Furthermore, the same content as (68) can be expressed by two conjoined clauses (although this way of coding its meaning is stylistically cumbersome):

(70) Babies can spot nice characters, and babies can spot nasty characters.

To conclude, the meaning of (68) is compositional, i.e. transparent: *and* has the same meaning as the logical connective '∧' (see Chapter 1).

The second sense of the *nice and Adj* pattern is based on the literal compositional sense, but it adds elements of idiomaticity that, as shown below, are derivable via pragmatic inferencing. The following examples (71)–(80), which instantiate the ten most frequent types of the *nice and Adj* construction, have been retrieved from the *iWeb* corpus. The focus of this section is on the idiomatic, i.e. non-compositional sense of the construction.[124]

(71) The rooms are nice and clean, but they are bit small.   (iWeb, hostelz.com)

(72) This step by step tutorial makes it nice and easy.   (iWeb, photoshopcafe.com)

(73) I love going to Houston Archery! Everyone is so nice and helpful.
(iWeb, macaronikid.com)

(74) I sanded [the wood plaques] with low grit sand paper until they were nice and smooth!   (iWeb, thediydreamer.com)

(75) The weather, even here in Brighton, is nice and warm.
(iWeb, marziaslife.com)

(76) The interface of this game is nice and simple [...].   (iWeb, n4bb.com)

(77) I do enjoy my experience with City University of Seattle! Professors are nice and friendly   (iWeb, ratemyprofessors.com)

(78) The fabric is nice and soft [...].   (iWeb, ladyvlondon.com)

(79) The villa is very nice and quiet, located near the center and the beach.
(iWeb, longtermlettings.com)

(80) While the temperature outside was around 30 degrees, inside was nice and cool.   (iWeb, nomadsworld.com)[125]

---

124. The *iWeb* corpus lists 92,488 tokens of the *nice and Adj* pattern.

125. The *nice and cool* examples include metaphorical uses of *cool* such as in *Altogether a great product with a really nice and cool design.* (iWeb, globalflyfisher.com)

In examples (71)–(80), the *nice and Adj* construction has the function of evaluating the second adjectival conjunct as GOOD or POSITIVE, i.e., the second conjunct inherits its positive quality from the first conjunct *nice*. This is the case even if the second conjunct is relatively neutral or has negative connotations in other contexts. As examples of properties that are not inherently viewed as positive, consider the uses of *chewy* in (81), *sad* in (82), and *depressing* in (83):

(81) The noodles were nice and chewy. (iWeb, kirbiecravings.com)

(82) The Little Mermaid is a nice and sad tale. (iWeb, storynory.com)

(83) Who doesn't like some nice and depressing quotes, especially post-Valentine's Day? (iWeb, brostick.com)[126]

In the online dictionary NOAD, the adjective *chewy* is defined as '(of food) needing to be chewed hard or for some time', and the dictionary illustrates this sense with the following example:

(84) [T]he bread was never quite fresh, always pretty chewy. (NOAD, s.v. *chewy*)

In (84), the bread's property of being chewy is obviously evaluated negatively. However, in (81), the positive quality of *nice* imposes a corresponding positive evaluation of *chewy* noodles. In the same way, in (82) and (83), *nice* coerces *sad* and *depressing*, respectively, into positively evaluated properties.

The conventionalized conceptual modifier function of *nice (and)* can be reconstructed stepwise as a series of pragmatic inferences. By way of example, recall the first clause in (71):

(85) The rooms are *nice and clean* → The rooms are *nice and, more specifically, clean*
It is a *nice property* of the rooms that they are *clean*.

The first cognitive step at work in (85) is a construal of the second conjunct, here *clean*, as a hyponym of the hyperonym *nice*. This sense elaboration is achieved by means of a metonymic shift from *and* as a purely truth-functional connective to the sense 'and more specifically'. The first conjunct *nice* expresses the superordinate property GOOD or POSITIVE, which is inherited by the second conjunct, here the adjective *clean*. Notice that the second adjective does not have to be inherently positive, as evidenced by expressions such as *nice and depressing*. Figure 6 is an attempt to generalize the inferential mechanisms from the literal coordinative source meaning, via an interpretation that metonymically shifts the "logical" meaning of *and* to the reading 'and more specifically', i.e. establishes a relation of

---

126. The erroneous spelling *post-Valentines Day* has been corrected.

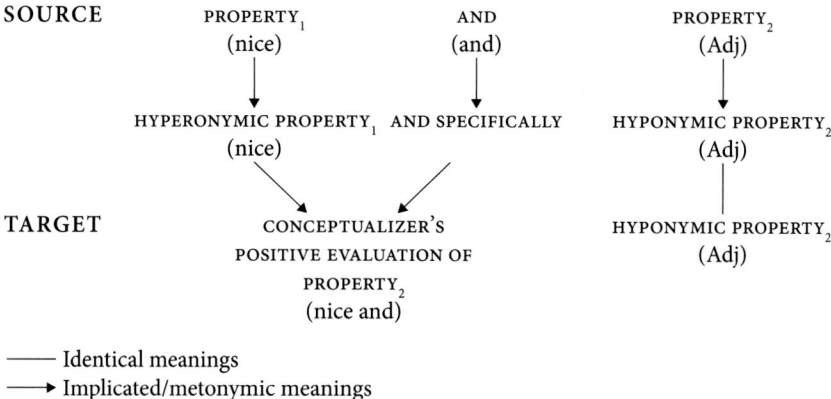

Figure 6. Metonymic derivation of the target sense of the *nice and Adj* construction

hyperonym-hyponym between *nice* and the following *adjective*, to an illocutionary target sense in which *nice* functions as an index of an act of positive evaluation of the property denoted the second adjective.

The thesis that the *nice and Adj* construction is semantically and pragmatically distinct from genuinely coordinative patterns of the form *Adj and Adj* is supported by the fact that sentences of the form *This N is nice and Adj* can be also coded as *what*-cleft sentences of the form *What is nice about NP is Adj*, whereas this transformation is blocked in cases of conceptually coordinative cases of the form *This N is Adj_1 and Adj_2*.

To see this, consider first some examples of the pattern *This N is nice and Adj*:

(86) This recipe is nice and simple [...]. (iWeb, scottishmum.com)
(87) [T]his gin is nice and dry [...] (iWeb, ginfestival.com)
(88) This place is nice and clean. (iWeb, palmbeachtan.com)
(89) This cake is nice and moist [...]. (iWeb, kitchenmeetsgirl.com)
(90) This park is nice and quiet (iWeb, campingroaddtrip.com)
(91) This sauce is nice and hot (iWeb, hotsauce.com)

Sentences (86)–(91) are truth-conditionally equivalent to the *wh*-cleft sentences (92)–(97), respectively:

(92) What is nice about this recipe is that it is simple.
(93) What is nice about this gin is that it is dry.
(94) What is nice about this place is that it is clean.

(95) What is nice about this cake is that it is moist.

(96) What is nice about this park is that it is quiet.

(97) What is nice about this sauce is that it is hot.

In contrast, consider coordinative structures of the form *This N is Adj₁ and Adj₂*, in which the two adjectival conjuncts are both formally and conceptually coordinative:

(98) This stemware is tall and elegant […]. (iWeb, villeroy-boch.com)

(99) [T]his recipe is delicious and easy! (iWeb, justhungry.com)

(100) [T]his necklace is elegant and classy. (iWeb, diamondsdirect.com)

(101) This course is useful and relevant. (iWeb, sqlskills.com)

(102) This website is excellent and informative. (iWeb, caffeineinformer.com)

(103) This book is intelligent and understandable. (iWeb, cjc-online.ca)

None of the examples (98)–(103) appears to allow the formation of a corresponding *what*-cleft construction, in which the first adjectival conjunct is being placed in the *what*-clause. Thus, the following seem to be pragmatically weird or even unacceptable:

(104) #What is tall about this stemware is that is elegant.

(105) #What is delicious about this recipe is that it is easy!

(106) #What is elegant about this necklace is that it is classy.

(107) ?What is useful about this course is that it is relevant.

(108) ?What is excellent about this website is that it is informative.

(109) #What is intelligent about this book is that it is understandable.

Here are additional corpus examples of the form *What is nice about X is Y* that provide evidence that *nice* has the function of signaling a speech act of positive evaluation.

(110) What is really nice about Google+ hangouts is that they are easy to use and the control aspects are very basic. (iWeb, wordtracker.com)

(111) What is nice about a question and answer broadcast is that it is easy, you already hold the answers to many frequently asked questions.
(iWeb, wordtracker.com)

(112) What is nice about this query syntax is that it's very clean and easy to read and understand. (iWeb, web-loh.west-wind.com)

In examples (110)–(112), *nice* occurs within a *wh*-cleft construction. The *what*-clause introduces a topic, which, through the workings of *nice*, indexes a positive evaluation of the content of the complement clause following the copula *is*. The *what*-clause conveys the *presupposition* 'x has a positive property', where *x* is a variable instantiated by the noun phrases *Google+ handouts* in in (110), *a question and answer broadcast* in (111), and *this query syntax* in (112). In the subsequent *focus* clause, the positive characteristics of *x* are specified more narrowly as *easy to use* in (110), *easy* in (111), and *clean and easy to read and understand* in (112). Importantly, the order of *nice* and the attributes occurring in the focus clause cannot be reversed, which supports the thesis that *nice* is the superordinate (hyperonymic) "evaluator" that imposes its positive connotation on the subsequent adjective(s):

(113) #What is really *easy* to use about Google+ hangouts is that they are *nice* [...].

(114) #What is *easy* about a question and answer broadcast is that it is nice [...].

(115) #What is very *clean and easy* to read and understand about this query syntax is that it's *nice*.

We have seen that *nice (and)* signals a speech act of positive evaluation. Analogously to *nice*, there are other adjectives of positive evaluation that can also be used in *wh*-cleft constructions, e.g. *excellent* and *unique*, as in (116)–(119):

(116) What is excellent about Stockholm is that you can go to really good concerts for free. (iWeb, sweden.se)

(117) What is excellent about this course is that it covers everything you need to do in order to succeed as a Clickbank affiliate [...]. (iWeb, graophic-design-employment.com)

(118) What is unique about this product is the fact that it has 4 separate button setting switches [...]. (iWeb, mameworld.info)

(119) What is unique about Expense Reduction Solutions is that it provides a turnkey solution [...]. (iWeb, harlandclarke.com)

Finally, another interesting aspect of the *nice and Adj* construction that deserves mention is that the positive evaluation signaled by *nice* does not hold unconditionally. To see this, consider examples (120)–(126):

(120) PDF is nice and well supported but it's a bitch to edit. (www.linux.com/feature/29685)

(121) Great quality soap but smells like a regular bath soap. Definitely nice and clean but not unique. (iWeb, stirlingsoap.com)

(122) The rooms were nice and clean but not true 5 star [...].
(iWeb, softvoyage.com)

(123) The Remington 710 is nice and serviceable but not a good starting point for a precision rifle. (iWeb, uzitalk.com)

(124) Nice and warm but not true to the size listed on the site.
(iWeb, aerotechdesigns.com)

(125) I was quite pleased with the results, certainly nice and edible but not quite as light as I would [have] hoped for. (iWeb, virtousbread.com)

(126) This is a photo of the original carpeted floor I had. It looked real nice and comfortable but not practical. Especially for cleaning.
(iWeb, doityourselfrv.com)

In (120)–(126), the *but* clause names one or more properties that are not "nice", i.e. positively evaluated. By way of example, consider (126). In the second sentence *comfortable* is obviously considered a positive quality of the carpet in question; however, in the *but* clause a negatively viewed property is introduced, i.e., the carpet is *not practical [...] for cleaning*.

5. Conclusion

This chapter has shown that syntactic structure can be motivated by semantic and pragmatic factors. The sources cited in the introduction to this chapter provide numerous additional language data that provide evidence of the conceptual and pragmatic motivation of grammatical phenomena. The relationship between conceptual content, pragmatic function, and morphosyntactic structure is a fascinating but also contentious topic in contemporary linguistics. Desiderata and proposals for further research are addressed in the final Chapter 12.

CHAPTER 12

Epilogue

1. To recap

My motivation for writing this book was both theoretical and practical. To start with the latter, I believe that it would be useful for advanced (graduate and postgraduate) students and interested scholars to be offered an introduction that relates central themes of cognitive linguistics to contemporary pragmatics, especially to Gricean and Neo-Gricean paradigms and speech act theory. My aim in this monograph has been to show that, in various respects, cognitive linguistics and contemporary pragmatics can be reconciled, i.e. coexist in harmony, and complement each other. A worthwhile research agenda would and should be to develop a unified theory of cognitive pragmatics. I do not pretend that this goal has been achieved in this book, but I hope that a few steps forward on the road to this destination have been taken.

The present book aims at working against a certain tendency towards fragmentation of linguistic theories whose proponents sometimes regard scholars of any other theoretical orientation than their own as "adversaries", rather than as co-researchers competing in a friendly way with the goal in mind to advance our knowledge of the formal and conceptual structure of language, and its use in communication. My own view is that interesting hypotheses have been advanced by linguists from "all walks of academic life", i.e. theoretical paradigms, be they formalist, functionalist, or cognitivist. In this monograph, I want to make a case for the thesis that cognitive linguistics and contemporary pragmatics can learn from each other and that they should cooperate rather than have heated arguments over whether e.g. metaphor should be analyzed in terms of pragmatic inferencing (implicature) or in terms of mappings across cognitive domains or conceptual frames.

The relationships between competing linguistic models are fundamentally of two kinds. First, different theoretical paradigms may be genuinely incompatible, i.e. offer descriptions and explanations that cannot be true at the same time. For example, the idea that syntax (or more generally, grammar), is a self-contained module organized according to its own rules and principles, is not compatible with functionalist, and more specifically, cognitive linguistic approaches postulating that morphosyntactic form is *motivated* to a certain extent by meaning and pragmatic function (see e.g. Croft 1995; Chapter 2 of this book). Second, and more importantly for the agenda of this book, theories differ in their descriptive and explanatory terminology. Notwithstanding, on closer inspection, these terminologies may be partially or even fully translatable into one another; i.e., they may turn out not to be mutually exclusive. I have argued in this book that, despite terminological differences, many tenets of cognitive linguistics are compatible with contemporary pragmatics, and vice versa. Furthermore, and this is also of significance concerning the relationship between cognitive linguistics and pragmatics, their objects of inquiry overlap and complement each other in ways that have been discussed in this book.

It must be kept in mind that the linguistic paradigm known as *cognitive linguistics* does not constitute a unified theory (see Panther & Thornburg 2009a). For example, Ronald Langacker's approach known as *cognitive grammar* (Langacker 2013) differs – not only terminologically, but possibly also conceptually – in certain respects from other cognitivist frameworks, such as the one developed by George Lakoff and Mark Johnson (see e.g. Lakoff 1987; Lakoff & Johnson 1999), which, in turn, is not in all respects congruent with Gilles Fauconnier's and Mark Turner's theory of *mental spaces* and *conceptual integration* (see e.g. Fauconnier 1997; Fauconnier & Turner 2002), and the model of *cognitive semantics* proposed by Leonard Talmy (2000a,b). However, the pluralism of theoretical frameworks can be seen as an advantage rather than a deficiency of cognitive linguistics, as long as the different schools of thought avoid the risk of theoretical compartmentalization and are open to inputs from other paradigms.

2. Themes and prospects

In the following, I briefly summarize the chapters of this book and pose some open questions and desiderata for future research that readers of this book might want to explore; especially, motivation (Chapters 2 and 11), inferencing (Chapters 3–5), metonymy (Chapter 8), and speech acts (Chapters 6, 9, and 10).

Chapter 1 was concerned with definitional issues of pragmatics, i.e. the discipline that studies the use of language-in-context, and the thorny issue of how (if at all) pragmatics can be distinguished from semantics, i.e. the study of linguistic meaning. In this connection, the chapter also contains a brief discussion of the role of truth – more precisely, *truth values* and *truth conditions* – in the construction of meaning. In cognitive linguistics, truth conditions are rarely addressed and possibly considered to be irrelevant to an adequate cognitivist theory of meaning. However, as philosophers of language and logicians have pointed out, truth conditions play an important part in the characterization of meaning of e.g. connectives such as conjunction ('∧'), disjunction ('∨',) and material implication ('⊃'), all of which have counterparts in natural language, i.e. 'and', 'or', and 'if … then', respectively. As was shown in Chapter 1, there are also important conceptual differences between e.g. the logical properties of '∧' and its counterpart in natural language, e.g. English *and*. However, these differences should not lead to the conclusion that truth does not play an important role in an adequate theory of meaning. Finally, Chapter 1 also provides a characterization of pragmatics that is inspired by scholars like Leech (1983) and Green (1989), as well as cognitive linguists such as Fauconnier (2006), Schmid (2012), and Langacker (2013). These scholars appear to be in agreement that a distinction between the objects of inquiry of semantics and pragmatics can be made; but, it can also be argued that the boundary between them is fuzzy.

Chapter 2 focused on language-internal and -external factors that may *motivate* linguistic structure and use. In particular, it discussed the question if and how the form of linguistic signs is shaped by their meaning and/or communicative function. The presumption that language is motivated is usually contrasted with the doctrine of *arbitrariness* of linguistic signs, as postulated by the Swiss structuralist Ferdinand de Saussure (1995) in the early twentieth century, who claimed that meaning and communicative function have little or no impact on the form of linguistic units. Phenomena such as sound symbolism or *onomatopoiea*, as manifested in lexical items like *cuckoo*, where the bird's call metonymically stands for the bird itself, are regarded as exceptions to the principle of arbitrariness. Basically, in this view, they are seen as confirming the thesis of the arbitrary relationship between form and meaning, rather than falsifying it. In contrast to the Saussurean model, in Chapter 2, I argue that the motivatedness of linguistic signs is a pervasive phenomenon – although, undeniably, arbitrary, i.e. unmotivated signs, are abundant as well (see e.g. Panther 2013, 2021 for overviews; on specific types of motivation, see e.g. Benczes 2019 on phonological motivation and Radden 2021 on iconic motivation.[127]

A central theme in this book has been the role of *inference* in the construction of meaning, a research subject to which especially scholars working in the tradition of Gricean pragmatics (e.g. Grice 1975; Levinson 2000) and relevance theory (e.g. Sperber & Wilson 1995) have made substantial contributions. The significance of inferential mechanisms in meaning creation, especially metaphoric and metonymic reasoning, has been recognized by some cognitive linguists (see e.g. Barcelona 2015 for an overview; and more recently Pérez-Hernández 2021). Nevertheless, what has been neglected in the cognitive linguistic literature is, to my mind, a focus on other *types* of inference than conceptual metaphor and metonymy that speakers "invite" and that hearers draw, usually fast and spontaneously, in communicative interaction.

---

[127]. It is worth noting in this context that Dingemanse, Blasi, Lupyan, Christiansen, and Monaghan (2015: 313) argue that even arbitrariness (between form and meaning) has a communicative function. According to these authors, "arbitrariness facilitates meaning individuation through distinctive forms."

The topic of inferencing in the construction of meaning was dealt with in detail in Chapters 3, 4, and 5. My view is that mechanisms of reasoning and inference, which have been well known in pre-cognitivist semantics and pragmatics, should be part and parcel of the descriptive apparatus of cognitive pragmatics, in particular, inferential types such as entailment, presupposition, and implicature. Chapter 5 focuses on commonalities and important differences among these inferential types, concerning properties such as suspendability, cancelability, and reinforcement, which have some effect on discourse structure and coherence. Among other things, Chapter 5 discusses the question, under what circumstances, reinforcement, i.e. explicit repetition of what has already been entailed, presupposed or implicated by preceding linguistic units in a sentence or piece of discourse does not produce an effect of redundancy or tautology. This is a subject that deserves further investigation (for acceptable tautological compounds, see e.g. Benczes 2014). The study of redundancy in language, apart from its theoretical interest, is also important from a socio-cultural perspective, and is relevant to the teaching of normative grammar as well as English as a foreign language.

Chapter 6 provided a succinct overview of speech act theory. Speech acts, in particular illocutionary acts, are crucial objects of inquiry, from the perspective of linguistic theory as well as its application in other fields, e.g. in foreign language teaching (see e.g. Pérez-Hernández 2021). In Chapters 6, 9, and 10 of this book, I proposed an approach to illocutionary acts and their senses that relies heavily on the notion of semantic or conceptual frame (see Fillmore 1982 and Ziem 2014). The frame-semantic approach to illocutionary meaning advocated in this book is an attempt to integrate what speech act theorists refer to as *felicity conditions* (see Chapter 6) into a cognitive linguistic framework (see also Thornburg & Panther 1997; Panther & Thornburg 1998). Building on the concept of illocutionary frame, in Chapters 9 and 10, the target senses of *indirect illocutionary acts* were described in terms of metonymic inferencing within illocutionary frames. An interesting research project would be to investigate, cross-linguistically, commonalities and differences in the exploitation of metonymies in indirect speech acts, and what the roles of linguistic and possibly socio-cultural factors are that influence the productivity or blocking of specific metonymies.

Chapters 7 and 8 were concerned with two central figures of thought and language: metaphor and metonymy. In cognitive linguistics, metaphor is usually considered as an instance of iconic and analogical reasoning and, following Lakoff and Johnson (1980) is described in terms of mappings *across* two distinct conceptual frames, while metonymy is defined as a kind of indexical relation that exploits associative relations *within* one frame. However, a clear distinction between what constitutes *one* single frame versus what counts as *two* distinct frames is not always easy to draw (see also Barnden 2010, who provides evidence that the connection between metaphor and metonymy is "more slippery" than hitherto thought). Further research and cooperation between pragmaticists and cognitive linguists on these issues are desirable. This includes the problem whether metaphor and metonymy can be reduced to specific kinds of Gricean implicature. As suggested above, this may turn out to be a pseudo-problem in the sense that *both* metaphor and metonymy may be regarded as *inferential* mechanisms.

As to metonymy, there are still various theoretical and applicational problems that await clarification and elucidation. There are definitional issues regarding the nature of metonymy that have not yet been resolved. As already pointed out in Chapter 8, one objective should be to develop a more precise and constrained definition of this central figure of thought and language (see also Ruiz de Mendoza Ibáñez 2021). Two ambitious projects should focus on the exploitation of metonymies from a cross-linguistic and typological perspective (see e.g. Panther & Thornburg 1999; Zhang, Geeraerts, & Speelman 2015) and investigate how metonymy and grammar interact (see Brdar 2017 on the relation between word-formation and metonymy).

Chapter 11 returned to the overriding theme of this book: the conceptual and pragmatic motivation of grammatical structure. The corpus data analyzed in the chapter are particularly relevant to the development of an adequate cognitive pragmatic model. I argued, like other functional linguists, that conceptual and pragmatic parameters that have an influence on linguistic form should be considered an integral part of grammar. Three case studies were presented in detail and analyzed in terms of their conceptual-pragmatic motivatedness. They were: (i) the impact of preposed negative adverbials on word order; (ii) acceptable violations of Ross's (1967) Coordinate Structure Constraint (CSC), and (iii) the shift from coordination to evaluative modification in the *nice and Adj* construction. In all three cases, the motivation from CONTENT/FUNCTION to FORM is mediated, at least in part, through metonymic inferencing. For example, admissible violations of the CSC can be seen as cases of *emergent grammaticalization*: the first conjunct undergoes a shift from a coordinated element to a grounding unit with an *aspectual* meaning (see e.g. Traugott 2012: 556–557 on the role of metonymy in diachronic processes of grammaticalization). Another interesting project would be to test the acceptability of CSC "violations" in other languages. It seems to me that, unlike in English, e.g. in my native German and in French, such violations are unacceptable and do not occur even in colloquial registers. What are the reasons for these contrasts? Are they rooted in language-specific grammatical differences and/or normative traditions of what constitutes "correct" or "good usage"? Answers to such questions are worthy dissertation topics.

3. Final thoughts

In the present book, my aim has been to make a case for a model of pragmatics that combines insights from contemporary pragmatics with a cognitive linguistic approach. I hope to have shown that such an approach can lead to new insights into language structure and use, and to open up new avenues of research into linguistic conceptualization, communicative function, and grammar, as well as the interaction among these fields of inquiry. In conclusion, my hope is that readers of this book will be inspired and "motivated" to pursue some of the research agenda formulated in this monograph.

References

Akmajian, A., Demers, R. A., Farmer, A. K., & Harnish, R. M. 2010. *Linguistics: An Introduction to Language and Communication*. 6th edition. Cambridge, MA: The MIT Press.

Aliseda, A. 2006. *Abductive Reasoning: Logical Investigations into Discovery and Explanation* (Synthese Library: Studies in Epistemology, Logic, Methodology, and Philosophy of Science 30). Dordrecht: Springer.

Allott, N. 2010. *Key Terms in Pragmatics*. London & New York: Continuum.

Ambler, E. 2001 [1937]. *Background to Danger*. New York: Vintage Books.

Ariel, M. 2008. *Grammar and Pragmatics*. Cambridge: Cambridge University Press. https://doi.org/10.1017/CBO9780511791314

Ariel, M. 2010. *Defining Pragmatics* (Research Surveys in Linguistics). Cambridge: Cambridge University Press. https://doi.org/10.1017/CBO9780511777912

Arnaud, A. & Lancelot, C. 1660. *Grammaire générale et raisonnée*. Paris: Pierre Le Petit. [Online access: http://gallica.bnf.fr/]

Athanasiadou, A. 2017. Irony has a metonymic basis. In: A. Athanasiadou & H. L. Colston, eds. *Irony in Language Use and Communication* (Figurative Thought and Language 1). Amsterdam & Philadelphia, 201–216. https://doi.org/10.1075/ftl.1.10ath

Austin, J. L. 1961. *Philosophical Papers*. Oxford: Oxford University Press.

Austin, J. L. 1962. *How to Do Things with Words*. Cambridge, MA: Harvard University Press.

Austin, J. L. 1971. Performative – constative. In: J. R. Searle, ed. *The Philosophy of Language*. Oxford: Oxford University Press, 13–22.

Bach, K. & Harnish, R. M. 1979. *Linguistic Communication and Speech Acts*. Cambridge, MA: M.I.T. Press.

Baicchi, A. 2012. *On Acting and Thinking: Studies Bridging between Speech Acts and Cognition*. Pisa: Edizioni ETS.

Barcelona, A. 2015. Metonymy. In: Dąbrowska, E., & Divjak, D., eds. 2015. *The Handbook of Cognitive Linguistics*. Berlin & Boston: de Gruyter Mouton, 143–167.

Barnden, J. A. 2010. Metaphor and metonymy: Making their connections more slippery. *Cognitive Linguistics* 21.1: 1–34. https://doi.org/10.1515/cogl.2010.001

Benczes, R. 2014. Repetitions which are not repetitions: the non-redundant nature of tautological compounds. *English Language and Linguistics* 18.3: 431–447. https://doi.org/10.1017/S1360674314000112

Benczes, R. 2019. *Rhyme over Reason: Phonological Motivation in English*. Cambridge: Cambridge University Press. https://doi.org/10.1017/9781108649131

Bergman, M. & Paavola, S., eds. 2014. *The Commens Dictionary: Peirce's Terms in His Own Words*. New Edition. [Term 'Metaphor' retrieved from http://www.commens.org/ dictionary/term/metaphor].

Bierwiaczonek, B. 2013. *Metonymy in Language, Thought and Brain*. Sheffield: Equinox.

Birner, B. J. 2013. *Introduction to Pragmatics*. Chichester: Wiley-Blackwell.

Blakemore, D. 1987. *Semantic Constraints on Relevance*. Oxford: Blackwell.

Borsley, D., & Newmeyer, F. J. 2009. On subject-auxiliary inversion and the notion "purely formal generalization". *Cognitive Linguistics* 20: 135–145. https://doi.org/10.1515/COGL.2009.007

Brdar, M. 2017. *Metonymy and Word Formation: Their Interaction and Complementation*. Newcastle upon Tyne: Cambridge Scholars.

Broccias, C. 2003. *The English Change Network* (Cognitive Linguistics Research 22). Berlin & New York: Mouton de Gruyter. https://doi.org/10.1515/9783110901207

Brown, P. & Levinson, S. C. 1987. *Politeness: Some Universals in Language Use*. Cambridge: Cambridge University Press. https://doi.org/10.1017/CBO9780511813085

Brown, K. & Miller, J. 2013. *The Cambridge Dictionary of Linguistics*. Cambridge: Cambridge University Press. https://doi.org/10.1017/CBO9781139049412

Brugman, C., & Lakoff, G. 1986. The semantics of aux-inversion and anaphora constraints. Unpublished paper: University of California at Berkeley.

Buchler, J. 1955. *Philosophical Writings of Peirce*. New York: Dover Publications.

Burgers, C., Konijn. E. A., & Steen, G. J. 2016. Figurative framing: Shaping public discourse through metaphor, hyperbole, and irony. *Communication Theory* 26.4: 410–430. https://doi.org/10.1111/comt.12096

Burkhardt, A. 1986. *Soziale Akte, Sprechakte und Textillokutionen: A. Reinachs Rechtsphilosophie und die moderne Linguistik*. Tübingen: Niemeyer. https://doi.org/10.1515/9783111371573

Cann, R. 1993. *Formal Semantics: An Introduction*. Cambridge: Cambridge University Press.

Carston, R. 2012. Metaphor and the literal/non-literal distinction. In: K. Allan & K. M. Jaszczolt, eds. *The Cambridge Handbook of Pragmatics*. Cambridge: Cambridge University Press, 469–492. https://doi.org/10.1017/CBO9781139022453.025

Choi, Y. 2012. Semantic comparison between English -er nominals and Korean -i nominals. *Discourse and Cognition* 19.3: 297–319. https://doi.org/10.15718/discog.2012.19.3.297

Chomsky, N. 1957. *Syntactic Structures*. The Hague: Mouton. https://doi.org/10.1515/9783112316009

Chomsky, N. 1959. A review of B. F. Skinner's *Verbal Behavior*. *Language* 35.1: 26–58.

Chomsky, N. 1975. *Reflections on Language*. New York: Pantheon Books.

Clark, H. H. & Clark, E. V. 1977. *Psychology and Language: An Introduction to Psycholinguistics*. New York: Harcourt Brace Jovanovich.

Cobley, P., ed. 2010. *The Routledge Companion to Semiotics*. Abingdon: Routledge.

Coetzee, J. M. 2016. *The Schooldays of Jesus*. Melbourne: The Text Publishing Company.

Comrie, B. 1988. Topics, grammaticalized topics, and subjects. In: S. Axmaker, A. Jaisser, & H. Singmaster, eds. *Berkeley Linguistics Society: Proceedings of the Fourteenth Annual Meeting*. Berkeley, CA: Berkeley Linguistics Society, 265–279. https://doi.org/10.3765/bls.v14i0.1798

Conant, L. L. 1931. *The Number Concept: Its Origin and Development*. New York & London: Macmillan and Co.

Croft, W. 1995. Autonomy and functionalist linguistics. *Language* 71.3: 490–532. https://doi.org/10.2307/416218

Croft, W. & Cruse, A. 2004. *Cognitive Linguistics*. Cambridge: Cambridge University Press. https://doi.org/10.1017/CBO9780511803864

Cruse, A. 2006. *A Glossary of Semantics and Pragmatics*. Edinburgh: Edinburgh University Press.

Crystal, D. 1997. *The Cambridge Encyclopedia of Language*. Cambridge: Cambridge University Press.

Crystal, D. 2008. *A Dictionary of Linguistics and Phonetics*. 6th ed. Malden, MA: Blackwell. https://doi.org/10.1002/9781444302776

Culicover, P. & Jackendoff, R. 2005. *Simpler Syntax*. Oxford: Oxford University Press. https://doi.org/10.1093/acprof:oso/9780199271092.001.0001

Dąbrowska, E. & Divjak, D., eds. 2015. *The Handbook of Cognitive Linguistics*. Berlin & Boston: de Gruyter Mouton. https://doi.org/10.1515/9783110292022

Dancygier, B., ed. 2017. *The Cambridge Handbook of Cognitive Linguistics*. Cambridge: Cambridge University Press. https://doi.org/10.1017/9781316339732

Dancygier, B. & Sweetser, E. 2014. *Figurative Language*. Cambridge: Cambridge University Press.

Davidson, D. 1978. What metaphors mean. *Critical Inquiry* 5.1: 31–47. https://doi.org/10.1086/447971

Davis, W. 2014. Implicature. In: E. N. Zalta, ed. *The Stanford Encyclopedia of Philosophy*. [Accessed at: https://plato.stanford.edu/archives/fall2014/entries/implicature].

Deane, P. D. 1992. *Grammar in Mind and Brain* (Cognitive Linguistics Research 2). Berlin & New York: Mouton de Gruyter. https://doi.org/10.1515/9783110886535

Denroche, C. 2015. *Metonymy and Language: A New Theory of Linguistic Processing*. New York & London: Routledge.

Deutscher, G. 2002. On the misuse of the notion of 'abduction' in linguistics. *Journal of Linguistics* 38: 469–485. https://doi.org/10.1017/S002222670200169X

Dingemanse, M., Blasi, D. E., Lupyan, G., Christiansen, M. H., & Monaghan, P. 2015. Arbitrariness, iconicity, and systematicity in language. *Trends in Cognitive Science* 19.10: 603–615. https://doi.org/10.1016/j.tics.2015.07.013

Dirven, R. & Verspoor, M., eds. 2004. *Cognitive Explorations of Language and Linguistics*. Amsterdam & Philadelphia: Benjamins. https://doi.org/10.1075/clip.1

Ducrot, O. 1969. Présupposés et sous-entendus. *Langue française* 4: 300–43. https://doi.org/10.3406/lfr.1969.5456

Ducrot, O. 1972. *Dire et ne pas dire: Principes de sémantique linguistique*. Paris: Hermann.

Durkin, P. 2009. *The Oxford Guide to Etymology*. Oxford: Oxford University Press.

Evans, N. 2007. Insubordination and its uses. In I. Nikolaeva, ed. *Finiteness: Theoretical and Empirical Foundations*. Oxford: Oxford University Press, 366–431.

Evans, N. & Watanabe, H., eds. 2016. *Insubordination* (Typological Studies in Language 115). Amsterdam & Philadelphia: Benjamins. https://doi.org/10.1075/tsl.115

Evans, V. 2007. *A Glossary of Cognitive Linguistics*. Edinburgh: Edinburgh University Press.

Evans, V. & Green, M. 2006. *Cognitive Linguistics: An Introduction*. Edinburgh: Edinburgh University Press.

Fauconnier, G. 1997. *Mappings in Thought and Language*. Cambridge: Cambridge University Press. https://doi.org/10.1017/CBO9781139174220

Fauconnier, G. 2006. Pragmatics and cognitive linguistics. In L. R. Horn & G. Ward, eds. *The Handbook of Pragmatics*. Malden, MA: Blackwell, 657–674. https://doi.org/10.1002/9780470756959.ch29

Fauconnier, G. & Turner, M. 2002. *The Way We Think: Conceptual Blending and the Mind's Hidden Complexity*. New York: Basic Books.

Faust, M. & Mashal, N. 2007. The role of the right cerebral hemisphere in processing novel metaphoric expressions taken from poetry: a divided visual field study. *Neuropsychologia* 45: 860–879. https://doi.org/10.1016/j.neuropsychologia.2006.08.010

Feist, J. 2012. *Premodifiers in English: Their Structure and Significance*. Cambridge: Cambridge University Press.

Fillmore, C. J. 1969. Verbs of judging: An exercise in semantic description. *Papers in Linguistics* 1.1: 81–117.

Fillmore, C. 1982. Frame semantics. In: The Linguistic Society of Korea, ed. *Linguistics in the Morning Calm: Selected Papers from SICOL-81*. Seoul: Hanshin Publishing Company.

Fraser, B. 1975. Hedged performatives. In: P. Cole & J. Morgan, eds. *Speech Acts (Syntax and Semantics 3)*. New York: Academic Press, 44–66. https://doi.org/10.1163/9789004368811_008

Garner, B. A. 2009. *Black's Law Dictionary* (9th ed.) St. Paul, MN: West.

Frege, G. 1892. Über Sinn und Bedeutung. *Zeitschrift für Philosophie und philosophische Kritik* 100: 25–50.

Geeraerts, D. 2010. *Theories of Lexical Semantics*. Oxford: Oxford University Press.

Geeraerts, D. & Cuyckens, H., eds. 2007. *The Oxford Handbook of Cognitive Linguistics*. Oxford: Oxford University Press.

Geis, M. L. & Zwicky, A. M. 1971. On invited inferences. *Linguistic Inquiry* 2.4: 561–566.

Gibbs, R. W., Jr. 1994. *The Poetics of Mind: Figurative Thought, Language, and Understanding*. Cambridge: Cambridge University Press.

Gibbs, R. W., Jr. 2005. *Embodiment and Cognitive Science*. Cambridge: Cambridge University Press. https://doi.org/10.1017/CBO9780511805844

Gibbs, R. W., Jr. 2006. Metaphor interpretation as embodied simulation. *Mind & Language* 21.3: 434–458. https://doi.org/10.1111/j.1468-0017.2006.00285.x

Giora, R. 2002. Literal vs. figurative language: Different or equal? *Journal of Pragmatics* 34: 487–506. https://doi.org/10.1016/S0378-2166(01)00045-5

Givón, T. 1993. *English Grammar: A Function-Based Introduction*. Vol. I. Amsterdam & Philadelphia: Benjamins. https://doi.org/10.1075/z.engram1

Goffman, E. 1967. *Interaction Ritual: Essays on Face-to-Face Behavior*. New York: Pantheon Books.

Goldberg, A. 1995. *Constructions: A Construction Grammar Approach to Argument Structure*. Chicago: University of Chicago Press.

Goldberg, A. 1996. Jackendoff and construction-based grammar. *Cognitive Linguistics* 7(1): 3–19. https://doi.org/10.1515/cogl.1996.7.1.3

Goldberg, A. 2006. *Constructions at Work*. Oxford: Oxford University Press.

Goldberg, A. 2009. The nature of generalization in language. *Cognitive Linguistics* 20(1): 93–127. https://doi.org/10.1515/COGL.2009.005

Goldsmith, J. A. 1985. A principled exception to the Coordinate Structure Constraint. In: W. Eilfort, P. Kroeber & K. Peterson, eds. *Papers from the 21st Meeting of the Chicago Linguistics Society*. Chicago: Chicago Linguistic Society.

Gordon, D. & G. Lakoff. 1975. Conversational postulates. In: P. Cole & J. L. Morgan, eds. *Speech Acts (Syntax and Semantics 3)*. New York: Academic Press, 83–106.

Grady, J. 1997. *Foundations of Meaning: Primary Metaphors and Primary Scenes*. UC Berkeley: Dissertations, Department of Linguistics. Retrieved from https://escholarship.org/uc/item/3q9427m2.

Grady, J. E. 2005. Primary metaphors as inputs to conceptual integration. *Journal of Pragmatics* 37: 1595–1614. https://doi.org/10.1016/j.pragma.2004.03.012

Green, G. 1989. *Pragmatics and Natural Language Understanding*. Hillsdale, NJ: Lawrence Erlbaum.

Grevisse, M. & Goosse, A. 2016. *Le bon usage: Grammaire française*. Louvain-la-Neuve: De Boeck.

Grice, H. P. 1975. Logic and conversation. In: P. Cole & J. L. Morgan, eds. *Speech Acts (Syntax and Semantics 3)*. New York: Academic Press, 41–58. https://doi.org/10.1163/9789004368811_003

Grice, H. P. 1989. *Studies in the Ways of Words*. Cambridge, MA: Harvard University Press.

Grundy, P. 2000. *Doing Pragmatics*. London: Arnold.

Heine, B. 1997. *Cognitive Foundations of Grammar*. Oxford: Oxford University Press.

Horn, L. R. 1988. Pragmatic theory. In: F. J. Newmeyer, ed. *Linguistics: The Cambridge Survey*. Vol. I: *Linguistic Theories: Foundations*. Cambridge: Cambridge University Press, 113–145.

Horn, L. R. 1989. *A Natural History of Negation*. Chicago & London: University of Chicago Press.

Horn, L. R. 1991. Given as new: When redundant affirmation isn't. *Journal of Pragmatics* 15: 313–336. https://doi.org/10.1016/0378-2166(91)90034-U

Horn, L. R. 2006. Implicature. In: L. R. Horn & G. Ward, eds. *Handbook of Pragmatics*. Oxford: Blackwell, 3–28. https://doi.org/10.1002/9780470756959.ch1

Horn, L. R. & Ward, G., eds. 2006. *Handbook of Pragmatics*. Oxford: Blackwell. https://doi.org/10.1002/9780470756959

Huang, Y. 2007. *Pragmatics*. New York: Oxford University Press.

Huddleston, R. & Pullum, G. K. 2002. *The Cambridge Grammar of the English Language*. Cambridge: Cambridge University Press. https://doi.org/10.1017/9781316423530

Huddleston, R. & Pullum, G. K. 2005. *A Student's Introduction to English Grammar*. Cambridge: Cambridge University Press. https://doi.org/10.1017/CBO9780511815515

Jäkel, O. 1997. *Metaphern in abstrakten Diskurs-Domänen: Eine kognitiv-linguistische Untersuchung anhand der Bereiche Geistestätigkeit, Wirtschaft und Wissenschaft*. Frankfurt am Main: Lang

Jäkel, O. 1999. Kant, Blumenberg, Weinrich: Some forgotten contributions to the cognitive theory of metaphor. In: R. W. Gibbs & G. J. Steen, eds. *Metaphor in Cognitive Linguistics: Selected Papers from the Fifth International Cognitive Linguistics Conference, Amsterdam, July 1997* (Current Issues in Linguistic Theory 175). Amsterdam & Philadelphia: Benjamins, 9–26. https://doi.org/10.1075/cilt.175.02jak

Janda, L. 2013. *Cognitive Linguistics: The Quantitative Turn: An Essential Reader*. Berlin & Boston: De Gruyter Mouton. https://doi.org/10.1515/9783110335255

Kahneman, D. 2011. *Thinking Fast and Slow*. New York: Farrar, Strauss and Giroux.

Karttunen, L. 1971. Some observations on factivity. *Papers in Linguistics* 5: 55–69. https://doi.org/10.1080/08351817109370248

Kiparsky, P. & Kiparsky, C. 1970. Fact. In: M. Bierwisch & K. E. Heidolph, eds. *Progress in Linguistics*. The Hague: Mouton, 143–173. https://doi.org/10.1515/9783111350219.143

König, E. 1991. *The Meaning of Focus Particles: A Comparative Perspective*. London & New York: Routledge.

Köpcke, K.-M. & Panther, K.-U. 1989. On correlations between word order and pragmatic function of conditional sentences in German. *Journal of Pragmatics* 13: 685–711. https://doi.org/10.1016/0378-2166(89)90074-X

Köpcke, K.-M. & Panther, K.-U. 2016. Analytische und gestalthafte Nomina auf -er im Deutschen vor dem Hintergrund konstruktionsgrammatischer Überlegungen. In: A. Bittner & C. Spieß, eds. *Formen und Funktionen* (Lingua Historica Germanica 12). Berlin & Boston, 85–101. https://doi.org/10.1515/9783110478976-006

Kövecses, Z. 2005. *Metaphor in Culture: Universality and Variation*. Cambridge: Cambridge University Press. https://doi.org/10.1017/CBO9780511614408

Kövecses, Z. 2010. *Metaphor: A Practical Introduction*. 2nd ed. Oxford: Oxford University Press.

Kövecses, Z. & Radden, G. 1998. Developing a cognitive linguistic view. *Cognitive Linguistics* 9: 37–77. https://doi.org/10.1515/cogl.1998.9.1.37

Lakoff, G. 1987. *Women, Fire, and Dangerous Things: What Categories Reveal about the Mind*. Chicago & London: University of Chicago Press. https://doi.org/10.7208/chicago/9780226471013.001.0001

Lakoff, G. 1993. The contemporary theory of metaphor. In: A. Ortony, ed. *Metaphor and Thought*. Cambridge: Cambridge University Press, 202–251. https://doi.org/10.1017/CBO9781139173865.013

Lakoff, G. 2008. *The neural theory of metaphor.* In: R. W. Gibbs, Jr., ed. *The Cambridge Handbook of Metaphor and Thought.* Cambridge: Cambridge University Press, 17–38. https://doi.org/10.1017/CBO9780511816802.003

Lakoff, G. 2016. *Moral Politics: How Liberals and Conservatives Think* (3rd. ed.). Chicago & London: Chicago University Press.

Lakoff, G. & Johnson, M. 1980. *Metaphors We Live By.* Chicago & London: Chicago University Press.

Lakoff, G. & Johnson, M. 1999. *Philosophy In The Flesh: The Embodied Mind And Its Challenge To Western Thought.* New York: Basic Books.

Lakoff, G. & Turner, M. 1989. *More Than Cool Reason: A Field Guide To Poetic Metaphor.* Chicago & London: The University of Chicago Press. https://doi.org/10.7208/chicago/9780226470986.001.0001

Langacker, R. 1987. *Foundations of Cognitive Grammar.* Vol. 1: Theoretical Prerequisites. Stanford, CA: Stanford University Press.

Langacker, R. 1991. *Foundations of Cognitive Grammar.* Vol. 2: Descriptive Application. Stanford: Stanford University Press.

Langacker, R. 2000. *Grammar and Conceptualization* (Cognitive Linguistics Research 14). Berlin & New York: Mouton de Gruyter.

Langacker, R. W. 2008. *Cognitive Grammar: A basic Introduction.* Oxford: Oxford University Press. https://doi.org/10.1093/acprof:oso/9780195331967.001.0001

Langacker, R. W. 2009a. *Metonymic grammar.* In: K.-U. Panther, L. L. Thornburg, & A. Barcelona, eds. *Metonymy and Metaphor in Grammar* (Human Cognitive Processing 25). Amsterdam & Philadelphia: Benjamins, 45–71. https://doi.org/10.1075/hcp.25.04lan

Langacker, R. W. 2009b. *Investigations in Cognitive Grammar* (Cognitive Linguistics Research 42). Berlin & New York: Mouton de Gruyter. https://doi.org/10.1515/9783110214369

Langacker, R. W. 2013. *Essentials of Cognitive Grammar.* Oxford: Oxford University Press.

Lausberg, H. 1990. *Elemente der literarischen Rhetorik: eine Einführung für Studierende der klassischen, romanischen, englischen und deutschen Philologie.* 10th ed. Munich: Huber.

Leech, G. 1983. *Principles of Pragmatics.* London & New York: Longman.

Levinson, S. C. 1983. *Pragmatics.* Cambridge: Cambridge University Press. https://doi.org/10.1017/CBO9780511813313

Levinson, S. C. 2000. *Presumptive Meanings: The Theory of Generalized Conversational Implicature.* Cambridge, MA: MIT Press. https://doi.org/10.7551/mitpress/5526.001.0001

Lipton, P. 2000. *Inference to the best explanation.* In: H. D. Newton-Smith ed. *A Companion to the Philosophy of Science.* Malden, MA: Blackwell: 184–193.

Littlemore, J. 2015. *Metonymy: Hidden Shortcuts in Language, Thought and Communication.* Cambridge: Cambridge University Press. https://doi.org/10.1017/CBO9781107338814

Littlemore, J. & J. Taylor, J. 2013. *The Bloomsbury Companion to Cognitive Linguistics.* London: Bloomsbury.

Lodge, A. 1998. *Is French a logical language?* In: L. Bauer & P. Trudgill, eds. *Language Myths.* London: Penguin Books, 23–31.

Maalej, Z. A. & Yu, N., eds. 2011. *Embodiment Via Body Parts: Studies from Various Languages and Cultures* (Human Cognitive Processing 31). Amsterdam & Philadelphia: Benjamins. https://doi.org/10.1075/hcp.31

Markert, K. & Hahn, U. 2002. *Understanding metonymies in discourse. Artificial Intelligence* 135: 145–198. https://doi.org/10.1016/S0004-3702(01)00150-3

Mashal, N. & Faust, M. 2008. Conventionalization of novel metaphors: a shift in hemispheric asymmetry. Ms., Bar-Ilan University.

Mazzone, M. 2018. *Cognitive Pragmatics: Mindreading, Consciousness, Inferences*. Boston & Berlin: de Gruyter. https://doi.org/10.1515/9781501507731

Menninger, K. 1969. *Number and Number Symbols: A Cultural History of Numbers*. Cambridge, MA: MIT Press.

Morris, C. W. 1938. *Foundations of the Theory of Signs*. Chicago: Chicago University Press.

Murdoch, I. 1999. *The Sea, the Sea*. London: Vintage.

Musolff, A. 2016. *Political Metaphor Analysis: Discourse and Scenarios*. London & New York: Bloomsbury Academic.

Newmeyer, F. J. 1992. Iconicity and generative grammar. *Language* 68: 756–796. https://doi.org/10.1353/lan.1992.0047

Newmeyer, F. J. 1994. A note on Chomsky on form and function. *Journal of Linguistics* 30: 245–251. https://doi.org/10.1017/S0022226700016248

Notley, F. E. M. 1881. *In the House of a Friend*. London: Ward, Lock & Co. Retrieved from: httspgoogle.books.com

Nöth, W. 1990. *Handbook of Semiotics*. Bloomington & Indianapolis: Indiana University Press. https://doi.org/10.2307/j.ctv14npk46

Ochs Keenan, E. 1976. The universality of conversational postulates. *Language in Society* 5: 67–80. https://doi.org/10.1017/S0047404500006850

Paavola, S. 2005. Peircean abduction: Instinct or inference. *Semiotica* 153–1/4: 131–154. https://doi.org/10.1515/semi.2005.2005.153-1-4.131

Panther, K.-U. 1981. Indirect speech act markers or why some linguistic signs are non-arbitrary. In: R. A. Hendricks et al., eds. *Papers from the Seventeenth Regional Meeting: Chicago Linguistic Society, April 30 – May 1, 1981*. Chicago: Chicago Linguistic Society, 295–302.

Panther, K.-U. 1997. Dative alternation from a cognitive perspective. In: B. Smieja & M. Tasch, eds. *Human Contact through Language and Linguistics*. Frankfurt/M.: Lang, 107–126.

Panther, K.-U. 2006. Metonymy as a usage. In: G. Kristiansen, M. Achard, R. Dirven, & F. J. Ruiz de Mendoza, eds. *Cognitive Linguistics: Current Applications and Future Perspectives*. Berlin & New York: Mouton de Gruyter, 147–185.

Panther, K.-U. 2008. Conceptual and pragmatic motivation as an explanatory concept in linguistics. *Journal of Foreign Languages* 3.5: 1–19.

Panther, K.-U. 2013. Motivation in language. In: S. Kreitler, ed. *Cognition and Motivation: Forging an Interdisciplinary Perspective*. Cambridge: Cambridge University Press, 407–432.

Panther, K.-U. 2014. Metaphor and metonymy shaping grammar: The role of animal terms in expressive morphology and syntax. In: G. Drożdż & A. Łyda, eds. *Extension and its Limits*. Newcastle upon Tyne: Cambridge Scholars, 10–38.

Panther, K.-U. 2015. Metonymien im Sprachvergleich. In: C. Spieß & K.-M. Köpcke, eds. *Metapher und Metonymie: Theoretische, methodische und empirische Zugänge* (Empirische Linguistik). Berlin & Boston: de Gruyter, 207–226. https://doi.org/10.1515/9783110369120.207

Panther, K.-U. 2016a. 'Quo vadimus?' from a cognitive linguistic perspective. *Chinese Semiotic Studies* 12.1: 93–116. https://doi.org/10.1515/css-2016-0007

Panther, K.-U. 2016b. How to encode and infer linguistic actions. *Chinese Semiotic Studies* 12.2: 177–214. https://doi.org/10.1515/css-2016-0018

Panther, K.-U. 2021. Motivation. In: X. Wen & J. R. Taylor, eds. *The Routledge Handbook of Cognitive Linguistics*. New York & London: Routledge, 297–313. https://doi.org/10.4324/9781351034708-20

Panther, K.-U. & Köpcke, K.-M. 2008. A prototype approach to sentences and sentence types. *Annual Review of Cognitive Linguistics* 6: 83–112. https://doi.org/10.1075/arcl.6.05pan

Panther, K.-U. & Radden, G., eds. 1999. *Metonymy in Language and Thought* (Human Cognitive Processing 4). Amsterdam & Philadelphia: Benjamins. https://doi.org/10.1075/hcp.4

Panther, K.-U. & Radden, G. 2011. Introduction: Reflections on motivation revisited. In: K-U. Panther & G. Radden, eds. *Motivation in Grammar and the Lexicon* (Human Cognitive Processing 27). Amsterdam & Philadelphia, 1–26. https://doi.org/10.1075/hcp.27.02pan

Panther, K.-U. & Thornburg, L. L. 1998. A cognitive approach to inferencing in conversation. *Journal of Pragmatics* 30.6: 755–769. https://doi.org/10.1016/S0378-2166(98)00028-9

Panther, K.-U. & Thornburg, L. L. 1999. The POTENTIALITY FOR ACTUALITY metonymy in English and Hungarian. In: K.-U. Panther & G. Radden, eds. *Metonymy in Language and Thought* (Human Cognitive Processing 4). Amsterdam & Philadelphia: Benjamins. https://doi.org/10.1075/hcp.4.19pan

Panther, K.-U. & Thornburg, L. L. 2001. A conceptual analysis English -er nominals. In: M. Pütz, S. Niemeier, & R. Dirven, eds. *Applied Cognitive Linguistic II: Language Pedagogy* (Cognitive Linguistics Research 19.2). Berlin & New York: Mouton de Gruyter, 149–200.

Panther, K.-U & Thornburg, L. L. 2002. The role of metaphor and metonymy in English -er nominals. In: R. Dirven & R. Pörings, eds. *Metaphor and Metonymy in Comparison and Contrast* (Cognitive Linguistics Research 20). Berlin & New York: Mouton de Gruyter, 279–319.

Panther, K.-U. & Thornburg, L. L., eds. 2003a. *Metonymy and Pragmatic Inferencing* (Pragmatics & Beyond New Series 113). Amsterdam & Philadelphia: Benjamins. https://doi.org/10.1075/pbns.113

Panther, K.-U. & L. L. Thornburg. 2003b. Metonymies as natural inference schemas: The case of dependent clauses as independent speech acts. In: K.-U. Panther & L. L. Thornburg, eds. *Metonymy and Pragmatic Inferencing* (Pragmatics & Beyond New Series 113). Amsterdam & Philadelphia: Benjamins, 127–147. https://doi.org/10.1075/pbns.113.10pan

Panther, K.-U. & Thornburg, L. L. 2003c. Metonymy and lexical aspect in English and French. *Jezikoslovlje* 4.3: 71–101.

Panther, K.-U. & Thornburg, L. L. 2005. Motivation and convention in some speech act constructions: A cognitive-linguistic approach. In: S. Marmaridou, K. Nikiforidou, & E. Antonopoulou, eds. *Reviewing Linguistic Thought: Converging Trends for the 21st Century* (Trends in Linguistics: Studies and Monographs 161). Berlin & New York: Mouton de Gruyter, 53–76. https://doi.org/10.1515/9783110920826.53

Panther, K.-U. & Thornburg, L. L. 2007. Metonymy. In: D. Geeraerts & H. Cuyckens, eds. *The Oxford Handbook of Cognitive Linguistics*. Oxford: Oxford University Press, 236–263.

Panther, K.-U. & Thornburg. L. L. 2009a. Introduction: On figuration in grammar. In: K.-U. Panther, L. L. Thornburg, & A. Barcelona, eds. *Metonymy and Metaphor in Grammar* (Human Cognitive Processing 25). Amsterdam & Philadelphia: Benjamins, 1–40. https://doi.org/10.1075/hcp.25.03pan

Panther, K.-U. & Thornburg, L. L. 2009b. From syntactic coordination to conceptual modification: The case of the nice and Adj construction. *Constructions and Frames* 1.1: 56–86. https://doi.org/10.1075/cf.1.1.04pan

Panther, K.-U. & Thornburg, L. L. 2012a. Conceptualizing humans as animals in English verb particle constructions. *Language Value* 4.1: 63–83. https://doi.org/10.6035/LanguageV.2012.4.4

Panther, K.-U. & Thornburg, L. L. 2012b. Antonymy in language structure and use. In M. Brdar, I. Raffaelli, & M. Z. Fuchs. eds. *Cognitive Linguistics Between Universality and Variation*. Newcastle upon Tyne: Cambridge Scholars, 159–186.

Panther, K.-U. & Thornburg, L. L. 2014. Metonymy and the way we speak. *Revista Española de Lingüística Aplicada* 27.1: 168–186. https://doi.org/10.1075/resla.27.1.07pan

Panther, K.-U. & Thornburg, L. L. 2017a. *Motivation and Inference: A Cognitive Linguistic Approach*. Shanghai: Shanghai Foreign Language Education Press.

Panther, K.-U. & Thornburg, L. L. 2017b. Metaphor and metonymy in language and thought. *Synthesis Philosophica* 64.2: 271–294.

Panther, K.-U. & Thornburg, L. L. 2018. What kind of reasoning mode is metonymy? In: O. Blanco Carrión, A. Barcelona, & R. Pannain, eds. *Metonymy: Methodological, Theoretical, and Descriptive Issues* (Human Cognitive Processing 60). Amsterdam & Philadelphia: Benjamins, 121–160.

Panther, K.-U. & Thornburg, L. L. 2019. Figurative reasoning in hedged performatives. In: M. Bolognesi, M. Brdar, & K. Despot, eds. *Metaphor and Metonymy in the Digital Age: Theories and Methods for building repositories of Figurative Language* (Metaphor in Language, Cognition, and Communication 8). Amsterdam & Philadelphia: Benjamins, 175–198. https://doi.org/10.1075/milcc.8.08pan

Panther, K.-U., Thornburg, L. L., & Barcelona, A., eds. 2009. *Metonymy and Metaphor in Grammar* (Human Cognitive Processing 25) Amsterdam & Philadelphia: Benjamins. https://doi.org/10.1075/hcp.25

Paradis, C. 2004. Where does metonymy stop? Senses, facets, and active zones. *Metaphor and Symbol* 19.4: 245–264. https://doi.org/10.1207/s15327868ms1904_1

Paradis, C. 2016. Corpus methods for the investigation of antonyms across languages. In: P. Juvonen & M. Koptjevskaja-Tamm, eds. *The Lexical Typology of Semantic Shifts*. Berlin & Boston: de Gruyter, 131.–156. https://doi.org/10.1515/9783110377675-005

Partridge, E. 1966. *Origins: A Short Etymological Dictionary of Modern English*. London & New York. Routledge.

Pérez-Hernández, L. 2021. *Speech Acts in English: From Research to Instruction and Tex*

Pople, H. E. 1973. On the mechanization of abductive logic. *Proceedings of the Third International Joint Conference on Artificial Intelligence, 20–23 August 1973*, Stanford University, Standford, CA, 147–152.

Posner, R. 1980. Semantics and pragmatics of sentence connectives in natural language. In: J. R. Searle, F. Kiefer, & M. Bierwisch, eds. *Speech Act Theory and Pragmatics* (Synthese Language Library 10). Dordrecht: D. Reidel, 169–203. https://doi.org/10.1007/978-94-009-8964-1_8

Postman, L. & Keppel, G. 1970. *Norms of Word Association*. New York: Academic Press.

Pustejovsky, J. & Bouillon, P. 1995. Aspectual coercion and logical polysemy. *Journal of Semantics* 12: 133–162. https://doi.org/10.1093/jos/12.2.133

Predelli, S. 2013. *Meaning without Truth*. Oxford: Oxford University Press. https://doi.org/10.1093/acprof:oso/9780199695638.001.0001

Radden, G. 2009. Generic reference in English: A metonymic and conceptual blending analysis. In: K.-U. Panther, L. L. Thornburg, & A. Barcelona, eds. *Metonymy and Metaphor in Grammar* (Human Cognitive Processing 25). Benjamins: Amsterdam & Philadelphia, 199–228. https://doi.org/10.1075/hcp.25.13rad

Radden, G. 2021. Iconicity. In: X. Wen & J. R. Taylor, eds. *The Routledge Handbook of Cognitive Linguistics*. New York & London: Routledge, 268–296. https://doi.org/10.4324/9781351034708-19

Radden, G. & Dirven, R. 2007. *Cognitive English Grammar* (Cognitive Linguistics in Practice 2). Amsterdam & Philadelphia: Benjamins. https://doi.org/10.1075/clip.2.additional

Radden, G. & Kövecses, Z. 1999. Towards a theory of metonymy. In: K.-U. Panther & G. Radden, eds. *Metonymy in Language and Thought* (Human Cognitive Processing 4). Amsterdam & Philadelphia: Benjamins, 17–59. https://doi.org/10.1075/hcp.4.03rad

Radden, G. & Kövecses, Z. 2007. Towards a theory of metonymy. In: V. Evans, B. K. Bergen, & J. Zinken, eds. *Cognitive Linguistics Reader* (Advances in Cognitive Linguistics). London & Oakland, CA: Equinox, 335–359.

Radden, G. & Panther, K.-U. 2004. Introduction: Reflections on motivation. In: G. Radden & K.-U. Panther, eds. *Studies in Linguistic Motivation* (Cognitive Linguistics Research 28). Berlin and New York: Mouton de Gruyter, 1–46.

Radford, A. 1988. *Transformational Grammar: A First Course*. Cambridge: Cambridge University Press. https://doi.org/10.1017/CBO9780511840425

Riemer, N. 2002. When is metonymy no longer a metonymy? In: Pörings, R. & Dirven, R., eds. *Metaphor and Metonymy in Comparison and Contrast* (Cognitive Linguistics Research 20). Berlin & New York: Mouton de Gruyter, 379–406. https://doi.org/10.1515/9783110219197.379

Riemer, N. 2005. *The Semantics of Polysemy: Reading Meaning in English and Walpiri*. Berlin & New York: Mouton de Gruyter.

Rivarol, A. 1857. *Oeuvres de Rivarol: Études sur sa vie et son esprit par Sainte-Beuve, Arsène Housset, Armand Malitourne*. Paris: Adolphe Delyhays.

Ross, J. R. 1967. *Constraints on Variables in Syntax*. Ph.D. dissertation. Cambridge, MA: Massachusetts Institute of Technology. Retrieved from http://hdl.handle.net/1721.1/15166.

Ruiz de Mendoza Ibáñez, F. J. 2000. The role of mappings and domains in understanding metonymy. In: A. Barcelona, ed. *Metaphor and Metonymy at the Crossroads* (Topics in English Linguistics 30). Berlin & New York: Mouton der Gruyter, 109–132.

Ruiz de Mendoza Ibáñez, F. J. 2014. On the nature and scope of metonymy in linguistic description and explanation: Towards settling some controversies. In: J. Littlemore & J. R. Taylor, eds. *The Bloomsbury Companion to Cognitive Linguistics*. London: Bloomsbury, 143–166.

Ruiz de Mendoza Ibáñez, F. J. 2021. Conceptual metonymy theory revisited: Some definitional and taxonomic issues. In: X. Wen & J. R. Taylor, eds. *The Routledge Handbook of Cognitive Linguistics*. New York & London: Routledge, 204–227. https://doi.org/10.4324/9781351034708-15

Ruiz de Mendoza Ibáñez, F. J. & Otal Campo, J. L. 2002. *Metonymy, Grammar and Communication*. Granada: Editorial Comares.

Ruiz de Mendoza Ibáñez, F. J. & Pérez Hernández, L. 2001. Metonymy and the grammar: Motivation, constraints and interaction. *Language and Communication* 21: 321–357. https://doi.org/10.1016/S0271-5309(01)00008-8

Sadock, J. 1978. On testing for conversational implicature. In: P. Cole, ed. *Pragmatics* (Syntax and Pragmatics 9). New York, etc.: Academic Press, 281–297. https://doi.org/10.1163/9789004368873_011

Saeed, J. I. 2009. *Semantics*. 3rd ed. Oxford: Wiley-Blackwell.

Saussure, F. de. 1959. *Course in General Linguistics*. (W. Baskin, Trans.) New York: Philosophical Library. (Original work published 1916)

Saussure, F. de. 1995 [1916]. *Cours de linguistique générale*. Paris: Payot

Schmid, H.-J. 2012. Generalizing the apparently ungeneralizable: Basic ingredients of a cognitive-pragmatic approach to the construction of meaning. In: H.-J. Schmid, ed. *Handbook of Cognitive Pragmatics*. Berlin: de Gruyter, 3–22. https://doi.org/10.1515/9783110214215.3

Searle, J. R. 1969. *Speech Acts: An Essay in the Philosophy of Language*. Cambridge: Cambridge University Press. https://doi.org/10.1017/CBO9781139173438

Searle, J. R. 1971. What is a speech act? In: J. R. Searle, J., ed. *The Philosophy of Language*. Oxford: Oxford University Press, 39–53.

Searle, J. R. 1972. Chomsky's revolution in linguistics. *New York Review of Books*. June 29, 1972.

Searle, J. R. 1975. Indirect speech acts. In: P. Cole & J. L. Morgan, eds. *Speech Acts* (Syntax and Semantics 3). New York, etc.: Academic Press, 59–82.

Searle, J. R. 1976. A classification of illocutionary acts. *Language in Society* 5: 1–23. https://doi.org/10.1017/S0047404500006837

Searle, J. R. 1979. *Expression and Meaning: Studies in the Theory of Speech Acts*. Cambridge: Cambridge University Press. https://doi.org/10.1017/CBO9780511609213

Searle, J. R. 2002. *Consciousness and Language*. Cambridge: Cambridge University Press. https://doi.org/10.1017/CBO9780511606366

Searle, J. R. & Vanderveken, D. 1985. *Foundations of Illocutionary Logic*. Cambridge: Cambridge University Press.

Sedley, D. 2003. *Plato's 'Cratylus'*. Cambridge: Cambridge University Press. https://doi.org/10.1017/CBO9780511482649

Sedley, D. 2013. "Plato's Cratylus". In: E. N. Zalta, ed. *The Stanford Encyclopedia of Philosophy* (Fall 2013 Edition). [Accessed at: at https://plato.stanford.edu/archives/fall2013/entries/plato-cratylus].

Senft, G. 2014. *Understanding Pragmatics: An Interdisciplinary Approach to Language Use*. London & New York. Routledge. https://doi.org/10.4324/9780203776476

Service, R. W. 2008. *The Spell of the Yukon and Other Verses*. [Retrieved from www.gutenberg.org. (EBook #207).

Sharifian, F., Dirven, R., Yu, N., & Niemeier, S., eds. 2008. *Culture, Body, and Language: Conceptualizations of Internal Body Organs across Cultures and Languages* (Applications of Cognitive Linguistics 7). Berlin & New York: Mouton de Gruyter. https://doi.org/10.1515/9783110199109

Siemund, P. 2018. *Speech Acts and Clause Types: English in a Cross-Linguistic Context*. Oxford: Oxford University Press.

Skinner, B. F. 1957. *Verbal Behavior*. New York: Appleton-Century-Crofts. https://doi.org/10.1037/11256-000

Sobrino Pérez, P. 2017. *Multimodal Metaphor and Metonymy in Advertising* (Figurative Thought and Language 2). Amsterdam & Philadelphia: Benjamins. https://doi.org/10.1075/ftl.2

Sperber, D. & Wilson, D. 1995. *Relevance: Communication and Cognition*. Oxford: Blackwell.

Sperber, D. & Wilson, D. 2002. Pragmatics, modularity and mind-reading. *Mind & Language* 17: 3–23. https://doi.org/10.1111/1468-0017.00186

Strawson, P. 1952. *Introduction to Logical Theory*. London: Methuen.

Sweetser, E. 1990. *From Etymology to Pragmatics: Metaphorical and Cultural Aspects of Semantic Structure*. Cambridge: Cambridge University Press. https://doi.org/10.1017/CBO9780511620904

Talmy, L. 2000a. *Toward a Cognitive Semantics*. Vol. 1: Concept Structuring Systems. Cambridge, MA: MIT Press.

Talmy, L. 200b. *Toward a Cognitive Semantics*. Vol. 2: Typology and Process in Concept Structuring. Cambridge, MA: MIT Press.

Taylor, J. 2002. *Cognitive Grammar*. Oxford: Oxford University Press.

Taylor, J. 2003. *Linguistic Categorization*. Oxford: Oxford University Press.

Thagard, P. 2007. Abductive inference: From philosophical analysis to neural mechanism. In: A. Feeney & E. Heit, eds. *Inductive Reasoning: Experimental, Developmental and Computational Approaches*. Cambridge: Cambridge University Press, 226–245.

Thibodeau, P. H. & Boroditsky, L. 2011. Metaphors we think with: The role of metaphor in reasoning. *PloS One* 6.2: e16782. [Retrieved from https://doi.org/10.1371/journal.pone.0016782]

Thornburg, L. L. & Panther, K.-U. 1997. Speech act metonymies. In: W.-A. Liebert, G. Redeker, & L. Waugh, eds. *Discourse and Perspective in Cognitive Linguistics*. Amsterdam & Philadelphia: Benjamins, 205–219. https://doi.org/10.1075/cilt.151.14tho

Tomasello, M. 2003. *Constructing a Language: A Usage-Based Theory of Language Acquisition*. Cambridge, MA: Harvard University Press.

Tomasello, M. 2009. *Why We Cooperate*. Cambridge, MA: MIT Press. https://doi.org/10.7551/mitpress/8470.001.0001

Tomlin, R. S. 1986. *Basic Word Order: Functional Principles*. London: Croom Helm.

Tóth, M. 2018. *Linguistic Metonymy: Implicitness and Co-Activation of Mental Content*. Berlin: Peter Lang. https://doi.org/10.3726/b14806

Traugott, E. C. 2012. Pragmatics and language change. In: K. Allan & K. M. Jaszczolt, eds. *The Cambridge Handbook of Pragmatics*. Cambridge: Cambridge University Press, 549–565. https://doi.org/10.1017/CBO9781139022453.030

Traugott, E. C. & Dasher, R. B. 2002. *Regularity in Semantic Change* (Cambridge Studies in Linguistics 97). Cambridge: Cambridge University Press.

Ungerer, F. & Schmid, H.-J. 2006. *An Introduction to Cognitive Linguistics*. Pearson & Longman: Harlow.

Vallauri, E. L. 2016. Insubordinated conditionals in spoken and non-spoken Italian. In: N. Evans & H. Watanabé, eds. *Insubordination* (Typological Studies in Language 115). Amsterdam & Philadelphia: Benjamins, 145–169. https://doi.org/10.1075/tsl.115.06val

Vanderveken, D. 2004. Success, satisfaction, and truth in the logic of speech acts and formal semantics. In: S. Davis & B. S. Gillon, eds. *Semantics: A Reader*. New York: Oxford University Press, 710–734.

Vendler, Z. 1957. Verbs and times. *Philosophical Review* 66.2: 143–160. https://doi.org/10.2307/2182371

Verschueren, J. 1999. *Understanding Pragmatics*. London: Arnold.

Verspoor, M. & de Bie-Kerékjártó, A. 2006. Colorful bits of experience: From bluestocking to blue movie. *English Studies* 87.1: 78–98. https://doi.org/10.1080/00138380500490819

Voßhagen, C. 1999. Opposition as a metonymic principle: In: K.-U. Panther & G. Radden, eds. *Metonymy in Language and Thought* (Human Cognitive Processes 4. Amsterdam & Philadelphia, 289–308. https://doi.org/10.1075/hcp.4.17vos

Wachowski, W. 2019. *Towards a Better Understanding of Metonymy* (Literary and Cultural Stylistics 44). Oxford: Peter Lang. https://doi.org/10.3726/b13365

Wehling, E. 2016. *Politisches Framing: Wie eine Nation sich ihr Denken einrichtet – und daraus Politik macht*. Köln: Halem.

Wierzbicka. A. 1985. Different cultures, different languages, different speech acts. *Journal of Pragmatics* 9: 145–178. https://doi.org/10.1016/0378-2166(85)90023-2

Wilson, D. 2005. New directions for research on pragmatics and modularity. In: S. Marmaridou, K. Nikiforidou, E. Antonopoulou, eds. *Reviewing Linguistic Thought: Converging Trends for the 21th Century*. Berlin & New York: Mouton de Gruyter, 375–400. https://doi.org/10.1515/9783110920826.375

Wittgenstein, L. 2009. *Philosophical Investigations* (G. Anscombe, P. Hacker, & J. Schulte, Trans.). Chichester, U.K.: Wiley-Blackwell.

Wunderlich, D. 1976. *Studien zur Sprechakttheorie*. Frankfurt a. M: Suhrkamp.

Ziem, A. 2014. *Frames of Understanding in Text and Discourse: Theoretical Foundations and Descriptive Applications* (Human Cognitive Processing 48). Amsterdam & Philadelphia: Benjamins. https://doi.org/10.1075/hcp.48

Name index

A
Akmajian, A. 197
Aliseda, A. 47–48
Ambler, E. 116, 175
Ariel, M. 42, 142, 236
Arnaud, A. 22–23
Athanasiadou, A. 182
Austin, J. L. 109, 111–116, 130, 196–197

B
Bach, K. 79
Baicchi, A. 195
Barcelona, A. 163, 236, 263
Barnden, J. A. 264
Benczes, R. 263–264
Bergman, M. 147
Bierwiaczonek, B. 163
Birner, B. 7
Blakemore, D. 12
Boroditsky, L. 161
Borsley, D. 237
Bouillon, P. 174
Brdar, M. 36, 176, 236, 265
Broccias, C. 96
Brown, K. 184–185
Brown, P. 191–192, 195
Brugman, C. 235–238
Buchler, J. 7, 181

C
Cuyckens, H. 28

D
Dasher, R. B. 9
Demers, R. A. 197
Dirven, R. 5, 28–29
Ducrot, O. 62, 107
Durkin, P. 41

E
Evans, N. 216
Evans, V. 16, 144, 178

F
Farmer, A. K. 86, 197
Fauconnier, G. 18–19, 171, 191, 262–263
Faust, M. 142
Fillmore, C. 55, 264
Fraser, B. 126
Frege, G. 111

G
Garner, B. A. 129
Geeraerts, D. 28, 144, 183, 265
Gibbs, R. W. 28, 39, 144, 192
Giora, R. 142
Goldberg, A. 17, 28, 237
Goldsmith, J. A. 241
Goosse, A. 28
Gordon, D. 219
Grady, J. 145, 251
Green, G. 15–16, 79, 263
Green, M. 16
Grevisse, M. 28
Grice, H. P. 9, 11, 13, 62–63, 65–66, 68–70, 73–81, 83–84, 88–89, 93, 104, 107, 140–141, 175, 238, 263
Grundy, P. 3

H
Hahn, U. 181
Harnish, R. M 79, 197
Heine, B. 27
Horn, L. R. 63, 67, 70–71, 77–80, 91, 94, 102
Huang, Y. 2–3, 9, 12, 77–78, 104
Huddleston, R. 10, 125

J
Jäkel, O. 139, 144
Janda, L. 17
Johnson, M. 36–38, 40, 139, 144–145, 151, 153, 163, 231–232, 236, 239, 242, 251, 262, 264

K
Kahneman, D. 69, 89
Karttunen, L. 200
Keppel, G. 182
Kiparsky, C. 200
Kiparsky, P. 200
König, E. 14
Köpcke, K.-M. 34, 36, 133, 201, 235–236
Kövecses, Z. 18, 156, 160, 168, 183–184

L
Lakoff, G. 17–18, 36–38, 40, 92, 139–140, 144–146, 151, 153–156, 160, 162–163, 168, 182–183, 219, 235–239, 242, 251, 262, 264
Lancelot, C. 22–23
Langacker, R. 15, 17, 26, 57, 95, 140, 184, 186–187, 190–191, 236, 262–263
Lausberg, H. 139, 149, 190
Levinson, S. C. 19, 45–46, 48, 63, 68, 70, 77–78, 84–85, 88, 90–92, 107, 175, 182–183, 191–192, 195, 263
Lipton, P. 47
Littlemore, J. 28, 163, 180–181
Lodge, A. 22

M

Maalej, Z. A.   178
Markert, K.   181
Mashal, N.   142
Mazzone, M.   81, 89, 170
Menninger, K.   28
Miller, J.   184–185
Morris, C. W.   1
Murdoch, I.   240
Musolff, A.   160

N

Newmeyer, F. J.   235, 237
Nöth, W.   21
Notley, F. E. M.   75

O

Ochs Keenan, E.   81
Otal Campo, J. L.   236

P

Paavola, S.   18, 47, 147
Panther, K.-U.   16, 18, 21, 24, 27–29, 34, 36–37, 39–40, 42–43, 64–65, 79, 99, 109–110, 120, 124, 126, 128, 133, 138, 145, 149, 158, 161, 164, 167, 171–174, 182, 186–188, 191, 201–202, 208, 217, 235–236, 242, 251, 254, 262–265
Paradis, C.   17, 95, 164, 173, 184–187
Partridge, E.   41
Pérez-Hernández, L.   195, 236, 263–264
Plato   21, 140
Pople, H. E.   45–46, 48
Posner, R.   11
Postman, L.   82
Predelli, S.   14
Pullum, G. K.   10, 125
Pustejovsky, J.   174

R

Radden, G.   18, 21, 24, 27–28, 34, 37, 40, 99, 168, 183–184, 191, 263
Radford, A.   235
Riemer, N.   179
Rivarol, A.   22–23
Ross, J. R.   239, 242, 246
Ruiz de Mendoza Ibáñez, F. J.   163, 171, 236, 265

S

Sadock, J.   91, 94
Saeed, J. I.   49, 51
Saussure, F. de   24–26, 30, 263
Schmid, H.-J.   16, 18–19, 263
Searle, J. R.   79, 109, 111–113, 115–120, 124–125, 128–133, 136, 138, 141, 187, 192, 196, 211, 216, 221, 231, 235
Sedley, D.   22
Senft, G.   81
Service, R.   150
Sharifian, F.   178
Siemund, P.   197
Skinner, B. F.   16, 140
Sobrino Pérez, P   164
Sperber, D.   63–64, 79–80, 263
Sweetser, E.   35, 144, 201, 213

T

Talmy, L.   262
Taylor, J.   16, 28
Thagard, P.   48
Thibodeau, P. H.   161
Thornburg, L. L.   16, 18, 21, 28, 36, 39–40, 42–43, 65, 79, 110, 120, 126, 128, 138, 145, 149, 161, 164, 167, 171–174, 182, 186–188, 191, 202, 208, 217, 236, 242, 254, 262, 264–265
Tomasello, M.   16, 68
Tomlin, R. S.   23–24
Tóth, M.   163
Traugott, E. C.   9
Turner, M.   151, 153, 171, 191, 262

U

Ungerer, F.   16

V

Vallauri, E. L.   216
Vanderveken, D.   10, 118, 128, 130–131, 136
Vendler, Z.   246
Verschueren, J.   2
Voßhagen, C.   182

W

Wachowski, W.   163
Watanabe, H.   216
Wehling, E.   160
Wierzbicka, A.   105–106
Wilson, D.   63–64, 79–80, 263
Wittgenstein, L.   109
Wunderlich, D.   10, 120

Y

Yu, N.   178

Z

Ziem, A.   110, 146, 264

Subject index

A
abductive instinct   47, 181
abductive reasoning   48, 164, 180–182, 193
abuse(s)   113–114
Anglo-American pragmatics   2
apodosis   7, 34–35, 57, 216, 235; see also *protasis*
arbitrary sign(s)   29–30; see also *motivated sign(s)*
associative (relation)   35, 47, 170–172, 178, 180, 193, 215, 264
associative connection   47
associative memory   170
associative reasoning   47, 193
autonomy of syntax hypothesis   17; see also *Autonomy of Syntax Principle*
Autonomy of Syntax Principle   235–236

B
background assumption(s)   53–54, 59
background information   59–60
breach of commitment   14

C
calculability   84, 89–90, 107
cancelability   84–85, 107, 264
cancelable   5, 68, 84–86, 88, 92, 97, 159, 248
cancelation   57, 85–86, 88, 238
cardinal numbers   5
code model (of communication)   63–65
coherence   4 ,8–9, 264
conceptual contiguity   172
conceptual frame   110, 138, 1461, 153, 168, 170–172, 182, 193, 195, 2013, 261, 264
conceptual scale   70
conceptually contiguous   33, 35
conditional clause   34, 201, 216–217
conditionality   53–54, 59, 131
consequent clause   7, 34, 57, 201, 216
constituent order   22–24, 124–125, 237–238; see also *word order*
constitutive rule   115, 117; see also *regulative rule(s)*
conventional implicature   83–84
conventional sign   25, 29–30
conventionalism   22; see also *naturalism*
conversational implicature   65, 68–70, 83–91, 103–107, 113, 141, 163, 182, 238, 248
Cooperative Principle   68–70, 75, 80
cultural model   11, 18, 39–40, 110, 151
culture/language-specific implicatures   104–105

D
declarative sentence   11, 197, 240
deductive reasoning   43–45
defeasibility   45, 46, 48, 72, 84–86, 103, 104, 107; see also *cancelability*
defeasible   46, 48, 68, 79, 84, 86, 88, 89, 93, 100, 174, 188, 199; see also *cancelable*
deictic   12, 26
deixis   12
demotivation   41
direct causation   37
direct illocutionary act   196–197; see also *direct speech act*
direct speech act   96
direction of fit   118–121

E
embodiment   18, 28, 39
entailment   43, 48–49, 51–53, 58, 61, 63, 68, 71, 77, 83, 86–87, 90, 93, 95–96, 100, 103–104, 107, 139, 151, 153, 156–159, 168, 173–175, 188, 198–199, 203, 231, 237, 264
epistemic qualification   53–54, 59
European Continental tradition (of pragmatics)   2
expert model   111
explicit performative utterance   126, 196–197, 205, 225, 233

F
factive verb   200
felicity condition   116–117, 121, 128, 264
flouting   70, 74
folk model   39, 40, 109–111
frame   59, 146, 149, 151, 153, 155, 158, 160, 162, 168, 170–172, 182, 193, 213, 223, 246, 264; see also *conceptual frame*
frame semantics   146

G
GCI   68, 85, 88, 92, 104
generalized conversational implicature   68, 84, 87; see also *GCI*
generative grammar   16–17, 28, 48, 235, 239–240
Gricean maxim   69–70, 77–78, 81; see also *maxim*

H

hedged performative   126, 196, 202, 208, 220, 224, 230, 232
Horn scale   70, 71, 77, 91

I

I-principle   78
icon   26, 47
iconic principle   37, 104; see also *iconicity*
iconic relation   26, 30, 37, 104, 139, 147, 153, 160, 170, 263–264; see also *iconicity*
iconicity   153, 250–251
illocutionary act   110–119, 125, 128, 133, 135, 192, 216, 219, 231, 233
illocutionary force   116–117, 121–127, 164, 187, 192, 195–197, 201–202, 207, 219–220, 225
illocutionary meaning   13, 126, 213, 264
illocutionary point   118–121
illocutionary scenario(s)   110, 128–129, 131, 137–138, 192, 195–198, 205, 208, 213, 215, 222–223
imperative sentence   10, 196, 231
implicature(s)   9–11, 13, 17, 62–63, 65–66, 68–70–76, 78–79, 83–93, 100, 102–107, 113, 139–142, 147–149, 151, 159, 163, 168, 174, 182–183, 199, 204, 238–239, 248, 250, 261, 264–265
index   12, 26, 113, 146, 170, 174, 177, 223, 246, 251, 257
indirect causation   37
indirect illocutionary act   79, 138, 192–193, 195, 197, 213, 215, 233, 264; see also *indirect speech act*
indirect request   3,61, 79, 191–192, 216–217, 222
indirect speech act   38, 192, 195–196, 203, 273; see also *indirect illocutionary act*
inductive reasoning   46
infelicity/infelicitous   94, 100, 109, 113, 122, 132, 249
inferential model of communication   63–65
inferential motivation   21, 42–43
insubordination   216
interrogative sentence   10, 53, 118, 125, 196, 206, 210, 217, 222, 224, 239–240, 242
interrogativity   53–54, 59
invited inference   3, 9, 10

L

language-independent factors of motivation   37, 42
Law of Least Effort   79
linguistic source   7
linguistic target   7
linguistic vehicle   146, 163, 166, 168, 170–171, 179, 181–184, 186–187, 195, 201, 207, 231–233
literal meaning   3, 39, 140–142, 146, 165, 192, 196, 218, 248–249; see also *literal sense*
literal sense   140, 143, 159, 181, 183, 218
locutionary act   111
logical conjunction   5, 11, 46, 48
logical connective   6, 11, 76, 255
logical disjunction   6

M

M-principle   78
Malagasy society   81
Malagasy speakers   81
Maxim of Relation   74–75, 79–80; see also *Maxim of Relevance*
Maxim of Relevance   74
Maxims of Manner   75, 79, 93
Maxims of Quality   73–74, 77, 140
Maxims of Quantity   70, 73, 77–79, 81
meaning-in-context   18–19, 42
meaning-in-use   1–2, 10, 42
mental organ   16
metonymic inference   92, 164–167, 174–175, 183, 188, 190, 197, 200–202, 207
misfire(s)   113–114
modus ponens   44–45, 90

modus tollens   44
motivated sign(s)   25, 32

N

naturalism   22; see also *conventionalism*
NECI   53–55, 57, 59, 61, 89
negation   44, 50–55, 57–59, 71, 78, 89, 91, 238, 243
new information   35, 60–61, 63, 80–81, 91, 93, 96, 101–104, 107, 202
non-cancelable   45, 76, 97; see also *indefeasible*
non-codability   85, 90, 107
non-conventional sign   25, 29, 33, 83–84, 90
non-detachability   84, 88; see also *non-detachable*
non-detachable   88–89
non-truth conditional meaning   12–13

O

old information   60, 63; see also *background information*
onomatopoeic words   26, 30, 32

P

particularized conversational implicature   68; see also *PCI*
PCI   68, 86
performative verbs   124–125; see also *performatives*
performatives   126, 196–197, 202, 220, 224, 226, 228–229
perlocutionary act   111–112
phatic act   111–112
phonetic act   111
polysemy   35–36, 185, 205
predicating   111–112
presupposition   43, 48, 51–61, 63, 68, 83, 86–90, 93, 100–104, 107, 114, 120, 133, 139, 151, 156–160, 168, 200, 223, 225, 259, 264
Principle of Relevance   79–80
propositional act   111–112
propositional content   35, 55, 116–127, 129–132, 136, 164, 187, 192, 196, 199–205, 207–208, 211–212, 218, 221–222, 238

protasis   7, 34–35, 57–58, 216
psychological state   119–121

Q
Q-principle   77–79

R
R-principle   79–80
reasonableness condition   217
referring   111–112, 176
regulative rule(s)   115, 117
reinforceability   85, 90–91, 93–94, 100, 103–104, 107
reinforcement   90–91, 93, 103, 264
relative motivation   24
Relevance Theory   63–64, 77, 79–80, 141–142, 263
rhetic act   111–112

S
satisfaction condition   10
semiotic system   17
signified   24, 26, 29–30, 144
signifier   24, 26, 29–30
sincerity condition   30, 73, 117, 119–120, 128–129, 198, 219, 223
statement   3, 5, 7, 12–13, 18, 59, 71–72, 74, 83, 86, 92, 100, 116, 125, 143, 154, 168, 184, 188, 197–198, 206, 213, 227
suspendability   72, 84–85, 107, 264
syllogism   44–45, 47
symbol   22, 29–30; see also *symbolic sign*
symbolic sign   25–26
symptom   26, 41, 157, 171, 177; see also *index*

T
topic continuity   8
truth condition   7–9, 10–11, 13–14, 49, 83, 262; see also *truth-conditional approach (to meaning)*
truth value   4–13, 44, 49–52, 58, 119, 197, 201, 245, 262
truth-conditional approach   4–5, 8

U
universal grammatical principles   17, 239
universal implicatures   84, 104–105
universal language   22
universal quantifier   45–48
unmotivated (signs)   24–25, 29–30, 33, 42, 263; see also *arbitrary sign*
utterance act   111–112

V
verbs of judging   55
violation of the CSC   240, 242, 244, 265
visual perception   38

W
what is implicated   4, 14, 63, 66–68, 83; see also *what is said*
what is said   4, 9, 13–14, 63, 66–68, 75–76, 78, 84–85
word order   22–24, 34, 125, 236–237, 265, 271, 278; see also *constituent order*